The Student Guide to Fellowships and Internships

Written by the students of Amherst College

E.P. Dutton   **New York**

For information contact: Elsevier-Dutton Publishing Co., Inc., 2 Park Avenue, New York, N.Y. 10016

ISBN: 0-525-93155-4, cloth;
       0-525-93147-3, paper

LCC: 80-67575

Published simultaneously in Canada by Clarke, Irwin & Company Limited. Toronto and Vancouver

10 9 8 7 6 5 4 3 2 1

First Edition

Director: Kenneth W. Banta

Editors-in-Chief: Philip Simmons
Rosanne Haggerty

Assistant Editors: Marcelle Van Amsterdam, Robin Avner, Michele Deitch, Ned Desmond, William Houston, Steven Lewis, Elizabeth McDermott, Joseph H. K. Osborn, Scott Ulm.

Contributors: Leo Arnaboldi, Margaret Bangser, Bruce Becker, Kirsten Cronin, Ann Dolinsky, Michael Flood, James Gelin, Deborah Hart, Gary Lee, John Marrella, James Mendelsohn, Diana Meservey, Kathy Meyers, Rowan Murphy, David Nicholas, Brian O'Connell, Richard Read, Jeanne Symmes, George Witwer, David Zonderman.

Business Manager: William H. Cohn

Special Thanks to: Bruce Becker, Mark Daniel, Judy Dayton, Eric Fornell, Michael Gorra, Dr. Robert Grose, Glen Kesselhaut, Deborah Marvel, David Moore, Dr. Donald I. Robinson, Emily Rubin, Sandra W. Soule.

Also: Susan Little, Janice Schell, and Peggy Stosz of the Amherst College Office of Career Counseling; Allison Dillon of the Smith College Career Development Office; Dr. Robert Ginn of Harvard University's Office of Career Services and Off-Campus Learning; the University of Massachusetts (at Amherst) Internship Office; the Options Office of Hampshire College; the Career Counseling Office of Mount Holyoke College; and the National Society for Internships and Experiential Education.

The editors would like to express their great appreciation of the contribution made by the many interns, fellowship winners and program administrators who offered their advice and comments.

Contents

Preface

This guide signals an important development on the educational landscape: the growing realm of experience between undergraduate life and professional career. The rapid growth of internships plus the more traditional fellowship opportunities have created a new option for students. A breathing space between school and work, a chance to sample a possible career before diving in, an opportunity to do work you never plan to do again — increasingly, this kind of break is being sought by students and organized by schools and businesses.

This experience is not just for the newly graduated: not long ago, the only internships undergraduates thought about involved photo-copying in Capitol Hill offices, while now, college students can find summer slots in everything from journalism to law to wooden-boat building.

Despite the phenomenal growth of interest and opportunity, vast ignorance prevails when it comes to the nuts and bolts of how, when, where, and why. This book fills the gap. It's not a catalogue. There are lots of publications on your library shelves which are: listings of Washington internships, listings of fellowships and scholarships, listings, listings, listings. Some are helpful; many are not.

This guide is different. You will find lots of programs described here, with plenty of information about when and where to apply. But you will also find much more. It is a guide to the entire *process* of getting into a program that you want, and which is right for you.

If you are a college student or recent college graduate, this book will help you to:
  —find an internship or fellowship that suits your needs, or create one that does
  —get accepted in the program of your choice
  —make the most of the program once you're in.

Here is the advice you really need—and almost never get. What are program administrators *actually* looking for? What can you do to present yourself in the best possible light? Will the job end up being more than three months of envelope-stuffing and answering the phone? You'll find answers to these and lots of other questions.

And you will find them answered by students, for students. The personal experience of hundreds of interns and fellowship winners has gone into these pages—general hints, do's and don'ts for different types of programs, and inside reports on specific programs—so that you can profit from their experiences, and avoid a lot of trouble for yourself.

Of course, we have also talked to program administrators. The official word which will make the application process as painless as possible is encapsulated here—but you will also find those off-the-record comments which cut through the officialese to tell you what they are really after.

How to Use the Guide

The Guide contains two different kinds of information, divided for convenience: 1) general advice on internship and fellowship hunting, and 2) rundowns on specific programs.

Our chapter, "Fellowships" is devoted to a special category of awards known as "national fellowships". Open to students across the country, these are the most sought-after awards, and are distinguished by an emphasis on non-academic as well as academic qualifications, the intensity of competition, generous stipends, and great prestige. But even if you've ruled out competing for one of the national fellowships, you will profit from the advice given here. Applications for graduate fellowship programs of all types ask for similar information, and the advice included here about recommendations, essays, and interviews will help you with *any* applications you make.

Internships are divided into chapters covering different fields— "Arts" and "Health" are two examples. Each chapter begins with an essay which gives an overview of the opportunities available in that field, and where to find them. In addition, these essays contain specific advice on getting accepted into programs and information on the "quality of life" you can expect to find once you've gotten in.

The descriptions of individual programs are designed to tell you at a glance if you'll be interested. The summary entries at the beginning of each listing give the basic dope—where you would work, who is eligible, when the job starts, whether and how much you would be paid—followed by the *General Description* of the program.

When you locate a program that seems to fit the bill, move on to *The Inside Word*. There you will find comments by students who have actually participated in the program, and often, the candid advice of program administrators. With tips on getting accepted into the more competitive programs, examples of the work you'd likely be doing, and even judgments about the social life, *The Inside Word* gives you a unique glimpse behind the application form to help you make the right decision.

But if you can't find exactly what you are looking for, don't give up. We have covered important and representative programs, selected with an eye to giving best possible insights into work in each general field. Many programs had to be left out. Many more are out there waiting to be discovered. And, as the section on *Making Your Own* points out, the most rewarding program may well be one you put together for yourself.

The entries here are meant to be suggestive, not exhaustive. We couldn't possibly list every environmental group in the country—but the internship experiences described here are representative of what you'll find in other programs around the nation. Both the general advice and specific examples will put you on the road to the kind of internship or fellowship you want—or quite possibly, will lead to experiences you never thought about before. This book will get you started in the right direction; your own imagination and initiative—the more of each the better!—will take you to your destination.

Let Us Hear from You

We want to keep up to date, but we can only do it with help from other students. Let us know what *your* experience has been—whether happy or harrowing—with the world of internships and fellowships. Use the handy forms at the back of the book or simply fire off a note to

> *Amherst Student Special Publications*
> *Box 234, Station #2*
> *Amherst, MA 01002*

Be sure to include your name and address so that we can get back to you.

All About Internships

If you were born after 1950, you've practically grown up in the classroom. For at least the first 20 years of your life, the world has been centered around going to school. As a result, students often feel set apart from the rest of the world. Educational institutions put the student in the role of observer, rather than participant, and contact with the world of work is all too often limited to summer stints at the car wash, until that fateful senior year when you sign your life away to a professional career you know nothing about. What has long been lacking is a way of bridging the gap—a way of sampling life in the workplace without making a career commitment.

In the past few years, internships have become the alternative. An idea that once had currency only as "Washington Internships" for high school and college good citizens, internships are fast becoming accepted in almost every field imaginable. For the graduating senior looking for a productive year between school and career or more school, and for the undergraduate looking for a challenging summer, internships are the answer.

Why the increasing popularity of the internship idea? Observers are scrambling for answers, but two reasons top the lists. First, "preprofessional fever" is raging around the country. At its worst a singleminded pursuit of a hot career, its better side is the realization that a short-term job experience can help you choose a satisfying career. And internships are sources of experience, training, and references, that do make you more desirable in a tight job market—and are a way out of the Catch-22 routine of personnel offices which tell you "we only want people with experience but we aren't going to give you any experience."

Which is part of the second reason internships are on the rise: organizations of every kind are finally realizing that students and recent graduates can provide enthusiastic and capable help at bargain-basement prices. Understandably leery of hiring people without experience, organizations are learning the benefits of short-term internship commitments. And who knows?—that summer intern everyone liked so much might just come back to the business for good in a few years. Not a bad deal, from the employer's point of view.

Everyone benefits from a good internship; it is truly a reciprocal relationship.

About Internships: What Are They?

An internship can be lots of things. It can be a chance to see a Congressional office in action, or an oceanographic research voyage off the coast of Southern California. Interns have positions writing memos for major corporations and they can be found every year pounding beats for local newspapers.

Diverse indeed, but there are some essential features which define the animal. An internship is

- —short term. Ranging from a few months to a few years, it is a limited commitment, with no strings attached regarding future employment.
- —a chance to observe and participate in a professional work situation.
- —an opportunity to gain on-the-job experience and training which can make a future job hunt in the same profession easier.

The most important result of an internship, however, is often psychological. For the undergraduate doing a summer internship, the experience proves that there is a world outside the university that he or she can succeed in. For the recent graduate, it provides invaluable breathing space, a time to assess interests and abilities, and to think—perhaps for the first time—about what directions to take in the future.

Jargon of the Trade

With the rapid increase in popularity of internships has come a parallel explosion of buzz words. As a result you are now likely to encounter a confusing tangle of terms rolling glibly from the tongues of various experts; some of the most common are defined below.

Some of this is merely the verbal driftwood which accumulates around experts in anything: some of it, however, can be helpful to you. Distinctions between types of programs, while they usually get blurred in practice, will help you decide which you want. More importantly, with these distinctions in mind, you will be able to work with your employer to make the internship work the way you want it to.

Externships. A hybrid genre devoted exclusively to *observation*. Based on the idea that you can sometimes learn most by watching closely what someone else does, externships are arranged so that you "shadow" a professional throughout the work day for a few weeks or months.

An interesting approach, but in practice it can be phenomenally frustrating, especially if the externship lasts more than a few weeks. It is, however, an excellent way of getting close to work you would have no hope of doing yourself as an intern—a television cameraman, or copy writer on a big account for one of New York's top advertising firms, for example. It can also be a back-door approach to hands-on work. An organization which says it can't use an intern will often succumb when you say you only want to *watch;* and once you're tagging along, the person you shadow will likely end up giving you real work to do. A bit sneaky, but sometimes the only way in when an organization thinks it doesn't need you.

Cooperative education and off-campus learning: Usually code-words for internships which are sponsored by an academic institution, often with academic credit attached. An exception to the summertime internships which undergraduates usually seek, these programs frequently operate during the school year. Justified by universities as "learning experiences," critics charge that these internships are undermining the academic basis of higher education. But their advantage is the great connections which university career and internship offices often have with the professional world. The official sanction of your school encourages organizations to take on interns, and the coordinating work done by your university office saves you the hassle of setting something up on your own. Best of all, these internships very often are designed to lead to a permanent position after graduation, so that this type of program has the greatest potential as a direct bridge between academic life and professional career.

Intern-trainee and paraprofessional positions. This is the twilight zone of the internship world, where the distinction between short-term commitment and full-blown career training is hazy. Examples include teaching internships and paralegal positions. While often the first step in a full-time job, in many instances the employer regards them as short-term positions, expecting you to leave within two years for more schooling or another job. For the college graduate willing to commit at least a year, these positions can offer major responsibility and an excellent preview of a career in the field.

Affirmative action: One recent trend has been the use of internship programs for affirmative action. Many businesses and organizations sponsor internships specifically to give minorities training—with the long-term hope that the interns will make a career in the field. Other programs not designed for minorities nevertheless make special provisions for minority applicants. If you fit the bill, it is well worth your time to inquire.

Internships can be an excellent route into fields where minorities have consistently been under-represented—in journalism, for example. For applicants whose education or background has denied them essential skills or experience, these programs often have another big plus, in the form of intensive training programs designed to fill those gaps.

Finding an Internship

Internship hunting is not usually fired with the thrill of the chase; more often, it is a slow slog. The program listings here will give you an idea of what you will find in different fields and some ideas about how to win a position in a place you'll like, but only you can bring home the bacon. The introductions to specific fields of internship opportunities which follow give hints on how to proceed in each field and will repay careful reading. Some advice, though, applies generally:

—Whether trying to "Make Your Own" internship or applying to a
formal program, be clear about your goals, the sort of work you
want, and the kind of organization you seek. When you do identify
who you want to work for and what you want to do, research the
organization to learn where you could fit in, and so you can impress
them with your informed interest. "More internship hunts are
frustrated by sloppy preparation and uncertain goals than any other
set of factors" sighs one internship expert: don't let that happen to
you. (See sections on *Making Your Own* and *Making the Most of
Yourself* for more on this important subject.)

—Do not be a slave to terminology. Concentrate on the substance of
the position, not its name. If a law firm says it has no internships,
hang up and call again, asking about paralegal work. Be nice and
use whatever language makes the organization happy, but the
important thing is what the language means.

—When you are in doubt whether an organization has a formal
program or are fairly certain it does not, go to the top with your
initial inquiry. Directories of firms and organizations with names
and titles of key individuals abound: find the appropriate source,
pick a likely name attached to a plausible title, and write. While a
secretary might say "sorry, no," the higher-up will think twice,
maybe even start a program for you.

—Use connections; they work. Useful connections are not only
knowing the president of the company; they are countless affilia-
tions of other kinds. Maybe you worked for a lab one summer as a
bottle washer, but got to know the research director in the process.
Now you want to do zoology. Ask the research director who you
might call, and whether he/she can give you a recommendation.

One source of help students often forget: college alumni.
Graduates of your college or university nearly always look fondly
on their juniors; some alumni associations even ask alumni if they
wish to be listed in a directory of grads willing to help out students
looking for summer jobs or career advice. Check with your alumni
office to see if such a directory exists; if not, consult the alumni
listings for grads living near you and/or in the field of your choice,
then write or call. Begin by asking only for *advice;* you'll find out
quickly if the alumnus can also offer an internship, and you'll avoid
embarassment if he or she cannot.

Other useful associations: fraternities and sororities, national clubs with campus chapters, hometown Rotary, Lions clubs,
especially if a friend or relative is a member.

—Some colleges give financial support to interns to allow them to
work in traditionally volunteer positions; Washington internships,
for example. Stipends are often awarded through a campus competition, in which case the selection committee supplies winners with
a valuable letter of recommendation. Check with the Dean's or
Careers office on campus.

Paid or Volunteer?

The big question. If you cannot survive without earning money, the decision is already made. But most people have some flexibility on this score, and the hard question is deciding how much stipend/salary is enough, or whether the experience alone is worth foregoing money altogether.

Traditional arrangements should be taken into account. Capitol Hill offices rarely pay summer interns; their budgets are limited, applicants can be had by the truckload, and licking stamps in a congressional office is considered an honor. Public interest groups, including environmental organizations and lobbyists of various persuasions also fall into the usually-volunteer category. These organizations regularly rely on volunteer help as a substantial portion of their work force.

A wise guideline is this: if you are doing work that the organization ordinarily pays people to do, then you should be paid for it too. If inexperience means you work more slowly, that means you should be paid less, not that you should get no wage at all. Especially in profit-making enterprises, if there is work worth doing, then it should be worth paying you to do it. A business that profits from your free labor is exploiting you.

Exception: in some field jobs are so tight and prospective interns so eager that it is customary to work for free despite the sometimes monstrous profits of the employer. Examples: publishing, broadcast and print journalism, big-time advertising, television and film. But it is also true that in these fields experience counts for everything, and that your internship position, if you can win one, is one of the few ways of breaking into a closed market. By all means fight for some cash, but remember that you are lucky to get any position at all, and that a future job may be your payoff in these fields.

Academic Credit

An increasingly common form of reimbursement is academic credit granted by universities and colleges for all manner of internships.

This can be beneficial to all involved. The sponsor benefits because the grades or evaluations used to determine credit encourage high quality work in interns. The intern benefits by having practical experience count toward a degree.

But be wary of the credit-offering institution. Says Dr. Robert Ginn, Director of Harvard's Office of Career Services and Off-Campus Learning, "these arrangements often constitute outrageous exploitation of students. They pay college tuition, while having no service rendered them by their college. Unpaid by their employer, they are meanwhile paying for college credit. It's a rip-off."

Liberal arts students should be especially wary of internships-for-credit: their skills are general, and getting credit for using them is rather like getting credit for Life. In more vocational fields—nursing, forestry, even accounting—on-the-job experience is an integral part of the degree, and academic credit in return for the work is justified.

If you do an internship for college credit, be sure you get what you pay for. The college should provide guidance and support in return for your tuition. That means continuing, regular contact with college faculty, integration of the internship experiences into your other coursework, and a final assessment of the internship with your faculty advisor upon its conclusion.

Recognizing a Good Program

Organized internship programs range from good to abysmal. It pays to nail down the details of the job before committing a summer or year to it. Because the very idea of an internship is new to many of the organizations now offering them, their ideas of what constitutes a "program" can vary drastically.

This checklist gives the basics. If most of these elements are lacking from the program you're looking into, think twice before signing up. If it does look like there are major deficiencies in a program with an organization that otherwise seems ideal, however, don't despair. Once you know what's missing, tell your contact at the organization. Perhaps they made no provision for a supervisor/mentor for you: that can probably be arranged. Possibly no schedule has been drawn up of what you can work on, with whom: try doing that over the phone.

The Good Internship Program Checklist

Not every good program will include all these points, but a program lacking many of them spells trouble.

1. A clear description of your duties plus a schedule of the work you will be assigned: either by category or by specific projects needing attention.

2. An estimate of how much clerical work you will have to do — filing, answering the phone, photo-copying, etc.

3. Assignment to specific individuals with whom you will work; or, if doing an independent project, assignment to a supervisor.

4. When not part of #3 above, assignment to a high-level mentor in the organization who will regularly check on your progress and happiness, and who has the power to change your schedule of work if problems arise.

5. Formal or informal opportunities to learn about the work of the

organization outside your area: meetings with department heads, seminars, lunch with top brass, etc.

6. Space provided for you—desk, telephone, etc. Although many organizations will have to move you from one spot to another as desks open up, organizers of a good program *are* aware that you need to be accommodated. Badly-organized programs can often be recognized on the basis of this seemingly obvious criteria.

On Using This Book

Finding a possible internship is relatively easy: any organization you can think of has room—or can make room—for an intern. *Getting* an internship, and making sure it involves doing what you want, where you want, is the hard part. That's why this book is based on giving useful advice, not merely addresses and phone numbers.

So before you turn to the listings for ideas, read the following sections carefully:

Making the Most of Yourself will prime you for the hunt. Internship-hunting is similar to job-hunting, but students have little experience with either, and the pursuit of internships has a few twists of its own that you will want to know about. Sample resumes, cover letters, and even advice on how to shake hands—it's all there, step-by-step.

More and more, businesses, government agencies, corporate offices —organizations of every kind—are using students to work on specific short-term projects, even though they have no formal internship program. It's a wide-open field, and tremendously exciting for a self-starting type with lots of ambition and definite ideas about what he/she wants to do.

Making Your Own will get you started: mapping out a practical strategy for infiltrating an organization, this section also provides case studies of successful ventures by self-made interns in the past.

Getting the Most Out of It: As with most things in life, getting there is only half the battle. Once you land an internship, you will be low man on the totem pole. In this section the fine points of self-defense in office politics are covered, and the experiences of other interns condensed into advice on how to make sure *your* internship is more than three months of envelope-stuffing and answering the phone.

Program listings: You will find them divided into chapters according to field; each chapter begins with an essay briefing you on the field's general characteristics, the range of internship opportunities offered, and the kind of work you can expect to do.

Be sure to check *all* sections where internships in your area of interest might be offered. Biologists, for example, are needed in Health Sciences as well as Environmental Sciences. Law has a section of its own, but you will find lots of law-related opportunities with Public Service groups as well. To help you out, check at the end of each section for cross-references to other listings that involve similar interests.

Remember that these listings are *not* comprehensive. Programs have been included because they seem both good *and* representative of other opportunities in the particular field. Your own search will lead you to some of these others, and for more help with addresses and phone numbers, consult the publications listed in the last chapter, "Additional Sources of Information".

Happy trails!

MAKING THE MOST OF YOURSELF

"Appearances are everything," a world-weary courtier once observed about succeeding at Versailles, and the same advice holds true—well, almost—of the internship game.

The real point, of course, is that if you have done the hard work of thinking about yourself and your objectives in seeking an internship, appearances will almost take care of themselves.

So, before assembling a resume or hitting the phone to organize interviews, look hard at yourself:

—What made you choose the programs you want to apply for?
—What are your strengths, and in what fields can they be applied best?

A close look at your extracurricular interests can produce surprises. For instance, a chemistry student thinking of interning as a scientific researcher should also consider a successful stint while in high school as a catechism teacher to fourth graders and two years' experience as a reporter for the college paper.

The result? An internship teaching biology at summer school turns out to be an additional option, or work as an editorial intern for a science magazine.

The moral: don't limit yourself to the obvious, and don't impose artificial limits on your own interests and abilities.

When determining your interests and skills, consider the kind of experience you want, and why. Jot down thoughts of jobs, schooling, responsibilities, etc., you have had in the past and their relative merits and demerits. Talk to your college career-counselor or someone who knows you well for advice in choosing an area of interest you would like to explore through an internship. "Establish a portrait of yourself," recommends one counselor. "See if a pattern of interests or activities emerges from your experiences. Consider any skills, abilities, or interests you have acquired through past experiences. Figure out what you've accomplished, what you're good at, and outline your range of interests as a means of arriving at internship, and, ultimately, career options."

This exercise will prepare you for the two-part process of seeking entrance into an internship program. As was stressed earlier (see section "All About Internships"), the challenges of writing an effective resume,

and using an interview to your best advantage will be met most successfully by taking time to focus on your interests and abilities and experiences
you have to support them.

Self-analysis, the key: The resume and interview are your means of
presenting yourself to an internship director, and convincing him/her that
you are as attractive to the program as the program is to you. Self-analysis
is the key. Said one director, "The applicants who impress me most, and
consequently, those who we hire, are precisely those whose resumes and
manner during the interview reflect careful thought and genuine desire to
take part in our program, over any other. This comes as the result of
having fully examined personal strengths and weaknesses, interests and
capabilities."

THE RESUME

The act of writing a resume has somehow and somewhere acquired
negative connotations. But the resume is important, and if it's vague and
disorganized you might not land that internship you're going after. It need
not be an agonizing process, however—which isn't to say it will be fun, but
it's not as bad as pulling teeth.

With the cover letter, the resume marks your first contact with a
prospective employer. First impressions are lasting, so carefully plan and
construct your resume.

The resume should be a written record of the conclusions you have
arrived at concerning your skills, experiences, and job interests. Your
thoughts about yourself will dictate the content of your resume. Know
what you want to do, why, and how your abilities can help make the
internship experience a successful one for you and for the hiring organization. Select experiences, refer to courses and describe skills which will
illuminate the range of your abilities, and which will suggest to the
internship director ways in which you might fit into the organization.

Not only is the resume your initial means of communication; the
entire application process hinges upon its substance and attractiveness.
Devote as much time as is necessary to get it into the best possible shape.
It is the basis of the all-important interview as well as a crucial factor in its
own right. It's to your advantage to make yourself look and sound as good
as you can on paper.

Be specific in your resume; don't generalize. In defining your
interests succinctly, the process of resume-writing can be an informative
experience personally. A focussed, concise listing of your educational,
work, and extracurricular experiences can be an invaluable asset in
narrowing your interests and career goals.

In your resume, include all relevant schooling, activities, jobs, etc.,
that you have had beginning in high school (for those people just into their
junior year of college) or since entering college (for those people who have
completed at least three years of college). These guidelines are fairly
flexible, but remember that if a 22-year-old person stresses high school

activities on a resume, there is usually good cause for suspicion. But if a high school activity or job experience has a direct bearing on the kind of internship you are seeking, by all means mention it. For example, a prospective intern in an environmental studies program should definitely include the fact that as a high school junior she participated in an Outward Bound program.

The ultimate purpose of your resume is to convince the prospective employer that you are qualified for the internship. As an employer will base his first judgment of you and your abilities on the quality and substance of your resume, give it the preparation time it deserves. In addition to listing education and activities, try to convey a sense of the responsibilities and skills that your experience involved.

Keep it to one page: The essence of a well-crafted resume is one in which listings are stated clearly and accurately in a confident, self-promoting way. Be honest, but don't overstate your case. A few well thought-out descriptive listings go a good deal further than a four-page record of every club, committee, team, etc., that you have ever given time to. The cardinal rule of resume-writing is that *resumes should never exceed one page.* Sacrifice what you must, but never allow your resume to exceed one side of a page. Your qualifications may fill several pages, but a lengthy resume may be given only a cursory glance. Choose your most significant credentials and state them briefly.

Make it look good: The appearance of your resume is as important as the content. A resume that is attractive and easy to read will be better received than an overlong, disorganized one. After the difficult process of preparing a resume, don't undermine your efforts with a sloppy typing job and jumbled arrangement. If your typing is not impeccable, have it done professionally. Otherwise, type the master copy on bond—not corrasable—paper. Use an electric typewriter with a clean ribbon. Select a good copying service. Have the resume photocopied or offset printed. The reader's attention will be drawn by information that is attractively spaced on the page for maximum readability. Use capitals, margins, underlines, headings, and spacing to achieve the most open, appealing, and interesting visual effect.

Always make the responsibilities of the job the focus of your statement. Waitressing/waitering jobs, for instance, may entail not only table service, but personnel work, scheduling, and management as well. Don't merely state "cashier at skating rink" when your responsibilities also included bookkeeping and billing. Define your past jobs so that they highlight your potential, skills, knowledge, adaptability, reliability, and desire to learn and excel.

"The Real Thing"

Here are three sample resumes. They all differ in approach and offer different advantages and disadvantages. Consider carefully which form will best serve your needs and highlight your past endeavors.

Chronological: This format lists education and experience in *reverse* chronological order. It is the style most widely used but has one obvious disadvantage in that it clearly displays any shortcomings in your education, job background, or activities. Additionally, it can be somewhat boring and because of its very conventional nature may appear quite routine.

Note on "chronological" resumes: Especially if your resume is very short, you may include brief descriptions of your jobs, interests, etc. Remember, however, that descriptions are generally used in "Functional" or "Combination" resumes, where fewer items are listed but with greater attention to detail. For example, under "Work Experience":

> Stock Assistant—Biology Laboratory, University of California at San Francisco. Researched and assisted in drafting group proposal on Recombinant DNA—Summer 1979.

Functional/Analytical: This format enables you to present yourself in a "thematic" way. It groups types of job and educational experiences together, covering any particular shortcomings with a general approach. A drawback to consider though, is that employers are often aware that this type of resume may indeed be glossing over some important experiences, or lack thereof.

In whichever form of resume you use, don't make excuses or apologize for any time spent out of school or out of the work force; rather, use this to your advantage. Describe your endeavors briefly and any skills you may have learned or utilized during those undefined periods. Your atypical experiences and credentials may well appeal to an employer, and, in any case, will set you apart from the rest of the applicant pool.

Another difficulty with this type of resume is its appearance. "Functional" resumes are often unfocussed and lengthy. The blocks of paragraphs become cumbersome and hard to read. As stated earlier, the best resumes are those which are most attractive visually, best organized, and easiest to read.

Combination: This format combines the two previously described approaches. It allows you to highlight specific areas of interest and skill, while retaining the more traditional and well-known aspects of the "Chronological" form. This form is recommended by many career counselors, as it reflects self-analysis and stresses the range and nature of one's skills and experiences.

NAME

PRESENT ADDRESS: PERMANENT ADDRESS:

PHONE: PHONE:

EDUCATION: Glenview College, Danforth, Illinois
                        Candidate for B.A. degree in June, 1980.
                        Major: Biology
                        Dean's list 1978-1980.

SCHOOL   Teaching Assistant—Department of Biology,
ACTIVITIES: 1979-1980.
                        Member, George L. Sussman Memorial
                          Society for Biological Inquiry, 1978-1980.
                        Varsity Swim Team 1977-1980.
                        Member of College Choral Society, 1977-1980.

WORK   Stock Assistant—Biology Laboratory,
EXPERIENCE: University of California at San Francisco.
                        Summer of 1979.

                        Assistant Manager—Rustic and Company
                        Pub, Berkeley, California. Summer, 1978.

                        Volunteer—Danforth Center for Needy
                        Children—8 hours per week.
                        1977-1980.

OUTSIDE   Member—National Association of Biological
EXPERIENCE: Researchers, 1978-1980.

REFERENCES: Available upon request.

<u>NAME</u>

<u>PRESENT ADDRESS:</u>   <u>PERMANENT ADDRESS:</u>

<u>PHONE:</u>   <u>PHONE:</u>

<u>JOB OBJECTIVE:</u> (OPTIONAL)

<u>EDUCATION:</u>

Amherst College, Amherst, MA. B.A. cum Laude, Political Science, concentration in Constitutional history. 1975-1979.

<u>EXPERIENCE:</u>

Salesperson—Colonial Camera Shop, Carmel, CA. Taught photography workshop for purchasers of equipment, conducted periodic inventories, oversaw general maintenance and operation of branch store. Summer of 1978.

Construction worker—S. Kane and Sons, Carmel, CA. Assistant supervisor of nine-hour, twelve person shift, specialized in carpentry and cement pouring, worked on renovation of two former office buildings into a shopping mini-mall and a community center, respectively. Summer of 1977.

Volunteer—coach in Monterey Summer Youth Basketball League, coach of 25 boys, ages 12-15, scheduling of 18-game season, instructor at basketball clinic for boys 7-10. Summer of 1977.

Campaign Assistant—State Senator Marc Citrin. Organized 75 volunteers to canvas three-town district. Wrote speeches, campaign literature, organized phone campaign. Summer of 1976.

<u>ADMINISTRATIVE AND STUDENT SERVICES:</u>

Served as dormitory resident counselor for 20 freshmen and 20 upperclassmen. Counseled students in academic social and personal concerns, while coordinating social events for the dorm. Coordinated student-faculty-administration forums to facilitate discussion of pertinent campus issues. 1978-1979.

Served as class representative for two consecutive years to the College Council. Researched success of transition to coeducation which Amherst undertook in 1974. Recommended future goals and specific projects to the college.

<u>REFERENCES:</u>

Available upon request.

NAME

PRESENT ADDRESS: PERMANENT ADDRESS:

PHONE: PHONE:

JOB OBJECTIVE: (OPTIONAL)

EDUCATION:

Trinity College, Hartford, CT. B.A., Psychology to be awarded May, 1981.

COUNSELING WORK:

Counselor, Vermont Society for Children (June 1979-August 1979).
—facilitated adjustment to group living
—assisted in group therapy sessions
—coordinated activities to develop childrens' ability to live, play and work together

Resident Advisor, Trinity College (September 1979-May 1980).
—advised students in problems relating to personal and academic life
—planned social activities for the dormitory and intra-college social council
—assisted in course planning as part of the new core curriculum adopted by the college

ACADEMIC RESEARCH:

Working at the present time on thesis proposal dealing with the adolescent life of the "only child." Thesis work entails:
—detailed development of thesis topic
—specific materials to be used
—interviews planned and justification for them
—compilation of information and writing of thesis
—thesis defense before the Psychology Department

Developed an independent research project (1978) on the effects of urbanization on the American family.

SUMMER EXPERIENCE:

Kitchen worker, Darien Country Club, Darien, CT.
Summers of 1978, 1979. Managed dining room and refreshment stand.

Traveled throughout Europe and North Africa, Summer 1977.

PERSONAL:

Enjoy playing guitar and performing semi-professionally.

REFERENCES:

Available upon request.

Basics: resume checklist

1. *Name.* Clearly and prominently displayed. Avoid nicknames.
2. *Address.* You may use both your home (permanent) and school (temporary) address.
3. *Telephone number.* Provide a telephone number for each address.
4. *Objective.* While stating an objective is not mandatory, if you have a specific objective in mind, i.e. "to become fluent in Spanish through work as intern with inner city planning commission," stating it will give an employer a better idea of how you might fit into the organization. Don't worry if you have no specific goal, but attempting to identify an objective is a good means of deciding on the kind of internship that is best suited to your interests.
5. *Education.* Usually presented in reverse chronological order, be sure to include:
   —degree you earned or are in the process of earning.
   —major(s) and possibly other academic foci.
   —dates degrees were, or will be, received.
   —schools and locations—again, try to determine whether or not you will be including high school experience on your resume. If so, include your high school in the education section of the form.
6. *Grade Point Average.* You may mention this if you like, but do so *only* if it is a good one. Including a poor or average one is foolish.
7. *Work.* This listing should include paid and volunteer work, and be listed in reverse chronological order.
8. *Outside Experience.* Major projects, programs or activities with which you were involved and have not yet listed. Include any courses you have taken which are pertinent to the field in which you hope to work.
9. *Extracurricular Activities.* These are separate from your "experiences," and should be listed afterwards. Include any extracurricular activities to which you devoted time and effort. But do not overstate your case by including *everything*, large and small.

In numbers 7, 8, and 9 remember to describe (unless you are using a "chronological" resume) your experience in terms of the responsibilities you had and the skills you developed which would be an asset to a future employer. Don't overdo it, but try to omit personal pronouns (i.e., "I did . . .") and begin phrases with an "action verb" (i.e., "coordinated the . . ."). This will draw the reader's attention to the responsibility entailed in the job. The saying "It's not what you say but how you say it" was probably originated by a career counselor conducting a seminar in resume writing. Effective wording is crucial. The more accurate and interesting your language, the better you sound.

10. *Additional Information.* (If needed and relevant). This may be presented under separate categories such as "honors", "special interests", "personal", etc. Try to develop headings that will be appropriate in light of the type of internship you are pursuing.
11. *More Additional Information,* such as birthplace, marital status, etc., is optional; it's important to some employers while irrelevant to others. As a general rule, it is just as well omitted.

12. *References.* The concluding part of your resume can simply state: "Available upon request." Select appropriate people to recommend you for a particular internship; people who know you well and are familiar with your abilities. A teacher, coach, former employer or co-worker are the best choices. When asking an individual to recommend you, discuss the prospective internship with him/her, including the reasons for your interest in the internship, your experience, and thoughts on what might be emphasized in a letter of recommendation. Provide your references with a copy of your resume and cover letter to refer to when writing. Recommendations should include how the person sees you as an individual, and very importantly, specific instances of your initiative, effectiveness, accomplishments, and motivation.

If you have an impressive list of "recommenders"—one that includes people involved in the field you hope to work in, list them by name on your resume, along with their titles and addresses. For instance, if your English professor is recommending you for an internship as an English teacher, it will be to your advantage to have that information on your resume and in the hands of a prospective employer. Should an internship organization require recommendations along with your application, notify your recommenders of this well in advance of the deadline. Just prior to the application date, check back with them to see that the references have been written and mailed. Provide your recommenders with addressed, stamped envelopes.

THE COVER LETTER

Along with the resume and interview, the cover letter is a necessary part of the application process. Include it with your resume. Its primary function is to introduce you to the prospective employer. In the letter, which should follow a business letter format, briefly describe your interests and any skills and experience you have which relate to the internship you are pursuing.

Send your cover letter and resume to a specific person. Call first or check any literature you have on the program or organization to determine who is in charge of interviewing and hiring interns. Addressing the letter, "To Whom it May Concern" denotes an element of ambiguity, as if this is one of 50 letters you are sending out. Although it may well be one of many, there is no reason why your interviewer should know that.

State your aims forcefully. This is the time to make a good impression and effectively demonstrate your writing skills, ability to state your case, enthusiasm, and initiative. In your letter suggest when you will call or visit for an informative session or interview.

Type each cover letter individually: appearance counts. A xeroxed letter of introduction will not create a positive first impression. As with the resume, be brief and to the point. Begin by identifying yourself and name the internship for which you are applying. Explain why you are interested in the program or organization and specify your reasons for wanting to participate in this type of internship. Refer to the enclosed resume; point out significant experiences or skills which qualify you for the internship. In the absence of specific experience, stress your abilities and the nature of your interest. In closing, express your interest in having an interview and state your phone number. You are responsible for following up the letter with a call on the appointed date to arrange an interview.

Keep copies of your letters so that you know who you have written to in each organization or office, and exactly what you said. Be organized; this can be your greatest asset in locating an internship. Keep files, lists, answers to your letters, resumes you have written, copies of letters of recommendation, etc. Not only will these be of help in keeping yourself organized during the process of searching, but you will most likely want to reuse them in the future.

THE INTERVIEW

"Of the 14 factors that most often lead to rejection of a job applicant, 7 are interview related" states the *New York Times,* citing a Northwestern University survey of 186 companies. "Chief among these pitfalls are the inability to demonstrate self-confidence, enthusiasm, and a clear set of goals." Don't let the figures scare you, though. The interview can work for you just as easily as it can work against you. Although an interview is primarily for hiring purposes, it is also an informative session for you. You are there to sell yourself and to prove that you are qualified. Ask questions that are well defined and specific; focus on gaining insight into where you will fit into the organization and what the organization deals with on a day-to-day basis. Bear in mind that the interview is actually a two-way conversation. Before an interview, do your homework. Appearances count, but so does intelligence and preparedness. Research the organization or firm so that you avoid obvious, irrelevant, or unimportant questions. Being knowledgeable about the internship shows interest and initiative. Familiarity with the internship program and organization will also make you feel more at ease and more comfortable conversing with your interviewer.

The way you dress can say a lot about you. For instance, if you arrive with greasy hair, dirty finger nails, wearing your most fatigued army jacket, the message is clear. Dress according to the standards of the given organization or firm. A prospective intern at I.B.M. is advised against wearing a t-shirt and sneakers, while a volunteer intern candidate at a neighborhood revitalization organization might feel out of place in a three-piece suit. As a general rule, women should plan to wear a dress or skirt and blouse—men a casual suit or jacket and tie. Note: don't mix purple with orange, plaids with stripes, or faded denim with anything. Wear something comfortable for the sake of being physically more at ease during the interview and to avoid squirming and itching.

Take a couple of deep breaths. Relax. Smile but don't appear plastic. Forget about "acting yourself." If you've ever been interviewed you know that it's bogus advice. Take comfort, however, in knowing you're prepared. If you've prepared, and know why you're there, you won't be caught flat-footed. When entering the office, keep your right hand free for a handshake. Have a resume with you just in case, even if you sent one ahead of time.

There are two forms of communication during an interview. One is verbal, the other, physical. Be conscious of both.

Talking: Speak clearly and concisely. Look at your interviewer while you're talking, and, more importantly, while he is. Ask questions. Don't let your preparation go to waste. Make him realize that you are genuinely interested. Smile, but don't overdo it. Have questions ready and be prepared to answer questions from your resume. Don't feel compelled to keep talking. Say what you have to say then stop. Be conscious of speech patterns ("well," "uh . . .") and be a good listener. Recall that an interview is foremost a two-way conversation. Attentiveness is a must. Try to put yourself in the interviewer's shoes and consider what you would like to hear and see, and how you would react to you in an interview situation.

Body language: This is not impossible to dictate or control. Slouching and scratching don't make it. Be consciously attentive to your mannerisms to reinforce the impression you are trying to create verbally. Be relaxed, but poised; even lean toward being formal. Bear in mind that you are seeking a job, and the way you carry yourself is important to an employer. Once hired, you will be representing that organization or company, so suit your manner to what the situation demands just as you would your dress.

Refrain from asking about salary, length or work day, etc.: it's tacky. If the interviewer has failed to mention the particulars of the internship, wait until the end of the interview when you are wrapping things up. Try your skill at euphemisms and tactfulness. Ask if there is a stipend with the internship, about the duration of the program, if it is a full or part-time position, who you would be working with, etc. If asked what you hope to earn, give a range of salary. Make sure you have considered beforehand (see section "All About Internships") how important it is that you be paid for your efforts.

Following the interview, write a short note to your interviewer thanking him for his time. The thank you note is an opportune time to reiterate your interest in the internship and enthusiasm for wanting to be part of the organization. Call to inquire about the status of your application only if you have not heard after the date on which decisions were to be announced. Don't call any earlier, however, or any more frequently. You will make an impression, certainly, but not necessarily a good one. Again, particularly if you are interviewing with many groups and organizations, keep a list of those whom you have called and written. Keep track of the contacts you make, for conveniences' sake as well as future reference.

MAKING YOUR OWN

Beyond the tended fields of organized internship programs lies a vast uncharted wilderness rich in opportunity and just waiting to be tamed: it is the world of the do-it-yourself internship. Is there a corporate law firm you're itching to work for? An advertising company in New York that says it only needs secretaries? Making your own program takes resourcefulness, *chutzpah*, charm, and a certain amount of good luck, but it *can* be done. The rewards are correspondingly great: doing the work you want to do, in the place you want to do it, and the satisfaction of knowing that credit for your success lies entirely with you.

This section outlines a strategy specifically for creating an internship where one did not exist before. But the problem of infiltrating an organization and securing a worthwhile position is met by interns in organized programs as well as by those who are creating an internship from scratch. Consequently, much of the advice given here will be useful to everyone seeking an internship.

The process of creating your own internship consists of 1) learning about an organization, 2) figuring out where you might fit in, and then 3) convincing them that it would be worth their while (and yours) to hire you. The steps outlined below should help you through that process. But be sensible: there are many ways to skin this particular cat, and the method below is an all-purpose technique. Adjust it to suit your circumstances, and abandon it if fortune throws a family friend in your direction who wants you to do whatever will make you happy in his Hollywood movie studio.

Sizing Up–The Initial Assault

The most vital skill required to successfully target and eventually capture a position is the ability to size up an organization. "Sizing up" consists of asking yourself the following more or less obvious questions about the company-clinic-factory-office-field you are interested in:
- —How big is it?
- —What does it do?
- —Who hires and fires?
- —Do the people who you would imagine yourself working for have the authority to hire and fire?
- —What bureaucratic prerequisites exist? (e.g., security clearances, civil service exams, academic degrees, etc.)
- —Is the company a rich or poor organization? How well can it afford luxuries like interns?

Answer these questions and a useful picture of the organization will emerge. This picture should first of all tell you whether you are still interested in working for the organization. Assuming you are, the most important thing is understanding *where the power to hire you is*. It is this person who you will have to talk into taking you on. As one self-made intern put it, ''Don't waste a lot of time talking to people who don't have the authority to hire you. Once you know what you want to do, find out who's in charge and go straight to them.''

But finding out what you want to do may take some time. Answers to some of your questions may be available in company reports, periodicals, job guides, and the like. When doing this initial research, always be on the lookout for information that will help you to sell yourself to the organization. You will want detailed information on those aspects of the operation that are in line with your interests. You may be interested in marketing, and you may know that IBM makes computers, but do you know what types compared with the competition? Often the kind of details you need to know can only be discovered through talking to people on the inside. Most people looking for an internship will start both their search and research at . . .

The Impersonnel Office–On the Front

Most interns try for a job in a large organization of one form or another because big usually translates to more opportunities. But big equals bureaucracy—which means a personnel office—that modern institution resembling a cross between a registry of motor vehicles and a state lottery commission. Personnel offices all have that ''have a nice day'' superficial friendliness, a propensity for files, records, and forms, and offer about the same odds for success as a state lottery. As a general rule, the personnel office is a sure route to another summer flipping burgers at the local set of arches.

Organizations tend to have two systems for finding people to fill jobs. There is the official route through the office with all the smiling secretaries and file cabinets. And there is the unofficial route through the people who actually work there. If you happen to be one of those people whose qualifications are so seductive that you are never turned down for anything by anyone, then you need not fear the smiling secretaries. But if you're like most of us, be sure to investigate the structure of this unofficial personnel system. If you are able to convince someone on the working level of a newspaper, congressional office, or laboratory that you are the sort of person they would like to have as a colleague, you'll stand miles ahead of the average naked resume. An excellent way to get a look at the operation from the inside is . . .

Interviewing for Information–Behind Enemy Lines

A valuable means to both learn about a field of work and to infiltrate a particular organization is simply to go in and ask someone about his or her job. Getting in the front door is usually rather easy since most people like to talk about what they do. Several strategies are possible:

  —Find out if you might legitimately know someone in or around your target organization. Consider college and high school ties as well as family connections. Alumni of most every shape and form are usually more than happy to give a few minutes of information to a student of their alma mater.

—Hunt up any personal acquaintances in the field or related fields. It is usually possible to come up with some sort of tenuous connection to a person on the inside of most any organization.

—If all else fails, go in cold. Call the switchboard and start asking questions. With a modicum of luck you will be connected to someone who will be able to help you. Above all else, be persistent. When you finally contact someone who seems to be involved in the work you are interested in, tell that person honestly why you are calling. While you *are* job hunting, stress that you are not asking for a formal interview, but need some information about what the field is like.

Let us assume that by hook or crook you have gotten a foot in the door and are now the bona fide holder of an appointment to meet informally with someone. Think carefully about why you are interested in journalism, law, lion taming, etc. The quality of your thought will help you to better express yourself as well as improve the quality of information you will receive. Bring along a nicely typed (or offset printed) copy of your current resume. And, last but not least, *do not put the person you are speaking with on the spot for a job.* In other words, do not throw yourself at his/her mercy, beg, plead, or otherwise seek to extort employment. Interviewing for information is precisely that: you are there to learn about how a given organization or field works. If you nail the school alum with whom you are speaking with a direct plea for a position, you are not only likely to blow your chance and embarrass the alum, but also prevent anyone else from trying this technique in the future in that particular office. Here are some practical questions you *can* ask:

—How does one get into this field? Ask the person you are speaking with for his/her personal history.

—How does this organization compare with others in the same field?

—Does this particular operation or any other like it ever hire people for summer or part-time or internish-type positions?

—If it does, what role do interns play? Are they usually peripheral, reserved for the performance of menial tasks, or do interns make a significant contribution?

—What work have interns done in the past that has been of value to the company?

—If the person you are speaking with does not really know (or seem to know) the answers to these questions, ask who might.

—Also, if the person you are speaking with is not really working in your field of interest, find out who in the organization is, and ask if you may go speak to them.

You may just find yourself back at the personnel office again. Only this time, you know a little bit more about what you are getting into, and about the people who make things work. You might have found an existing semi-formal arrangement that suits your needs, e.g., a laboratory that has no intern program but hires assistants who are given significant responsibility. If you were not so lucky, however, now is the time to start selling yourself. Assuming that you have decided an internship with this outfit is for you, you now face the problem of all members of the army of prospective interns: convincing an *employer* that an intern is for *him*. You must convince whoever has the authority to hire you that taking on an ambitious, bright, hardworking, swell, nice person will be a) a tremendous service to humanity, and b) a smart business move because you are high-quality goods at a low price. In other words, you are preparing for . . .

The Hype

Since by this point in your search you should be rather familiar with the operation of your target organization, try to figure out where you might fit in. Bear in mind that what you propose must be both useful to the organization and worthwhile for you. Your options are often broader if you are willing to settle for a volunteer internship. Working for free—if you can afford it—has its advantages. First, there is the obvious plus that anybody is more likely to chance an unknown commodity (you) if they do not have to pay for it. Secondly, once you are in, an employer is less likely to give you clerical and other not-so-fun jobs if they are not paying you—they aren't obliged to get their money's worth out of your expensive hide. On the other hand, the old adage that a job that doesn't pay isn't worth doing often holds true. In organizations where there is very little need for "volunteer-type" help—where secretarial and clerical tasks are minimal and already handled easily by permanent staff—your job is likely to be substantive only if you are being paid for it. Your decision has to be based on a careful estimation of how the operation would use a volunteer intern.

As you consider where you could squeeze yourself into a job, remember that for most organizations the jobs done by inexperienced people (like you) are probably clerical, i.e., filing, answering the phone, etc. You have to convince them that letting you do other kinds of work as well will be as valuable to them as it will be to you. The burden of proof is on you—after all, why should they trust a college student with tasks usually performed by permanent employees? There are essentially two strategies for freeing yourself from trivial work; both of them require using your detailed knowledge of the organization:

Find a need and fill it. Point out how you could help with certain routine but non-trivial tasks that would provide you with an idea of what is going on and be of some real use to your prospective employers. Are there letters that need writing, experimental measurements in a lab that must be taken regularly? Learn the rudiments of legal research or discover what trade news must be summarized—chances are there is something you could become sufficiently expert at to be of real use. Then convince your doubting interlocutor that you can do it. *But:* be sure that the job you have found (or created as the case may be) will not require all of your time. It is essential to have enough free time that you can take on some of the more interesting things that will inevitably come up once you have proven you won't bungle everything you touch. Having a regular, important, yet not crucial job to start with is a perfect opportunity to show that you are competent. From there you should be able to move in to other more interesting and important tasks as they come along.

An alternative strategy is to create a project that will be interesting to work on full-time and useful to the organization. This gambit is a little harder to pull off since you have to sell yourself as a complete package, the results of which will probably not be seen until the term of your employment is up. This plan has the advantage of freeing you to do exactly what you want. Unfortunately, working on an independent project necessarily isolates you from some of the routine of a line of work—an important aspect of learning about a field from an internship. The trickiest part of this strategy, however, is the first-class selling job it requires. As you draw up your proposal for a project, essential points to remember are:

Keep it reasonable—Make sure that you are capable of fulfilling, and fulfilling well, every requirement of the project you are proposing.

Keep it small—Unless the opportunity to work on this project is all you want from an internship, plan to spend part of your time doing other things within the organization that will help you learn about what goes on in several different departments. An especially well-designed project might take you through several departments in the course of working on it.

Keep it sweet—Be sensitive to the nature of the organization and who does what for whom. A great idea for a project may just horn in on somebody's territory—a profoundly bad scene for intern-types who depend completely on insiders' good will.

Case Studies

So far we've laid out a general game plan for making your own internship. Remember that, at best, it is only a set of suggestions, and putting our ideas into practice requires improvisation on your part. The following case studies will give you an idea of how the *Making Your Own* strategy works in the real world. The three examples are taken from fields where self-made internships are often the only way to go: Architecture, Hospital Administration, and Capitol Hill offices in Washington. Perhaps the best lesson to be learned from them is that any of a number of approaches can work; the one you select must fit your own particular circumstances. Take our ideas and the methods described below as *general* suggestions, then play it by ear. Above all, be creative!

Case study #1: This student wanted to spend January of her sophomore year working in an architectural firm. Because she had no course experience in architecture, she set out looking for a firm that would take her on as a volunteer.

Acting on a tip from an advisor at school, she sent off a letter to a large architecture firm in Boston in which a school alumnus was a senior partner. Following up the letter with a phone call, she was unable to get an interview. According to the secretary, the alum was much too busy to see her. Realizing that she would never be given an appointment, she decided that the only thing to do was to walk in the front door. Armed with a portfolio of drawings and paintings, she drove the three hours to Boston and presented herself to the receptionist. She explained who she was, and said that she had been sent by her advisor at school who was a close personal friend of the senior partner (not entirely true). She then explained that she had made the three-hour trip solely for this interview (another lie, but an effective one). Within five minutes, our intrepid intern found herself talking to the senior partner.

The man (a school alum) was floored by her gumption, and just happened to need an extra hand right then. She explained that she would work for free in order to gain exposure to the field, and that she would help out wherever she could, as long as she didn't have to be just a secretary (her typing was lousy, besides). She stressed her ability to think fast on her feet, and promised to stay out of people's way. The alum took her on, and she spent a very worthwhile month with the firm. Among her activities were building models of proposed buildings, some graphics work, and researching building codes for a major development project. This student went on to major in architecture, and is now working for an architect in Boston before she applies to architecture schools.

Case study #2: One college sophomore sent out 15 letters to hospitals in Boston and Chicago, asking for a volunteer position as an administrative aide for the month of January. The letters stated that he was interested in a career in Hospital Administration, and that he was pursuing a business/economics curriculum (even though at the time he had taken only one course in each). He mentioned specific areas of interest, such as public relations, policy, and the government-affected aspects of hospital administration.

Of great importance was the fact that he had had three summers' experience in hospital work. Though his letter did not mention that this work had been in the minor capacity of a patient transporter, it did state that his experience had given him a feel for patient needs and an understanding of the hospital working environment.

The 15 letters netted him six replies, including three requests for interviews. The first interview was conducted over the phone, during which he restated his reasons for wanting the internship and maintained a "comfortable, relaxed tone." It went well enough to land him a position with a major urban teaching hospital, where he spent the month working on an evaluation of the hospital's implementation of Section 504 of the Rehabilitation Act (prohibiting discrimination against the handicapped). The project was completely his own, allowing him to work independently while observing the goings-on in the hospital's administrative office. It proved to be an extremely educational month.

Case study #3: Capitol Hill is a forest of "make-your-own" opportunities. One student started his search for a summer internship by doing some background research on the congressman from his home state. A helpful publication was the *Almanac of American Politics* (Dutton, New York, Annual), which gives some basic information on every member of Congress. The key thing was to be both interested and knowledgeable concerning the congressman's favorite issues. The student managed to get past the receptionist and talk directly to the Administrative Assistant. As the one who hires and fires, the "AA" is the most important person in the office to the prospective intern. The student explained who he was, why he was there, and—with caution—what he might do in the office. His familiarity with the congressman's activities, and his ability to make modest suggestions as to possible projects, made him appear a worthwhile addition to the office. His offer to help out with clerical work to a *limited* extent made him seem less of a freeloader and more of an earnest helper.

Though he did end up doing a fair amount of routine office work—helping on mailing campaigns and answering inquiries from constituents (sometimes interesting)—he was also asked to analyze certain sections of the federal budget. He wrote up his evaluations, which were included in the congressman's final report as part of a yearly budget evaluation. Using a bit of aggressiveness to get out from under the burden of clerical work, he ended up with a very satisfying summer.

MAKING THE MOST OF IT

Once you have finagled your way into an internship, the next step is to make it worthwhile. This means establishing a good working relationship with those around you, and taking full advantage of your position as an intern to learn and gain exposure to your field of interest. While this is more a matter of art than of science, there *are* some basic considerations to keep in mind as you approach an internship.

The piece of advice most frequently given by interns is: "be flexible." Realize that interns, unlike most regular employees, do not usually stick to any strictly defined job. Being flexible means two things. First, always keep your eyes open for new things to do. If you see a task to be done that you think you can handle, and would add to your experience, ask if you can do it. Second, always appear eager to take on new work if it is asked of you. As one intern said, "If your boss asks you to do something, just *do* it, even if you don't completely understand what's going on." The important thing is to show them that you are ready and willing to take on new tasks, and that you can think on your feet. When given something new to do, "Don't ask a lot of questions right away, just give it your best shot and then find out later what you did wrong."

A cardinal rule is *never be in the way*. This means tackling new jobs with a minimum of explanation, and making the most efficient use of your supervisor's time. One strategy is to write down whatever questions you have, wait until your supervisor is free, then go to him with a whole list of questions at once. "The most important thing was to show them I could work independently," says one student who did a volunteer internship, "you don't want to get in the situation of having to ask someone a question every ten minutes."

Sticking closely to your original job description could mean foregoing some exciting opportunities. If you turn down every offer of a new task, the offers will not continue. And three out of four times a new job offered to interns will be more challenging than the previous one. Why? Because, as you become better known to an organization they will be more inclined to trust you with significant jobs. Many an intern has been busier with more important tasks during the last two weeks of his/her summer job than during the first six.

Stay sensitive to new possibilities, and push yourself in the direction of a job you might want to do. Keeping track of other people's schedules is one way of doing this. When the person who normally edits international news for the newspaper you are working on is planning a vacation, it's time for you to ask if you might "cover" the position for the duration of his/her absence. If the job you want to try is too big or complex, ask if you could assist whoever is officially taking over the position. Organizations of all kinds are usually hard-pressed by a regular employee's vacation. They are usually more than happy to have an intern's help—and interns usually end up with real responsibility and a feel for the job that never comes from observation or busy-work.

Office Politics

Office politics can often determine whether your stay is pleasant or hellish. The sooner you catch-on to office relations, the better off you'll be.

Figure out who does what for whom; the pecking order. There will be both a visible and an invisible power structure which may not coincide. If you figure out these structures early on, your chances of asking the right questions of the right people, and generally getting things done are vastly increased. *Secretaries* in almost any organization are near the heart of the invisible power structure: getting to know them and keeping them happy will pay you back in spades. They know which levers to push in the corridors of power, and if you can get them pushing a few for you, so much the better.

Obviously, the amount of clerical work you will be expected to do will depend on how the particular organization works. In some offices everyone is more or less expected to handle his or her own paperwork, whereas others rely more heavily on secretarial help. Whatever the case, you should make it clear at the outset that you do not want your internship to consist of clerical work only. This should be done during your initial interview with your employer. Making the most of an internship usually means being more than a secretary, and you should inform your employer of this. Express your willingness to help out where needed, but make it clear that you want to spend time on jobs which give you the kind of exposure to the field that you're after.

Never underestimate the help of a mentor. As the one person in the social structure who has no official status, your best bet is to be associated with someone who does. To the extent circumstances permit, keep a steady connection with one figure in the hierarchy high enough up to wield authority. Not only will that connection tend to ensure that the work you are given is challenging and broad in scope, but it will help protect you from an overload of busy work. As a mere "office intern," no one will think twice about asking you to watch the phone all morning. As summer assistant to the vice president, you will strike lots of people as too busy to bother. Of course, the best way to establish that connection is from the very start, when you talk about doing the internship in the first place. An upper-echelon guardian angel will also serve you well in two other important ways:

—In even the best internship there are "dead" periods when absolutely nothing is happening. If you have a mentor, then you can always pester him or her for something to do. His or her advice can also be very useful in shaping a long-term project so that it is worthwhile when finished. A mentor can offer the insight you need when you are working independently; without it, you could easily be wasting your time.

—When you wrap up your internship and return to the ivy walls of Podunk U., your experience will go with you. Yet someday, possibly someday very soon, you will need a reference who will describe and evaluate what you did. A detailed recommendation from a heavyweight based on the "you" in the work world outside the classroom could help win you the job that starts your career.

Architecture

Architecture is an extremely competitive field. Interns are a dime-a-dozen, and many internship-type positions that were once available to college undergraduates are now filled by the hordes of students graduating from architecture schools each year. One student, who graduated from Williams College with that school's architecture prize, searched for eleven months in Boston and New York before finding even a temporary architecture job as a gap-filler before applying to grad schools in architecture. During her search, she found that many Boston firms were staffing their drafting rooms with Harvard Design School graduates—a discouraging discovery in a field where the question "can you draw?" is the equivalent of "can you type?" for most firms.

Landing an internship in architecture—especially if you are an undergraduate with relatively little training—takes determination. Unless you are willing to settle for helping out with secretarial work in order to at least *see* the inside of an architect's office, some technical drafting, graphics, and modelling skill is a must for securing a substantive position. Drawing is the bread and butter of an architectural office, so without some basic skills you will have difficulty convincing someone to take you on.

Because architecture firms are constantly bombarded with pleas for jobs, few bother to run formal internship programs. Almost all of the opportunities involve creating your own position, so the advice contained in the section on *Making Your Own* is especially applicable to this field.

How to Fit In

Let's assume for the moment that by some combination of genius, chutzpah, and connections you have managed to land a job with an architect for the summer. There are several areas in which interns can make themselves useful. Most of these are in support capacities—involving tasks peripheral to the actual design and drawing of buildings that is done by the professional architects.

Many architects emphasize the use of scale models of their plans to portray three-dimensionally what their concepts will look like. These models are the things you often see in museums, with the parsley trees and midget buildings. One intern spent two months building models of the same site. Eventually his architect took it to Mayor Byrne of Chicago, who liked it enough to authorize the construction of four new high-rise buildings designed by the firm.

Other interns do the lettering on blueprints: "If someone is really good at lettering, then there is a lot he can do," said one architect. Specifications, dimensions, captions, and often the firm's logo are copied from other sketches. Lettering is a tedious but satisfying job because interns get to see—and in a small way participate in—the designs that take shape and substance in front of them.

Graphics and working up presentations is another area where interns are a great help. Almost all of the structures designed have to be explained to interested laymen before they are built. Developers, bankers, and tenants all want to know what their building is going to look like, and often they don't know much about blueprints. Consequently firms create presentations, with photos of the site, carefully constructed models, and slick graphics, to sell their proposals.

Interns can put most of these things together. They "zip" drawings—laying down patterned tape to highlight particular areas. They make titles, border the drawings, cut the paper, darken walls on the plans (to give them more "substance"), and paste the exhibit together.

Things can get feverish when a presentation is needed quickly. The interns "really get a sense of urgency—they are in the middle of it." Other times, things can be slow and dull as nails. "Every office has its moments," one intern explained, and the only thing to do when a project gets tedious is to finish it quickly.

What about drafting? As we said above, architects—especially in large firms—can usually get architecture students to fill in in the drafting room, so if you are an undergraduate, don't expect to do too much of it. An architect is interested in your drafting ability only to see that you have some manual dexterity, familiarity with plans, and a demonstrated interest in the field. Beyond that—unless you are unusually gifted—it is unlikely that your drafting talents will be put to much use.

Small Versus Large

Your experience as an intern will to a large extent depend on the size of the firm you are working in. The consensus seems to be that large firms teach the interns better architectural technique but restrict them to a particular specialty. "Large offices offer good technical training. But in a short period of time, you're likely to get a narrow view of the profession." Small firms, on the other hand, offer a jack-of-all trades, master-of-none perspective on the entire process from design to finishing construction. "You're likely to get a better overall picture in a small firm, but in many cases we don't 'do' the profession as well," suggested an architect from a small office.

Getting Hired

The key to landing a job with an architecture firm is getting an interview with the right person, i.e., whoever has the power to hire you. As always, connections are often the only way to get to the person in charge.

The personal recommendation really does help. "If someone calls ahead, then I pay attention, look hard at him," said an interviewer. At the same time, however, a stranger's telephoned recommendation carries little weight. "Some of the worst assessments I get come from Deans," said one architect.

An architect interviewing you for an internship is looking for a few simple qualities. Primarily, he/she wants to know whether you can draw. "It's virtually impossible to get a job in a firm if you can't draw, or do model and graphics work," one architect put it. So, *bring your drawings to the interview*. They will speak louder and clearer than any grades or descriptions of courses that you can offer. Barring drawings, bring layouts, advertisement mock-ups—anything to show your graphics ability.

Secondly, the architect is hiring students whom he hopes to encourage to go into architecture, and who will perhaps eventually come back to the firm. So make sure that you can clearly express and convincingly demonstrate a sincere interest in architecture. To the firm, an internship is not just a summer job to give students spending-money for school.

By the end of your interview, the architect should have a pretty good idea of where you could fit into the firm, but he/she will also be curious to see what you think you can offer. In your response, present a clear, cogent expression of your own talents, interests, and goals, and how they relate to the firm. Be sure, though, not to boast about your architectural design solutions. Architects emphasize that "It's stupid to think that you are going to design—you just don't know enough." Instead, explain why you are interested in the field. One architect hired an intern who had worked the past three summers putting up dry wall. The intern had said, "I like putting up dry wall straight and getting the corners just right!" Architects appreciate this kind of pride in construction. Especially if you are a liberal arts student, i.e., untrained for everything, then the burden is on you to explain how you're qualified to work in the office.

A note to women: Architecture is a stubbornly male profession. Less than one percent of registered architects in this country are women. As a woman entering the field, realize that you are a pioneer up against extremely tough odds. The times are only slowly changing, and you are likely to have to work extra hard to prove yourself every step of the way.

Other Opportunities

Aside from jobs in architectural firms themselves, students can put their interest in architecture to work in various organizations that are out of the main stream. The Brown, Donald & Donald Summer Planning Internship (listed below) is an example of the architecture-related opportunities available in private planning firms. Other research-oriented organizations, of which the American Institute of Architects Research Corporation is a good example, study various social aspects of architecture. The Nacul Center (also listed below) is one of a growing number of firms approaching basic architectural design problems from an ecological and environmental perspective.

Also included in this section is the program at the Institute for

Architecture and Urban Studies. Though the program requires that you pay tuition (making it more of a course than an "internship"), it is listed here because of its value in providing a bridge between undergraduate study and architecture school or work in an architecture-related field.

Planning agencies: There are abundant opportunities with local, urban, and regional planning agencies. Planning agencies are notoriously understaffed, and therefore interns are often welcomed. Many agencies will allow interns to work on flexible schedules. With alertness and motivation, interns can work their way into the heart of the planning process.

Of course the type of work you'll do in a planning agency will depend on what kind of area the agency is planning *for*. For example, one intern in a suburban planning agency spent his summer designing parking lots and preparing pamphlets on the care of trees and shrubs. Below we've included descriptions of internships with four planning agencies serving very different types of areas. The East Tennessee Design Center serves both rural and urban communities, and ranks as one of the largest private non-profit design and planning centers in the country. The Cleveland Heights program serves a very small and exclusively suburban community. San Mateo County is in between the two in size, serving one, primarily urban, county. The Lake Tahoe planning agency serves a unique area, containing wilderness territory and a large resort community.

Finding an internship in architecture will not be easy. Below you'll find some more detailed information on internships with large architectural firms that should give you a better idea of how to approach your job search. If working with a large firm is what you're set on, then be prepared for a hard struggle. If you *do* land a position, however, it is bound to be worth the effort.

But perhaps the best piece of advice would be to remain open to the other less competitive opportunities that exist in architecture-related work. Perseverance and attention to the full range of possibilities will add greatly to your chances of finding a worthwhile internship.

THE TYPICAL LARGE ARCHITECTURAL OFFICE INTERNSHIP

ELIGIBILITY: *Undergraduates and architecture students*
DURATION: *Usually summer*
ACADEMIC CREDIT POSSIBLE: *No*
REMUNERATION OR FEE: *Volunteer to minimum wage*
POSITIONS OFFERED: *None to 12*
APPLICATION DEADLINE: *3 to 5 months in advance*

General Description

Working for one large architectural office is like working for any of them. Granted the personalities are different, but, in general, application procedures and responsibilities are the same all over the country.

Students can be helpful in drafting, building models, and preparing presentation set-ups. Some firms are compartmentalized so that interns can get stuck in a specialized area. If you can, choose your section carefully.

Internships in large offices are competitive. Typically, three or four dozen will apply for eight or ten summer openings. Strictly defined, architectural "internships" are for architecture students. Applicants who are *not* in architecture school are looking for "summer jobs." As the jobs open to college undergraduates are not likely to be part of any regular program, you would do well to read the chapter on "Making Your Own" for some general advice that applies well to this situation.

The jobs can begin and end any time, though the vast majority of them are for the summer. Be sure to apply early—three to five months in advance of when you wish to begin.

Apply for jobs with the traditional cover letter, resume, and follow-up phone call form. Of most importance is the interview. Bring your drawings and be modest but persuasive about your talents! Remember though, very few college students get hired. So don't be distraught if the first five or six architects turn you down, and definitely use any connections that you may have.

The Inside Word

Finding a job: For a summer job with an architect, write and call many firms. Address your correspondence to someone in particular. If nothing else, pick one of the partners from the firm's title. But in any case be sure to secure an interview, preferably with someone who has the power to hire you.

When you visit any firm, *be sure to have a portfolio ready.* "Architects depend on getting ideas across visually, and they want to see if you have the drawing ability," one intern explained. Your portfolio should ideally consist of architectural presentations, but, lacking these, use whatever you have: sketches, paintings, photos of sculptures, anything!" explained an intern. One suggestion is that students interested in an architectural job get a portfolio together and talk to *any* architect about it. "Even if he's not offering a job, he might have ideas for improving it or, if it's already good, maybe he'll keep you in mind when he *does* have an opening." This is the best way of developing the contacts leading to a summer architecture job.

In addition to a well-developed visual sense, architects are looking for "a sense of responsibility" and a "true desire for the job." Most applicants meet these qualifications. Consequently, friendship plays a large role. As one intern put it, "I had a roommate whose father was president of the firm, which may have helped me. . . ." You should use whatever leverage you might have—through family ties, school alums, etc.

Two types of firms: Large offices divide into two types—design team and compartmental. Design teams work as a group to plan a building all together, allowing input from all levels into the design process. Compartmental buildings are designed by a series of specialists, passing the plans from one department to another. Design team projects are more exciting because interns get to see the whole process, from start to finish. Compartmentalized employment develops interns' technique, as they become well practiced at their small contribution.

Interns in a design team are usually assigned to a project for a couple or three weeks: building models, drafting, and sometimes working up presentation graphics. Much of the work is monotonous but an intern explained that "we were constantly made aware of the ideas that were being thrown around, and were able to comment freely on them."

In compartmentalized firms, the tediousness of the work really depends on what department an intern is thrown into. One intern spent his time stenciling in the toilets of each bathroom on the plans of a high-rise. Another worked in the graphics department, doing titles, layout, and production work for the firm's brochures. In short, the work you do really depends on your interests and where a large firm places you.

AMERICAN INSTITUTE OF ARCHITECTS (AIA) RESEARCH CORPORATION
Work/Study Internship
Washington, D.C.

ELIGIBILITY: *Undergraduate and graduate*
DURATION: *Summer, fall, or spring*
ACADEMIC CREDIT POSSIBLE: *Yes*
REMUNERATION OR FEE: *$5.00/hour*
POSITIONS OFFERED: *Varies*
APPLICATION DEADLINE: *Varies*

General Description

The AIA Research Corporation is an organization devoted to the research of national problems and policy of the built environment. Their projects cover a wide range of concerns including energy conservation and the sociological implications of architecture.

The purpose of the internship is to give students academic and work experience in architectural research. The intern participates as a research assistant in one of the current projects and is also required to complete an independent project, proposed in his/her application, equivalent to university work at the student's individual level. Students do 25 hours of paid work each week on the assigned project and are expected to devote the remaining 15 hours of the work week to research on their individual project.

Admission to the internship is competitive, and the number of interns accepted depends upon the workload at the time. The primary criteria for selection is a proposal which shows the student's interests and/or skills in architectural research. The deadlines vary depending upon which term the student is applying for.

The Inside Word

Because it is a research organization, interns' projects at AIA will be mostly theoretical. One intern worked on redesigning the space surrounding the Union Station area into one large plaza "incorporating classical and neo-classical motifs." Though the project will never be built, the intern claimed that the two months she spent working on it were extremely worthwhile.

Of the internship, one student commented, "The Research Corporation is a flexible organization and I was impressed with their willingness to help me design a program around my particular interests. They want you to get as much, and more, out of the opportunity as you do." They stress individual initiative and encourage the use of the unique resources of both the Research Corporation and Washington, D.C.

Contact:

ASC/AIA
1735 New York Avenue, N.W.
Washington, DC 20006

BROWN, DONALD & DONALD   *Farmington, Connecticut*
Summer Planning Internship

ELIGIBILITY: *Undergraduate and graduate*
DURATION: *June 1 to September 1*
ACADEMIC CREDIT POSSIBLE: *No*
REMUNERATION OR FEE: *$400 to $600 per month*
POSITIONS OFFERED: *1*
APPLICATION DEADLINE: *Varies*

General Description

The Brown, Donald & Donald Summer Planning Internship is an extremely competitive opportunity for an individual to assist in a cross-section of the urban planning process. The person chosen is involved in at least one significant planning project during his or her three-month stay. Fifteen to 40 people apply each year for the one position available. Sometimes the intern is asked to stay on as a full-time employee after the internship is over.

The Inside Word

Getting accepted: The application process is simple and competitive. To apply, send the firm your resume and arrange for an interview. Find out, by calling or writing, what projects are going to be "in the office" that you can work on. "If we take someone, there will be something for them to do . . . It really does depend on how much work we have to do."

As there are many applicants from all over the country for the single spot offered each summer, those that get the internship must have a good background in urban planning and must have strong research and writing skills. Brown, Donald & Donald is looking for interns with a good generalized background and with strong potential to handle a variety of research tasks. The interns hold "such eclectic responsibilities that we generally want somebody with a little bit of everything."

Daily life: In the office, the interns get a sharp view of the planning process. Mostly, they do research; this means things like spending a week reading housing studies by the firm, gathering data by sitting in on meetings with the Regional Planning Agency, and interviewing real estate salespeople. After that interns put together a comprehensive report complete with all the "compilation" of data.

For an internship at B,D&D to go well, students must work well on their own. "You really have to be an independent and self-motivated person to have a self-designed internship be of value . . . One should always be ready to ask questions and speak up when ideas are requested." The projects are generally the individual's responsibility. An intern explained that "I was nearly always on my own, with access to other people for help if I needed it." The supervision was good—the staff was "helpful, informative, and pleasant."

Contact:

Dennis W. Brown and/or
Robert W. Donald
Brown, Donald & Donald
Spring Lane
Farmington, CT 06032

THE CITY OF CLEVELAND　　　　　　　*Cleveland Heights, Ohio*
HEIGHTS' Urban Administration
Internship Program

ELIGIBILITY: *Senior through graduate*
DURATION: *Semester or year*
ACADEMIC CREDIT POSSIBLE: *Yes*
REMUNERATION OR FEE: *None*
POSITIONS OFFERED: *Up to 20*
APPLICATION DEADLINE: *2 to 3 weeks in advance of
    desired starting date*

General Description

An internship in the City of Cleveland Heights planning department is an experience in the mechanics of suburban planning. Interns in this office will plan for a 55,000-person bedroom community on the outskirts of Cleveland. According to the director, an intern's activities depends upon the intern's skills. "We give them every opportunity to act as a staff member."

Interns typically spend their time applying for federal block grants for the city, collecting data on commercial development, and studying rezoning. As one administrator pointed out, there is "no decision-making involved in the internship."

The Inside Word

Getting accepted: There should be no problem getting an internship. Cleveland Heights receives few applicants, and welcomes those who apply, "unless they're anti-social," one administrator added. An application including references and writing samples is required.

General comments: As a suburban community, Cleveland Heights spends most of its time maintaining a commercial and residential environment. Do not expect to be making plans which will significantly alter the character of the community. One intern categorized his work experience in the following manner: "I did demographic work—traffic surveys, block grant proposals, preliminary feasibility studies for making public buildings accessible to the handicapped, put together a pamphlet for residents on the care of trees and shrubs, redesigned some parking lots, and did a little "gofer" work, too. This is not an internship for those who wish to alter urban design, but it is a first-hand experience in how suburban communities plan for the future.

Contact:

Howard R. Maier
Planning Director
City of Cleveland Heights
2953 Mayfield Road
Cleveland Heights, OH 44118

EAST TENNESSEE COMMUNITY DESIGN CENTER INTERNSHIP

Knoxville, Tennessee

ELIGIBILITY: *Undergraduate and graduate*
DURATION: *Semester, quarter, or year*
ACADEMIC CREDIT POSSIBLE: *Yes*
REMUNERATION OR FEE: *None*
POSITIONS OFFERED: *3 to 10*
APPLICATION DEADLINE: *1 month in advance of
    desired starting date*

General Description

The East Tennessee Community Design Center provides a 16-county area with both planning and design services. The size of the center should not intimidate the prospective intern, as impressive opportunities are available. Hired by various communities, the design center attempts to translate grass-root concerns into low-cost community-conscious design programs. Work ranges from interior house renovation to small-town/neighborhood planning projects in both urban and rural communities.

Each intern should expect to take on considerable responsibility. An intern is the primary—in fact the only—staff person for each project. Consequently, interns' activities include research, client liaison work, organizing meetings, grant proposals, measuring, photographing, and designing. Interns can expect to tackle two to five projects depending on the length of their stay.

To ensure that proper supervision is provided, the Design Center has each intern work with a local professional. Architects, planners—whatever professional is relevant to the project—are recruited by their professional organizations to aid the center. In short, an intern gets expert advice and comprehensive practical experience.

Applications and recommendations are required, but there is no interview.

The Inside Word

Getting accepted: Getting into the program should be little trouble for the "reasonably well qualified" applicant. According to one Center administrator, "an intern should have skills in communications, interpersonal relations, and design planning in order to be qualified." The majority of interns do come from the University of Tennessee's social work, architecture, and urban studies programs or from the Vista volunteer program. Should you be accepted through the University of Tennessee, there is the possibility of qualifying for work-study funds. Should you apply through Vista, be sure you advise them that you want to work at the Center, and that you have the appropriate skills to do so. Furthermore, if applying through Vista, apply months in advance, and expect to be accepted for an

October to October stint; all Vista Volunteer programs require a one-year commitment and most programs begin with the beginning of Vista's fiscal year in October. (There is some small financial support from Vista; (check with them for details.)

Projects: Expect to have some choice of which projects you tackle. There isn't a surplus of interns, so they're needed in many areas. Expect to be exposed to all of the political, economic, and social forces which affect a design proposal. One intern had the following project: an upcoming exposition of alternative energy sources in Knoxville required a community adjacent to the exposition area to renovate a series of dilapidated buildings. Exposition forces did not come up with a design which satisfied the community. The community contacted the Design Center, and the design center began drafting an alternative design.

General comments: The center is not a shoddy operation. The people are dedicated. They expect their interns to be capable of working independently, though they do not neglect them. More than in many closely-supervised programs, the success of the program depends upon the intern's motivation. It is the intern's work which alone determines the success of each project.

The design center appears to be one of those rare places where creativity is harnessed for social needs. It takes motivated interns to make such a center thrive, and motivated interns will have a good experience there.

Contact:

Annette Anderson
East Tennessee Community Design Center
1522 Highland Avenue
Knoxville, TN 37916

THE INSTITUTE FOR ARCHITECTURE AND URBAN STUDIES   *New York, New York*

ELIGIBILITY: *Graduate only*
DURATION: *September through May*
ACADEMIC CREDIT POSSIBLE: *No*
RENUMERATION OR FEE: *$2500 tuition*
POSITIONS OFFERED: *15*
APPLICATION DEADLINE: *Early April*

General Description

The Institute for Architecture and Urban Studies, a non-profit educational institution, offers a course for college graduates. Interns spend the mornings working on design problems and the afternoons working on Institute projects and apprenticeships. The program is a full-time activity, over 40 hours per week. Interns spend approximately 30 to 40 hours each week on academic work: they attend lectures, work on assignments, draw plans or build models, and bring assignments to class for critiques from three professors. They also spend from five to twenty hours per week working on projects, such as an Institute publication, helping an architect build models, or participating in the lecture series—an educational program held four evenings each week.

This program is designed for students interested in architecture, architectural publications, planning, development, research, and architectural history. People who have graduated from a four year liberal arts college from three months to five years prior to their date of application are eligible. Applicants must submit letters of recommendation and a letter of intent; an interview is necessary. Approximately 25 people apply for 15 positions.

The Inside Word

A unique opportunity: Interns say that the education at the Institute is different from that of any other architecture school. It is an open system: there are no grades, so that any evaluation of an intern's progress—and much of the learning besides—depends upon the professors' critiques of the assignments. The assignments are very conceptual; the students often work in abstractions. For example, one assignment was to pick three volumes of any shape and distort those shapes so as to create architecture. Interns say that the ideas behind these assignments are what make the learning experience so unique and valuable. Interns also learn concrete skills: an early assignment asked interns to trace a plan for a villa, an exercise that helped develop their drawing skills.

Daily life: The afternoon and evening projects are not related to the academic work. Some interns get to build models and draw plans for architects' projects, but many do clerical work. We talked to one intern who works on the magazine published by the Institute; he types, edits and acts as "go-fer." Others, he told us, go to the lecture series, take notes and take tickets at the door. He said that he doesn't mind the lack of independence in these projects, and he doesn't think the other interns do either; "architecture is so new to most of us that we probably wouldn't know what to initiate even if initiation were encouraged."

Future prospects: Administrators and interns say that the Institute has a good record of placing its students in graduate school. Administrators stress that they try to help interns find the school that is most suited to their particular needs. One intern said that graduate schools are impressed with the well-known professors who write interns' recommendations, and that because the program at the Institute is so unique, interns' portfolios are usually more novel and well-rounded than those from other institutions.

Getting in: Interns say that enthusiasm is the key to getting accepted into the program. The Institute does not ask for transcripts when making selections, nor does it assign grades; the emphasis, we are told, is on ideas. As one intern told us, "philosophy and so much more than architecture is brought into the classroom." Interns say that a well-rounded liberal arts background and the desire to learn are perhaps the most important admissions criteria.

Contact:

FOR APPLICATION MATERIALS:

Jill Silverman
Administrator of Educational
*   Programs*
Institute for Architecture
*   and Urban Studies*
8 W. 40th St.
New York, NY 10018

FOR MORE INFORMATION:

Peter Eisenman
Director of Internships

(same address)

THE NACUL CENTER   *Amherst, Massachusetts*
Roots, Principles and Design of
Ecological Architecture

ELIGIBILITY: *Undergraduate and graduate*
DURATION: *1 or more semesters*
ACADEMIC CREDIT POSSIBLE: *Yes*
REMUNERATION OR FEE: *Varies*
POSITIONS OFFERED: *6 to 8*
APPLICATION DEADLINE: *Varies*

General Description

This program stresses environmental design as well as the basics of architecture—model building, graphics, drafting. Depending upon their experience, interns learn or develop architectural skills or help the director of the program, Tulio Inglese, with his projects. Basically, these projects involve the research and design of energy efficient buildings and neighborhoods.

Interns independently arrange the length of their involvement with Nacul Center. Most interns stay there the length of one school term, but those who are not affiliated with a school may work from ten weeks to a couple of years. The number of work hours per week is also flexible, but most work between 20 and 40 hours per week. Schedules of fewer than 20 hours per week may be arranged by special permission.

There are no special requirements for admission, but candidates should have *some* architectural skills. Beginners who have no architectural skills must pay a tuition fee of $200 per month until they become effective contributors to the Center. Most of the interns don't have to pay this tuition, nor do many interns receive payment for their work. However, highly advanced architecture students may be paid from $4 to $7 per hour.

Students majoring in architecture, environmental design and ecology have the backgrounds best suited to the program. Applicants must submit a resume and a portfolio. An interview is necessary.

The Inside Word

Getting accepted: The director of the program says that he tries to admit candidates who seem mature, self-motivated and "able to set aside their egos for a little while." He warns applicants that, if accepted, they will be fitting themselves into projects that are not their own, projects conceived by and probably already initiated by other people. "Our interns," he says, "must be able to be part of a team."

A valuable approach: Interns say that this program is important because it emphasizes the environment rather than purely technical skills. This emphasis, one intern writes, enables one to "carry a spiritual sense into the studio." Interns stress the ethical value of this program over and above the personal career advantages of it, but they also say that the career advantages are by no means small. One intern claims that this internship got him into the Yale School of Architecture. Another writes: "If you're interested in working with a visionary architect (Tulio Inglese) in the tradition of Wright and Soleri—do it. If you're interested in developing architectural skills—do it. It's also a good stop before graduate school and a good way to spend a year off."

Daily life: Interns spend their days drafting, designing, building, visiting sites, making models, and estimating. They say that the range of activities keeps the internship from being boring. In addition, once projects are started, interns are allowed to work fairly independently. The projects are very interesting; a recent project is Solstice One, an energy efficient building that will include 25 households and house approximately 90 people.

Both interns and administrators stress that although working hours are arranged to fit individuals' schedules, once established they are rigidly maintained. The director of the program says "We are pretty demanding: interns have to stick to what they've proposed or they just won't see me.". One intern writes that the atmosphere at the Center is "very informal yet serious and productive at the same time."

Contact:

Tulio Inglese, Director
Nacul Center
592 Main Street
Amherst, MA 01002

SAN MATEO COUNTY PLANNING AND DEVELOPMENT DIVISION
Student Internships

Redwood City, California

ELIGIBILITY: *Undergraduate and graduate*
DURATION: *Semester or quarter*
ACADEMIC CREDIT POSSIBLE: *Yes*
REMUNERATION OR FEE: *None*
POSITIONS OFFERED: *10*
APPLICATION DEADLINE: *1 month in advance of desires starting date*

General Description

The San Mateo County Internship program reads like a good recipe: Construct a well-staffed planning office. Service an area small enough (one county) to handle problems well. Provide a dynamic atmosphere for learning and make internships available to any interested college or graduate student. (There hasn't been a surplus of applicants yet.) Now offer college credit year-round for 16-20 hours of weekly work and set the interns loose under competent supervision. "Serves ten people."

San Mateo is an urban county surrounding San Jose, California. Consequently, work involves planning for an urban environment. San Mateo's program offers considerable opportunity, but the internship can be good or bad depending upon the intern's curiosity and motivation. Interns are assigned to a single project planner whose area of expertise coincides with the intern's skills and interests. For example, interns working with the long-range land-use planner might spend time in the following manner: collecting population and socioeconomic statistics, making field surveys, analyzing specific site conditions, doing research on solutions and techniques used in similar situations in the past, or gathering information on proposed capital improvement plans. There are other types of planning work to be done. One intern spent her time analyzing problems associated with converting apartments into condominiums. Her work culminated in the adaption of codes restricting such conversions. About the only thing an intern will not do is design.

An application, references, and writing samples are required.

The Inside Word

Getting accepted: The following advice was relayed by an intern: be sure to specify your interests to the planning people. Ask for an interview, and give them verbal and written indications of your interest. There aren't many interns, so chances are you'll be able to pick your area. Find out who's on the Board of Supervisors at the time you want to intern. The Board's political leanings will determine much of the planning policy. (Every piece of work done in the planning office goes to the Board for approval.)

General comments: The minor hurdles of applying done with, you should be in for a pleasant and educating experience. "Fantastic" was the word one intern used to describe her experience. Her mentor on the staff was "as dynamic as she could be." Any discussions, programs, or conferences related to planning that came to the attention of the office were brought to the intern's attention; any invitation the office received was an invitation to the interns as well. Interns were invited to all staff meetings—a policy that one intern considered quite out of the ordinary. Interns' ideas were well received and their duties much more than clerical. Furthermore, interns felt that the office staff was extremely competent.

Contact:

Mark Duino
Senior Planner
Planning and Development Division
San Mateo County
County Government Center
Redwood City, CA 94063

THE TAHOE REGIONAL PLANNING AGENCY
South Lake Tahoe, California

ELIGIBILITY: *Undergraduate and graduate*
DURATION: *Usually summer*
ACADEMIC CREDIT POSSIBLE: *Yes*
REMUNERATION OR FEE: *None*
POSITIONS OFFERED: *Up to 5*

APPLICATION DEADLINE: *Beginning of April for
summer, or 4 to 6 weeks in advance of desired
starting date*

General Description

The Tahoe Planning Agency concentrates on land-use planning. Situated in wilderness land bordering on resort territory, the planning agency is one of the few public offices in the area which attempts to prevent large-scale, unorganized development. Almost from the beginning, an intern will be expected to take on large responsibilities, to work alone when necessary, and to be an effective innovator.

The Tahoe Planning Agency is looking for interns to help out a seven-person staff attempting to do work formerly done by 24 people (a consequence of Proposition 13). Those figures speak for themselves. A description of an intern's assignments reads something like this: "Working in close coordination with the staff, an intern will take on a three-month project in areas such as air quality, water quality, traffic analysis, and land use. At the end of the three-month period, the agency would expect the intern to have acquired sufficient skills to work more independently." (They would also expect a finished work product.) "Interns will be responsible for preliminary or cursory review of projects; they will not have sole responsibility, but will occupy an assistant's position." One agency administrator added this was not a strict rule. A fast-learning, responsible intern could conceivably do the work of a permanent staff member.

Most interns come for the spring and summer months, but the agency welcomes interns at all times of the year. They expect to have a maximum of five interns at any one time.

State of the agency: As has been mentioned, this agency has been hit hard by Proposition 13. Do not expect any money. Three years ago the agency had a budget of $750,000. The current budget is $300,000. They have no California-state supporting funds and work-study is unavailable.

The Inside Word

Getting in: The desperate need for people has *not* forced this agency to throw open their doors to any willing worker. If anything, they have toughened their standards. " 'Coordination' is the key word here. Often all seven of us will throw ideas back and forth to each other. With seven trying to do the work of 24, we have to be able to use our time very efficiently. We can't spend a lot of time worrying about interns." The Tahoe people will not ignore an intern. They simply can't afford to nurse anyone.

Applicants send in a resume that includes course work completed and goals for the job and afterwards. Then, the seven staff members get together with the applicant for an informal interview session. "This is to make sure everyone is compatible with everyone else." The staff emphasizes they have no desire to drag anyone into a job unsuited to their interests. If everyone gets along in the interview, the prospective intern will most likely be accepted.

Future prospects: Interns have had good luck finding jobs upon leaving the agency. One administrator said that, "Every motivated intern who has left the agency has been employed in either the public or private sector. Across the Board. And I mean within two to three months of leaving." The administrator himself was an ex-intern, as was one other member of the staff.

General comments: The job will involve an intern with one of the most controversial areas of planning on the current scene. The conserving of wilderness land versus commercial development interests is an area of planning which always brings up the word "compromise." Involvement with such a political issue can be a frustrating experience. But, if you're sharp, this could be an educating and exciting internship.

Contact:

James P. Dana
Tahoe Regional Planning Agency
P.O. Box 8896
South Lake Tahoe, CA 95731

OTHER PLACES TO LOOK:

Business
The Greater Washington Business Center, Inc.
International Association for the Exchange of Students for Technical Experience (IASTE)

Environment
Environmental Intern Program

Public Service
Institute for Local Self-Reliance

The Arts

In the arts, where apprenticeships have historically been the way to train young artisans, a confusion of terms results with the application of the word "internship" to describe various work/learn situations. Don't let the jargon throw you—the term "apprenticeship" generally continues to retain its historical meaning; a period of close work with or observation of a skilled craftsperson in order to learn a specific trade. "Internships" in the arts include a broader range of experiences, from learning museum administration to producing graphics for a traveling theatre company.

In the fine arts and in art-related fields, formal programs for interns *and* apprentices are abundant and diverse. Museums, public galleries and historical societies frequently offer formal intern programs of a non-remunerative nature. Many art-related businesses, institutions, and publications take on interns and apprentices as well. However, informal programs, arranged privately with individual artists or institutions, are the most common and fruitful means of gaining first-hand experience in the applied arts field.

Determination and an early start are the keys to fiinding art internships, particularly in the fine arts and crafts. Generally, art internships fall into three main categories: general interest museum/gallery internships, specialized or applied arts apprenticeships, and high-powered academic programs.

General Interest Museum/Gallery Internships

These include museum, public gallery, and historical society internships open to students with a general interest in the arts. These are by far the most numerous. They offer experience in the administration and operation of a museum or gallery, including taking inventory, arranging exhibits, and dealing with artists and clients.

The smaller museums and galleries (e.g. The Worcester Art Museum, the Brattleboro Museum and Art Center) generally offer volunteer internships. Often there is no formal, structured program and most of what the intern does depends on his or her own interests and educational goals. The Brattleboro Museum, for example, relies heavily on volunteer support and has a small staff. Therefore, interns have a good chance to contribute and work on self-initiated projects. Such programs are considerably less competitive than those offered by larger museums, and more readily available.

Specialized Applied Arts Internships and Apprenticeships

Apprenticeships and internships in the applied arts demand skilled work in particular art forms (painting, sculpture, photography).

47

Some formal internships exist: the Mass PIRG Graphic Design Internships, for example, in which students with some experience in graphic design, photography, or illustration assist a professional graphic artist in the production of flyers, posters, pamphlets, and a quarterly newsletter. However, informal programs arranged with individual artists or institutions remain the most widespread means of obtaining on-the-job experience.

Programs labeled "apprenticeships" in the arts are often the only bridge between an academic arts background and professional arts or crafts. The distinction between "apprenticeships" and "internships" is sometimes rather fuzzy. The term "apprenticeship" denotes close one-to-one work with an individual artist, learning one specific skill, for example, making cloth at Patrician Yuhas' wool farm.

For the fine arts or crafts person, apprenticeships with practicing artists are ideal. Students are exposed first-hand to artists practicing their art in a professional business setting. Apprentices will learn technique, may teach, and are introduced to the range of professional possibilities within a particular art field. Most positions are unsalaried. Nevertheless, benefits are substantial—access to studios, teachers, artists and contacts, and a place to live.

You must search hard for an apprenticeship! Opportunities are limited. Resources include art journals, artists, schools, and state art councils. Books will provide listings of craft programs, schools and publications. *By Hand,* by John Coyne and Tom Herbert (E.P. Dutton, 1974) is a guide to schools and craft programs, listed by state and offerings. The annual *Craftworkers Market* (Writer's Digest Books, 9933 Alliance Road, Cincinnati, Ohio 45242) also has extensive listings. For listings of applied arts publications, study programs and internships, check the back pages of art journals such as *Craft Horizons* and *American Craft*.

A *Directory of Periodicals* is available from the American Crafts Council, Publications, 22 West 55th Street, New York, New York 10012. You may also advertise your search by placing a classified ad in some of the craft periodicals.

Another search avenue is to contact crafts people directly at craft events—fairs particularly. A national calendar of craft events is contained in many craft journals. Other valuable resources are state art councils, state internship offices, and state-funded craft organizations. Becoming acquainted with those in your area is a good way to meet craftspeople. These groups often publish newsletters listing job opportunities. The National Endowment for the Arts also has a formal paid internship program described in the listings section of this chapter.

High-Powered Academic Programs

The high-competition internships are found at major museums and galleries (e.g. National Gallery of Art, Hirshhorn Museum). These programs are generally more structured, have more stringent eligibility requirements, and offer remuneration. Serious interest in an art career, course work completed in art history, art education, or studio art and a good academic record are important admissions factors for these over-subscribed programs. For example, Hirshhorn will only consider students who have completed twelve semester hours of art history, and applicants must send a transcript, resume and letters of recommendation.

However, if museum work interests you, don't be discouraged by the stiff competition for internships at the larger, more prestigious institutions. Similar experience and programs are often available at museums of different sizes and specialties. The exposure and ambience might be more exciting at the Guggenheim or the Hirshhorn, but your specific responsibilities may be greater and more varied at a smaller museum.

Private Galleries

Private art galleries rarely offer formal internships, but often need extra help. Informal arrangements made by the individual are the best means of exploring this area. The first place to look for a gallery internship is New York City, the hub of the gallery world. If you are able to approach gallery owners in midtown Manhattan and SoHo, you are likely to find work, probably non-paying, but with the considerable fringe benefit of establishing worthwhile future contacts. Clusters of galleries are also located in major cities throughout the country, as well as in popular resort and tourist spots from Palm Beach to Palm Springs.

Before you accept a non-paying gallery position, find out what your specific responsibilities will be. The daily routine of a small gallery is often slow. You will learn a great deal just spending time at a gallery, but being directly involved with specific functions and customer dealings will be more rewarding. Formal programs for gallery interns are scarce, yet the field is ripe for motivated students willing to structure their own internships. (See the section on *Making Your Own* for ideas on how to direct your interests toward creating your own specialized program.)

Performing Arts

Internship programs in the performing arts are limited and usually are production-related. They involve work on lighting, set design, costumes, promotion and publicity (e.g. North Shore Music-Theatre). Very few formal acting internships exist—that at the New Jersey Shakespeare Festival being a notable exception—and even these combine production work into an acting intern's schedule. Competition for organized programs is usually rugged and most such internships are unpaid.

In the absence of organized programs, major theaters, ballets and orchestras will often take on one or two students interested in some very specific aspect of work. Landing one of these internships will take some research on your part as to what kinds of things actually go on at the theatre or ballet.

Often the performing arts department of your university, or a local theatre group or arts council can be of help and may have recommended or employed interns in the past. The initiative is up to you—you have to call up the organization, talk to schools, hang around and talk to actors, workers, musicians, etc. and get an idea of what the possibilities are.

Other Possibilities

A wide range of internships are available in the applied arts or with art-related businesses. Areas to consider are the performing arts, commercial art, communication and media, education, administration, architecture, etc. In mass media and communications, outlets exist with television and radio stations, newspapers, magazines and other publications. *The Student Guide to Mass Media Internships,* by Ronald H. Claxton and Buddie Lorenzen (Intern Research Group, University of Colorado School of Journalism, Boulder, Colo.) is a comprehensive national listing of internships by state in specific areas of mass communications, complete with descriptions and contact addresses. These internships will appeal to students interested in combining art skills with communications or public relations work. Advertising, photo-journalism, and public affairs design work are among the opportunities available.

Public relations staff at non-profit service agencies often have interns produce original illustrations and graphic designs for magazines, posters, or flyers for the agencies' promotional campaigns or special events. Interns find that they develop an awareness for public support of the arts and a personal appreciation for performing and visual arts through this type of art internship. The opportunity to enhance your portfolio and publish art work are exciting attractions to these positions. These internships are numerous, though non-salaried as a general rule.

If you are a practicing artist, you may be interested in pursuing a state, federal or foundation grant instead of an intership program. The National Endowment for the Arts Visual Arts Program (Washington, D.C. 20506), The Foundation Center (888 Seventh Avenue, New York, New York 10019) and The Washington International Arts Letter (P.O. Box 9005, Washington, D.C. 20003) all issue publications that list grants and offer hints on finding and procuring them. The National Endowment for the Arts has grant monies for artists pursuing independent projects—particularly for art graduate students or experienced crafts people needing financial support to sit down and work intensely at developing and perfecting their skills. The application is extensive, and you must wait six to twelve months for a grant decision.

The Grantsmanship Center (1015 W. Olympic Boulevard, Los Angeles, California 90015), a non-profit educational center, offers week-long group workshops in many cities dealing with how to find funds and how to write an effective grant proposal. The Center also publishes reprints of how-to information and source articles that have appeared in their magazine, *The Grantsmanship Center News*. In addition, it's worth looking up "Grants: Where To Find Them and How To Get Them," an article by Diane Hines which appeared in the July 1979 issue of *American Artist* magazine.

State funding of the arts is inconsistent, but most states do have organized arts councils. Make use of these councils and any other organizations supportive of the arts, not only as information banks but as possible employers or sponsors. They can provide you with the inside word on where, who, and what major projects are being funded, and suggest how to go about arranging an internship.

ALEXANDRIA ARCHAEOLOGICAL RESEARCH CENTER

Alexandria, Virginia

ELIGIBILITY: *Junior through graduate*
DURATION: *1 semester*
ACADEMIC CREDIT POSSIBLE: *Yes*
REMUNERATION OR FEE: *None*
POSITIONS OFFERED: *9 per year*
APPLICATION DEADLINE: *Varies*

General Description

The Archaeology Center researches and catalogues archival and archaeological resources and works on the conservation of sites. Interns may become involved in archaeological lab or field work, historical preservation, museum administration or museum education. The duration of the internships is flexible, but most run for a semester. Interested students should apply by the end of the semester if they wish to intern the following semester.

Applicants must submit a resume, a letter of recommendation and a letter of intent outlining a project they hope to pursue. Interviews are required. During the interview applicants must submit writing or research samples and further discuss their proposed projects. Interns' projects will be coordinated with the resources available at the Center. Interns are encouraged to publish the results of their projects.

The Inside Word

There is a lot of independence in this program. The only structure to the internship is the requirement that the project correspond to some work going on at the Center and that interns have a paper or presentation to show for their work; the interns provide the rest of the structure themselves. An intern told us, "There are not a lot of authority figures. My paper was evaluated by a panel, but I saw and worked with members of that panel every day on an equal footing."

The program is designed loosely enough to allow interns to work in many fields; conserving artifacts, managing exhibits, investigating funding sources, handling public relations, graphics and exhibit design. The intern we talked to had two projects: he designed and constructed an exhibit and wrote a paper on collections management. As a result, he did everything from painting the walls for his exhibit to researching museum policy. He told us "I feel very qualified for a museum career because I've experienced so many aspects of museum management, from the practical to the theoretical." Later, parts of his paper were incorporated into a presentation the Research Center made at a symposium.

This intern felt that the Research Center is a unique opportunity: "It is one of the few practical, contemporary projects in the United States. Unlike Williamsburg, for example, they have an ongoing urban program."

Directors of the program look for applicants who have demonstrated their interests and abilities in related fields. The project proposal is an important part of the selection process. It demonstrates an individual's competence and shows how he/she would fit into the Center.

Contact:

Catherine West
Alexandria Archaeology Research Center
City Hall, Box 178
Alexandria, Virginia 22313

AMERICAN CONSERVATORY THEATRE
San Francisco, California

ELIGIBILITY: *Undergraduate and graduate*
DURATION: *9 months*
ACADEMIC CREDIT POSSIBLE: *Yes*
REMUNERATION OR FEE: *$65/week stipend*
POSITIONS OFFERED: *7 to 9*
APPLICATION DEADLINE: *Mid-April*

General Description

The American Conservatory Theater offers internships in many aspects of production: stage managing, costuming, props, lighting and sometimes sound. Students with a B.A. in theater arts and some undergraduates are eligible. Interns work at least 40 hours per week for the whole season, which runs from September to May.

Approximately 100 people apply for the positions. Applicants must submit a resume, reference letters and a cover letter. Interviews are required.

The Inside Word

One intern we talked to was involved in stage managing. She helped run rehearsals at the main stage (the Geary Stage) and was responsible for writing prop lists and scene breakdowns. In addition to helping with the major productions, she stage managed two plays—new works being developed. This system allowed her to work with the professional Geary Stage performers and crew while having some major responsibilities of her own.

This intern had also worked with off Broadway and off off Broadway theaters. She enjoyed working at the American Conservatory Theater because she had the chance to work with a paid professional crew. "The American Conservatory Theater is the perfect place to learn how a professional repertory company works," she said, and was impressed with how well everyone worked together.

She felt she was hired on the basis of her experience and a successful interview. A director of the program said that he is looking for applicants who "have decided to make theater their field" and who have had good training. Grades, he said, are not a major concern.

Contact:

The Internship Program
American Conservatory Theater
1150 Geary Street
San Francisco, CA 94102

THE APPRENTICESHOP
Introduction to Wooden Boat Building
The Apprentice Program

Bath, Maine

ELIGIBILITY: *High school through graduate*
DURATION: *6 weeks for beginner's course; 2 years for apprentice program*
ACADEMIC CREDIT POSSIBLE: *No*
REMUNERATION OR FEE: *$575 fee for course*
POSITIONS OFFERED: *15 for course; 8 for the apprentice program*
APPLICATION DEADLINE: *Varies*

General Description

The Apprenticeshop offers two programs for students of boat building: the Introduction to Wooden Boat building, a six-week course for beginners, and The Apprentice Program, a two-year program for those who have completed an introductory course either at The Apprenticeshop or elsewhere. The two programs are linked because the more experienced apprentices work with and help teach the beginners.

Both programs are offered during different sessions staggered throughout the year. Everyone devotes 40 hours per week to the development of modeling, carpentry and building skills. Applicants with backgrounds in marine architecture or maritime history, or those who have had previous experience in building boats are eligible. Beginners need submit only a resume, but those who want to be apprentices must also have completed an internship or some related volunteer work. Interviews are not necessary. About 10 percent of all applicants are admitted to the programs.

The Inside Word

Interns and apprentices stress that these programs are very relaxed. After the instructor has given a demonstration or helped a student with a problem, the interns and apprentices are free to work on their own. Sometimes projects are simply assigned, but self-initiated projects and creativity in building are encouraged.

When problems arise, the interns and apprentices very often put aside their individual projects to help each other. One apprentice writes "priorities are placed on the *how* of getting somewhere, not so much on end results." "The ability to work with others" is cited as one of the prime learning experiences of the program as well as an admission criterion. In fact, apprentices are part of the staff that selects the new interns. As a result, they feel a responsibility to the program and to the new interns: "Apprentices help make newcomers feel very much welcome and at home."

There is a "pitch in" atmosphere at The Apprenticeshop. In addition to the carpentry work, interns and apprentices cut and split wood, carry dirt, and haul materials. One apprentice advised that applicants get involved in the program with these attitudes: "Set no goals; do the work to help someone else or the shop; let yourself fall into the rhythm here (a bit chaotic); relax with the knowledge that you're here to learn and money is far away."

Contact:

Lance Lee
The Apprenticeshop
Maine Maritime Museum
375 Front Street
Bath, Maine 04530

THE ARTS COUNCIL OF WINDHAM COUNTY
Brattleboro, Vermont
Arts Administration and Graphic Arts Internships

ELIGIBILITY: *Undergraduate and graduate*
DURATION: *Varies*

ACADEMIC CREDIT POSSIBLE: *No*
REMUNERATION OR FEE: *None*
POSITIONS OFFERED: *2 to 4*
APPLICATION DEADLINE: *Open*

General Description

The Arts Council is a non-profit organization which promotes arts development in the community by introducing art programs to schools, rest homes, and rural locations, and by attracting performers to the area.

The Council offers two internships in arts administration. These are fairly competitive, full-time, non-salaried positions. Interns must work a minimum of forty hours per week, with flexible schedules. An interview is mandatory. Academic record is less important than interest, commitment, and a willingness to learn.

Intern projects vary with the time of year, duration of the internship, and the intern's particular skills. Possible projects include writing and design work on publications and grant research. Opportunities for teaching and direct contact with schools are offered only to those working on a long-term basis (a year). Interns must have enough time to develop a rapport with the people in order to perform these tasks.

Internships in graphic design and photography are also available. These are full-time positions paid through CETA grants or federal funds. In graphic arts, full production knowledge and skills are required of the intern. This includes design, layout, paste-up and final production techniques. One intern worked on a journalism program to help school children construct class newspapers. Other projects might include designing and producing *Lively Arts,* a calendar of arts events sponsored by non-profit organizations in the County. The photography internship consists of photographing people, artists and performers involved with Council events. Printing and developing skills are required.

The Inside Word

Interns find that "the freedom to be employed while exploring various aspects of a particular art field through contact with outside people and artists is invaluable." Brattleboro is an artist's community, and "a good place to find out what's going on in your field."

Contact:

Phyllis Odessey
Executive Director
Arts Council of Windham County
67 Main Street
Brattleboro, VT 05301

CHELSEA HOUSE FOLKLORE CENTER, INC.

Brattleboro, Vermont

ELIGIBILITY: *High school through graduate*
DURATION: *6 weeks*
ACADEMIC CREDIT POSSIBLE: *Yes*
REMUNERATION OR FEE: *$180 tuition; $50 deposit*
POSITIONS OFFERED: *2*
APPLICATION DEADLINE: *Varies*

General Description

The Chelsea House is a non-profit educational institution dedicated to the preservation of traditional music, dance, folklore and folk arts. Interns manage and program the Folklore Center, coffee houses, concerts, school programs and festivals. Special events include the Annual Brattleboro Folk Festival and Traditional Craft Fair and the Annual Chelsea House Anniversary Weekend. Among intern responsibilities are writing press releases, public programming, bookkeeping, archive maintenance, and working sound systems.

Interns may work for any number of six-week sessions. The summer session is the most popular and the most difficult to get into. Chelsea House is open 9:00 to 5:00 Tuesday through Friday, and interns generally work all 32 hours in addition to helping with evening concerts. Tuition covers room and board. The rooms are group living arrangements; interns are expected to share housing responsibilities.

Applicants must submit an application form and a letter describing their interests and experiences. Interviews are necessary.

The Inside Word

Interns and staff members stress that self-motivation is an important part of this program. An intern told us that the Center has a "pitch in" atmosphere; there is a lot of pressure to do things before certain deadlines, but everyone works together and cares about their work. "I am here because of a real interest in the Center," one intern said.

Staff members and interns meet twice each week to choose the projects the Center will do. "Interns are not spoon fed," said a director of the program. "How well they do and how much they learn depends upon their motivation." She added that interns are given as much responsibility in as many areas as possible. "We prefer that interns learn from mistakes rather than not learn at all."

The required interview is a joint interview. Prospective interns are encouraged to be certain that the program is what they are looking for. What the staff members are looking for, said director Carol Levin, is interns who are imaginative, dependable, flexible, who don't mind working long hours and have the ability to think as well as to be able to work with others."

Contact:

Carol Levin
Box 1057
Chelsea House Folklore Center, Inc.
Brattleboro, Vermont 05301

COOPER-HEWITT MUSEUM · New York, New York
Internship Program

ELIGIBILITY: *Undergraduate and graduate*
DURATION: *Varies*
ACADEMIC CREDIT POSSIBLE: *Yes*
REMUNERATION OR FEE: *Varies*
POSITIONS OFFERED: *Varies*
APPLICATION DEADLINE: *Early April for summer,*
   open for other

General Description

The Cooper-Hewitt is the Smithsonian Institution's National Museum of Design. Throughout the year it offers to students who have completed two years of college individually designed internships. During the summer there is a formal internship program in which about 20 volunteer interns and three fellows (each receiving a $500 stipend) participate. Participants must spend a minimum of twenty hours each week at the museum. Volunteer interns can design the schedule and length of their programs. The three summer fellows must work for ten weeks: from mid-June to mid-August. The fellowships are usually given to students who do not have prior experience in museum work.

Summer interns and fellows go through a short orientation; then they are assigned to a department where they work with staff and on their own. Curatorial work is the focus. The departments interns work in are: drawings and prints; decorative arts; wallpaper; exhibitions; education and membership; public relations and business.

The Inside Word

Writing and researching skills are essential. Typing is also handy. Interns said they spent about 60 percent of their time doing curatorial work (research, writing, work on exhibitions) and 40 percent doing office work. Past interns stressed that it is not easy for the museum to immediately incorporate students into curatorial work, but they were given a chance to do it anyway, along with "less glamorous work." The Cooper-Hewitt is a small museum—interns thought this was to their advantage: "It is a small, but active museum. You find yourself working on 17 seemingly unrelated projects, but you are learning a lot."

They felt the internship taught them all aspects of museum work and would be a great experience for anyone interested in the field: "Enter with an open mind, understand it may not always be glamorous, but you will get deep into museum work."

Contact:

FOR APPLICATION MATERIALS:
Coordinator, Internship Program
Cooper-Hewitt Museum
2 East 91st Street
New York, New York 10028

FOR MORE INFORMATION:
Ms. Mary Kerr and
Ms. Linda Currie
same address

CORCORAN GALLERY
Summer Internship Program

Washington, D.C.

ELIGIBILITY: *Undergraduate and graduate*
DURATION: *7 to 10 weeks*
ACADEMIC CREDIT POSSIBLE: *Yes*
REMUNERATION OR FEE: *None*
POSITIONS OFFERED: *7 to 10*
APPLICATION DEADLINE: *Late March*

General Description

The Corcoran Gallery of Art, with an extensive collection of American art, a collection of European art and many temporary exhibitions throughout the year, offers a nine-week internship from June to August, for students of art history. Graduate students and undergraduates who expect to complete their junior or senior years by June are eligible to apply.

A background in American art and/or American studies is desirable. Approximately seven to ten students are chosen from 50 to 100 applicants. The internship is a highly structured program designed to give the intern a general understanding of museum operations, a knowledge of the specific functions of one department, and familiarity with the history of American art. These objectives are accomplished through routine gallery assignments, a specialized project supervised by a staff member, study assignments on the Corcoran's collections, and field trips to area museums and art related organizations. The intern program is directed by the Assistant Curator of Collections and the Curator of Education.

The museum offers no remuneration and interns must provide for their own living accommodations. An application fee of $5.00 is required; in addition, applicants must provide college transcripts and a statement describing their abilities and interests. A recent term paper can be submitted as a writing sample.

The Inside Word

Getting accepted: Students with a strong background in American art and art history have the best chance of being accepted. At the required interview, "be organized and efficient" at presenting yourself.

Daily life: The Corcoran summer internship program is highly structured and carefully supervised. "The Corcoran attempts to fit students to projects, choosing a project that will benefit both the museum *and* the student." The only problem interns seemed to face was abandoning their romantic conceptions and coming to grips with what actually goes on at an art museum. Said one intern: "It's not always glamorous. You may be disillusioned; working at a museum may not be what you think." "I had a great time," said another, "because I knew what it was like and knew that was what I wanted to do."

Although interns are assigned to one specific department, interns are rotated to allow them to have the chance to spend some time in each department. Said one intern, "it allowed me to get a general feeling of how the museum is run."

General comments: The Corcoran is a relatively small museum, compared to the nearby Smithsonian, and interns felt the benefit of this. "You can really get to know people's names," said an intern. "There is a general feeling of congeniality, and during the rush to get a big project done on time, people really pitch in, even the directors."

Interns found a high level of professionalism at the Corcoran. Said one: "Coming in contact with and understanding the level of professionalism at a major museum, as well as learning how a museum really runs from the inside, can be valuable experience for finding a job later on."

Contact:

Barbara S. Moore
Curator of Education
Education Department
Corcoran Gallery of Art
7th Street & New York Avenue, N.W.
Washington, D.C. 20006

DALLAS MUSEUM OF FINE ARTS
Summer Internship

Dallas, Texas

ELIGIBILITY: *Juniors*
DURATION: *Mid-June to Mid-August*
ACADEMIC CREDIT POSSIBLE: *No*
REMUNERATION OR FEE: *$750 stipend for 8 week period*
POSITIONS OFFERED: *1*
APPLICATION DEADLINE: *Early April*

General Description

This program focuses on curatorial and education work. Applicants must have completed three years of college, but may not yet be enrolled in graduate school. Preference is given to art history majors and Dallas area residents. Each year about 20 people apply for the internship.

The full-time program combines independent work with work supervised by staff. The intern assists in educational programs and learns techniques of cataloguing, exhibiting, conservation, and research.

A resume, three recommendations, a personal statement of interest in museology, a description of the main interest to be pursued during the internship, and an interview are required of applicants.

The Inside Word

This internship is fairly structured, yet interns have freedom to vary their daily program. One past intern wrote: "I proposed and worked on a project in European Painting; however, if I desired to help any staff member on his/her project I was free to do so."

The general consensus is that the staff is friendly and energetic; one ex-intern wrote: "It was an invaluable opportunity to learn about museum work and to further my knowledge of art history."

Contact:

Dr. Anne R. Bromberg
Curator of Education, Education Department
Dallas Museum of Fine Arts
P.O. Box 26250
Dallas, Texas 75226

DAUGHTERS OF THE AMERICAN REVOLUTION MUSEUM
Internship Program

Washington, D.C.

ELIGIBILITY: *Seniors and graduates*
DURATION: *1 or more semesters*
ACADEMIC CREDIT POSSIBLE: *Yes*
REMUNERATION OR FEE: *None*
POSITIONS OFFERED: *6 to 8*
APPLICATION DEADLINE: *Varies*

General Description

Interns at the DAR Museum, an American arts and crafts museum operated by the Daughters of the American Revolution, work in either the decorative arts program, researching and cataloging items in the collection, or in the education department, giving tours and preparing programs for grade-schoolers. Most students work in decorative arts. They use sources in the museum's library and information given by donors to prepare historical resumes of furniture, clothing, accessories, ceramics, samplers, etc. The interns in the education department also use the museum's library resources to prepare presentations for school groups.

Most interns work at the museum for one school term, but those not affiliated with schools sometimes stay longer. Interns work between 20 and 40 hours each week, and may schedule their own shifts. Generally, the museum accepts only graduate students, but in some cases highly qualified seniors may be accepted. Applicants must submit a resume and have an interview.

The Inside Word

Interns say the research work that goes into the cataloging for the decorative arts has its ups and downs. Sometimes a number of similar items come in at one time and interns have to complete sheafs of folders about the same thing. As one woman told us: "By the sixth handkerchief, you're a little bored." However, interns often prepare folders for antique contrivances they've never seen before, in which case the work becomes interesting. They measure the object carefully, check it for minute markings, pore through books and information given by donors and try to establish who made it and when. As one intern told us, "this forces you to look and read very carefully—valuable disciplines to develop."

One administrator said that sometimes the particular interests of the intern can be accommodated; if someone is interested in samplers, for instance, he/she may be assigned to work in that area. Most of the time, however, interns work on projects that are in progress. Once given their projects, however, they are allowed to work independently.

The education department has a very small program; often one intern works closely with the director. This intern has some individual projects as well. For instance, he/she may have to research a particular colonial craft and prepare to play the role of that craftsman before a group of students.

Interns have the opportunity to work in all aspects of the museum operation. One intern said that she enjoyed her internship at the DAR Museum better than one she had had at a more prestigious museum precisely because she was given a larger variety of responsibilities.

Administrators say that they accept the applicants who seem most interested in the museum. They judge this interest on the basis of applicants' academic and work experience.

Contact:

Jean Federico, Director
DAR Museum
1776 D. Street, N.W.
Washington, D.C. 20006

FOUNDATION FOR THE COMMUNITY OF ARTISTS
New York, New York

ELIGIBILITY: *High school through graduate*
DURATION: *Varies*
ACADEMIC CREDIT POSSIBLE: *Yes*
REMUNERATION OR FEE: *None*
POSITIONS OFFERED: *Varies*
APPLICATION DEADLINE: *Open*

General Description

The Foundation aids artists in obtaining grants, provides counseling, and publishes *Art Workers News*. The internship is not highly competitive; it is open to anyone who wants to learn through working with the Foundation. Every aspect of the internship is flexible. There are no specific requirements of interns: each internship is individually designed.

The Inside Word

It is hard to generalize about intern's experiences, owing to the variety of work they have done. One intern did research in funding possibilities and wrote funding proposals. She said: "the work I did required strong writing skills and budgeting experience." Another answered artists' questions, did clerical work, wrote articles for the paper, and conducted interviews. Much of the work was tedious, but there were high points, and she said "the atmosphere was friendly and relaxed." One intern did all of her work outside of the office; she wrote, "I fully enjoyed it, because I was free-lancing. I was given complete freedom in designing each proposal. I learned a lot about the administration and grant-seeking process of visual arts organizations. This opens up a new job field; I had not worked in the visual arts or on a service organization previously. Be motivated; this internship is only what you make of it."

Contact:

Ms. Melodie Begleiter
Foundation for the Community of Artists
Suite 412
280 Broadway
New York, NY 10007

HIRSHHORN MUSEUM AND SCULPTURE GARDEN

Washington, D.C.

ELIGIBILITY: *Juniors and seniors*
DURATION: *10 weeks, summer*
ACADEMIC CREDIT POSSIBLE: *Yes*
REMUNERATION OR FEE: *$1000 stipend*
POSITIONS OFFERED: *5*
APPLICATION DEADLINE: *Early March*

General Description

The Hirshhorn Museum and Sculpture Garden is part of the Smithsonian Institution, making these internships both very prestigious and very popular. Between 120 and 200 undergraduates apply each year for the five positions. The lucky five get full-time jobs, lasting from mid-June to mid-August. Their responsibilities include learning about the museum's collections and general operations, and participating in ongoing projects within specific museum departments.

Only those students who have completed twelve semester-hours of art history will be considered. There is no application form, but applicants must send in an official college transcript, a resume including prior academic and work experience, a statement of intent—reasons for wanting an internship at Hirshhorn, including areas of greatest interest—and three letters of recommendation from people personally acquainted with the applicant's academic qualifications. Personal interviews are not required.

The Inside Word

Getting accepted: The key to getting accepted into the program is being specific. When writing your letter of intent, include your reasons for wanting to work at Hirshhorn rather than at other museums. Provide those writing your recommendations with details about your qualifications and about the museum program itself. Spend a lot of time on your resume and dwell on your unusual and particular skills.

The caliber of students who are accepted is very high: generally art history majors with good academic records and impressive work experience. One intern had a 3.7 academic average and had worked four summers for the Corps of Engineers and two semesters for her art history professor.

Daily life: The amount of freedom interns have depends on what department they work in, but every intern spends a lot of time doing researching and writing. A typical project involves studying a collection and its history, then writing general summaries geared to the public: labels, informative handouts, and speeches for gallery guides.

In addition, every intern faces a good share of tedium: answering phones, addressing and stuffing envelopes, etc. and sometimes absorbing the overflow from their supervisors' crowded desks. One intern said that there was little time for independent work because of the large amount of required work, but she added that whenever possible, her supervisors encouraged her to browse in the gallery, in museum storage, and in other museums.

Another intern was not too busy for independent projects, and found a need for them: "The internship can be very worthwhile as long as you have something to offer. You have to take the initiative to suggest programs, projects, etc.; otherwise you can spend a lot of time sitting on your thumbs."

These variations are bound to crop up because interns work in different departments under different supervisors. However, all interns agreed that this program offers unique opportunities. In addition to the work, interns have talk-tours with the supervisors of each department and special behind-the-scenes tours in other museums in Washington, Virginia, and Maryland.

Future prospects: Interns feel that this inside look at the museum world is both stimulating and beneficial in establishing connections. But the value of the internship will depend a lot on the work you do. One intern said that when she applied for other jobs, interviewers were impressed by the Hirshhorn name, but they were disappointed by the small amount of responsibility she had there. "Career-wise," she said, "programs at other museums may be better because they give interns more valuable training."

Still, the program is bound to be a good time. Said one intern: "Working on the National Mall at the Smithsonian Institution has the same feel that I imagine working at Disneyland must have—plus the added excitement of working in a museum of art—I loved it."

Contact:

Edward P. Lawson
Education Department

Hirshhorn Museum and Sculpture Garden
Smithsonian Institution
Washington, D.C. 20560
(202) 381-6710

LOON AND HERON   *Boston, Massachusetts*
CHILDREN'S THEATRE

ELIGIBILITY: *Undergraduate and graduate*
DURATION: *Varies*
ACADEMIC CREDIT POSSIBLE: *Yes*
REMUNERATION OR FEE: *None*
POSITIONS OFFERED: *Varies*
APPLICATION DEADLINE: *Open*

General Description

The Loon and Heron Theatre is a touring children's theatre, also offering
school programs in the performing arts for children. The Theatre is
composed of professionals in theatre and education, and performs in
schools, community centers, and theatres throughout New England,
including their own resident theatre: Family Performance Center in
Cambridge.

The Theatre accepts interns in the areas of graphic design, costume
design and public relations/booking assistant, although positions vary
seasonally. Internships are structured according to the student's interests.
A minimum of twenty hours per week is required, with flexible daily
schedules. Competition for internships at the Theatre is small. All
positions are volunteer.

Graphic design interns should have experience or working knowledge
of production techniques including design, layout and paste-up, and basic
knowledge of the printing process. Specific tasks include production of
touring and performance brochures, posters, and other promotional
materials. The intern will also supervise the video library, arrange for
video documentation of all new productions and for photographic coverage of all events.

Costume design interns will gain experience in mask-making, clay
work, props and costume design skills. Interns learn on the job, working
closely with a supervisor.

Free acting classes are offered. Interns may eventually perform small
parts in productions.

The Inside Word

Internships with the Theatre are not competitive. Applicants should have some experience in theatre arts, and must show their work. Personality is equally important, however. The Theatre wants people who work well with others.

One past intern's advice about the internship: "forget your own ideas for a while. Be prepared to do anything—run errands or tasks not related to the workshop; 25 percent of an intern's work is tedious but the internship is a great experience. You learn useful skills, develop confidence in your abilities and eagerness to try new things. It's also good work experience to include on a resume. The internship was worthwhile and I recommend it."

Contact:

Joan Schwartz
Co-Artistic Director
Loon and Heron Theatre
169 Massachusetts Avenue
Boston, MA 02115

MEREDITH CORPORATION   *Des Moines, Iowa*

ELIGIBILITY: *Juniors*
DURATION: *3 months*
ACADEMIC CREDIT POSSIBLE: *Yes*
REMUNERATION OR FEE: *Varies*
POSITIONS OFFERED: *12*
APPLICATION DEADLINE: *Early April*

General Description

The Meredith Corporation offers graphic arts and advertising internships in several of its publications. These include *Better Homes and Gardens*, *Successful Farming*, *Apartment Life*, and various special interest publications. Interns are recruited to fill various department needs and the type of work they do varies between departments. Interns who are interested in art rather than journalism generally do layout and design work.

Administrators prefer to hire interns who plan to continue working at Meredith after their internships are over. Competition for the positions is stiff; 200 to 300 people apply for the 12 places. Applicants must submit a resume and work samples.

Although Meredith does not provide housing, it does assist interns in finding a place to live.

The Inside Word

One administrator said that the interns do a lot of "go-fer" work. They often run errands and pick up materials. Most of the work is office-related rather than creative. "However," she added, "the work depends largely upon the person. There is a lot to do, a lot to learn, and many opportunities."

Because competition for the positions is stiff, applicants' grades are important. Those with impressive transcripts are the most likely to be accepted. The admissions board also places importance on the applicants' particular academic preparation and previous work experience.

Contact:

The Internship Program
The Meredith Corporation
1716 Locust Street
Des Moines, IA 50336

MINNESOTA MUSEUM OF ART   St. Paul, Minnesota
Museum Education Internships

ELIGIBILITY: *Undergraduate and graduate*
DURATION: *Varies*
ACADEMIC CREDIT POSSIBLE: *No*
RUMERATION OR FEE: *None*
POSITIONS OFFERED: *Up to 4*
APPLICATION DEADLINE: *Varies*

General Description

The Minnesota Museum of Art offers museum education internships at various times of the year, depending on the preference of the applicants and the needs of the museum. The program is open to undergraduate and graduate students with interests in fine arts, art history, art education, and public relations.

Depending on their interest, students may work in the museum education department or curatorial department. Education department opportunities include work with education programs for St. Paul school groups, after-school art programs, and the adult art school. Curatorial department responsibilities include assisting in cataloging and checking the condition of the collection, doing research on pieces, and helping with the development of the collection.

There is little competition for acceptance into the program; the museum tries to accommodate any interested students into one or more of its programs. A resume and a letter of interest are required. A 50 percent discount on museum art classes and invitations to all museum events are offered to all interns, but the museum offers no other remuneration.

The Inside Word

The chance for a variety of museum experiences is the strong point of the Minnesota Museum of Arts program. Interns assisting in one area (for example, museum administration) often find the chance to explore many facets of museum work. The museum has a "very friendly atmosphere on all levels of authority," wrote one intern, "at no time did I feel out of place." "I was in touch with the many facets of museum art and education. I was an active member of staff meetings and helped prepare art school exhibitions, and many of my ideas were used in future programs." Interns do get stuck "occasionally cleaning cabinets, running errands and doing mailings," but "even much of the phoning and errands were enjoyable as I represented the museum, even if at the bottom of the totempole."

Interns have found the education they received at the museum applicable to their future activities. One intern found ways to apply arts administration knowledge to a teaching job, another kept up contacts with the museum and was able to find employment some time later at the museum on a CETA contract.

Contact:

Ms. Nell McClure
Museum Education Internships
Minnesota Museum of Art
30 E 10th Street
St. Paul, Minnesota 55101

MUSEUM OF AFRICAN ART   Washington, D.C.
Academic Internship Program

ELIGIBILITY: Undergraduate and graduate
DURATION: Varies
ACADEMIC CREDIT POSSIBLE: Yes
REMUNERATION OR FEE: None
POSITIONS OFFERED: Varies
APPLICATION DEADLINE: Open

General Description

Internships at the Museum of African Art last for a semester, January term, or summer, and can be scheduled as either full-time or part-time positions. Interns work in the curatorial department, where they participate in the ongoing operation of the Museum; in registration, exhibition, insurance, and security, as well as in researching the histories of Museum pieces. In the photographic archives, which house an extensive collection, interns are given responsibility for acquiring, selling, and loaning slides, negatives, and prints, as well as preparing exhibitions. Interns have also worked with the library, administration, and education departments with positive results; however, those positions are not normally available.

The Inside Word

Getting accepted: Interns should have finished two years of college, and must submit a resume, college transcript, and recommendation from an academic advisor when applying. Students interested in anthropology or African art are sought, and generally benefit most from the experience.

Daily life: During part of the program, interns research a special topic, and prepare a final paper on their findings. "It is a valid Museum enterprise rather than a hypothetical study," said one former intern of his experience.

The Museum is small, which in the opinion of the staff and interns, makes for a more rewarding experience. Interns work closely with full-time staff members, and, consequently, "don't get lost," said one current intern. "There is a good working atmosphere, the staff is very accepting—the intern is not made to feel incidental."

Contact:

Ms. Gretchen Jennings
Internship Coordinator
Department of Higher Education
Museum of African Art
316-318 A Street, N.E.
Washington, D.C. 20002

NATIONAL ENDOWMENT FOR THE ARTS   Washington, D.C.
National Endowment Fellowship Program

ELIGIBILITY: *Undergraduate and graduate*
DURATION: *13 weeks; spring, summer, or fall*

ACADEMIC CREDIT POSSIBLE: *Yes*
REMUNERATION OR FEE: *$2,660 stipend plus round-trip air fare*
POSITIONS OFFERED: *45 each year*
APPLICATION DEADLINE: *Varies*

General Description

The National Endowment for the Arts (NEA) is federally and state funded. The Fellowship Program introduces participants to the policies, procedures, and funding operation of the National Endowment and gives them an overview of arts activities in this country. Three 13-week sessions are offered each year (spring: February to May, summer: June to August, fall: September to December). A different group of 15 fellows participates in each of the sessions.

To apply, each candidate must be sponsored by a college or university, state or local arts agency, or other non-profit, tax-exempt arts organization. Fellows are selected on the basis of academic and professional background. Most have M.A.'s or Ph.D.'s, but undergraduates are also accepted. About 1200 people apply for the 45 fellowships each year. The application consists of a resume, college transcript, letters of recommendation, and an essay describing interests and reasons for attending the program. Fellows can arrange for academic credit through their own institution.

Fellows work in one of the Endowment's grant-making offices: Architecture, Planning and Design; Challenge Grants; Dance; Education; Expansion Arts; Federal-State Partnership; Folk Arts; Literature; Media Arts; Museums; Music; Opera-Musical Theatre; Special Projects; Theatre; or Visual Arts.

About two-thirds of fellows' time is spent working as members of the professional staff to gain a functional view of the Endowment and to assist programs and offices in their daily operations. Activities include work with grant applications, panel review sessions, and individual project research on policy and grants. The remainder of the time is spent in guest speaker seminars, field trips, panel meetings, and National Council on the Arts meetings. Fellows are in contact with artists, journalists, federal officials, and leading arts administrators.

The Inside Word

The Fellowship is an entrance to the world of nationally-supported arts programs. Each fellow has some background in the arts, either through formal study or working experience. Fellows learn about policy development, grant-making procedures, and administration of Endowment programs. Each experience is unique depending on the department of NEA the fellow works with and the project designed with a staff member supervisor.

The personal essay is an important part of the application. According to a staff member of the NEA, "it should articulate how the fellowship will help in their future career in the arts." NEA staff suggests that fellows have a clear sense of what aspects of the federal funding they want to learn about. They encourage fellows to make contacts, talk with program directors, understand the federal grant process from the inside out.

Fellows have found the program helpful and have enjoyed nearly all aspects of it. Past fellows are now working with state and municipal arts agencies, professional theatre, opera, and dance companies, universities, arts centers, museums and media organizations.

Contact:

Kathleen Bannon
Fellowship Program Officer
National Endowment for the Arts
2401 E Street, N.W.
Washington, D.C. 20506

NATIONAL GALLERY OF ART   Washington, D. C.
Summer Internship Program

ELIGIBILITY: *Graduates*
DURATION: *Mid-June to Labor Day*
ACADEMIC CREDIT POSSIBLE: *No*
REMUNERATION OR FEE: *$800/month*
POSITIONS OFFERED: *15*
APPLICATION DEADLINE: *Mid-March*

General Description

The National Gallery of Art's Summer Internship Program lets interns do independent research and writing, work with members of the Gallery's senior staff, and learn how a large museum operates. Each of the 15 interns is assigned to one of the following departments, depending on their background, interests, and stated preference: American Painting, Graphic Arts, Northern European Painting, Conservation, Exhibitions and Loans, Education, and others. Interns must have a B.A. in art history or museum work—or be enrolled in a graduate art program—have a grade point average of 3.5 or better, and intend to continue their education during the next academic year.

Either a Gallery curator or department head directs the interns' work. In addition to work in their assigned departments, interns spend three hours per week in briefings on curatorial work and connoisseurship.

To apply, submit a completed application, a college transcript, a letter of recommendation from a college professor, and a personal letter stating reasons for wanting the internship.

The Inside Word

Getting accepted: The National Gallery is one of the country's major museums; it draws interns of the highest caliber. Each year about 75 apply for the 15 available spots. Past interns stress that the application should be filled out carefully or it may be discarded. They also recommend that you persevere in obtaining a place. One intern applied three years in a row before finally being accepted. Many interns in the program have had prior experience in museum work, usually at smaller galleries.

Daily life: All the interns we spoke with emphasized the flexibility allowed them in their independent work. However, one intern pointed out that "self-initiated projects had to have a precise bearing on the gallery's function." As always, self-initiation is adamantly advised by past interns. Said one: "Don't be scared to say that you're having problems with your project. If you are, get on a different project early—my mistake was that I didn't." Said another: "After I realized that the person with whom I was supposed to work was not there, I did lots of lobbying to get myself reassigned. I was probably able to tailor my work more to my interests than the other interns."

Contact:

William J. Williams
Summer Employment Coordinator
Personnel Office
National Gallery of Art
6th and Constitution Avenue, N.W.
Washington, D.C. 20565

NATIONAL TRUST FOR HISTORIC PRESERVATION
Stockbridge, Massachusetts
Chesterwood Summer Intern Program

ELIGIBILITY: *Undergraduate and graduate*
DURATION: *1 to 3 months*
ACADEMIC CREDIT POSSIBLE: *Yes*
REMUNERATION OR FEE: *None*
POSITIONS OFFERED: *2 to 5*
APPLICATION DEADLINE: *February or March*

General Description

The Chesterwood Summer Intern Program gives undergraduates and graduate students the opportunity to work in various aspects of a historic house museum. Interns may be involved in research, curatorial care, and property interpretation (otherwise known as giving tours). Students majoring in art history, studio art, history, landscape architecture, decorative arts, education, sculpture and museum studies are eligible for the program.

The internships are very flexible in format, generally running from May to September. The program allows interns to determine their own time commitment. Some interns have continued their projects during the fall; others have worked part-time or full-time up to 35 hours per week.

Intern duties vary from day to day. One could be involved with research or be active in conserving furniture. The program's major responsibilities are the interns' independent designs and projects on which they work separately until completion.

The Inside Word

Getting accepted: Admission to this program is fairly competitive. About 10 to 25 people apply for 2 to 5 positions. Applicants must submit their college transcripts and letters of recommendation, and an interview is required. There is no specific deadline for applications, but the bulk of applications are handled in the late winter or early spring. Sculptors must send in a portfolio.

Most often interns are selected because of their special interests or previous experience: they are often paired with the upcoming projects the supervisors have planned. Specialization in a particular area is usually the admission key. For example, one woman was selected because she could demonstrate obsolete bronze casting and clay-to-plaster mold processes. Interns also report that the interview is very significant. An interest in the preservation of history is a valuable admissions asset. Knowing something about historical preservation will give you a better idea of the functions and goals of the Chesterwood Program as well.

Daily life: Interns stress that the degree of independence makes the Chesterwood Program very enjoyable. The individual projects are challenging, interesting, and worthwhile, and provide a sense of real accomplishment. One intern's project involved planning the restoration of a garden to its 1925-1931 appearance. Another located and began restoration of an abandoned nature trail. An intern writes, "The portion of the historic structure report that I prepared was solely my work. It was not changed by my supervisor and I was given full credit for the work."

Not all of the work is exciting. Interns assist in the maintenance of gardens and furniture, "important but tedious" in the opinion of one intern. Another aspect of the job involves property interpretation: giving tours, explaining to the public the significance of certain objects or buildings, etc. Said one intern, "I didn't particularly enjoy being a property interpreter because it's hard to be enthusiastic for seven straight hours on your feet. However, that was the only drawback to the internship."

While supplies are provided and expenses covered, the program is unsalaried. The parent organization, the National Trust for Historic Preservation, has provided work/study funding in the past, however, for individuals who have sought such aid on their own.

Contact:

Paul W. Ivory
Museum Director
Chesterwood Summer Intern Program
Box 248
Stockbridge, Massachusetts 01262

NEW JERSEY SHAKESPEARE FESTIVAL
Theatre Design Internships

Madison, New Jersey

ELIGIBILITY: *High school through graduate*
DURATION: *5 to 6 months*
ACADEMIC CREDIT POSSIBLE: *Yes*
REMUNERATION OR FEE: *None*
POSITIONS OFFERED: *50 to 80*
APPLICATION DEADLINE: *March 1*

General Description

The Shakespeare Festival is a repertory company located on the Drew University campus performing classical and modern plays. The Festival is an Equity company with professional actors. Each season internship openings are available in all areas of theatre production. These include openings for actors, designers, technicians, administrators and publicity personnel.

The internship is an intense and comprehensive program of theatre instruction. Interns work an average of fifteen hours per day, six days a week. Interns work in crews, which rotate weekly to gain exposure to all areas of the production process.

The internships are competitive. About 1000 people apply, with 50 to 80 accepted each year. Most positions are acting internships, but these include work in all areas of theatre production. Limited openings are available in the design areas—scene design, lighting design, costume design, plus business administration. The technical positions are less competitive than the acting internships, and several scholarships are awarded.

The Inside Word

"This is an intense and worthwhile program," says one acting intern. An average day might proceed as follows: 9:00 to 10:30 acting class; 10:30 to 12:30 fencing class; 1:00 to 5:30 acting class; dinner, 7:00 to ? performances. If you are on the change-over crews, responsible for changing and dismantling stage sets for nightly productions, work is late, sometimes until 2:00 AM.

Other interns recall the program as "rigorous and a tremendous amount of work" with mixed or negative reactions about the merits of the internships. The drawbacks include a system of allocating points for class attendance, etc., which affects days off, a policy barring acting interns from being cast in productions and requiring them to do technical stage work, and a $75 deposit returned only upon completion of the internship.

Contact:

Paul Barry
Artistic Director
New Jersey Shakespeare Festival
Madison, NJ 07940

NORTH SHORE MUSIC-THEATRE
Apprentice Training Program

Beverly, Massachusetts

ELIGIBILITY: *High school through graduate*
DURATION: *12 weeks, summer*
ACADEMIC CREDIT POSSIBLE: *Yes*
REMUNERATION OR FEE: *None*
POSITIONS OFFERED: *15*
APPLICATION DEADLINE: *Open*

General Description

The North Shore Music-Theatre, located 18 miles north of Boston, is a 1700 seat theatre-in-the-round where musicals, comedies and concerts are performed. Under the supervision of professional staff members, North Shore apprentices participate in all aspects of production, such as scenery, costumes, lights and props. Each week they are assigned to a different department. Apprentices generally do not perform in the productions, although some occasionally appear on stage as extras. They do help run the technical aspects of the shows.

The hours are long; the work begins at 9 AM and continues until 11:30 PM after the performance. Weekends are particularly busy because new shows are prepared and performed then. Apprentices ordinarily have a free day during the week. In addition, apprentices must report to the theatre two weeks before the season opens in order to become familiar with the staff and to help prepare for the first production. An apprenticeship usually runs from early June to early September.

Apprentices must pay their own living expenses, which are estimated to be $600 for the summer. Most members of the company pay $25 per week for rooms in private homes. Expenses for food and transportation (the theatre is three miles from town) are approximately $30 per week. A limited number of grants are awarded on the basis of an individual's need and qualifications. These grants are usually $300 for the summer.

The 15 candidates are selected from hundreds of applicants. Candidates must submit an application form and at least one personal and one professional letter of recommendation. Interviews are strongly recommended, but if an interview is impossible, the letters of recommendation are used to determine suitability for the program.

The Inside Word

Members of the North Shore staff feel that these apprenticeships are particularly valuable because the apprentices have the opportunity to train with a fully professional company. One woman said, "We are considered one of the best summer theatres in the country." Administrators cite North Shore's 25 years of experience in training apprentices as an asset. They also say that because their theatre is not the tent-type they can use advanced equipment and techniques which "assure the highest professionalism."

However, being an apprentice requires "a tremendous amount of stamina," said one staff member. The hours are long and the work is not glamorous. One administrator advises, "The stars in your eyes may disappear when you realize the work and dedication required for success."

Because admission to the program is competitive, applicants who have experience in many areas of production besides acting are most likely to be accepted. Staff members stress dedication and discipline as being the requirements for and the rewards of a summer at the North Shore Music-Theatre: "Regardless of the direction your future takes, the values of self-discipline, dedication and pride in your work gained during the summer will remain."

Contact:

Apprenticeship Training Program
North Shore Music-Theatre
Box 62
Beverly, MA 01915
(Those hoping to be costume trainees
should write to the Costume Department.)

OHIO OUTDOOR HISTORICAL DRAMA ASSOCIATION
New Philadelphia, Ohio

Summer Internship

ELIGIBILITY: *Undergraduate and graduate*
DURATION: *Summer*
ACADEMIC CREDIT POSSIBLE: *Yes*
REMUNERATION OR FEE: *$50/week and up*
POSITIONS OFFERED: *About 5*
APPLICATION DEADLINE: *March 31*

General Description

The Ohio Outdoor Historical Drama Association is one of America's major outdoor theatre companies. Each summer they put on a production of *Trumpet in the Land,* the historical symphonic drama by the Pulitzer Prize winner Paul Green. The show is played under the stars in a 16,000 seat outdoor amphitheatre, and requires a crew of over 20 technicians and 70 actors. The play tells the story of the American Revolution on the Ohio frontier, with the help of galloping horses, gunfire, and artillery explosions.

Interns work directly under professional directors, costumers, stage managers, and technical directors. Opportunities are available in all aspects of the production—including acting and singing—depending upon the interns' interest and background. For example, an intern interested in technical lighting would work directly with the master electrician.

The company holds an Actors Equity Association Contract, and thus belongs to the professional union of actors. In addition to the major production each summer, the company provides free workshop classes to the public, and does occasional children's theatre, dance concerts, and choral work.

The Inside Word

Getting accepted: The program directors are looking for interns with fairly extensive technical experience. They are mainly interested in college graduates, but would accept well-recommended interns with two years undergraduate training in a good drama department. Besides those interested in the technical aspects of the production, the company will accept experienced actors, dancers, singers, and people to work in public relations.

Dynamite: One intern in the pyrotechnic department was in charge of the guns and explosions. Though he had had only a little training in firearms before he came to the program, he learned to build and set charges equivalent to four sticks of dynamite.

Interns claim that compared to other Actors Equity houses, *Trumpet in the Land* allows them to take on much greater responsibility. "At most Equity houses, interns aren't even allowed to flip a light switch without someone's permission. Here we were given a lot more freedom."

The personnel available to teach interns was described as "excellent." "If there is something you want to learn, you have the time—and the personnel—to teach you." Interns are allowed to drift to different areas during the course of the summer, so that they can learn a range of technical work. "You get a lot more overall experience here than you would in other types of theatres," said one intern who had previously spent a good deal of time working in dinner theatres.

Daily life: Once the initial rehearsal period is over, the work schedule is pretty open-ended. Interns are given specific daily responsibilities, but it is up to them to get them done on their own time. "I work for however long it takes me to do what I have to do—then I go home," said one intern.

The program director states that in addition to giving students training in particular technical skills, "interns leave the program with a much more professional attitude towards theatre than when they come in."

Contact:

Ohio Outdoor Historical Drama Association
Box 275
Dover, OH 44622

HELENA RUBINSTEIN FELLOWSHIP IN   New York, New York
ART HISTORY AND MUSEUM STUDIES
Independent Study Program

ELIGIBILITY: *Undergraduate and graduate*
DURATION: *2 semesters*
ACADEMIC CREDIT POSSIBLE: *Yes*
REMUNERATION OR FEE: *$800 tuition; $1,200 stipend
    per semester*
POSITIONS OFFERED: *10 to 20*
APPLICATION DEADLINE: *Early April for fall term;
    early November for spring term*

General Description

The Helena Rubinstein Fellowships at the Whitney Museum of American Art give advanced undergraduates and graduate students the opportunity to initiate and organize exhibitions on their own. Fellows handle every step of mounting an exhibition, from deciding what to exhibit to making final catalogues. Most of the fellowships are two semesters long, starting in September and ending in June, but a few one-semester fellowships are available.

Students who have or who are working towards a B.A. in Art History or Museum Studies are eligible. Applicants must submit a resume, a college transcript, letters of recommendation and writing samples. Interviews are not necessary, but they are recommended if feasible. This program is very competitive: over 100 people apply for the 10 to 20 positions. Only those with high academic records and good recommendations are likely to be accepted.

There is an $800 tuition charge, but tuition aid is available. Fellows also receive $1,200 per semester in grants on a bi-weekly basis. The fellowships are full-time commitments of 40 hours per week.

The Inside Word

Administrators and fellows tell us that the amount of independence and responsibility of these fellowships is unique. Fellows literally run the whole show. As a result, they learn a great deal about every aspect of curating and administrating exhibitions and museums, right down to the actual acquisition of loans.

Some fellows say that they were expecting the structure and organization of an academic institution and were surprised when they were called upon to provide that structure and organization themselves. One intern told us that the problem with this system is all of the fellows have to work together like a democracy to get anything accomplished and as a result there is inevitably "the tyranny of the majority."

This democratic method can be troubled by the nature of the interns themselves. One intern told us that the high caliber of students working at the Whitney can create the problem of too many chiefs and not enough Indians. She warns "There's a lot of ego there. But you find people you like and some you don't like in any group of ten."

Getting accepted: Administrators say that they accept students who have displayed academic excellence, who are enthusiastically recommended by their professors and who seem willing and able to initiate projects. One administrator stresses that this third criterion is very important: "Because we rely heavily on the initiative of participants, we look for people who seem self-directed and mature. And some experience helps."

Future prospects: Other fellows complain that they've been spoiled by their Helena Rubinstein Fellowships. They say they can't find positions as challenging and exciting as their fellowships were. Yet most of the fellows move on to equally stimulating jobs. They are excellent candidates for curator and director positions because of the practical experience they've had. One woman who runs the program had had a fellowship there herself. She told us "We have a very good track record. Our graduates are quite illustrious."

Contact:

David Hupert
Independent Study Program
Whitney Museum of American Art
945 Madison Avenue
New York, New York 10021

THE SHAKER MUSEUM   *Old Chatham, New York*
Student Internships

ELIGIBILITY: *High school through graduate*
DURATION: *Varies*
ACADEMIC CREDIT POSSIBLE: *No*
REMUNERATION OR FEE: *None*
POSITIONS OFFERED: *1 to 3 per year*
APPLICATION DEADLINE: *Open*

General Description

The Shaker Museum houses the world's largest collection of Shaker materials, including furniture, looms, fabrics, tools, and industrial equipment. The museum accepts students year-round from secondary school upward who are interested in Shaker history, culture, and crafts.

The museum's internship program is not formally structured, but in the past, students have done research and cataloging in the museum's reference library, given tours and developed educational programs, and worked on craft projects including weaving and cabinet making on the museum's period equipment.

Competition for work opportunities at the museum is not intense, though a resume and interview are required.

The Inside Word

Although specialized in its focus on Shaker culture and history, the Museum does provide an opportunity for students to become integrally involved in the workings of a small museum. The program is informal, meaning anyone with a serious interest and a willingness to do work has a good chance of being accepted.

"Students have enjoyed working at the museum," says program director Peter Laskovski. "Being a small organization, the museum offers a chance for students to become directly involved with museum professionals and do work of real impact on the museum and public."

Contact:

Peter Laskovski
The Shaker Museum
Old Chatham, New York 12136

TRURO CENTER FOR THE ARTS AT   Truro, Massachusetts
CASTLE HILL WORK/STUDY PROGRAM

ELIGIBILITY: *High school through graduate*
DURATION: *5 or 10 weeks between mid-June and
    Labor Day*
ACADEMIC CREDIT POSSIBLE: *Yes*
REMUNERATION OR FEE: *Free tuition to classes*
POSITIONS OFFERED: *About 6*
APPLICATION DEADLINE: *Varies*

General Description

The Work/Study Summer program at Truro's Center for the Arts allows
artists, sculptors, and craftspeople to exchange their skills and labor for
intense art training and unlimited studio use. Apprentices work twenty
hours each week at the Center doing odd but necessary jobs in lieu of
tuition. The program can last either five or ten weeks: from June 20 to July
27; or July 30 to September 1; or from June 20 to September 1.

Located near Provincetown, Massachusetts (on Cape Cod), the
Center does not provide housing, yet many comfortable, reasonably-
priced living units are available nearby. Academic credit may be arranged
through the Massachusetts College of Art. The application deadline is
open, and each application must enclose a resume and recommendations.

The Center is a community of well-trained artists working in a variety
of mediums. Apprentices take courses, receive in-depth studio instruction, and have access to the facilities at all times—in exchange for
performing general maintenance work in the studios. All apprentices are
allowed to create their own work schedule as well as choose the kind of
work they will do. Chores include recycling clay, firing kilns, and general
studio maintenance. Skills in electronics and carpentry come in handy, but
the majority of the assignments are very basic.

The town of Truro, a noted gathering-spot of artists and artisans,
particularly during the summer months, draws a variety of people from
artistic backgrounds on a year-round basis as well. The Center boasts
some nationally known instructors and offers a range of courses in such
areas as resin-bonded sand casting, foundry work, Japanese ink painting,

rug weaving, and frame loom weaving. More general courses are offered in oil painting, watercolor, figure drawing, graphics, and ceramics. There is also a group of miscellaneous courses, including mime and stained glass work.

The Inside Word

The general concensus on Castle Hill's summer apprenticeship is that you can learn as much as your interest dictates. Although the work itself is not rewarding, the opportunity to be a dedicated student at the Center makes the effort well worthwhile. One ex-apprentice recalls, "The work got sort of dull by the end of the summer, but the quality of the teachers was outstanding. I felt perfectly free to utilize all available classes and facilities—ranging from clay to textiles to foundry work."

Cape Cod is known as a perfect artist's setting, and all of the apprentices raved of the Center's lovely location. There were varied reactions, however, to the problem of combining work duties with artistic efforts at the Center. One apprentice felt, "it's lots of work and one doesn't always have the time and energy left to take full advantage of the classes—it's not a vacation on Cape Cod." Another apprentice continued, "Don't expect a very high-caliber, intense scene, but lots of time to think and create as you wish in a positive environment."

Contact:

Ms. Joyce Johnson
Truro Center for the Arts
Box 756
Truro, Massachusetts 02666

THE WORCESTER ART MUSEUM   Worcester, Massachusetts

ELIGIBILITY: *Undergraduate and graduate*
DURATION: *1 or more semesters*
ACADEMIC CREDIT POSSIBLE: *Yes*
REMUNERATION OR FEE: *None*
POSITIONS OFFERED: *Up to 6*
APPLICATION DEADLINE: *Early November for spring
    semester; early May for fall semester*

General Description

The Worcester Art Museum does not have a formal internship program, but internships with the curatorial, conservation and education departments may be arranged depending upon the needs of the Museum. Interns in the curatorial departments are expected to answer requests for information about the art collection, prepare bibliographic research for exhibitions and prospective acquisitions, give tours, help install exhibitions, catalog artwork, write explanatory labels, and do some clerical work. Those working for the conservation department prepare varnishes and adhesives, stretch linen, assist conservators and do occasional clerical work. Education department interns prepare and present tours, write explanatory material about the collection and the Museum's music and film programs, prepare interpretive material on the exhibitions, and do occasional clerical work. Every intern works at least eight hours per week for one or more semesters.

Approximately ten people apply for one to six positions each year. Applicants for curatorial internships should be majors in art history or a related field and preferably be able to read French or German. The conservation department requires that interns be art history or science majors (preferably chemistry) and have "proven manual dexterity." Applicants for the education department should be art history or related majors and be able to write and speak clearly and effectively. All applicants should have "superior" academic records. Candidates must submit a resume stating qualifications, a letter of intent indicating which department they want to work in, and two references. Interviews are necessary. Selections will be made within 30 days after the application deadline.

The Inside Word

Getting accepted: Interns advise that applicants show their enthusiasm for the Museum. They say that the administrators like dedicated workers, and that the more persistent and interested an applicant seems the more likely he/she is to be chosen. Have a reason for wanting to intern at Worcester; a specific person you want to work with, a part of the collection you want to study, etc. Make personal contact before you write a letter.

Daily life: Interns working in the curatorial and education departments say that they are given a lot of responsibility and are allowed to work on their own most of the time. The most popular work is the research. One intern said that when the Museum had a show of French landscapes, she researched and wrote biographies of all the artists.

Interns in all of the departments say that the routine tasks are not always boring. For instance, one woman had to sort through all the Museum's prints to make certain that the files on them were correct. She told us: "Some people might think that it's boring to sort through prints like that, but I found it interesting and exciting just to be handling such great art."

Although there are usually only one or two working at the Museum at the same time, interns say that they don't feel excluded. Some said that because they worked alone a lot, it took them a week or so to feel as if they fit in. One intern remarked, "The people in my department do a lot together, and I feel very welcome."

Contact:

Internship Committee
Worcester Art Museum
55 Salisbury Street
Worcester, Massachusetts 01608

PATRICIA YUHAS' WOOL FARM   *Martinsville, New Jersey*

ELIGIBILITY: *High school through graduate*
DURATION: *Varies*
ACADEMIC CREDIT POSSIBLE: *Yes*
REMUNERATION OR FEE: *None*
POSITIONS OFFERED: *1 or 2*
APPLICATION DEADLINE: *Open*

General Description

Patricia Yuhas operates a farm on which she raises sheep, grows vegetables, processes wool and linen, spins yarn by hand, weaves and knits clothing and sells the produce from the farm. Between the shoppers at her fruit and vegetable market and the school groups learning how wool and linen are processed, spun and made into clothing, the farm is an active place. Members of her family and three or four other workers help her wind yarn, demonstrate spinning and sell produce.

Although she does not offer a formal internship or apprenticeship program, she accepts applications from students interested in working on the farm and learning from her. Applicants should write her a letter of intent and include their phone numbers. She will contact applicants and discuss the possibilities of arranging an apprenticeship. Apprenticeships can be structured for any duration at any time of the year except February.

Yuhas is unable to provide room and board for her workers, so apprentices must arrange their housing in nearby Somerville or Rutgers (both about five miles away). They must also provide their own transportation.

The Inside Word

The value of these apprenticeships is not just in the spinning and weaving skills taught; they expose students to "a way of life," as Yuhas says. She feels that "it's important to understand how to put together cloth before you start working on some sort of unusual op-art. Feeding the sheep whose wool you are spinning is also important."

One of the workers told us that she feels "like family." She called the farm "very relaxed and friendly—everyone is able to laugh at their mistakes." Because of the friendly rapport among co-workers, tasks like packing vegetables and winding yarn aren't too painful. "You do have to be willing to work," said one intern.

Contact:

Patricia Yuhas
Patricia Yuhas' Wool Farm
1020 Wash Valley Road
Martinsville, NJ 08836

OTHER PLACES TO LOOK:

Business
American Association of Advertising Agencies

Environment
Aquarium of Niagra Falls Sea Research Foundation, Inc.
Rochester Museum and Science Center

Journalism
Saturday Review

Public Service
Atlanta Urban Corps

Business

Business, or its liberal arts equivalent—economics—is the most popular major on college and university campuses today. The reason is simple: the vast majority of good jobs available to college graduates is in business. Despite the hordes of undergraduates preparing for careers in the business world, formal business internship programs are few and far between. This is not to say that there aren't plenty of opportunities for internship-like experiences; they simply aren't always neatly labeled as "internship programs." Some of the best programs are simply called "Summer Employment" or "Summer Development" programs, and some of the best experiences we know of come from the odd summer jobs offered by businesses.

A formal internship program requires recruiters, administrators, and a well-organized program for the intern—in short, internship programs are expensive deals for the firm. As far as most businesses are concerned, the incentives for an internship program—talent hunting and community relations—can be bought more cheaply. This is especially true now, when the boom in the number of business-bound college graduates has flooded the labor market—a situation much to the liking of employers. They get the pick of the crop to start at entry level, and at bargain basement prices. In this rarefied atmosphere, internship programs do exist but they always occupy the lowest priority on a firm's list of expenditures. As one program director remarked, "When business is tight, the first thing they axe in the board room is the internship program."

There are two types of formal internship programs in business. First are the internships designed for students interested in industrial science. These are the largest and most numerous programs, offered by companies like 3M, Dupont, Texas Instruments and Phillips Petroleum. The programs of these high technology firms usually call for majors in engineering, math, physics, chemistry, and geology. As a rule, the opportunities for business majors in these firms are "minimal." Second are the internship programs designed for business and economics majors. Again, it is usually the big firms which offer these programs, but they are much smaller and scarcer than their counterparts in industrial science. These two types of programs have one important aspect in common. As far as the firms are concerned, the purpose of the programs is to find, train, and test prospective employees. They don't look on the program as providing liberal-arts intellectuals with simply another fun, but non-committal adventure into the real world.

For the business or economics student who is not yet ready to get locked into a particular field, there is an out. There are two other valuable kinds of internship experiences—odd jobs, and summer employment programs. Usually these do not demand the gung-ho attitude of most formal internship programs. You are expected to work as hard as in a formal internship program, but the difference is that the incentive for offering the program or the odd job revolves around the need for extra and temporary help—usually during the summer months when many full-time staffers are on vacation.

Formal Business Internships: Industrial Science

These internship programs abound for a simple reason: the supply end of the labor market in industrial science fields is tight compared to the supply end of the business labor market. One program director said, "Without internship programs to locate, train, and try out candidates for jobs in our departments, I can't imagine the chaos the employment office would face." The programs are huge by most standards—often accommodating several hundred interns. These internships are a dream come true for undergraduates planning a career in industrial science. They pay well and the prospects for a full-time job offer afterwards are outstanding.

Nearly every large high technology firm offers this sort of internship program and the listings here are far from comprehensive. If you are qualified and interested in this kind of internship, it will pay off to locate and check out other programs. If there is a nearby plant or office of a firm whose work interests you, contact their employment or recruitment office—or college relations office if they have one—and inquire about an internship program. It is a good idea to write or call the head office of a firm as well, but don't expect that they will necessarily know all there is to know about the firm's internship program. One firm's employment office director said flat out that he didn't have much information on the firm's internship program because they were located in each of the more than twenty plants that this firm operates throughout the country.

Also, many large firms try to simplify their recruiting of interns by concentrating on certain colleges and universities. This makes the job of the internship admission director easier because he can become acquainted with the science faculty who will be recommending candidates. Check with your career office to see if any firms look favorably on your school. Be sure to ask your faculty advisor if he/she or any other members of the science departments might have useful contacts with a high technology firm.

Formal Internship Programs: Business

Like the programs in industrial science, most of the formal internship programs in business are offered by big firms. That these programs exist at all might be seen as a contradiction to what we've already said about the business labor market. Why would a firm foot the bill for a formal business internship program when entry-level M.B.A.'s can be had by the truckload? There are about as many answers as there are programs—a fact which makes it difficult to generalize. One incentive for these programs that holds true for many firms is the improvement of community and corporate relations.

The words "community" and "corporate" imply some sort of limited eligibility to the program. Limited eligibility is exactly what students interested in many of these programs must face. The limitations are commonly placed on the applicant pool. The first is that the applicant be from certain universities or colleges—usually in the area of the firm's home office or plant. This is a constructive "good neighbor policy," but recruiting from a set number of local schools also helps cut down on program administration and recruitment expenses since the applicant pool and recruitment areas are limited.

The second limitation stipulates that the applicant be the child of an employee—hence, good "corporate relations." A huge firm like GM gets an enormous number of applications despite these two conditions. The New York Stock Exchange Internship Program also stipulates that a parent of the applicant be a member of the exchange. There aren't untold thousands of Stock Exchange members, so in this case the policy is just a case of nepotism. But one should realize that, while nepotism may be anathema to a politician—it is not a dirty word in the business world, especially at the entry level. As the top executive of one small company which doesn't explicitly stipulate this limitation but tends to practice it said, "Sure, we'll take anybody's application, but you're crazy if you don't think the boss's daughter has the best chance of all."

The programs we have listed have none of these limitations, but if your school or your family puts you in a position to take advantage of an internship, by all means scoop it up. When strings can be pulled, pull them!

The few large businesses that *do* have formal internship programs believe that they—like the programs in industrial science—help to locate and train prospective employees—and are well worth the expense and administrative headaches. Aetna Life and Casualty Insurance Company is a good example of this. Aetna believes their program can produce excellent candidates for permanent jobs with the firm, but with a minimum of risk. (Aetna also only hires students from specific schools to which they send recruiters.) Because their internship program is short (one summer), bad apples can be spotted and simply not hired for full-time positions, whereas a one- or two-year entry level training program would force the company to keep a bad apple for a longer period.

The important thing to remember in formal business internship programs is that a real commitment to the field is expected. You won't be accepted if there is any question of your interest. In this respect programs like Aetna's are very similar to those offered by high technology firms.

Formal Internships: Some Additional Options

There are two other important alternatives to consider. The first are the organized international reciprocal job internship exchange programs offered by AIESEC and IAESTE (see listings). These programs are invaluable means to foreign work and travel experience. If you are interested in working abroad it is nearly impossible to get through the red tape without their help. One government major had a great time and learned a lot in the City Planning agency in Helsinki through AIESEC. The second alternative to consider is a government internship. Many of these at the state and federal level require business backgrounds. Look at the government section for programs, and also find out if your state has a central clearinghouse for government internships. While the pickings in business may seem slim, the fact is that the internships are out there even if they're not advertised. Do not neglect the business needs of every other sector of our economy—from the accounting for a radio station to the administration of a zoo—the possibilities are endless.

Formal Internships: Some Hints on Applying

Battling your way into Big Business internships is tough. The programs are extremely competitive. For instance, Monsanto Corporation asked that they not be listed here because they already receive 10,000 applications for 75 positions. These are typical—and certainly not comforting—odds. Nevertheless, if you pay attention to two closely-linked pointers you may help your application to rise above the glut.

First, realize that the internship program is designed to single out prospective employees. A stellar academic record that isn't accompanied by an unequivocal statement of plans for a career in the field will mean nothing to the program's admission's director. Second, the admission's director will try to find some substantiation of that unequivocal statement. Anyone can profess to have been fascinated with calculators since the age of four. Try to back up your statement by showing how course work has taken you in this direction, what outside reading you've done pertaining to industrial science or business, and what relevant job experience you've had. Be thorough, detailed and concise.

Whether you are applying for a formal or informal internship, it is a good idea to have a resume in hand when you go to your interview. Also, have a thorough idea of what the firm does or produces, how large it is, etc. It always helps to impress the employer in this way. One way to do this homework is to study published reports and financial statements available from the corporate secretary's office, personnel office, or public relations office.

Informal Internships: The Summer Employment Program and the Odd Job

So your father isn't the president of United Technologies, no firm recruits at your school, and you can't honestly say what area of business you want to pursue. Don't feel left out—you're probably in the majority. Many good opportunities for internship-like experience aren't formal internship programs. Some firms, especially smaller ones which are not willing to take on the responsibility and expense of a formal internship program, operate

"Summer Development" or "Summer Employment" programs. Typically, a firm makes room in its budget for the employment of a few interested and qualified undergraduates to serve as extra bodies around the office in the summer. These extra employees help fill in for vacationing help in a variety of capacities.

It is not unusual for these programs to be somewhat unstructured, and, because the formality of a program administrator is dropped, you may find yourself in the perplexing situation of not knowing what work is expected of you. This may be the result of intentional conniving on the part of the employment office to find another typist—but more often the confusion is the result of innocent inattention. The employers usually don't worry about the extra body until it materializes. This situation can be turned to your advantage. One summer employee ended up as the personal assistant to the president of the company. Even if you are not this lucky, entering a confused situation presents an excellent opportunity to use your curiosity and initiative to prove your abilities. If you end up as a faceless entity in the typing pool it is usually your own fault. For some hints on how to impress your employer, take a look at the chapter on "Making Your Own."

Finding the odd job is more difficult—but it can be at least as rewarding as any other internship. An example of this is an architecture/fine arts major who landed a job as a draftsman for a large architecture firm. "I was lucky to find it through a friend. What an experience! I gained practical experience as a draftsman and designer I never would have gotten in school, and I learned how tough and competitive it would be to work in a big company like that."

Although odd jobs require that a specific spot in the firm be filled, there are plenty of opportunities to broaden your scope by observing the goings-on around you. Don't plan on any promotions in one of these jobs, so be sure that any job you accept will be interesting enough to get you through the summer.

Informal Internships: Where to Look, What to Ask For

When you inquire about the availability of internship programs with a business, it is important to be flexible in your request. Don't harp on the word internship. When inquiring at a personnel office or school placement office ask whether there are any internship programs, summer employment programs or short-term jobs available for undergraduates in your field. The point is to find some piece of jargon that rings a bell with the employer.

There are innumerable places to look. Begin by asking family and friends—everyone knows that the easiest way to get a job is through connections. For formal internship programs and summer employment programs call a firm's local and home offices (See Formal Internships, above). Also inquire at your school placement office and ask your professors if they have any contacts in the business world, or know of any programs. For odd jobs be sure to check the help wanted ads in the newspapers.

AETNA LIFE & CASUALTY INSURANCE CO.
Hartford, Connecticut

Summer Internship and Cooperative Education Program

ELIGIBILITY: *Undergraduate and graduate*
DURATION: *3 to 8 months*
ACADEMIC CREDIT POSSIBLE: *Yes*
REMUNERATION OR FEE: *$4.50/hr.*
POSITIONS OFFERED: *75*
APPLICATION DEADLINE: *Varies*

General Description

Aetna uses its summer internship and term-time cooperative education program to train and test prospective permanent employees. Their hiring criteria attests to this. Aetna hires interns only from those schools at which they recruit. You must apply through your school's placement service or cooperative education office. Aetna has no specific program for minorities, but minorities do receive special consideration.

The internship lasts for three months, May to September, and the cooperative education program is conducted during the school year. Occasionally interns work both during the summer and following semester.

To be accepted, you must have above a 3.0 grade point average, good verbal and written skills, and an aptitude for math. Students of business, data processing, and humanities are eligible. Most interns work in insurance-related areas; i.e., claims, experience rating, and actuarial. However, there is also a large number of interns who work in data processing, public relations, accounting, purchasing and personnel. The training occurs on the job and most interns work in several departments to gain as broad an experience as possible. Most of the interns hired work at Aetna's home office in Hartford, Connecticut. Interns are also placed in branch agencies around the country where they usually process claims. You may state a regional preference in your application.

Inside Word

The administrator acknowledged several weaknesses in the program. "The limitations are in housing out-of-town students, and a misunderstanding of the purpose of the program in some departments. At times interns are viewed as fill-in clerical employees. Fortunately, this situation has not occured often.''

One intern felt that the program's structure was somewhat restrictive. Since the interns work in a variety of departments, often the work was challenging only because of its novelty. ''Once I became familiar with the function of a department, the work got boring.'' Another major drawback was that interns were not allowed to work on self-initiated projects, and their assignments were closely monitored. ''Aetna felt we needed close supervision since we were being trained to do this work.''

Despite these drawbacks, the balance of the experience was positive for the interns. As a business and insurance major, one intern did gain invaluable experience doing group experience rating, analyzing past years' policies, auditing, taxes and bond investment. ''It's a way to get into a major corporation, and I might not have had the chance otherwise. It's an opportunity to meet influential people who will help promote my career.''

Contact:

Roy B. Snyder, Manager
Recruiting Office
Aetna Life & Casualty Insurance Co.
79 Farmington Avenue
Hartford, CT 06156

AMERICAN ASSEMBLY OF COLLEGIATE SCHOOLS OF BUSINESS   Washington, D.C.

ELIGIBILITY: *Junior through graduate*
DURATION: *Summer, semester, or 2 semesters*
ACADEMIC CREDIT POSSIBLE: *Yes*
REMUNERATION OR FEE: *None*
POSITIONS OFFERED: *1 to 5*
APPLICATION DEADLINE: *Varies*

General Description

Interns work in the areas of international and governmental affairs and assist the staff in placing business school faculty members in one-year assignments with the U.S. government; aid in the development of a worldwide clearing-house for the exchange of business school faculty; program planning and execution in the public policy realm as well as for a series of regional workshops to internationalize the business school curricula.

Interns must have completed their junior year in college and can be students of government, international affairs, business administration, and educational administration. They must be self-motivated to handle the independent work. Special consideration is given to women, minorities, and the handicapped. Send a letter expressing your interest along with a resume and references when you apply.

The Inside Word

The best way to be accepted into the program is to be an MBS candidate. "The ideal intern has the economic background and analytical skills to handle the assignments."

The main office of the AACSB is in St. Louis, but the Washington office, where interns are placed, is very small. This makes for an extremely comfortable working atmosphere, although at some times you can feel what one intern called "the ivory tower effect." One intern felt so much at home that he took over the Assistant Director's work when she was away.

The Assistant Director asked interns to fill out weekly reports evaluating their work and the supervisor's efforts, in order to improve the quality of the internship. One intern worked on two major projects: first, recruiting business faculty for positions in government, and second, an independent project developing a proposal for a paper to be presented to UNESCO. The intern was given a great deal of responsibility with the latter project.

One intern concluded: "Consider the internship a learning experience, like school—you can get out what you put into it."

Contact:

Ms. Terri Rosenblatt
Assistant Director
International and Governmental Affairs
American Association of Collegiate Schools of Business
1755 Massachusetts Avenue, N.W., Suite 320
Washington, D.C. 20036
(202) 483-0400

AMERICAN ASSOCIATION OF ADVERTISING AGENCIES
Minority Student Fellowship Program

New York, New York

ELIGIBILITY: *Undergraduate and graduate*
DURATION: *10 weeks, summer*
ACADEMIC CREDIT POSSIBLE: *No*
REMUNERATION OR FEE: *Undergraduates, $150/week salary plus room and board; Graduates, $275/week salary plus room and board*

POSITIONS OFFERED: *About 30*
APPLICATION DEADLINE: *Beginning of February*

General Description

The American Association of Advertising Agencies (AAAA) sponsors a "Minority Student Fellowship Program" each summer. The program places interns in a Chicago or New York advertising agency. Any minority student in an under-graduate program, who will have completed his or her junior year by the start of the program, can apply. Graduate students must have completed 50% of their graduate studies and be enrolled in a full-time program to be considered. The AAAA's objective is to select students who will be returning to campus after the program ends, hoping that they will spread the word about the opportunities available in advertising. Those students who will graduate from undergraduate programs will be considered only if they have plans for full-time graduate work.

Dormitory facilities and meal plans, paid for by the participating agencies, are provided for non-local students where necessary. In addition, transportation costs are paid for the trip to and from the internship.

The program is designed to provide interns with a realistic job experience in an advertising agency. The intern's summer position is determined by the needs of the participating agencies and the student's field of interest. In the past, assignments have been in account management, art direction, copywriting, research, media, and television production. Every effort is made to match the job assignments with the student's background and interests. The program begins with a week-long orientation. After this, individual assignments may vary, with some agencies preferring to host the intern in one department, while other agencies construct assignments that allow the intern to work in various departments during the ten weeks. In addition to the work experience, interns participate in weekly seminars, at which a specialist discusses in depth one aspect of the agency.

Competition for the program is keen. The initial pool of 500-plus applicants is screened and narrowed down to 100, then to 50, and finally to approximately 30. About 22 positions are located in New York and eight are offered in Chicago. There are no restrictions regarding academic majors, but the applicant's interest in the marketing and advertising business is a criterion for selection. A completed application is required. It is advantageous to include any support materials (i.e., portfolios, writing samples) and a letter of recommendation from a faculty member or school administrator, although these are not required.

The Inside Word

Getting accepted: The AAAA is looking for someone with business aptitude, though not necessarily business experience. A former intern, who is now involved in the administration of the program remarked, "We need someone who has enough sense to sell himself. The key to the advertising industry is selling ideas. If you can't sell yourself, you can't sell ideas.'' It is important to be straightforward in the interview and to assert your interest in the advertising business. "The most common negative comment from an interviewer is, 'They don't seem to show enough interest.' "

Supervision: The program is heavily supervised, with few opportunities for interns to work on self-initiated projects. Rather than seeing this as a negative aspect of the program, a former intern said, "I didn't have enough background or experience to start anything." The program is "well organized and substantive," causing one intern to remark that the program was "engaging and exciting" on the whole.

Contact:

Ruth S. Walter, Secretary
Special Committee on Equal Employment Opportunities
American Association of Advertising Agencies
200 Park Avenue
New York, NY 10017

CONTROL DATA SUMMER INTERNSHIP PROGRAM
Minneapolis, Minnesota

ELIGIBILITY: *Undergraduate and graduate*
DURATION: *June to September*
ACADEMIC CREDIT POSSIBLE: *No*
REMUNERATION: *Salary varies*
POSITIONS OFFERED: *Varies*
APPLICATION DEADLINE: *Varies*

General Description

Control Data Corporation is looking for students with backgrounds in computer science and engineering to participate in their summer program. Special consideration is given to minorities. The internship focuses on independent work on various projects. The internship is held at Control Data facilities across the U.S., but mainly in Minneapolis. The intern is paid a basic salary, as well as compensation for work-related travel and initial transportation to the site of the internship. The main purpose of the program is to develop the internship into a permanent position.

The Inside Word

An intern commented that race, sex, year in school, previous internships, course work, and grades all played an important·role in getting accepted into the program. Knowing a former intern may also help. The working atmosphere was characterized as "good," but the physical surroundings were "somewhat cramped". However, the Control Data internship is "an excellent opportunity to learn what it is like to work within a corporate structure."

The supervision at Control Data is helpful, not stifling, and interns are entrusted with significant tasks. "My supervisor was willing to assign projects that carried a lot of responsibility. I like the responsibility and the pay."

Contact:

Robert Martinez, Personnel Administrator
Control Data Corporation
8100 34th Avenue South
Mailing Address/Box 0
Minneapolis, MN 155440
(612) 853-6470

DEKALB SEED SALES MANAGEMENT INTERNSHIP
DEKALB SEED PRODUCTION MANAGEMENT INTERNSHIP

Dekalb, Illinois

ELIGIBILITY: *College juniors*
DURATION: *3 months*
ACADEMIC CREDIT POSSIBLE: *Yes*
REMUNERATION OR FEE: *$205/week plus travel expenses*
POSITIONS OFFERED: *15*
APPLICATION DEADLINE: *Varies*

General Description

DEKALB Agresearch, Inc. is a major supplier of hybrid corn, sorghum, and wheat seed. DEKALB offers internships in sales and in production. These internships are for agronomy, agricultural business and agricultural economics majors between their junior and senior years.

Sales interns work with the district manager to recruit new DEKALB dealers. Production interns help to conduct production research and make field stand counts. Interns' activities are minimally supervised. Both internships are full time and most interns work 45 hours per week.

Admittance into the program is competitive—there are 300 applicants for the 15 positions. Those with a strong interest in agriculture are most qualified for the internships. A completed application and resume are required.

The Inside Word

The program administrators are looking for self-starters: "Any way that you can demonstrate this quality will make you stand out in the applicant pool."

Students can make significant contributions in this program and a number return to the company as regular employees. However, one administrator finds that the program can be limited when, "Occasionally, the manager supervising an intern does not take full advantage of the intern's capabilities." This is reflected in the experience of one intern, who said "There were no opportunities for self initiated projects and there was a minimum of challenge." That same intern called 75% of his work uninteresting in spite of a "very pleasant" working atmosphere and an "outstanding" supervisor.

Contact:

Gregory L. Olson, Personnel Director
DEKALB Agresearch, Inc.
Sycamore Road
Dekalb, Illinois 60115
(815) 758-3461

DUPONT SUMMER PROFESSIONAL PROGRAM

Eastern U.S.

ELIGIBILITY: *Undergraduate and graduate*
DURATION: *Summer*
ACADEMIC CREDIT POSSIBLE: *No*
REMUNERATION OR FEE: *Salary varies*
POSITIONS OFFERED: *200 to 500*
APPLICATION DEADLINE: *Varies*

General Description

The DuPont Summer Professional Program is designed to give practical experience to students of chemical, mechanical and electrical engineering, chemistry, accounting and business. While DuPont *is* interested in testing prospective employees, this is not a formal training program.

Interns work in the various DuPont plants and laboratories located on the East Coast, in the Southeast, and on the Gulf Coast. DuPont prefers juniors in college through graduate students and bases the salary on the nature of the intern's work and his/her level of education. Applicants face stiff competition: there are 2,000 to 3,000 applicants for the 200 to 500 spots. DuPont arranges housing for the interns. Each intern is supervised by an experienced employee with a similar academic background.

The program features a two-day national symposium where all the summer interns are flown to the home office in Wilmington, Delaware. There they hear speakers from DuPont, and student interns report on their work.

The Inside Word

One electrical engineering intern was able to do independent research in audio distortion. His department was a small operation of eight employees involved in product development. There was a general consensus among interns that the larger departments were not as interesting to work in.

One intern found that as an EE major he was not fully prepared for the mechanical engineering work he was expected to do, but he learned quickly, and soon after was given free rein to pursue a self-initiated project. "I made good use of my previous skills, and my work here gave me a better idea of my career goals."

The general opinion seemed to be that "DuPont is a good company—it really treats their employees well."

Contact:

Dr. Donald L. Dinsel
Summer Coordinator
Employee Relations Dept.
DuPont Company
1007 Market Street
Wilmington, DE 19898

FEDERAL RAILROAD ADMINISTRATION   National
Intern Program

ELIGIBILITY: *Minority or Female, junior through graduate*
DURATION: *Summer, semester, quarter, or full year*
ACADEMIC CREDIT POSSIBLE: *Yes*
REMUNERATION OR FEE: *Salary varies*
POSITIONS OFFERED: *Varies*
APPLICATION DEADLINE: *Varies*

General Description

The FRS Railroad intern program is in its nascent stages. The program is designed to assist minorities and females in attaining managerial and professional level positions in the railroad industry. Currently, twenty cities are targeted for programs. These cities are serviced by Union

Pacific, Conrail, Amtrak and Southern Railroad. The salary will be paid by the railroad. The duration of the internship is flexible: it can be a full year beginning with full-time work during the summer and continuing part-time during the school year; a semester or quarter internship; cooperative-education rotation; or summer internship. Also, there is the possibility of the internship developing into a permanent position.

You can apply to this program only if your school has been invited to participate. This is contingent on whether your school is located in one of the railroads' selected cities. If so, your career placement office and faculty will be notified, and faculty members will be asked to pre-select qualified students. Contact your school's placement office to see if you are eligible. Work supervisors will then interview candidates and make the final selections. Academic advisors and work supervisors will collaborate to monitor the interns' activities and to build a permanent relationship for continued internship program development.

The specific academic areas the program is related to are: business administration, computer science, sociology, marketing, and especially engineering. The interns will be placed in mid-level managerial positions with the railroad local outreach centers of the FRA's Minority Business Resource Centers, and with minority businesses and major suppliers to the railroads.

The long-range goals of the FRA's Intern program are to increase the percentage of minority managers in the railroad industry, as well as the number of minority sales and marketing positions in suppliers of the railroads.

Contact:

Naomi M. Stauber, Program Director
FRA Railroad Intern Program
A. L. Nellum & Associates
1990 M Street, N.W.
Washington, D.C. 20036
(202) 862-9300

THE GREATER WASHINGTON BUSINESS CENTER, INC.
Internship Program

Washington, D.C.

ELIGIBILITY: *Sophomore through graduate*
DURATION: *Summer, quarter, or semester*
ACADEMIC CREDIT POSSIBLE: *Yes*
REMUNERATION OR FEE: *None*
POSITIONS OFFERED: *4 to 6*
APPLICATION DEADLINE: *Varies*

General Description:

The Greater Washington Business Center, Inc. provides a wide range of technical services to minority businesses in Washington, D.C. It offers internships in the fields of management and business consulting. MBA candidates with business undergraduate degrees are the ideal interns. Otherwise, a background in economics, management, engineering or architecture is suitable. Academic credit is sometimes arranged by students with their individual schools. Work-study stipends have also been arranged for these voluntary positions.

Interns work one on one with a supervisor, and after a brief introduction are given their own clients. The work involves client assessment, marketing studies, arranging and reviewing expansion loans, and even such involved tasks as working with construction and contracting firms to find a suitable site for a business, and establishing an advertising campaign. There is the possibility of the internship developing into a permanent position.

The Inside Word

One intern said that applicants should be sharp, self-confident, have organizational skills, and work well with people. "Because there is fairly little direction from the staff, you need to have some self-confidence to get through the difficult starting period." Interns see this as one flaw in the program; they begin with very little practical experience and have to quickly familiarize themselves with business accounting. Two interns wished they had more structured guidance in the beginning. "Although in the end I probably learned more from it, it was rough to have a loan package thrown at me and have to figure it out for myself."

Interns feel that the GWBC offers substantial on-the-job experience to students in business—a rarity in business internships. One intern offered the following reasons: "Since it is a non-profit organization there is less pressure than in a private firm with high paying clients and equally high expectations." He felt a little guilty towards his clients because of his lack of experience, but he learned quickly. His only regret was that he didn't begin the internship with more experience so that he could get to the "meaty stuff" sooner.

One good feature is the pleasant working atmosphere of the office. Each intern is given his own office, and the rest of the staff is extremely helpful and willing to answer questions.

The relevance of the practical experience in business was invaluable to one intern. "I was working with clients' money, real dollars and cents." His perspective towards economics changed from macro to micro when taken from the academic world and put in the business world.

Contact:

Marvin L. Doxie, Sr.
Assistant Vice President

The Greater Washington Business Center, Inc.
1705 DeSales Street, N.W.
Washington, D.C. 20036
(202) 833-8960

INTERNATIONAL ASSOCIATION FOR THE EXCHANGE OF STUDENTS FOR TECHNICAL EXPERIENCE (IAESTE)

World-wide

ELIGIBILITY: *Sophomore through graduate*
DURATION: *2 to 3 months during summer*
ACADEMIC CREDIT POSSIBLE: *Yes*
REMUNERATION OR FEE: *$50 application fee; stipend during traineeship*
POSITIONS OFFERED: *Varies*
APPLICATION DEADLINE: *December 15*

General Description:

IAESTE is an international reciprocal exchange program of practical training held in one of 46 member countries. Students in the natural and physical sciences, engineering, mathematics, architecture, or agriculture may apply. If you have finished your sophomore year in good standing at an accredited four-year college, but are not yet finished with your doctorate, you are eligible.

Students receive a stipend to cover living expenses during their traineeship. However, IAESTE estimates that an additional $700-900 are needed to cover expenses such as air fare, passport and visa fees, and free-time travel. The traineeship generally lasts two to three months during the summer, although programs lasting up to a year may be available. Some countries require fluency in the native language, and it is helpful for all other countries.

In this exchange program your skills are matched with voluntary employers in foreign countries. The terms of the offer are then sent to you between February and April. If you accept, IAESTE will help to arrange the necessary work visa. If at all possible, the traineeship will be in a country of your choice. It is important to note that the number of openings abroad for American students is directly related to the number of openings found for foreign students in this country. While it is not a prerequisite, and does not guarantee placement, students who find openings with American employers for foreign trainees will be given preference for traineeships in other countries of their choice.

IAESTE calls their program a "career vacation abroad," since it offers practical work experience in a specialized field, while placing you in a foreign country where you will have some free time to travel. In addition to the U.S., the member countries of IAESTE are: Argentina, Australia,

Austria, Belgium, Brazil, Canada, Colombia, Czechoslovakia, Denmark, Egypt, Finland, France, Germany, Ghana, Greece, Guyana, Iceland, India, Iraq, Ireland, Israel, Italy, Japan, Korea, Lebanon, Libya, Luxembourg, Mexico, Netherlands, Nigeria, Norway, Philippines, Poland, Portugal, South Africa, Spain, Sudan, Sweden, Switzerland, Syria, Thailand, Tunisia, Turkey, United Kingdom, Yugoslavia.

The Inside Word

It is impossible to give an overview of the type of experience that an intern will have in an IAESTE-arranged internship—the locations and the employers are too widely varied. IAESTE does its best to find good internships, but ultimately the success of the internship depends on the employer and the intern. Several people we contacted—ranging from a career guidance counselor to a previous IAESTE intern who worked as a hotel management trainee in Toronto—were very pleased with the work IAESTE had done for them. They hastened to point out that without IAESTE's help in lining up a job and obtaining a work visa, finding work in a foreign country would be next to impossible.

Contact:

IAESTE/US
217 American City Building
Columbia, MD 21044
(301) 997-2200

INTERNATIONAL ASSOCIATION OF STUDENTS IN ECONOMICS AND BUSINESS MANAGEMENT (AIESEC)
Traineeship Exchange

World-wide

ELIGIBILITY: *Sophomore through graduate*
DURATION: *2 to 18 months*
ACADEMIC CREDIT POSSIBLE: *No*
REMUNERATION OR FEE: *$200/week stipend*
POSITIONS OFFERED: *3000 world-wide (400 in U.S.)*
APPLICATION DEADLINE: *Varies*

General Description

AIESEC is a student-run international job internship exchange program for students of economics and business management. It allows students with one year of economics to apply theoretical training to practical situations in any of 55 countries on six continents. In order to work abroad, students must work on their school's AIESEC committee. The number of traineeships available in foreign countries relates directly to the number of local traineeships found by AIESEC members. AIESEC members go out into the local business community and locate traineeships for foreign students, whose educational training is matched up with an employer's management-related needs. There are presently AIESEC committees at 60 colleges in this country. If your school does not have one, contact other schools in your area to see if you can work on theirs.

Knowledge of a host country's language is helpful, but not always required. The traineeships can last anywhere from two to eighteen months, but are usually for the summer. Students are paid a stipend for living expenses by their employers, while the host AIESEC committee arranges visas, housing, and provides a social and cultural reception program.

Local AIESEC committees sponsor forums and lecture on business related topics for members and for the general student body. These serve to increase the interaction between student members and the academic and business world. In addition, AIESEC/US sponsors an annual National Leadership Training Seminar, and an International Congress. To attend, you must apply through your school's AIESEC committee. For more information, read the several AIESEC publications obtainable through your local committee or by writing to AIESEC/US, Inc. (see contact addresses).

The Inside Word

The ability to combine practical work experience with a foreign location was considered the best part of the AIESEC program by two members. "The social life was great, thanks to the AIESEC committee in Helsinki. I met trainees from all over the world at the numerous receptions held for the 70 trainees working in the city." One intern worked in the city planning agency, doing independent research in order to culminate her traineeship with a report on city planning. "I was lucky since this involved interviewing people in departments all over the city."

One intern explained why businesses hire trainees: "The U.S. employers stand only to benefit from hiring foreign trainees—since the selection process is so competitive in foreign countries they only send top-notch graduate students. They bring an objective view and a fresh perspective. The novelty of a foreign co-worker also improves the spirit in the office."

Another intern learned more about the country she worked in than any technical skills: "I learned how the Polish socialist system works—and saw first hand some of the numerous problems that no one likes to talk about. We were mainly given 'show and tell' tours of the Polish food production and distribution system, and asked to describe our respective countries' methods. They were especially interested in my opinions since I was the only American."

Another intern felt the program opened her mind to different perspectives, since the trainees often discussed international politics. "I heard a lot of varied opinions about America, and I had to continually defend America." Another pointed out the costs involved: "The traineeship was very expensive—I didn't make any money, but the experience of working abroad was well worth it."

Contact:

FOR APPLICATION MATERIALS:
Contact your school's
AIESEC committee.

FOR MORE INFORMATION:
AIESEC/US, Inc.
622 Third Avenue
New York, NY 10017
(212) 687-1905

C. PAUL LUONGO COMPANY   *Boston, Massachusetts*
Internship Program

ELIGIBILITY: *Undergraduate and graduate*
DURATION: *Varies*
ACADEMIC CREDIT POSSIBLE: *Yes*
REMUNERATION OR FEE: *None*
POSITIONS OFFERED: *1*
APPLICATION DEADLINE: *Varies*

General Description

This public relations internship program is personally directed by the firm's president, Mr. C. Paul Luongo. Especially welcome are students interested in English, business and economics.

The C. Paul Luongo Co. provides corporate, product and financial publicity services throughout North America and Europe for both consumer and industrial clients. In its publicity coverage, the agency produces special news programs, TV coverage, and feature articles for newspapers, magazines and other media sources.

Interns must have excellent writing and research abilities, and must be able to type. Any media experience will aid the intern in his or her duties. The intern needs good telephone skills, since much of the research and business is conducted by phone. Past interns have helped Mr. Luongo research biographies for his book, *America's Best!*

You must apply directly to Mr. Luongo, and along with an interview, provide a resume, college transcript, letters of recommendation, writing samples and, if possible, a portfolio.

The Inside Word

Most of C. Paul Luongo's interns have been students from Wellesley or Harvard, due only to these schools' proximity to the company. Mr. Luongo has continued the program because of the excellent performance of past interns. The savvy and confidence characteristic of "P.R. men"—as well as the hectic pace of public relations work is reflected in Mr. Luongo's criteria for selecting interns: "The intern must be a protean type—extremely quick. Yes, my interns must be simply brilliant . . . and be able to type."

Contact:

C. Paul Luongo Company
441 Stuart St.
Boston, MA 02116
(617) 266-4210

MASSACHUSETTS STATE BANKING DEPARTMENT CONSUMER ASSISTANCE DIVISION
Volunteer Internships

Boston, Massachusetts

ELIGIBILITY: *Undergraduate and graduate*
DURATION: *June to August; September to December; January to May*
ACADEMIC CREDIT POSSIBLE: *Yes*
REMUNERATION OR FEE: *None*
POSITIONS OFFERED: *6 per year*
APPLICATION DEADLINE: *Varies*

General Description

The consumer assistance division of the state banking department of Massachusetts handles the research, analysis and mediation of consumer bank disputes.

The hours are flexible during the term-time programs, ranging from 15 to 40 hours per week. The summer program is full-time, however. Academic credit is usually given by the interns' schools for their work.

Students with a background in economics and an interest in tackling banking, economic and legal matters while in a public role should apply.

Interns mediate complaints made by consumers about state-chartered financial institutions. By reading applicable laws, conferring with the legal department, and contacting the parties involved, the intern helps determine the solution to a complaint. Another part of the intern's job is to summarize and chart previous complaints to detect any general developing trends. A few times a week an intern is required to do paper work or telephone duty—answering inquiries or sending out complaint forms. Telephoning is a necessary part of the job, so a good telephone voice is essential. Oral and written skills are needed, as well as an ability to deal with the public. The intern must be consumer-oriented. An economic background, plus research and analytic skills are important.

Competition for positions is pretty stiff; only six positions are available for the 50 or so applicants each year. An interview and writing samples are recommended.

The Inside Word

One intern asked the program administrator why he was chosen. She said it was because she felt he had the "oomph." "During my interview I asked her as many questions about the banking department as she asked me," said the intern. He worked in a pleasant office where he felt "in place from day one."

Independent work and self-initiated projects are two advantages of the internship. "I was on my own nearly all of the time and was allowed to follow my interests. I became involved with mortgages and real estate practices and prepared a folder on condominium problems for the office." While the intern did not learn a great deal about applied economics, he did become familiar with state financial legislation, the mechanics of state government, and the politicking involved. "And as an actual representative of the Commonwealth of Massachusetts I learned the responsibilities of the position: responsibilities to banks, collecting agencies, and the public.

While corresponding with the public and banking associates, one intern said he ran into his share of "loonies." This experience fortified his confidence in his ability to deal with all different sorts of people. He also found that a good sense of humor got him a long way. "The office is dignified and responsible, but everyone likes a good laugh."

Contact:

Vicki Gintis, Coordinator
Massachusetts Department of Banking and Loans
Consumer Assistance Division
100 Cambridge St.
Boston, MA 02202
(617) 727-2102

PHILLIPS PETROLEUM INTERNSHIP PROGRAM

Southwestern U.S.

ELIGIBILITY: *Sophomores and juniors*
DURATION: *3 to 6 months*
ACADEMIC CREDIT POSSIBLE: *Yes*
REMUNERATION OR FEE: *Salary*
POSITIONS OFFERED: *600*
APPLICATION DEADLINE: *January 1*

General Description

Phillips Petroleum offers one of the largest internship programs in the country. If you are interested in oil, and currently a sophomore or a junior in college you are eligible to apply. Phillips gives preference to applicants from the Southwest, especially those at schools where they recruit. The length of employment is flexible, but it usually lasts from three to six months, beginning in the summer and continuing into the following semester. You must work for a minimum of 10 weeks. The pay for a 40 hour week depends on the intern's work. Academic credit is sometimes arranged, usually for engineering students who work through the semester.

Of the 600 summer employees hired, 200 are arbitrarily chosen to work in a semi-professional capacity as engineers, computer programmers, geologists and other technical positions. The remaining 400 employees work as "red-neck labor," even though they have the same qualifications as those employed in technical positions. Phillips believes that future professionals should experience manual labor, to better understand the kind of work they might otherwise not come in contact with. Phillips has found that these overqualified laborers have enjoyed their work nonetheless, and appreciate the insights gained. There are negligible openings in the business areas. Interns work in various locations throughout the Southwest. Phillips Petroleum considers this a program to find new talent, and only hires students who express a firm interest in the petroleum business.

Contact:

W. M. Hutchinson
Phillips Petroleum Co.
Bartlesville, Oklahoma 74004

TEXAS INSTRUMENTS   *Massachusetts*
Summer Development Program   *Tennessee*
                                                        Texas

ELIGIBILITY: *Junior through graduate*
DURATION: *Summer*
ACADEMIC CREDIT: *Possible*
REMUNERATION OR FEE: *Varies*
POSITIONS OFFERED: *20 in each of 8 locations*
APPLICATION DEADLINE: *June*

General Description

Texas Instruments (TI) Summer Development Program is designed to give
selected students a general knowledge of TI operations as well as
experience in their particular fields of study. The program is run in six
locations in Texas (see Contact addresses), as well as in Attleboro,
Massachusetts and Johnson City, Tennessee. Often, assistance in locating
housing is provided by TI. For instance, in Attleboro, interns are housed
in apartments and at nearby colleges.

Curricula of principal interest to TI are in the engineering fields,
chemistry, physics, computer science (hardware/software), math and
accounting. The individual TI locations have different criteria for selecting
interns. For instance, the Lubbock Texas Consumer Group is involved in
the design, development, and production of consumer and professional
calculators and microelectronic time instruments. As a result, the Lubbock group is primarily interested in students with the following types of
educational backgrounds: electrical engineering, mechanical engineering,
industrial engineering, computer science (hardware/software), and plastics engineering.

The intern's activities are directed by a supervisor, and whenever
possible, the intern is paired with an employee working in the intern's
field. At the end of the summer, the interns are expected to give a
presentation on their work experiences.

Acceptance to the TI program is highly competitive. There are 20
applicants for every position offered. Students must have completed their
junior year and be in the upper 25% of their class. To apply, send your
resume, including grade point average and class standing, to the location
of your interest. The screening begins around the end of February and runs
until June. Generally, applications will be accepted up until that time.

The remuneration offered for the intern's work is based on the
intern's educational level. The intern is also eligible for many company
benefits such as life insurance, medical insurance, short and long term
disability insurance, unemployment benefits, workman's compensation,
social security, and paid holidays. Paid vacation is accrued only if a
student returns to the company. When interns leave at the end of the
summer, they are not terminated, but retain their service status. One

Company representative sees the fact that many students do return to the company as strong evidence of its being a highly successful program.

The Inside Word

The TI program is used to try out prospective employees. Seen as essential criteria for acceptance into the program were good grades and a well-rounded personality. One former intern advises, "Make good use of the program, it is easy to slouch by, but the experience can be very beneficial if you apply yourself." The interns spoke of the advantages of project-oriented work. "You are given a goal and then you work toward it. The ways and means are yours. I enjoyed the responsibility." The Texas Instruments name carries a lot of clout in the business community, so even if the summer program does not develop into a full-time position, the experience will look very good on your resume.

Contact:

FOR MORE INFORMATION
George Berryman
Texas Instruments
P.O. Box 225474, MS 67
Dallas, TX 75265

FOR APPLICATION MATERIALS:
Listed after each address are the educational backgrounds in which each TI Group is interested:

Dallas, Texas
Semiconductor Group:

Bill Rigsby
Texas Instruments, Semiconductor Group
P.O. Box 225212, MS 11
Dallas, TX 75265

EE, ME, IE, Chem. E., Computer Science (hardware/software), Chemistry, Solid State Physics.

Equipment Group and Information Systems and Services:

Ruth Lodowski
Texas Instruments, Equipment Group
P.O. Box 226015, MS 222
Dallas, TX 75266

Computer Science (hardware/software), Management Information Systems, Mathematics, Accounting-Computer Science minor; EE, ME, IE, Computer Science.

Central Research Laboratories and Facilities Engineering:

Helen Meltzer
Texas Instruments, Corporate Staff
P.O. Box 22534, MS 217
Dallas, TX 75265

EE, ME, Computer Science, Physics, Chemistry, Systems Research; IE,
CE, Ch.E., Structural Engineering.

Sherman, Texas
Equipment Group and Semiconductor Group:

Dick Malnory
Texas Instruments
P.O. Box 84, MS 806
Sherman, TX 75090

EE, ME, IE, Ch. E., Engineering Physics, Engineering Science, Plastics
Engineering, Chemistry, Materials Science.

Austin, Texas
Digital Systems Group and Equipment Group:

Lee Cooke
Texas Instruments
P.O. Box 2909, MS 2208
Austin, TX 78769

EE, ME, Computer Science, Ch. E., Chemistry.

Houston, Texas
Digital Systems Group and Semiconductor Group:

Merv Galloway
Texas Instruments
P.O. Box 1443, MS 605
Houston, TX 77001

EE, ME, IE, Computer Science, Engineering Physics, Materials, Science.

Lubbock, Texas
Consumer Group, Semiconductor Group and Front End Processing
(FEP):

Connie Wharton
Texas Instruments
P.O. Box 10508, MS 5501
Lubbock, TX 79408

EE, ME, IE, Computer Science (hardware/software), Plastics Engineering; Ch. E., EE, IE, Physics, Computer Science.

Temple, Texas
Digital Systems Division:

Dan Bartell
Texas Instruments
P.O. Box 180, MS 3209
Temple, TX 76501

EE, ME, IE, Computer Science.

Attleboro, Massachusetts
Metallurgical Materials Division and Control Products Division:

Michael Smith
Texas Instruments
34 Forest, MS 12-3
Attleboro, MA 02803

EE, ME, IE, Metallurgical Engr., Engineering Science, Engineering Mechanics, Engineering Physics, Chemistry, Materials Science, Math.

Johnson City, Tennessee
Control Products Division:

Pat Aulson
Texas Instruments
P.O. Drawer 1255
Johnson City, TN 37601

EE, ME, IE.

3M COMPANY COOPERATIVE WORK-STUDY PROGRAM

St. Paul, Minnesota

ELIGIBILITY: *Undergraduate*
DURATION: *1 semester*
ACADEMIC CREDIT: *Yes*
REMUNERATION: *$239 to $306/week*
POSITIONS OFFERED: *Varies*
APPLICATION DEADLINE: *Varies*

General Description

3M hopes that by offering a carefully planned co-op program, students will eventually return as career employees upon graduation. Their work-study program is available to students enrolled in an engineering or chemistry curriculum. The program is administered only by certain schools, so applicants must work through school channels at all times. The majority of 3M's co-op students are assigned to the home office location in St. Paul, Minnesota, although many programs are being developed in new locations. 3M assists interns in finding housing—some apartments near 3M are reserved for co-op students.

Opportunities for co-op employees are available in Process Development, Equipment Engineering, Process Instrumentation and Control, Engineering Research, and Manufacturing Engineering. According to 3M the assignments are project-oriented: "under proper supervision the intern is given a meaningful project to work on." While the project assignments are mostly technical, there are also assignments in areas such as journalism.

The co-op student is eligible for many company benefits, including medical and life insurance, paid holidays, sick pay, and paid transportation to the initial site. Salaries reflect the educational level of the co-op trainee; they are carried on the payroll as full-time employees. When trainees return to school, they are placed on an educational leave of absence, rather than termination.

Contact:

Staffing and Employee Resources
3M Company, Bldg. 224-1W
3M Center
St. Paul, Minnesota 55101

3M COMPANY SUMMER TECHNICAL PROGRAM

St. Paul, Minnesota

ELIGIBILITY: *Graduate and third year technical undergraduate students*
DURATION: *Summer*
ACADEMIC CREDIT POSSIBLE: *Yes*
REMUNERATION OR FEE: *See below*
POSITIONS OFFERED: *Varies*
APPLICATION DEADLINE: *Early February*

General Description

3M Company is one of America's most diversified companies. The company markets 45 major product lines. For the summer program held in St. Paul, candidates must have completed a minimum of three years of technical training. Curricula of principal interest are chemistry and physics; plus chemical, mechanical, electrical, metallurgical and ceramic engineering. Limited opportunities also exist in other fields. The pay is graduated—reflecting the intern's educational level. Include details of your educational background and your interests when you request an application.

3M Company assigns projects to interns that require application of fundamentals learned in school. All of the assignments are typical of industrial laboratory and manufacturing situations, involving everyday use of laboratory equipment, contact with other employees, and carrying out an independent project. Upon completion of summer employment, the student submits a progress report summarizing the status of the project and recommending further action. The summer intern is under the guidance of a 3M scientist or engineer.

In addition to work experience, interns also participate in "Meet 3M Days." These include a tour of 3M facilities, and seminars presented by 3M technical personnel.

3M Company's technical program benefits the company as well as the student. The student receives on-the-job training and the company gets a look at potential technical employees, often basing their decision to offer the student a permanent position on their work as interns.

Contact:

Summer Employment (TSTE)
3M Company, 3M Center
St. Paul, MN 55101

WAKEFIELD WASHINGTON ASSOCIATES   *Washington, D.C.*
Career Development Internship

ELIGIBILITY: *Undergraduate and graduate*
DURATION: *Varies*
ACADEMIC CREDIT POSSIBLE: *Yes*
REMUNERATION OR FEE: *None*
POSITIONS OFFERED: *3 to 6*
APPLICATION DEADLINE: *Varies*

General Description

Rowan Wakefield oversees this internship in his small management consulting firm composed of managers, research associates and assistants. This program is unique in that only liberal arts majors are hired. The program runs year-round and can be done on a semester basis, in the summer, or even during the January interterm that many schools schedule. While there is no monetary remuneration, Mr. Wakefield feels that an "exchange of services" takes place. In exchange for the intern's work, the intern is able to make contacts and receive counseling in career development.

Wakefield's firm often acts as a liaison between private businesses, schools and government. Intern assignments include: editing and publishing *American Family* newsletter, and special projects in the management consulting field—energy and public policy, appropriate technology information systems, and market surveys. Skills required for the program include being able to write and speak well, reasonable self-confidence and self-motivation. If you're interested, write a letter to Mr. Wakefield telling him why you want the internship. Later, an interview will be necessary.

The Inside Word

This program gets rave reviews from former participants. Seen as pluses were the extensive writing experience and the wide range of contacts made through the program. One English major worked on projects which included organizing a library and filing system for an energy library, acting as a liaison between universities and the government in arranging grants, as well as in marketing and promoting sales for the *American Family* newsletter. She characterized the working atmosphere as ''very close— like a family.''

While hard-pressed to find negative aspects of the program, the interns were frustrated at not being able to see their long-term projects through. One intern added that it was difficult to choose among the many projects—she could not possibly handle them all. They also criticized the cliquishness of the Washington social circuit, by working for a small firm, they were out of the mainstream of interns who worked together on ''the Hill.''

One intern called the program ''ideal for anyone from a liberal arts background—it helps you narrow down your interests.''

Contact:

Wakefield Washington Associates, Rowan Wakefield, President
1129 20th Street N.W., Suite 504
Washington, D.C. 20036
(202) 833-9880

WAUSAU INSURANCE COMPANIES   Wasau, Wisconsin
Summer Fellowship

ELIGIBILITY: *Juniors*
DURATION: *12 weeks, summer*
ACADEMIC CREDIT POSSIBLE: *No*
REMUNERATION: *$900/month salary*

POSITIONS OFFERED: *2 to 6*
APPLICATION DEADLINE: End of April

General Description

Wausau Insurance Company's internship generally runs from mid-June to mid-August. Interns must be juniors in college. The program starts with a one week orientation that provides a general overview of the insurance business. The program involves insurance-related studies such as Actuarial studies, Accounting, and Management. Interns choose their area of work from among sales, marketing, education, and underwriting. For further training, company representatives give lectures on their areas every two weeks. In addition to the salary, the intern receives compensation for work-related travel and the cost of the initial transportation to the site of the internship. Usually there are five applicants for every position available. To apply, send your resume and college transcript to Wausau. Faculty recommendations and an interview will increase your chances of being accepted.

The Inside Word

One intern, though he did join Wausau Insurance in an entry-level position after his internship, maintained that the summer program is not a training program—just a summer internship to acquaint the student with the insurance business. As an introduction to insurance, it is thorough. One intern said, "The internship was custom-made; Wausau matched up my skills and interests with an appropriate area." The interns are given a lot of independent work, which is later reviewed by their supervisors. An intern who worked under the director of education said, "It is a unique company. I felt that my supervisor paid a lot of attention to me and respected my work."

Contact:

Betty Donovan, Coordinator, Recruiting and Placement
Wausau Insurance Companies
2000 Westwood Drive
Wausau, WI 54401
(715) 842-6596

OTHER PLACES TO LOOK:

Public Service
Consumer Affairs Department, Giant Food
National Consumer Affairs Internship Program

Education

Internship opportunities in education are primarily to be found in teaching programs at prep schools. However, there are other places where educational experience can be gained in a non-classroom situation. Museums, historical societies and environmental foundations are some of the institutions which offer internships in public education. These programs are less prevalent than prep school teaching jobs; but they offer a very different and refreshing alternative for those interested in education, but not necessarily teaching.

Prep school teaching internships tend to have a lot in common. Most prep schools, but not all, are located in the Northeast, the majority of these in small towns. Secondary schools (grades nine through twelve) predominate. These are usually coeducational boarding schools which also accept day students.

Besides location and the ages of the students, the size of the school is another factor to be considered. Enrollments range from three hundred to about a thousand, with small and large schools each offering certain advantages. In a smaller school it is much easier to get to know all your students very well, which is, ideally, what teachers should do. Larger schools, on the other hand, offer more choices of elective courses, sports, activities and facilities.

Most internships are year-long programs which run from September to June. These probably give the most accurate picture of a teacher's life. In addition, a few private schools offer summer programs which range from five to seven weeks. While these are less representative of prep school life, they are also less of a commitment for those considering other careers besides education.

Full-year internships generally provide room, board, and a stipend of $3000 to $5000, while summer programs pay $700 to $850 and also include food and lodging. It is obvious from these figures that money is not the primary motivation for the job. Still, living expenses are small.

Unlike public schools, which require certification, a B.A. or B.S. is generally the only requirement for teaching at prep schools. Year-long internships usually go to men and women directly out of college. Summer interns are usually students who have just completed their junior year or who have just graduated. The application deadlines for most programs are between January first and February first.

What the intern actually does varies somewhat according to the individual program. All internships include training but some emphasize this more than others. In some schools, the intern eases into his role gradually by starting as an observer, tutor, and an assistant to a seasoned teacher. By the second semester or trimester the intern is ready to teach his own class or section. In other programs, the intern plunges right in, teaching his classes alone the first day. Many interns seem to prefer this latter system "so there is no question in students' minds, (or in yours) as to who is in charge."

Internships also vary according to the individual assignments. Schools try to match interns' knowledge, interests and experience with their present needs. For instance, if the school lacks English and biology teachers, football, swimming and tennis coaches, a choir director and an outing club leader, interns with these skills will be chosen. Schools' needs vary from year to year so there is a certain amount of luck involved—you sometimes have to be the right person with the right talent at the right time.

Nevertheless, internship directors are not merely trying to fill gaps in their permanent staff. Schools can be flexible about what courses they choose to offer. Often, permanent faculty members teach the required courses while interns teach electives which can change from year to year. Occasionally, interns are allowed to design their own courses. Also, teaching an elementary or high school level course does not require a tremendous depth of knowledge in that field. As one intern put it, "College students know more about everything than kids that age anyway." Thus, the applicant with a fairly broad liberal arts background has a better chance of getting an internship than the applicant who specializes in one or two areas.

An intern's experience is also affected by the faculty he or she works with. Usually, interns are paired with one supervisor, although this in no way prevents him from observing or seeking advice from other teachers. Generally, interns report that their supervising teachers are very understanding, helpful, and happy to have the intern's assistance. Most are very fair in dividing the workload so that the intern has as much responsibility as he/she feels can be handled. This occasionally includes some busy-work, but no one escapes this.

Teaching internships require considerable time, energy, and emotional commitment. They are not 9 to 5 jobs where one can knock off at the end of the week and put work out of mind until Monday morning. An internship at a boarding school is a round the clock job. Besides the time spent teaching two courses and observing other courses, interns coach sports at least two out of three seasons. Like other teachers, they share duties such as proctoring study halls, checking students into their dorms approximately three nights a week, and chaperoning occasional Saturday night activities. In addition to these scheduled commitments, much of an intern's "free" time is spent preparing lectures, correcting tests and papers and talking with students in their dorms.

This last role is especially important for interns because they have a unique relationship with students. Although all teachers are still learning, this is particularly true of an intern who is young and only recently out of school. The enthusiasm of doing something new, not to mention being closer in age to the students than most faculty members, can help make the intern very aware and responsive to students' problems.

The time commitment and the emphasis on the counselor role results in a situation for the intern which is called both "the warm, close-knit community" and, less cheerfully, the lack of privacy. While lasting personal friendships between teachers and students are certainly one of the best things about teaching in a small school, everyone needs time to be alone. Unfortunately, privacy is sometimes in short supply.

Whereas the intern's age can be an advantage, it can also put him in an awkward position between young and old. Like any teacher, an intern must uphold and enforce the typically strict school rules. These rules include curfews, prohibitions on drinking and smoking, and sometimes dress codes. This is not always easy for someone just out of college. Interns sometimes feel that their authority is unnervingly precarious, especially since some of the students are as little as three years younger.

On the other hand, interns may feel out of place with the faculty, who are usually older and married. The social life is usually very family-oriented, which can be quite limiting for a young, single adult. Although one intern greatly enjoyed his experience, the social facet of prep school teaching was enough reason for him to postpone making a commitment to teaching until later in his life.

Program directors look first for enthusiasm, personality, and a liking for and ability to get along with young people. The ability to relate to students and other faculty members is regarded as much more important than any other consideration. As a result, personal recommendations and interviews are crucial.

The applicant's academic record is also important, but it is not necessary to have graduated Summa Cum Laude. A "B" average will do. Prep schools draw very heavily from the more prestigious Eastern colleges, although they try to avoid accepting too many from the same school.

Athletic ability and especially any experience at coaching or teaching a sport is also very helpful. While it is fairly easy to find someone who can teach math or coach lacrosse, it is rare to find someone who can do both well. Unfortunately, great athletes sometimes make terrible coaches and great mathematicians can be lousy teachers. If you have taught tennis or coached little league or even worked at a camp, get a recommendation that will show that you can do more than just play a sport.

In short, teaching at a prep school requires adequate ability in a number of fields, but most of all, a love of young people and dedication to helping them. As a result, internship directors look for the enthusiastic "jack of all trades" who is willing to get involved.

GROTON SCHOOL   *Groton, Massachusetts*
Teacher-Intern Program

ELIGIBILITY: *Graduate only*
DURATION: *September 8 to June 10*
ACADEMIC CREDIT POSSIBLE: *No*

REMUNERATION OR FEE: *$4500 plus room and board*
POSITIONS OFFERED: *2*
APPLICATION DEADLINE: *February 2*

General Description

The Groton School Teacher-Intern Program is an ideal opportunity for those who would like to work in the close environment of a small prep school. Groton is a coeducational boarding and day school of about 300 students in grades 8 to 12 (not the usual secondary school of grades 9 to 12). The student body is approximately two-thirds boys and one-third girls.

The teaching assistant's responsibilities include teaching under the guidance of an experienced member of a department, observation of other classes, and independent work in one's academic field. Interns also help coach athletics during at least two, but preferably three seasons; and they supervise the dorms two evenings a week and every third Saturday. They are encouraged to put their interests and talents to work in other school activities and organizations.

Interns are chosen first on the basis of their love of and ability to relate to young people, and secondly, by their ability to contribute to the athletic program. There is a real need for teacher-coaches, especially women. One man and one woman are accepted each year as interns. College seniors and recent graduates should write a letter describing previous employment, academic background and athletic experience, preferably before February 1st. Letters should be accompanied by college transcripts and letters of recommendation. Candidates who are then chosen for interviews will be informed so by February 15th.

The Inside Word

Interns were very pleased with the "family atmosphere" that is found in a small school. Faculty and administration offered both guidance and freedom to Groton interns. The course-load allowed time for experimentation and extracurricular activities. However, a noticeable shortcoming was the lack of a social life for a young, single person at such a small, rural school.

Contact:

Charles C. Alexander
Groton School
Groton, MA 01450
(617) 448-3363

THE MOSES BROWN TEACHING AND COACHING INTERNSHIP

Providence, Rhode Island

ELIGIBILITY: *Graduate only*
DURATION: *September to June*
ACADEMIC CREDIT POSSIBLE: *No*
REMUNERATION OR FEE: *$3000 stipend plus room and board*
POSITIONS OFFERED: *2*
APPLICATION DEADLINE: *May or June*

General Description

Moses Brown is a coeducational day and boarding school for students at the nursery level through twelfth grade. Only high school-age students are accepted as boarders, however. The enrollment is approximately 700 students, the majority of whom are boys.

The title of this program, The Moses Brown Teaching and Coaching Internship, is indicative of the unusual emphasis placed on athletics. In fact, coaching is placed on an equal par with involvement in the classroom. Interns coach at least one sport, often more, all three seasons of the school year. The intern's entrance into classroom participation is more gradual than on the athletic field. The fall semester is spent sitting in on other teacher's classes. Interns give occasional guest lectures, tutor individuals and small groups during the winter, and finally teach independently in the spring.

The applicant's area of academic competence is a secondary consideration, partly because of the emphasis placed on one's athletic skills. Special consideration is given to women and minorities because of a general shortage of women coaches.

There is a good chance that this internship will turn into a full-time teaching post should the intern decide that independent school life is right for him or her.

The Inside Word

Most interns seem pleased with the experience the Moses Brown internship provides. One intern said, "communicating with a class was much harder than I expected, but I am being given every opportunity to be creative and am well supported by the faculty." The program is good in that it involves the intern in all aspects of school life. However, one intern noted that this can go too far. The intern is often used to fill in for virtually any task so that the school doesn't have to hire substitutes. One intern reported, "I had to say 'no' on various occasions when asked to do some fairly mindless duty, because I was already overloaded with work."

While some interns were pleased that they had much preparation and observation before they were expected to teach on their own, others were impatient and eager to do some real teaching much earlier. Still, there is enough flexibility in the system to allow for an intern to teach sooner if he or she and the faculty agree that he or she is ready.

Moses Brown is currently in need of coaches, so stress your athletic experience when applying. The application must include a resume and a college transcript, and be received by late spring.

Contact:

David Burnham, Headmaster
Moses Brown School
Providence, RI 02906

NEW CANAAN COUNTRY SCHOOL   New Canaan, Connecticut
Apprentice Teacher Training Program

ELIGIBILITY: *Undergraduate and graduate*
DURATION: *August 24 to June 15*
ACADEMIC CREDIT POSSIBLE: *No*
REMUNERATION OR FEE: *$2500 to $3300 stipend;*
   partial board
POSITIONS OFFERED: *10 to 15*
APPLICATION DEADLINE: *Open*

General Description

The New Canaan Country School is a day school for kindergarten through ninth grade. Previously, teaching apprenticeships existed only in the lower school, but now the teacher training program has been expanded to include grades seven through nine. Interns in the first five levels teach general subjects in a specific grade, in addition to participating in a multi-age classroom. Those who have chosen to teach in the Upper School concentrate on a specific field of knowledge.

To qualify, candidates must have completed their junior year and be working towards a B.A. or B.S. Four years of college is preferable and older applicants interested in teaching are also welcomed. While there is no formal application, candidates should write a letter describing their educational background, work experience and interest in teaching.

Each student teacher is assigned to observe and assist an experienced teacher. Independence increases throughout the year as the intern gains experience. Besides helping prepare for and leading classes, they supervise the playground activities of the younger children and help coach sports in the upper levels. Assistant teachers also supervise lunch tables and field trips and attend faculty meetings. In addition, interns attend workshops with teachers, division heads, school psychologists and the headmaster to share experiences and frustrations and discuss child development theories.

Although New Canaan Country School can offer no credit, interns who have enrolled in Universities to work for their master's degree have received credit for student teaching. Also, some interns take undergraduate courses at nearby colleges.

The Inside Word

Interns are attracted to the school because of its many different grade levels: this diversity helps one experience and choose which grade levels one would most like to teach in the future. One intern commented that, while at first she thought she wanted to teach younger children, she learned through coaching Upper School sports that she preferred older students. Three interns we talked to chose to return for a second year and gain experience at a different level.

There is a general feeling of enthusiasm about the school and its faculty. Interns do run some errands such as getting coffee or photocopying, but, in general, there is much room for creativity. As one student put it, "The feeling of openness, the ability to share ideas with peers and experienced teachers and to implement programs, teaches you much about yourself and a possible career."

Contact:

Nicholas S. Thacher, Headmaster
P.O. Box 997
New Canaan Country School
New Canaan, CT 06840
(203) 972-0771

NORTHFIELD MOUNT HERMON   Northfield, Massachusetts
Summer School
Teaching Fellow Program

ELIGIBILITY: *Junior through graduate*
DURATION: *June 26 to August 11*
ACADEMIC CREDIT POSSIBLE: *No*
REMUNERATION OR FEE: *$750 stipend plus room and board*
POSITIONS OFFERED: *About 30*
APPLICATION DEADLINE: *January 1*

General Description

The Northfield Mt. Hermon Summer School enrolls approximately 350 students drawn primarily from public secondary schools and private day schools. The program aims to give these students a taste of boarding school life. The majority of the kids are from New York and New England although 29 states and 20 foreign countries were represented in 1978. No credit or grades are given for the summer courses; rather, the emphasis is on learning for its own sake. The summer school, which enrolled 91 foreign students in '78, places a great deal of emphasis on international matters. The curriculum includes The American Language Academy, which teaches English as a second language to foreign students.

The Teaching Fellow plays an unusually important role in the program. In fact, because of the very high percentage of interns among the faculty and because of the nature of the program, it is fair to say that the summer school is shaped around the Teaching Fellows. The program's director estimates that interns put between 60 and 70 hours a week into the job. Each intern is assigned to a master teacher under whose direction he/she plans a course, holds conferences with students and takes on some classroom teaching responsibilities.

An average day would run something like this: The intern teaches for three hours in the morning, six days a week. The early part of the afternoon is spent leading a workshop for which Teaching Fellows are often fully responsible. These include journalism, photography, dance, and wilderness activities. The rest of the afternoon is spent helping to coach sports. Interns are in charge of study time in their dorms two evenings a week. This involves checking attendance and maintaining quiet. In addition, they share the responsibilities of organizing and supervising social events.

Two interns are exceptions to the above in that they are assigned administrative responsibilities, assisting either the director of Athletics or Student Activities. Applicants interested in either of these positions should say so.

Northfield Mt. Hermon accepts applications from undergraduates who have completed their junior year and from recent graduates. After a primary screening, candidates are notified as to whether to schedule an interview. Representatives from the school hold interviews at many area colleges. If you do not attend one of these, you must make an appointment for an interview at Northfield Mt. Hermon. A resume, college transcript and two letters of recommendation also play a large part in the selection procedure. Applicants should stress all their skills and use imagination in designing a workshop they could lead. There is a particular need for lifeguards, water safety and tennis instructors, so those with such skills are especially encouraged to apply.

The Inside Word

The feature which former interns mention most is the incredible amount of time and energy which the job demands. As one intern noted "on paper, the schedule doesn't seem that demanding, but in reality it was." For most, the program was well worth the feeling of exhaustion at the day's end because so much was accomplished in such a short time.

However, one intern pointed out how easy it is to use one's "busyness" as an excuse for overlooking students' personal needs which are often unspoken. "I would emphasize how very, very important it is to get priorities straight, to take time out for close, one-to-one contact with staff and students, to not get sucked into the delusion that constant activity equals accomplishment." Others lamented the lack of time for themselves or to relax with one's fellow interns and teachers.

Most interns agreed that they profited immensely from working with experienced teachers but felt they could have used more guidance and structure in leading their workshops. "Teaching under the guidance of experienced faculty members has been a rewarding experience, but the workshop was definitely frustrating."

As one Teaching Fellow said, "Don't bother to bring along a new book to read." You probably wouldn't have time to read it, but then again, you probably wouldn't want to.

Contact:

William R. Compton
Northfield Mt. Hermon Summer School
Northfield, MA 01360

THE PARK SCHOOL   *Brookline, Massachusetts*
Intern Program

ELIGIBILITY: *Undergraduate and graduate*
DURATION: *September to June*
ACADEMIC CREDIT POSSIBLE: *No*
REMUNERATION OR FEE: *Varies*
POSITIONS OFFERED: *6 to 8*
APPLICATION DEADLINE: *July*

General Description

The Park School is a coeducational day school enrolling approximately 420 children in Nursery through ninth grades. Students come from the communities of Greater Boston and go on to prep schools after graduating from Park. The school promotes a family atmosphere by encouraging parental participation and enrolling siblings.

The Park School Intern Program offers teaching experience in many different age levels and subjects. Because students are young, in-depth knowledge is not necessary in teaching most subjects. Each term (fall, winter, and spring), interns are assigned to one of the school's four age levels: nursery and kindergarten, the primary grades (1 to 3), Middle school (4 to 5) and Upper School (6 to 9). Thus, by the end of the year, they will have been exposed to three of the four age levels and will have some idea of which they most enjoy teaching.

The Inside Word

Interns work with a different master teacher each term and also meet regularly with Department Chairmen and the Director of the Intern Program. They observe and help conduct classes and workshops, tutor individuals, coach from 3 to 4:30 in the afternoon and participate in the faculty professional development days.

Although there is no stipend offered, interns have opportunities to earn money. They are paid for coaching and can work in the after-school program for grades nursery through first from 12 to 3:00. Also, if they are deemed qualified by their cooperating teacher, they can do substitute work when a faculty member is sick. Some interns have lived with a family and received room and board in exchange for babysitting.

Those interested should send a resume, college transcript, and letters of recommendation. Interviews will be scheduled in April, May and June. The Park School makes every attempt to help those who complete the internship to find teaching jobs in private and public schools. The intern experience satisfies most state's requirements for practice teaching.

Contact:

Mr. Robert S. Hurlbut, Jr.
Headmaster
The Park School
171 Goddard Ave.
Brookline, MA 02146
(617) 277-2456

PHILLIPS ANDOVER ACADEMY   Andover, Massachusetts
Andover Summer Session
Teaching Assistants Program

ELIBILITY: *Single college seniors*
DURATION: *June 26 to August 7*
ACADEMIC CREDIT POSSIBLE: *No*
REMUNERATION OR FEE: *$850 for 6 weeks*
POSITIONS OFFERED: *Approximately 30*
APPLICATION DEADLINE: *February 1*

General Description

A Teaching Assistantship at Andover Summer Session is six weeks of intensive teaching under the direction of a permanent staff member. The intern's other duties include leading afternoon activites, coaching sports, and house counselling. The Summer Session is very competitive and students are usually very bright. Teachers spend 6 mornings a week in the classroom and attending school meetings. Afternoons are filled with sports and activities that include community service, photography and drama. In addition, checking students into the dorm at night occupies two to three evenings a week.

Single college seniors who are interested in a career in teaching and are willing to work hard are encouraged to apply. Transcripts, application and two recommendations are due the first of February. A preliminary selection occurs within two weeks after all material is received. Those who make it past this first cut must have an interview in late February or early March. By mid-March, the program directors should know in which fields of study Teaching Assistants are needed and can then make final decisions. Competition is stiff; there are about two hundred applications each year for thirty positions.

The Inside Word

Former Teaching Assistants consider their summer's experience invaluable, challenging, and lots of fun. In fact, some enjoyed it enough to return as permanent summer staff. Most of all, they stress that there is a great deal of work accomplished in a short time, and because of this intensity, one quickly forms close friendships with students from a myriad of backgrounds. Interns also speak very highly of their fellow teachers, labelling them "intelligent, creative, and very sociable."

One intern commented that, while most students are very likeable and intellectually motivated, some are more interested in the prestige a school like Andover has to offer. Many come from wealthy backgrounds and, having never been away from home before, expect to be waited on.

Another drawback was that house counseling can become a burden. "After a full day of work, enforcing rules is far from the best way to unwind." However, most teachers were usually good about scheduling dorm supervision so that interns had most of their weekends off.

On the whole, interns recommended that "if you're looking for a nice, relaxing summer job, be a lifeguard. But if you are interested in becoming a part of a teaching-learning community, this is a great opportunity."

Contact:

John Richards, Acting Dean of Faculty
Phillips Andover Academy
Andover, MA 01810
(617) 475-3400

PHILLIPS ANDOVER ACADEMY   *Andover, Massachusetts*
The Andover Teaching
Fellowship Program

ELIGIBILITY: *Graduate only*
DURATION: *September to June*
ACADEMIC CREDIT POSSIBLE: *No*
REMUNERATION OR FEE: *$5000 stipend plus room and board*
POSITIONS OFFERED: *10 to 12*
APPLICATION DEADLINE: *January 15*

General Description

Phillips Academy, commonly known as Andover, is one of the larger, more competitive secondary prep schools in the country. Because of the school's large size—1088 boarding and day students—and the quality of its students, the faculty is able to offer a broad variety of courses, including advanced college level subjects. Also, because of the school's proximity to Boston, students and faculty are able to take advantage of the city's museums, concerts and plays.

Teaching Fellows have much freedom in their responsibilities. They usually teach two courses under an advisor from their department. Afternoons and evenings are filled with coaching, counselling students, directing extracurricular activities and sharing dorm duties.

Phillips Academy accepts applications from graduates interested in a career in teaching immediately following the internship or after graduate school. Candidates must be willing to give freely of their time and energy and relate well to young people. Applications should be accompanied by a resume, college transcripts, and letters of recommendation. The school will make final decisions by April 30th.

The Inside Word

Interns feel that their experience as Teaching Fellow at Andover was a good mixture of flexibility and structure. One intern said, ''My department is very willing to help me if I ask for it, but otherwise I am free to do things according to my own judgement.''

Interns warn future applicants of the great amount of time the job consumes. As one Teaching Fellow said, ''I would like to stress the fact that the working day, if you have an eight o'clock class and have dorm duty can be as long as 15 hours. That is not to say that you are busy every minute; however, you may not have much time to yourself.''

Overall, interns agree on the rewards of the program, both personal and professional. One intern said, ''A day of good classes makes you want to sing.'' Also, the experience is definitely a great ''in'' to a full time teaching job.

Contact:

Peter Q. McKee, Associate Headmaster
Phillips Andover Academy
Andover, MA 01810

PHILLIPS EXETER ACADEMY
Teaching Fellow Program

Exeter, New Hampshire

ELIGIBILITY: *Undergraduate*
DURATION: *Early September through early June*
ACADEMIC CREDIT POSSIBLE: *No*
REMUNERATION OR FEE: *$5000 stipend*
POSITIONS OFFERED: *2 to 4*
APPLICATION DEADLINE: *February 1*

General Description

The Teaching Fellow Program at Phillips Exeter is a year-long opportunity to work at one of the most prestigious prep schools in the country. Although they have less of a teaching load than full-time teachers, interns gain experience in all aspects of school life including teaching classes, coaching sports and dorm supervision. Teaching and other assignments are determined according to the school's need and the individual's interest and experience. Besides training and supervision, interns receive a stipend of $5000, as well as housing in a dormitory and board in the dining hall.

Teaching Fellows put in an average of 40 to 50 hours a week teaching two courses and coaching two out of three seasons (although some choose to coach all three.) In addition, they have a supervisor whose classes they observe. Like regular teachers, interns are on duty two to three evenings a week in their dorm. This entails checking students in at seven, nine and ten o'clock. Approximately every third weekend interns are needed to check students in by eleven p.m. and occasionally chaperone Saturday night activities. A great deal of "free" time is spent planning courses, correcting papers and tests and talking with students in the dorm.

Exeter is one of the largest private secondary schools, with an enrollment of about 1000 students. The school tries to attract a diverse student body through such scholarship programs as A Better Chance, English-Speaking Union and American Field Service. Because of the competitive nature of the school, students are generally bright, talented and motivated towards college.

Like the school itself, the internship program is extremely competitive. There are about 100 applicants each year for only two to four positions. Most teaching fellows are accepted directly out of the more prestigious New England Colleges. Although they come from similar schools, there is a definite tendency not to accept many people from the same college. The application emphasizes extra-curricular activities, academic ability, and asks for three letters of recommendation. Personality is important. Therefore, an interview is a crucial part of the process if one makes it past the first screening.

The Inside Word

Interns agree wholeheartedly on the high quality of the teachers, students and fellow interns and the value of their experience at Exeter. They were allowed to be as creative as they liked while advice from experienced teachers was always available. They are also unanimous in the opinion that the job was demanding in terms of time and energy. One restriction frequently noted is the lack of privacy and the social limitations of living in a dorm. One intern concluded, "In fact, my internship did a great deal to convince me that I would probably like to be teaching at Exeter or a comparable school in another couple of years. The only drawback that I see, at this point, is the social one for a young person."

Contact:

Louis Hitzrot, Headmaster
The Phillips Exeter Academy
Exeter, NH 03833

ST. MARK'S SCHOOL   *Southborough, Massachusetts*
Teaching Internship

ELIGIBILITY: *Graduate only*
DURATION: *September 1 to June 15*
ACADEMIC CREDIT POSSIBLE: *No*
REMUNERATION OR FEE: *$3000 stipend plus room and board*
POSITIONS OFFERED: *1 to 2*
APPLICATION DEADLINE: *Late February*

General Description

St. Mark's is a small, coeducational boarding and day school for grades 9 through 12. Southborough was formerly the home of two separate schools—St. Mark's for boys and the Southborough School for girls, but the two are now merged. Approximately 70 girls and 230 boys live on separate campuses but take courses together and share in all school activities.

Each year, the school hires one or two interns to teach under an experienced teacher, live in and supervise a dorm, chaperone social events, and coach athletics. In addition, interns attend chapel services and faculty meetings as do regular teachers. Interns are given a great deal of independence, although advice and direction from the faculty is available.

The St. Mark's internship is designed not to fill gaps in the faculty but to be a separate position. Unlike a regular teacher, an intern is expected to take part in nearly every aspect of the school. So, while interns usually have a reduced course load, the additional duties they take on such as assisting other teachers, organizing activities, filling in for other teachers and little things such as delivering mail, keep them extremely busy.

Anyone with a B.A who is willing to get involved in every aspect of boarding school life is welcome to apply. A resume, college transcript and references are required; an interview is essential. There is a good chance, judging from the experience of past interns, that those accepted for the year-long program will be asked to return as full time teachers after their internship.

The Inside Word

One intern remarked that for someone who is not really sure of what aspect of education they want to pursue, the all-inclusiveness of this internship is ideal. However, for someone who already knows what they want to teach and wants to teach only that subject, the experience can be frustrating. For example, if you are expecting to specialize in music and direct the choir, you may be quite shocked to find that you are also expected to coach intramurals, assist in editing the newspaper and help organize student activities. During an interview, the applicant should ask lots of questions about what exactly is expected, so that there are no surprises.

Another small drawback of the program was the lack of feedback from teachers and department heads; the intern could get advice but he or she had to go and look for it. In most cases, the intern was treated as a regular teacher with little supervision. All of the interns agreed that because so much was expected of them, they learned a great deal about virtually every aspect of boarding school education.

Contact:

Headmaster, St. Mark's School
Southborough, MA 01732
(614) 485-0050

ST. PAUL'S SCHOOL   *Concord, New Hampshire*
Advanced Studies Program

ELIGIBILITY: *Undergraduate only; must have*
    completed junior year
DURATION: *June 20 to August 4*
ACADEMIC CREDIT POSSIBLE: *No*
REMUNERATION OR FEE: *$800, plus room and board*

POSITIONS OFFERED: *20 to 25*
APPLICATION DEADLINE: *January 15*

General Description

The St. Paul's Advanced Studies Program is different from that of almost any other summer school. Therefore, the opportunities it offers its teaching interns are quite unique. The program is solely for students from the New Hampshire public school system who are highly motivated and intellectually promising. The six week course at St. Paul's strives to provide its students with advanced courses which they probably would not receive in their high schools. Those who intern at St. Paul's have the chance to work with gifted students and a talented faculty in a strong academic environment.

Each high school in New Hampshire nominates a few students and the 200 most qualified are selected. Nearly half of these are on scholarship.

There are approximately 25 faculty members drawn from St. Paul's as well as other public and private schools and colleges. Each of these is matched with an intern according to their fields of academic concentration and interests. Interns spend about four hours in the classroom, six days a week. Actual responsibilities vary according to the subject but they include leading some classes, correcting tests and papers, lecture preparation and the inevitable, less interesting duties such as photocopying tests and assignments. The amount of independence each intern is granted varies considerably with the individual master teacher and the intern's abilities and motivation.

Outside of the classroom, interns are responsible for dorm supervision every third night, library supervision and counselling several students. In addition, four afternoons a week are spent working in the sports program. The intern's coaching role here is emphasized less than in other programs since the school hires a professional physical education teacher to direct the athletic activities. Applicants are not penalized if they do not have a strong background in any sport as they can sometimes substitute another activity in lieu of athletics.

The internship is available only to men and women who have just completed their junior or senior years and who are considering education as a career. It is not open to graduate students or those who have been working in other fields. There are usually about a hundred applicants each year. From these, some are selected for interviews on the basis of the application, transcript and recommendations which are due on January 15th. Interviews are an essential part of the final selection and are held either at the candidate's college or at St. Paul's.

The Inside Word

Interns speak very highly of the program and especially of the quality of students involved. Although not every one is brilliant, they are almost all highly motivated and attending the Advanced Studies Program because they want to. Many come from very small, rural schools and have never been exposed to college-oriented courses. Interns find it very refreshing and rewarding to be able to accomplish so much. However, one intern noted that it is not fair to use this ideal, exceptionally intellectual atmosphere as an example of the average teaching experience. Most students are not so eager to learn or do not possess such basic talent as these few.

The very intellectual quality of the Advanced Studies Program is not considered ideal by every intern. One commented, "Most of these students are overachievers, both in the classroom and on the playing fields. Because the program attempts so much in such a short time, this can lead to intense competition which takes some of the fun out of the summer."

One other drawback which bothered a few interns was the flexibility each master teacher had in delegating responsibilities to interns. While most were more than fair and very helpful, a few were less than generous in sharing the more interesting teaching duties. However, this was the exception rather than the rule; most interns felt that their teaching experience at St. Paul's was an ideal opportunity.

Contact:

Alan N. Hall, Director
Advanced Studies Program
St. Paul's School
Concord, NH 03301
(603) 225-3341

ST. PAUL'S SCHOOL   Concord, New Hampshire
Intern Teaching Program

ELIGIBILITY: *Graduate only*
DURATION: *September to mid-June*
ACADEMIC CREDIT POSSIBLE: *No*
REMUNERATION OR FEE: *$4500 stipend plus room and board*
POSITIONS OFFERED: *1 to 4*
APPLICATION DEADLINE: *End of January*

General Description

St. Paul's School is made up of about 500 boys and girls, both boarding and day, and approximately 80 teachers and their families who are required to live on the school grounds.

The Intern Teaching program assumes a lack of experience but does not assume that all interns have the same abilities or needs. An intern is assigned his or her academic work by the head of the department in which his or her interest lies. They usually begin by attending a variety of classes taught by many different teachers and discussing afterwards the strengths and weaknesses of those classes. In this way, interns get maximum exposure and much flexibility in choosing teaching methods that are best for them.

As the fall term progresses, interns may teach a class on a given day or for several days, at first with the master teacher present but later, on their own. By the winter term, if both the intern and regular teacher agree that he or she is ready, the intern teaches alone. During this time, roles are reversed and other teachers often sit in on the intern's classes and discuss them afterwards. In this way, the Teaching Fellow receives constructive criticism while the older teachers may get new ideas for their own classes. In addition, interns often attend classes in which they've had little training or need refreshing.

Of course, the intern's responsibilities extend outside the classroom. They include coaching, being a "group-master" (advisor to the students on one's dormitory floor,) and presiding over a table at four dinners a week. Interns also attend faculty meetings and required Chapel Services.

The Inside Word

Interns were generally highly complimentary about the school and the internship program. The flexibility in assigning classroom duties allowed some to teach a full course load in their final term without overloading those who were not ready to do so or who chose to emphasize other activities such as sports or clubs. Still, this lack of rigidity did not prevent the program from meeting what one intern called "the central requirement for an effective internship—that it be an organized whole, not an ill-conceived amalgamation of errands."

Most interns had just graduated from well-known private colleges, but there were exceptions to this. Also, one intern, who was a minority in that he had not attended a prep school himself, felt that an independent school background would have been an advantage in applying. One's prospective employer assumes, probably with much justification, that this familiarity with prep school life is helpful in the beginning.

Contact:

Miss Virginia S. Deane
Vice Rector, St. Paul's School
Concord, NH 03301

OTHER PLACES TO LOOK:

Arts

See museum listings. Most museums have education departments.

Business
American Assembly of Collegiate Schools of Business

Environment
Aquarium of Niagara Falls Sea Research Foundation, Inc.
The Atlantic Center for the Environment, Quebec-Labrador Foundation
Audubon Society of Rhode Island, Caratunk Wildlife Refuge
Chesapeake Bay Center for Environmental Studies
The Conservation Foundation
National Audubon Society Naturalist Training Programs and Audubon
  Nature Centers
National Wildlife Federation
New England Aquarium
Squam Lakes Science Center

Government
Robert F. Kennedy Memorial Youth Policy Institute

Health
DeKalb Mental Health and Mental Retardation Center
Devereux Foundation Career House
Devereux Foundation Institute of Clinical Training
C.B. Wilson Center

Public Service
Atlanta Urban Corps
Youth Opportunities Upheld, Inc.

The Environment

With a strong base of grass-roots support in the 1960's, environmental issues were pushed high up on the nation's agenda. Since then, concern for man's effect on the environment has had a major influence on a wide range of policy decisions on all levels of government. The field maintains a grass-roots orientation, and is characterized by the youth, enthusiasm and dedication of the people working in it.

It is a field built around interns. The great majority of environmental lobbyist organizations, conservation groups, and environmental education centers relies heavily on both paid and volunteer interns to accomplish a substantial amount of their work. If you are in your late teens to early twenties, you are likely to find yourself surrounded by people of the same age group—or not much older—wherever you choose to work in this field. The pervasive youth of the field makes it a fun and exciting area to be involved in.

It is also hard work. Along with youth and enthusiasm comes dedication and a serious commitment to solving environmental problems. The long hours and hectic pace typical of environmental organizations are fired by optimism. Said one intern involved in lobbying for solar energy, "We know we're going to win." A grass-roots orientation means keeping up contacts with a large number of organizations and individuals, and disseminating great volumes of information to the public, which means—a lot of envelope stuffing. It is impossible to escape having to do *some* routine office work in this field. An office manager of a major conservation organization said, "We *all* get roped into it at one time or another."

There are enough opportunities so that students of almost any academic background and a serious interest in environmental work can get involved. Environmentally-related organizations can be roughly broken down into three orientations: science, education, and political advocacy.

For students with backgrounds in the physical and life sciences, there is a host of opportunities to perform both laboratory research and field work relevant to environmental problems. For laboratory work, see the program at Woods Hole Oceanographic Institution, listed in the "Sciences" Chapter. Check the same chapter for programs at Department of Energy labs. Many of these labs perform basic research on the environmental and health effects of energy production and transportation. Organizations such as the Chesapeake Bay Center (listed in this chapter) perform field work on basic ecological problems.

Environmental education is carried out in two ways. The first is through publications and films. Some, such as the Conservation Foundation, make this their primary activity, but most every environmental group puts out at least a newsletter informing members and the general public of current issues and activities. Writing articles for these publications is one common aspect of intern work. The second type of education is that performed by nature centers, museums, wildlife refuges, and other environmental visitors' centers. The Caratunk Wildlife Refuge, the New England Aquarium, and the environmental education centers run by the National Audubon Society are good examples of these. Others, such as the Atlantic Center, run programs that send interns out to schools, libraries, and community centers to give lectures and show films on environmental issues. For a listing of nature centers nationwide, get a hold of *Directory of Nature Centers and Related Environmental Education Facilities*, put out by the National Audubon Society's Nature Center Planning Division.

The third aspect of environmental work involves advocacy and lobbying for environmentally-related legislation. This work goes on at both the state and federal level, performed by such groups as the Sierra Club, Friends of the Earth, and the Solar Lobby. These groups regularly use interns to research specific issues, attend legislative hearings, draft testimony, and generally keep tabs on legislative activity relating to the environment. For a listing of conservation groups, see the *National Wildlife Federation Conservation Directory*.

One word of caution: be wary of outfits with little funding and little real organization. Some organizations working on the grass-roots level simply do not have the resources to provide adequate support and direction for their interns. The programs we've listed here were chosen because they *do* provide worthwhile internships, while others were not included because of inadequate supervision and funding of interns' activities. See our tips on "How to Recognize a Good Program" in the introductory section on "Internships" (at the beginning of the book) for more help in this area.

There is enough activity in this field so that you are sure to find a place to fit in. The catch—many of the intern positions open to undergraduates are volunteer only. As a volunteer intern, you should not feel exploited— you'll have lots of company, and the work is bound to be rewarding.

ENVIRONMENTAL INTERN PROGRAM

Northeast
Lower Great Lakes
California

The Environmental Intern Program (EIP) is the place to start when looking for environmentally related internships. EIP is a non-profit educational program that each year places hundreds of undergraduates and graduates in paid internships with government agencies, non-profit organizations, and corporations across the country. The internships usually last three months, and take place year-round. EIP works with the interns' sponsors to see that the projects lined up for them are well organized and properly supervised. In addition, the program provides for interaction between interns, sponsors, and professionals in the field, through workshops and seminars. Interns are required to submit an evaluation of the program at the end of their internship, and are required to publish an article relating to the internship in a local newspaper, newsletter, or similar publication. Interns generally receive a stipend of between $100 and $150 per week.

EIP uses a broad definition of the term "environmental" when seeking sponsors for the program. Interns may be placed in organizations concerned with architecture and urban affairs, as well as in programs concerning pollution control and resource management. Opportunities exist for work in all aspects of both the natural and the man-made environment. Consequently, students from a very wide variety of backgrounds may be accepted. Positions are available for young scientists, writers, educators, public relations specialists, anthropologists, and artists, to name just a few.

The program operates in three distinct regions: the Northeast (New England and New York); the Lower Great Lakes (Ohio, Indiana, Michigan, western Pennsylvania); and California. Write to the EIP office in your region of preference for application materials and a listing of available internships. The application consists of a completed application form, two letters of recommendation, a resume, an optional writing sample, and a five-dollar application fee. The exact starting and ending dates are worked out between the intern and sponsor once the intern is accepted. The application deadline for summer programs is in mid-March.

Contact:

EIP/New England, New York
Massachusetts Audubon Society
Lincoln, MA 01773

EIP/California
681 Market Street
San Francisco, CA 94105

EIP/Lower Great Lakes
Institute for Environmental Education
8911 Euclid Avenue
Cleveland, OH 44106

AQUARIUM OF NIAGARA FALLS   *Niagara Falls, New York*
SEA RESEARCH FOUNDATION, INC.

ELIGIBILITY: *Undergraduate and graduate*
DURATION: *Minimum 6 weeks*
ACADEMIC CREDIT POSSIBLE: *Yes*
REMUNERATION OR FEE: *None*
POSITIONS OFFERED: *About 12 per year*
APPLICATION DEADLINE: *Varies*

General Description

Interns at the inland aquarium care for aquatic animals and their habitats and present them to the public. The Aquarium accepts interns year-round and requests that interns stay at least six weeks. The number of positions available varies with the time of year, but there are usually one or two per department. Applicants at higher educational levels receive preference.

Interns' responsibilities depend upon the department they work in: Art, Education, Exhibits, Training, Sales, or Maintenance. Art interns use graphics to publicize the Aquarium; education interns supervise the "Touch Tank" in which children can examine invertebrates. Interns in the Exhibits department work on the approximately 45 tanks and learn the aquarium's complex feeding process. Training department interns handle and train marine mammals. Each department provides a training period. All interns work 35 to 40 hours per week.

Request application in writing and arrange an interview with the General Manager, Bela Babus, as well as with the particular department head.

The Inside Word

An intern in the Exhibits department with a strong Biology background found this internship enjoyable and useful for her future career in environmental protection. She took care of fish: changed tanks, tested pH and chlorine levels, but also had time to pursue studies of her own. "Once you have the routine down in your department, then you have time to use the library and the lab (for research)."

Contact:

FOR APPLICATION MATERIALS:

Bela Babus, General Manager
Aquarium of Niagara Falls, USA
701 Whirlpool Street
Niagara Falls, NY 14301
(716) 285-3575

DEPARTMENT HEADS:
Exhibits—Albert Clifton, Jr.
Training—Donald Viele
Education—Nancy Corra
Maintenance—Richard Krull
Art—Cynthia Mis

THE ATLANTIC CENTER FOR THE ENVIRONMENT QUEBEC-LABRADOR FOUNDATION   *Ipswich, Massachusetts*

ELIGIBILITY: *Over 21, undergraduate and graduate*
DURATION: *3 months*

ACADEMIC CREDIT POSSIBLE: *Yes*
REMUNERATION OR FEE: *See below*
POSITIONS OFFERED: *10 to 20*
APPLICATION DEADLINE: *Open*

General Description

Atlantic Center interns investigate, publicize, and recommend solutions to environmental resource problems affecting the Atlantic region (New England and the Canadian Atlantic Provinces). Most of the work is self-designed, implemented, and documented. Typically, interns spend one month at the Center (in Ipswich) planning their projects, one month in the field implementing them, and then the third month compiling the results.

Projects often center on public education concerning wildlife and resource issues. Interns may teach short courses in schools, libraries, and community centers, or may be involved in fostering informed dialogue between industry and government officials concerning land use and resource conservation.

The Center prefers to interview all applicants, giving those from the east coast an advantage. Individuals with interest and background in environmental education, natural history, resource management, public information planning, ecology, or the biological sciences are eligible for the internships. Some knowledge of French is helpful but not required.

While there is no pay, the Center provides housing and kitchen facilities in Ipswich and arranges transportation, food, housing, and insurance for interns' work in the field. In addition, there is occasionally funding available in the form of research grants for interns' projects.

To apply, request application forms and descriptions of available internships. Send the completed application, resume, and letters of recommendation to the Center.

The Inside Word

The key to this program is self-motivation. According to one intern, the Center supervisors are there to "help structure the programs, provide the resources to get it going, and review the work in progress. They are good people for providing moral support and constructive advice." But the program's success depends mainly on the intern's organizational skills and individual effort. An intern noted that "while the Center is behind you 100 percent, sometimes no one thinks through the problems in advance of the interns, and some of the work ends up being done haphazardly."

An expedition: A group of four Atlantic Center interns completed a 450-mile canoe trip down the St. John River in Maine and New Brunswick. When not canoeing, their days were spent talking to people about resource issues in the watershed. They spoke with representatives from industries (pulp and paper, food processing, agriculture, energy) and government officials (dept. of natural resources, forestry, fish and wildlife, etc.). They also chased down historians and old-timers to learn more of the history, culture, and life style of the region.

General comments: Not only those on the River Expedition, but all of the interns we heard from thought the internship was worthwhile. They polished their skills in education, public speaking, and organization, in addition to gaining extensive experience in their individual subject areas. One intern learned a great deal about designing and planning an environmental education center.

Said one intern, "The Atlantic Center is staffed with very warm and friendly people—great folks to work with. There is a very low cash flow for the amount of work you do, but the experience makes up for it ten times over."

Contact:

The Atlantic Center for the Environment
The Quebec-Labrador Foundation
951 Highland Avenue
Ipswich, MA 01938
(617) 468-4423

AUDUBON SOCIETY OF RHODE ISLAND CARATUNK WILDLIFE REFUGE

Seekonk, Massachusetts

ELIGIBILITY: *High school through graduate*
DURATION: *Summer, year, other*
ACADEMIC CREDIT POSSIBLE: *Yes*
REMUNERATION OR FEE: *Some work-related travel expenses*
POSITIONS OFFERED: *6 per year*
APPLICATION DEADLINE: *Varies*

General Description

The Rhode Island Audubon Society manages the 159-acre Caratunk Wildlife Refuge (CWR), a relatively new environmental education center located seven miles from Providence, Rhode Island in Seekonk, Massachusetts. Interns with interest in environmental interpretation and education learn how this center functions and are encouraged to implement their own ideas into its operation.

Interns help the Center educate school children, teachers, and the general public on environmental issues, publish a quarterly newsletter, and instruct participants at the natural history summer camp.

The Center's needs determine the length of an intern's tenure. Academic credit has been granted to past participants, but must be arranged by individuals with their own schools. Presently, CWR provides funds only for limited work-related travel, but program directors will assist interns in locating reasonably-priced housing nearby.

The Inside Word

Getting accepted: Program administrator Carolyn Stefanik suggests that applicants have some background in teaching, possible career goals in environmental education, and a desire to heighten public awareness and appreciation of the natural environment. "The program is noncompetitive," explained Stefanik. "We will arrange internships with interested students as they apply." Interested students are advised not to apply for positions during winter months—"there simply won't be anything for an intern to do."

Daily life: The summer positions involve a wide range of responsibilities, including planning and supervising CWR's environmental education program. "The program is most applicable to students interested in the teaching and interpretive aspects of our work," advised Stefanik. Prospective interns should submit a school transcript and letters of recommendation along with their application. Interviews are important; students should make the necessary arrangements for visiting the Center or conducting a phone interview.

Contact:

Carolyn Stefanik and Suzanne Wienmann, Co-directors
Caratunk Wildlife Refuge
Brown Avenue
Seekonk, MA 02771
(617) 761-8230

CENTER FOR RENEWABLE RESOURCES   *Washington, D.C.*

ELIGIBILITY: *Junior through graduate*
DURATION: *Varies*
ACADEMIC CREDIT POSSIBLE: *Yes*
REMUNERATION OR FEE: *$75/week stipend*
POSITIONS OFFERED: *4 to 8*
APPLICATION DEADLINE: *Open*

General Description

The Center for Renewable Resources is a rapidly growing organization that originally evolved from Sun Day, an international celebration of solar energy. The Center organizes and conducts educational activities nationwide to promote the use of renewable energy resources. Interns compile publications, perform nationwide research studies, organize conferences, research regulations, gather public comments, and perform administrative tasks.

Interns can also work in the Center's companion organization—the Solar Lobby—lobbying and maintaining contact with all relevant sectors of the federal government. The Center's office manager says that they try to "maintain grass-roots contacts as well as contacts with Capitol Hill."

The Center will help interns who wish to receive academic credit, by providing schools with written evaluations of interns' projects.

The Inside Word

One intern we spoke to said that her internship was "terrific. It's the best experience I've ever had." She described the Center as "fast-moving, energetic. There are always new things to do, and most everything that comes along is interesting." The Center is also very well organized—"much better than Nader's group." She described the program as having "structure, but not pressure. You are allowed a fair amount of independence and time to work on your own projects."

Interns in the publications department are currently putting together a book of essays by noted advocates of renewable energy sources such as Barry Commoner, Amory Lovins, and Dennis Hayes. Interns may also research specific issues, such as the utility financing of residential solar energy systems.

To get hired as an intern, it is recommended that you visit the Center at least once and talk to the office manager.

Contact:

Jim Broyles, Office Manager
Center for Renewable Resources
1028 Connecticut Avenue, N.W.
Suite 1100
Washington, DC 20036
(202) 466-6880

CHESAPEAKE BAY CENTER FOR ENVIRONMENTAL STUDIES
Work / Learn Program

Edgewater, Maryland

ELIGIBILITY: *Undergraduate, graduate*

DURATION: *Fall, spring, summer, year, other*
ACADEMIC CREDIT POSSIBLE: *Yes*
REMUNERATION OR FEE: *Undergraduates, $40/week
    plus housing; graduates, $80/week plus housing*
POSITIONS OFFERED: *About 15*
APPLICATION DEADLINE: *April 1 for summer, July 1
    for fall, December 1 for spring*

General Description

The Chesapeake Bay Center, a subsidiary program of the Smithsonian Institution, incorporates interns into its research and environmental studies projects. While interns are primarily responsible for an individually assigned research project, they also participate in the Center's ongoing maintenance and educational activities. The program's starting date and duration are flexible and arranged between the supervisor and intern upon hiring, but projects are generally scheduled to coincide with fall and spring academic semesters as well as the summer. Most interns with the Work/Learn Program receive some form of academic credit from their college or university. In addition, living quarters are provided, although students must arrange for their own meals.

The Center is active in evaluating aquatic and terrestrial analyses, and studying man's effects on the ecosystem. Interns are responsible for completing one of a variety of projects involving these issues during their tenure at Chesapeake Bay. Interns at the Center, located on the Rhode River, seven miles south of Annapolis, Maryland, have focused on updating research on the river's watershed and estuary, other environmental research, news reporting, and education research.

The application of the Work/Learn Program is somewhat involved. An interview is optional, yet the Center does require an application, school transcripts, two reference letters, an essay concerning academic and non-academic interests, as well as a statement of personal goals and how they apply to the Chesapeake Bay program.

The Inside Word

The interns we contacted felt that visiting the Center was advantageous in gaining admittance to the program, particularly as the interview is not required. So, if you are interested in this competitive program, seriously consider making a visit. Only 15 students are chosen each year from an applicant pool of about 100. Said one intern, "My visit to Chesapeake Bay really paid off. I got to see what went on there and to meet the people I'd be working with. They knew I was interested."

The atmosphere is relaxed, say interns, although some supervisors, with whom the interns work closely, were not particularly helpful or supportive. Students can usually consider a range of projects, but are sometimes automatically assigned to programs on the basis of their academic backgrounds and work experience. Interns past and present agreed that the program is worthwhile. Said one, "I didn't realize the wealth of opportunities in environmental studies, until my experience with the detailed investigations pursued at Chesapeake Bay."

Contact:

Dr. John Falk, Program Director
Chesapeake Bay Center for Environmental Studies
Smithsonian Institution
Route 4, Box 622
Edgewater, MD 21037
(301) 798-4424

THE CONSERVATION FOUNDATION   *Washington, D.C.*

ELIGIBILITY: *Undergraduate and graduate*
DURATION: *12 weeks*
ACADEMIC CREDIT POSSIBLE: *Yes*
REMUNERATION OR FEE: *$165/week salary*
POSITIONS OFFERED: *5 to 7 per year*
APPLICATION DEADLINE: *Early April for summer,*
    open for other

General Description

The Conservation Foundation is a well-established environmental organization boasting three decades of impressive achievement. The Foundation conducts inter-disciplinary research and communicates its views and findings—through films and publications—to policy makers and opinion leaders. The Foundation is *not* a lobby organization, it does not have members, and it does not buy or sell land.

Internships are available to students with backgrounds in marine science, economics, law, natural resources management, and agricultural lands management. The positions are generally given to graduate students, but the Foundation occasionally makes use of exceptionally well-qualified undergraduates. Interns work on specific assignments as full members of the project staff. Internships can run at any time of the year, and those students able to work on a volunteer basis are particularly encouraged to apply.

A resume, college transcript, three to five letters of recommendation or names of reference, and a writing sample are required of applicants. The best time to apply for summer internships is late January through early April.

The Inside Word

Getting accepted: Interns stress that it is very important to narrow down your interests before applying to the program: "You should know what area you want to work in, whether it is land resources, toxic chemical substances, water or air quality—your specific background is very important here." One intern recommended talking directly to the people involved in projects in your area of interest—by calling up as well as writing. Interns are selected to fill a particular gap, so that your skills must be well matched to the Foundation's current needs.

Daily Life: The Foundation is very well organized, and provides excellent exposure to the field. Interns work directly with project leaders, performing background research, reviewing legislation, writing, and telephoning. One intern involved in a flood-plain management project was responsible for evaluating data and writing up the findings in addition to other duties. The internships also involve editing, and what one intern referred to as a fair amount of "academic go-fer work." Recommended one intern, "Not only do interns learn a lot from the experience, but they have the opportunity to make valuable contacts for the future."

Contact:

Gordon Binder
Assistant to the President
The Conservation Foundation
1717 Massachusetts Avenue, N.W.
Washington, DC 20036

FRIENDS OF THE EARTH (FOE)
Internship Program

Washington, D.C.
Denver, Colorado
Boston, Massachusetts
San Francisco, California
New York, New York

ELIGIBILITY: *Undergraduate and graduate*
DURATION: *Varies, at least 10 weeks*
ACADEMIC CREDIT POSSIBLE: *Yes*
REMUNERATION OR FEE: *None*
POSITIONS OFFERED: *2 to 5 per year*
APPLICATION DEADLINE: *Open*

General Description

Friends of the Earth, an activist environmental lobbying organization, offers internships at all five of their principal offices throughout the U.S.

Interns work both independently and with the senior staff. Projects center around environmental protection, and deal with such issues as nuclear power, endangered wildlife habitats, pesticides, coasts, transportation, and recombinant DNA research. Interns may be asked to do clerical work, research background information, or lobby for FOE-supported legislation.

FOE offers internships at various times; application deadlines vary accordingly. The issues in which FOE is involved at the time largely determine the interns' specific responsibilities. Hours can be negotiated, but FOE prefers full-time involvement (35-40 hours per week). FOE does not pay a salary, however, some FOE programs provide supplies and funds for work-related travel.

To apply, submit a resume and writing samples if possible. An interview is not necessary, although advised.

The Inside Word

This program requires strongly motivated individuals who know what issues interest them. "Eighty percent of the time I was working on my own," said one intern. Another advises, "Look carefully at what type of work will be expected of you and what staff will be available to ensure a successful program." The program director said that "this is not an envelope-stuffing job, although we all get roped into that at one time or another."

An internship with FOE can definitely be a rewarding experience, but a lot depends on the organization of the office where an intern works and the specific issues of the time. Suggested an intern, "Ask questions before taking the internship; it helps to know what to expect."

Contact:

FRIENDS OF THE EARTH

3 Joy Street
Boston, MA 02108

72 Jane Street
New York, NY 10014

620C Street, S.E.
Washington, DC 20003

124 Spear Street
San Francisco, CA 94105
(415) 495-4770

2239 East Colfax Avenue
Suite 209
Denver, CO 80206

THE GEORGIA CONSERVANCY

Atlanta, Georgia
Savannah, Georgia

ELIGIBILITY: *High school through graduate*
DURATION: *10 weeks*
ACADEMIC CREDIT POSSIBLE: *Yes*
REMUNERATION OR FEE: *Funds for work-related travel*
POSITIONS OFFERED: *6 per year*
APPLICATION DEADLINE: *Varies*

General Description

The Georgia Conservancy offers interns the opportunity to follow legislative activity affecting the environment. Interns are accepted at four times during the year for ten weeks starting in January, March, June, and September. Positions are offered in Atlanta and Savannah.

Interns research legislation, maintain files on pending bills, and draft letters informing Conservancy members of national and state-level environmental concerns. The intern may work part-time or full-time depending on the needs of the program and the availability of the intern.

The Inside Word

Interns said that this program allowed them to see how the legislative process works. "I saw all sides of environmental issues instead of just one aspect played up in a newspaper," said one.

Interns enjoyed the low-key atmosphere. "Most of the people at the Conservancy were in their 20's or early 30's and genuinely concerned about my progress and contributions." Another said that the clerical aspects of the job "were not so time-consuming as to become tedious."

Contact:

Barbara M. Smith, Program Director
The Georgia Conservancy
3110 Maple Drive Suite 407
Atlanta, GA 30307
(404) 262-1967

INTERNATIONAL CRANE FOUNDATION
Education Assistants and Agriculture Internships

Baraboo, Wisconsin

ELIGIBILITY: *Undergraduate and graduate*
DURATION: *3 months, 6 months, or 1 year*

ACADEMIC CREDIT POSSIBLE: *Yes*
REMUNERATION OR FEE: *Varies*
POSITIONS OFFERED: *1 or 2 per year*
APPLICATION DEADLINE: *Varies*

General Description

The International Crane Foundation (ICF) is a center for research on cranes from around the world. Interns conduct independent research in wildlife biology of endangered species, assist staff members with continuing projects and serve as envoys for the ICF. The Foundation prefers interns with some knowledge of research methods. It is also useful to have a background in wildlife ecology, biology, zoology, or ethology. The ICF particularly desires interns who can communicate well with the staff and are receptive to supervision.

The beginning and ending dates and the internships' durations are flexible. The two interns receive a weekly salary, tools and supplies for research, and reduced housing and board costs.

To apply, send a resume, college transcript, letters of recommendation, and writing samples. ICF prefers in-person interviews, although a telephone interview may suffice.

The Inside Word

Applicants are encouraged to visit Baraboo to discuss research project possibilities with the program director and other staff members.

The hours depend upon the intern's project. One intern "got up around 4:30 each morning in order to observe the behavior of Australian cranes in simulated monsoon season conditions." Besides spending a lot of time in blinds making observations, this intern did "the rounds" which included checking water tanks, food supplies, and conditions of the cranes.

Interns praised the program, particularly the wealth of information at the center, but advised applicants to be prepared to work hard.

Contact:

Steve Schmidt, Program Director
International Crane Foundation
City View Road
Baraboo, WI 53913
(608) 356-9462

NATIONAL AUDUBON SOCIETY *California, Connecticut, Ohio*
Naturalist Training Program
Environmental Education Internships

ELIGIBILITY: *Undergraduate and graduate*
DURATION: *13 weeks; September to December, January to March, March to June*
ACADEMIC CREDIT POSSIBLE: *Yes*
REMUNERATION OR FEE: *Usually free housing*
POSITIONS OFFERED: *About 10*
APPLICATION DEADLINE: *4 to 6 months before start of program*

General Description

The National Audubon Society offers a Naturalist Training Program for anyone interested in both nature and education. The interns participate in many aspects of nature center maintenance but especially the public education programs. There are presently five Audubon Centers and the interns' responsibilities vary in each. In general, the teacher-naturalist trainee assists experienced staff in informal classes, workshops, and field trips with visitors of all ages. This type of teaching is ideal for anyone with a serious interest in the outdoors, less structured education, and working with people of all ages.

The Naturalist Training Program is designed to familiarize college students, graduates, and other adults with all the roles of a nature center. The internship is 13 weeks long, either fall, winter or spring. Applicants should have a serious interest in a career as a naturalist. Apply early, between four and six months before the internship's beginning date; A personal interview is desired.

Participants are eligible to compete for the John H. Baker Scholarship which allows them to further their experience by attending Audubon Camp. The Scholarship's purpose is to reacquaint less recent graduates of the Training Program with the Audubon philosophy after they have been away from the Program for several years.

The five Audubon Centers are located throughout the country. Each offers its interns different study and work opportunities. Prospective interns should examine the programs at each Center to find the situation which best suits their interests.

The Audubon Center in Greenwich: The Audubon Center in Greenwich, Connecticut, is a 485-acre sanctuary, 52 acres of which are designated a natural area by the state. The area—an old farm site—includes a pond, stream, field, forest, marsh and swamp. Man-made facilities include a small museum, Teacher Resource Center, Environmental Bookshop, a demonstration classroom, and a resident facility.

The program's emphasis is on teaching students of all ages, adults, and especially other educators. Interns help the staff with guided walks, children's programs, consultations, volunteers' training courses, and newsletters. Besides teaching, trainees help in habitat management, writing educational and promotional materials and trail interpretation. A two-week orientation program familiarizes the intern with the various aspects of the Center. Afterwards, the trainees design their own program in cooperation with the other naturalist-teachers.

College training in ecology and some teaching experience are helpful but not necessary for applying. Experience in hiking and forestry is also helpful.

Contact: Audubon Center in Greenwich, 613 Riversville Road, Greenwich, CT 06830

Aullwood Audubon Center: Aullwood Audubon Center is a 70-acre National Environmental Study Area including old fields, a stream, pond, marsh, hardwood forest, wetlands and a stand of conifers. Interns take part in the Center's diverse informal educational program by planning and conducting one-week classes for school children, leading field trips for children and adults, conducting adult education classes, and working with teenagers. Also, trainees help manage the sanctuary, operate the bookstore, care for the Center's live animal collection and greet visitors. In addition, they become fairly familiar with native plants and animals in the sanctuary.

Contact: Aullwood Audubon Center, 1000 Aullwood Road, Dayton, OH 45414

Aullwood Audubon Farm: The Aullwood Audubon Farm is the agricultural part of the National Environmental Study Area. It provides corn, oats, and hay for the sheep, cattle and other livestock in the Farm's barns and pastures. There is also an orchard and an herb garden. Besides being an operational, productive system, the Farm strives to portray human beings as part of a delicate, ecological system. It trys to enlighten the public to the fact that there are no simple solutions to complex ecological problems.

Interns take part in both educational programs and farming operations. Participants first observe and later lead one and one-half hour school tours, work with teachers and parents in planning and guiding longer class visits, organize and participate in workshops and displays, and make trail signs. Interns are encouraged to contribute their own ideas as much as possible. The other half of the training program consists of farm chores, such as bailing hay, cleaning barns, repainting fences and caring for livestock, in which all staff members share.

Contact: Aullwood Audubon Farm, 9101 Frederick Road, Dayton, OH 45414

Sharon Audubon Center: The Sharon Audubon Center is a 590-acre forest and wildlife sanctuary amidst the rural, dairy farming area of northwestern Connecticut. The staff hopes to educate the people who come to the Center on environmental concerns.

There is a great deal of flexibility in the program's format. The interns' actual duties vary according to their interests and the Center's needs. The first week is spent getting acquainted with the staff and the countryside. Then, interns sit down with staff members and choose a project which interests them and benefits the community. Interns have a variety of roles to choose from, including historian, exhibit maker, teacher and amateur veterinarian. The program emphasizes teaching natural history, although interns also help with the caretaking of the Center.

Contact: Sharon Audubon Center, Route 4, Sharon, CT 06069

George Whittel Education Center: The George Whittel Education Center is part of the Richardson Bay Sanctuary in Tiburon, California. The Center offers one internship position as Administrative Assistant to the Manager for someone from the Bay Area who can supply his or her own housing and transportation.

The internship is a full-time commitment for an academic semester or a quarter. Naturalist-teacher trainees teach classes to all age groups, conduct nature walks, and prepare and conduct lectures and slide shows. They also work behind the scenes, developing training materials, planning activities, and leading workshops. They help patrol and maintain the Sanctuary's natural habitat. Interns also participate in environmental research.

Interns often receive credit through their colleges. Applications should be accompanied by a resume, and an interview is also necessary. The competition is stiff since about 50 people usually apply for one position. A background in biology is helpful.

Contact: Philip Schaeffer, Director, Richardson Bay Wildlife Sanctuary, 376 Greenwood Beach Road, Tiburon, CA 94920

NATIONAL WILDLIFE FEDERATION   *Washington, D.C.*
Conservation Internships

ELIGIBILITY: *Graduates*
DURATION: *6 months*
ACADEMIC CREDIT POSSIBLE: *Yes*
REMUNERATION OR FEE: *$3,240 stipend*
POSITIONS OFFERED: *10*
APPLICATION DEADLINE: *Varies*

General Description

The National Wildlife Federation is the world's largest non-profit, non-governmental conservation education organization. It takes on interns to work in its Resources Defense Division, which has five major program areas: Energy, Public Lands and Land Use, Wildlife and Fisheries, Pollution and Toxics, and Transportation and Public Works.

In addition to researching environmental policy issues, interns attend congressional hearings, draft testimony to be presented by the Federation to congressional and executive panels, lobby on environmental legislation, comment on environmental impact statements, write for Federation publications, and do a small amount of routine office work.

Five of the six-month positions begin in early January, although the exact starting dates are flexible. The application deadline for these positions is in mid-November. The other five positions begin in late June, and have an application deadline in early April. There is a possibility of arranging a volunteer internship if you are turned down for one of the regular paid positions. These non-stipend positions may vary in length, but must be a minimum of 12 weeks in duration.

The program seeks interns with strong independent research and writing skills, as well as some prior experience in working for the federal government. To apply, submit a letter stating your special interests, a resume including three to five names of reference, and a short, non-technical writing sample.

Contact:

Shirley Strong
Coordinator, Conservation Internship Program
National Wildlife Federation
1412 16th Street, N.W.
Washington, DC 20036

NEW ENGLAND AQUARIUM (NEA)   Boston, Massachusetts
NEA Volunteer Program

ELIGIBILITY: *High School through graduate*
DURATION: *Summer, year, other*
ACADEMIC CREDIT POSSIBLE: *No*
REMUNERATION OR FEE: *Free parking*
POSITIONS OFFERED: *1 or 2 per year*
APPLICATION DEADLINE: *Varies*

General Description

Interns at the New England Aquarium give tours, care for the fish and exhibits, and conduct independent research. The volunteer program takes interns at several times during the year: January-June, June-September, September-Christmas break. Interns can participate one day per week for a semester or for five days per week for four weeks. A background in

Biology, Education, Fisheries, Veterinary Science, or museum work is useful but not required.

The Coordinator of Volunteers and the Gallery Manager supervise and instruct interns. A completed application and an interview are required of all prospective participants.

The Inside Word

According to interns, Vida Poole, the Volunteer Coordinator, is always ready to offer suggestions and help. "She allows you to grow with the program and to develop your own potential in the areas you want to pursue." Interns also recommend the more drawn-out semester program which allows participants to devote time to personal projects.

Contact:

Vida Poole, Coordinator of Volunteers
New England Aquarium
Central Wharf
Boston, MA 02110
(617) 742-8830

NEW ENGLAND FORESTRY FOUNDATION, INC. RICE SANCTUARY FOR WILDLIFE

Peru, Massachusetts

ELIGIBILITY: *Undergraduate*
DURATION: *Summer, September and October*
ACADEMIC CREDIT POSSIBLE: *No*
REMUNERATION OR FEE: *Housing*
POSITIONS OFFERED: *2 in summer, 2 in fall*
APPLICATION DEADLINE: *Early February*

General Description

Interns generally run the 273-acre Rice Sanctuary for Wildlife in Peru (near Pittsfield), Massachusetts which is managed by New England Forestry Foundation. Interns maintain wildlife habitats and nature trails, provide information to visitors, and conduct studies. The sanctuary provides an excellent opportunity for ecological population studies and data collection.

Interns are usually undergraduates studying forestry and/or wildlife. The Foundation runs one program from June to August and another during the months of September and October. This program is usually conducted as work/study, however, other arrangements can be negotiated. Interns live in the Visitors Center, a cabin with a large reception room, fireplace, kitchen, and outdoor shower.

An internship may lead to a permanent position with the Program. To apply, send a resume; an interview is sometimes necessary.

The Inside Word

By living and working at the sanctuary, interns "constantly learned" from the environment. Past interns have enjoyed the independence the program provides and the assistance given by supervisors on their weekly visits.

One intern urged applicants to call John Hemenway, Executive Director, to discuss the program. He is "a super guy and really willing to help."

Interns enjoyed the work and the public contact. Said one, "Rice Sanctuary is secluded, but there is a lot of public interest, from those really interested in the habitat and its wildlife, to berry pickers out looking for unexploited patches."

Contact:

John Hemenway, Executive Director
New England Forestry Foundation, Inc.
One Court Street
Boston, MA 02108

NEW ENGLAND SIERRA CLUB   *Boston, Massachusetts*

ELIGIBILITY: *Undergraduate and graduate*
DURATION: *Summer, fall, spring, year*
ACADEMIC CREDIT POSSIBLE: *Yes*
REMUNERATION OR FEE: *None*
POSITIONS OFFERED: *1 to 4 per term*
APPLICATION DEADLINE: *Open*

General Description

Interns with the New England Sierra Club (one of eight regional Sierra Club offices) participate in on-going projects in environmental advocacy. Interns work within one of the club's committees: Alaska, Energy, Environmental Education, Wilderness, Offshore Oil, Outing, Publications, and Wildlife. Work includes becoming knowledgeable on a particular issue and writing articles for *The New England Sierran*, a newsletter. The club sets no specific dates for the internships, which can be as long as a year. The program is designed to attract applicants interested in environmental studies, natural sciences, and economics.

Interns work 10 to 25 self-scheduled hours per week, generally on their own. The program requires no special skills, however, the interns receive a certain amount of on-the-job training in environmental advocacy. A sincere concern for the environment and an ability to deal effectively with people are essential. A resume and an interview are required, and submitting writing samples is recommended.

The Inside Word

Interns comment that initiative in research and writing determines this program's degree of success. "The staff is quite willing to offer suggestions and ideas, but it was really up to me to follow through on projects." The Sierra Club's major projects during the time of the internship shapes the experience of each participant, but motivated interns can also investigate their special interests. There is some flexibility. The student plays an active role in developing a job description for the internship.

One intern comments that the frantic activity and the element of disorganization in the large office added to the excitement. "These people seemed honestly concerned about their work and the positive effects their efforts will have."

Contact:

Marsha Rockefeller, Office Manager
New England Sierra Club
3 Joy Street
Boston, MA 02108

FOR ADDRESSES OF OTHER REGIONAL OFFICES:
Information Services
National Offices
Sierra Club Headquarters
530 Bush Street
San Francisco, CA 94108
(415) 981-8634

ROCHESTER MUSEUM AND SCIENCE CENTER

Rochester, New York

ELIGIBILITY: *Graduate*
DURATION: *1 year*
ACADEMIC CREDIT POSSIBLE: *No*
REMUNERATION OR FEE: *$6,000 stipend*
POSITIONS OFFERED: *Two*
APPLICATION DEADLINE: *May 1*

General Description

Rochester Museum and Science Center (RMSC) offers two internships per year, one in the Rochester Museum and one in the Strasenburgh Planetarium. RMSC accepts college graduates, preferably students with backgrounds in history, anthropology, natural science, technology, or exhibit design. The Planetarium program seeks applicants interested in astronomy, computer science, and audio-visual communications. Interns perform administrative functions, arrange and maintain exhibits, serve the public, work on publications, and keep records.

Independent projects are a major aspect of this program and require much input by interns. The museum intern designs and arranges one major exhibit; the Planetarium intern produces a 15-minute show. The director, and other staff members, supervise the interns.

RMSC provides materials for projects, limited funds for work-related travel, and a $6,000 stipend distributed in bi-weekly allotments. This full-time program runs from the first Wednesday after Labor Day to the last day of the following August.

The Inside Word

Getting accepted: RMSC selects only two interns each year from an applicant pool of 100. Ideal applicants have museum or science-related work experience, possess special skills, and submit application materials early. Send a completed application, a statement of purpose, college transcript from your graduating institution, and three letters of recommendation no earlier than January 1 and no later than May 1. Interns strongly advise having some relevant experience, either paid or volunteer, before applying. Researching the RMSC program and stating in the application how your career interests are compatible with the program appears to pay off. According to past participants, a strong interest in a career in museum or planetarium work and demonstrated initiative in designing independent projects are essential to getting into the program.

Daily life: "I was on my own 95% of the time with periodic meetings with supervisors to discuss progress and/or problems," recalls one intern. Internships generally involve monthly projects, such as performing inventory on collections, curatorial responsibilities, designing and installing temporary exhibits, cataloguing in the museum, and working in the education department.

Future prospects: "Through this internship I not only gained skills from working in various departments," said one intern, "but I learned about the interrelation of departments and the competition and division between them. The internship encouraged me to continue in a museum career."

Contact:

Mr. Charles F. Hayes III
Museum Director
Rochester Museum and Science Center
657 East Avenue
P.O. Box 1480
Rochester, NY 14603
(716) 271-4320

SQUAM LAKES SCIENCE CENTER

Holderness, New Hampshire

ELIGIBILITY: *Undergraduate and graduate*
DURATION: *Summer, January term or 10 to 20 weeks of any season*
ACADEMIC CREDIT POSSIBLE: *No*
REMUNERATION OR FEE: *$100 total stipend plus housing*
POSITIONS OFFERED: *About 6 per year*
APPLICATION DEADLINE: *Varies*

General Description

The Squam Lakes program is geared toward students with a major in Outdoor Education, Environmental Education, Conservation Education, Environmental Science, Biology, or Veterinary Science. Preference is given to graduates and college seniors.

Interns lead field trips in natural history and ecology for all age groups, feed and care for the Center's native New Hampshire animals, design and develop nature trails and exhibits, and work on staff projects. Interns can design their programs around their specific interests and needs. The director of Squam Lakes supervises the interns' activities and the permanent staff provides feedback.

Squam Lakes provides the intern with a private bedroom, bath, and kitchen facilities. The Center supplies special equipment and funds for work-related travel as well as a $100 stipend.

The Inside Word

Although a resume, letters of recommendation, and a completed application are required, the word is that a successful interview is key to getting an internship.

Past interns praised the excellent working conditions and the helpful staff. One remarked, "The staff really went out of their way to help 'newcomers.' '' The variety of responsibilities kept the weeks interesting and full.

One intern said that the teaching load was sometimes so heavy that she did not have time to develop an outside project in the area of her special interests. Prior teaching experience was valuable to another intern who discussed the constant flow of busloads of all ages coming to the Science Center. "An intern simply must be able to relate to all ages."

Contact:

FOR APPLICATION MATERIALS:
Squam Lakes Science Center
P.O. Box 123
Holderness, NH 03245

FOR MORE INFORMATION:
Robert Nichols, Director
Squam Lakes Science Center
Holderness, NH 03245

TECHNICAL INFORMATION PROJECT, INC.
Washington, D.C.

ELIGIBILITY: *Sophomores*
DURATION: *Varies*
ACADEMIC CREDIT POSSIBLE: *Yes*
REMUNERATION OR FEE: *Varies*
POSITIONS OFFERED: *1 to 2*
APPLICATION DEADLINE: *Open*

General Description

Technical Information Project, Inc. is a Washington-based organization devoted to examining the effects of nuclear waste and toxic substances on the environment. The permanent staff of four to five researchers investigates environmental policy and promotes public energy education in addition to their scientific research.

Interns participate in all phases of the organization—from acting as research assistants to completely producing the agency's newsletter. A resume, three references, and a statement of purpose are required of all applicants.

The Inside Word

Getting accepted: Applicants from scientific or environmental studies backgrounds with good writing skills are the most successful candidates for admission. The program is largely non-competitive, however, directors are eager to locate talented and enthusiastic assistants, and when logistically possible, will arrange positions for all those who are well qualified and committed to the Project's work.

Daily life: The program for interns at Technical Information Projects, while involving a great deal of responsibility and wide range of experience, is somewhat loosely structured. Interns are quickly assimilated into the organization's workings, and treated as regular staff members. Consequently, participants can expect to do office work, as well as be given more involved and challenging assignments. According to Dr. Arthur H. Purcell, Director of Research at the center, initiative is a must. Often, interns assist in collecting data for agency publications. Recently, three interns developed a guide for people considering converting their home heating systems to plans more ecologically sound.

Future prospects: Of those interns who have completed the program at Technical Information Project, one is currently studying on a Fulbright scholarship, another is working as a nuclear programmer, and others have gone on to careers in environmental studies.

Contact:

Dr. Arthur H. Purcell, Director of Research
Technical Information Project
1346 Connecticut Avenue, N.W.
Room 217
Washington, DC 20036

OTHER PLACES TO LOOK:

Architecture
San Mateo County Planning and Development Division
The Tahoe Regional Planning Agency

Public Service
Institute for Local Self-Reliance
New Castle County Department of Parks and Recreation

Government

With government the largest employer in the nation, it stands to reason that internship possibilities in the public sector are limitless. As might be expected of bureaucratic administration, however, opportunities to serve your nation, state, or community tend to be as disorganized as they are abundant. Particularly on the local level, it pays to do some digging. Talk to friends, play your connections for all they are worth, and make a few phone calls to discover what openings are available or can be made available by creating your own internship (see section on *Making Your Own.*) On the national level, interning has become so popular that while internship programs are more formalized, they are also more competitive.

Metropolitan Washington, the hub of the federal government and home to a plethora of related agencies and organizations, is an intern's paradise. Paid positions may be hard to come by, but interesting, responsible, and worthwhile opportunities abound for the student able to work for experience's sake instead of pay. Congressional offices, government agencies, and lobbying groups are some of the many organizations which rely heavily on intern participation. Most require a degree of *Making Your Own* strategy—your Congressman will undoubtedly hire interns for the summer, but the success of *your* bid will depend largely on your initiative in contacting him or her and making the most of your abilities. Agencies and lobbying organizations, on the other hand, generally have formal application procedures. Working in these areas may not sound as glamorous as interning in a Congressional office, but your chances of getting the position you want, and of ending up with some real responsibility, are much greater.

Get on the ball early for any Washington program you are interested in, whether paid or volunteer, congressional or civil service. Application deadlines can be as early as October 31 for internships the following summer.

There are four basic types of internship offerings in the D.C. area: positions on Capital Hill, internships with one of the multitude of lobbying groups, "merit evaluation" internships, and those educational jobs or "work assignments" available through the Civil Service Commission.

CAPITOL HILL INTERNSHIPS

Everyone wants to spend a summer in Washington, D.C. working for his or her Congressman. This is as reliable a fact about students as their dislike of the humid Washington climate once they get there. Consequently, internships "on the hill" are the most eagerly sought positions, and the most difficult to come by. Internships with members of Congress are awarded completely at the discretion of each Congressman, and the criteria for hiring varies greatly. "The Congress is a loose amalgam of 535 baronies. Each Congressman and Senator has complete control over the hiring and firing of his staff, including interns," warns Harrison Fox in *The Directory of Washington Internships* (published by The National Center for Public Service Intern Programs; See the chapter on "Additional Sources of Information.") Recent legislation has made it easier to find intern positions, however, by making it simpler for Congressmen to hire summer interns. The LBJ Internship Program, established some years ago by President Lyndon Johnson to involve youth in Federal government, provides each Congressman with $650/month for two months to employ interns. The program is open to anyone who has spent the previous semester in school. But this program has been updated by recent legislation which creates three new classifications of Congressional staff people. The "temporary help authorization," "part-time," and "interns" categories expand the usual limit on the number of employees each Congressman is allowed. The "interns" ruling also provides additional funding for office space. Additionally, the $650 monthly allowance is available 12 months each year instead of just two. Congressional staff can allocate that amount in any way they choose—funding one intern for a full year, or several interns for limited periods.

Representatives give strong preference to residents of their home districts, and when the competition is toughest, or during re-election campaigns, they may discard the out-of-district applicants. In any case, apply early, particularly if you hope to work for a senator. "Finding a good internship was strictly connections, but connections are only what you make of them . . . it's the willingness to tap these resources that gets you the job," offered a Congressional intern.

The best spots to be had in Washington, however, are on the staffs of a Congressional Committee or subcommittee. In these situations, one deals with legislation, background hearings, and reports. The responsibilities are more substantive and closer to Congressional policy-making than the work done by most interns in Congressional offices. The Committee internships are particularly hard to find. Apply through the Committee or subcommittee chairman. Like Congressional positions, applicants from the Chairman's home state or district have the inside track.

Lobbying Groups

Another way to participate in the decision-making process of the federal government is through the wide variety of lobbying groups that work with Congress, the President and his staff, each of the Cabinet departments (H.E.W., State, Treasury, Agriculture, etc.) and the regulatory agencies (F.D.A., Consumer Safety Commission, etc.). The responsibilities an intern assumes vary from office to office. One intern spent her January winter-term "developing an intimate relationship with a Savin 7000" photocopy machine. Others have assumed somewhat more challenging tasks—from monitoring bills to completely producing agency newsletters.

The Better Government Association, Americans for Democratic Action, and National League of Cities are among the many such lobbying organizations. See the section on "Public Service" internships for more.

Merit Evaluation Internships

Merit evaluation is a general term applied to Federal departmental internships (e.g., Federal Summer Intern Program) in which applicants are often screened first by their own schools, then evaluated by an admissions committee. Though selection criteria vary, the process is usually highly qualitative. Generally, applicants are expected to submit essays to demonstrate their writing skill, and must have excellent academic records.

Civil Service Work Opportunities

Civil Service bureaus throughout the country frequently offer interesting, short-term jobs and/or projects "designed to provide educationally related work assignments for students in nonpay status." Internships are of the merit evaluation type, and prospective interns must apply through their college or university. The short-term jobs offered are outlined in the Civil Service's *Summer Jobs* booklet, available every spring from local Civil Service Offices. The descriptions in the booklet are so vague, however, that finding a good position is harder than hunting migrating geese in a dense fog. Try to identify those that seem appealing, and pursue your interest by calling or writing to the local office. Interns must take the Civil Service Exam before placement can be made.

Volunteer projects with the Civil Service are part of a new program which allows college students to work in the Federal government without having to take the exam. "The positions are meaningful jobs," said one Civil Service executive, and recommended that interested students approach the personnel office of the agency they want to work with. Explain that you are available and interested, and leave a copy of your resume. Applicants should specify what positions they want, but indicate their flexibility as well.

State Government Internships

Internships in government are by no means limited to the Federal level. Many governors' offices and state legislatures offer programs for politically active and aware students. Write to your governor or local representative for information on what is available. Most programs are open only to state residents, and can be quite competitive.

Government Clearinghouses

There are a number of clearinghouses organized to publicize the vast array of government internship opportunities available, to help interns find housing, and to orient interns to the Washington political scene. The

National Society for Internships and Experiential Education, and the Washington Center for Learning Alternatives are two of the best known agencies, both with impressive histories of aiding students in locating and surviving in Washington internships.

Many colleges, universities, and private organizations have programs that offer similar help. First, exhaust the resources of your schools's career counseling office, then make very liberal use of the numerous clearinghouses in the D.C. area (check the chapter, "Additional Sources of Information" of this book.)

Several states have clearinghouses which provide information about internship opportunities and which help place interns in state and local governments. California, North and South Carolina, Illinois, Kentucky, Massachusetts, Nebraska, Washington, and the District of Columbia are among these states; contact the state governers office for addresses. Residents of other states can find similar stores of information by checking with public service organizations for a listing of lobbying groups, and with state senators or representatives to determine what opportunities are available in state and local government.

ADA (AMERICANS FOR DEMOCRATIC ACTION) YOUTH CAUCUS
January Internship Program
Washington, D.C.

ELIGIBILITY: *Undergraduates*
DURATION: *January 3 to January 30*
ACADEMIC CREDIT POSSIBLE: *Yes*
REMUNERATION OR FEE: *None*
POSITIONS OFFERED: *30 to 40*
APPLICATION DEADLINE: *November 15*

General Description

The ADA is a private, non-profit organization dedicated to achieving liberal, progressive change. Undergraduates accepted into the program are placed in congressmen's offices or public interest groups, depending on what aspect of government they are interested in. Interns in the January program, however, do not work directly for the ADA.

Once the intern reports to his/her place of work, the only contact he has with the ADA is a series of workshops sponsored by the program at which legislators, journalists, and labor leaders address the interns and answer questions.

According to program director, Mitchell Edelstein, interns often answer mail, sit in on meetings, and do routine office work. Competent interns may have the opportunity to write briefing papers and undertake projects. Two interns recently completed a study on how great a monetary advantage the incumbent has in an election due to free mailing privileges, staff phones, etc.

Admission to the program is based on a resume and a fifteen minute phone interview. Of the 73 interns who applied for the 1980 session 40 were accepted; twelve of these were placed in Congressional offices while the remainder worked for environmental groups, consumer protection agencies and other public interest groups.

The Inside Word

Getting accepted: Edelstein is looking for people with a realistic conception of how the political process operates. Students, he says, who come to Washington with the expectation of participating in earth-shattering legislation are bound to be disappointed. Most of the work in a Congressional office involves the political necessity of keeping in touch with the constituency. Edelstein went on to say that interns are "used and even sometimes abused," for Congressional offices rely heavily on interns to do office work. One intern felt this apparent drawback was enlightening; he was surprised by the degree to which a congressman is propped-up by his staff and interns.

Daily life: The intern need not be doomed to a month of photo-copying to learn the disillusioning truth of how a Congressional office works. Initiative is definitely needed, according to one intern: "I'd come into the office, quickly dispose of my filing, and then ask for a project. Usually they'd give me something challenging to do."

Opinions of the ADA-conducted workshops were mixed. Many thought speakers like Congressman Toby Moffet, and Tom Braden of *The Washington Post* were effective. Others stressed the negative aspects, complaining that the speakers discussed topics irrelevant to their own work. Even these malcontents, however, felt the workshops provided a good opportunity to meet other ADA interns.

Contact:

ADA Youth Caucus
January Internship Program
1411 K Street, N.W., Suite 850
Washington, DC 20005
(202) 638-6447

AMERICAN ENTERPRISE INSTITUTE FOR PUBLIC POLICY (AEI)

Washington, D.C.

ELIGIBILITY: *Undergraduates and graduates*
DURATION: *June through August*

ACADEMIC CREDIT POSSIBLE: *Yes*
REMUNERATION OR FEE: *$540/month for
    undergraduates, $650/month for graduates*
POSITIONS OFFERED: *10*
APPLICATION DEADLINE: *March 1*

General Description

The AEI is a private, non-profit research organization which seeks to assist policy makers, scholars, business people, the press, and the public by providing analyses of national and international issues. Studies are commissioned in the areas of economics, foreign affairs, government, health, law, and legislation. The institute's aim is to foster competition of ideas rather than taking positions on policy issues. AEI also publishes a number of periodicals including public opinion and regulation magazines.

Interns are accepted into one of AEI's ten research programs and assist a project director in accumulating pertinent data for forthcoming studies. For example, one intern's research culminated in the discovery that over the past five years increasingly more money has been allotted to the Government Credit Program, which does not appear on the federal budget. Other interns have written critiques of recent legislation related to their research. Depending on his/her capabilities, the intern may have the opportunity to write for AEI publications. In the summer of 1979, eight interns out of twenty-four managed to have articles published.

Special Assistant John Rogers feels the AEI summer program differs from Congressional internships in the respect that students are expected to be vigorous researchers. Interns, however, are sometimes asked to do office work. The more independence, motivation, and intelligence an intern shows the more time he will be able to devote to his research projects. Yet Rogers estimates that of the twenty-four 1979 interns, seven or eight spent the majority of their time doing busy work.

Admission to the program is extremely competitive; over 300 applied for the ten positions available. Selection is based on a transcript, resume, cover letter, and references. Interviews are not required but will be granted if the applicant so desires. Demonstrated academic ability is essential for admission to the program.

The Inside Word

The AEI interns were quite positive about their experiences overall. They stressed that the quality of the internship depends to a large degree upon one's program director. When one intern's director left for Europe, she worked for another whom she felt had her doing irrelevant research. When her original director returned mid-way through the summer she became engaged in an interesting project involving the Constitution.

Despite the organization's *raison d'être* of promoting discussion through objective analysis of national and international issues, AEI publications inevitably have a conservative slant, championing the virtues of the free market. One intern pointed out: "AEI is for the Republicans what the Brookings Institute is for the Democrats—a place to go when they're not in power and stay sharp on the issues." Yet this intern who described himself as a liberal felt his ideas were just as well received as those of his conservative counterparts.

An internship with AEI could be a stepping-stone to a more permanent job with the organization. One former intern, who was doing graduate work in Washington, was asked to stay on part-time. Furthermore, after the completion of her graduate work she may be offered full-time work at the institute.

Some advice for admission: apply as early as you can, write a good cover letter, and have a couple of strong references ready from professors and former employers.

Contact:

John Rogers, Special Assistant
American Enterprise Institute
1150 17th Street, N.W.
Washington, DC 20036
(202) 862-5800

THE BETTER GOVERNMENT ASSOCIATION   Chicago, Illinois
Internship Program

ELIGIBILITY: *Undergraduate and graduate*
DURATION: *School term or summer*
ACADEMIC CREDIT POSSIBLE: *Yes*
REMUNERATION OR FEE: *Travel and lunch money*
POSITIONS OFFERED: *20 to 25 a year*
APPLICATION DEADLINE: *3 to 4 months in advance for*
the summer; 2 to 3 months for the fall, winter,
and spring

General Description

The Better Government Association (B.G.A.) is a Midwestern watchdog organization dedicated to exposing waste and corruption in state and local government. Working closely with the news media, the B.G.A. wields a team of lawyers, investigators, and interns headed by a former Special Attorney of the Department of Justice, Organized Crime and Racketeering Section. Last year they investigated abortion racketeering in major downtown abortion clinics, forced further research on Chicago's massive $8 billion "Deep Tunnel" sewage project, exposed major abuses in nursing homes, and prodded the State of Illinois into cracking down on the Talwin and Pyribenzamine—"T's & Blues"—drug distribution.

Interns work on the investigations; locating documents, analyzing, and interviewing to develop the evidence. They receive lunch and travel money, but the positions are unsalaried. Internships can be arranged on a part-time or full-time basis, and generally last the summer or a school term.

Twenty to 25 positions are offered each year, for which 40 to 50 people apply. Applications must be arranged with an intern's "field instructor"—a professor at the intern's college or graduate school who is willing to oversee the internship. Consequently, interns often receive academic credit. Apply three to four months in advance for the summer, and two to three months before for the fall, winter, and spring.

The Inside Word

Getting accepted: These internships are almost always obtained through an intern's college field instructor, college internship coordinator, or office of career counseling. They arrange the academic credit aspect after recommending qualified students.

Apply with a cover letter and resume. Expect an interview. Students majoring in government or political science, journalism, economics, urban affairs, or history are generally given priority.

Aggressive individuals, "self starters" who are "mature" and "reliable," are needed to work in-depth on the investigations. A background in journalism is helpful, as often the interns work with reporters and on issuing press releases.

Daily life: Interns learn how the "system," in this case, government or private agencies serving the public, works and doesn't work. They function as junior investigators, usually working on their own, locating public documents, going through legal files, and studying documents obtained through the Freedom of Information Act. Interns are assigned occasionally undercover work—infiltrating suspect organizations.

Interns said that working for the B.G.A. was a challenging test of their abilities to work independently. They improved their research and writing skills, in addition to receiving the unique training in the workings of state and local government.

Contact:

David Protess
Research Coordinator
Better Government Association
230 N. Michigan Ave., Suite 1710
Chicago, IL 60601

BUREAU OF EUROPEAN AFFAIRS OF *Washington, D.C.*
THE DEPARTMENT OF STATE
Student/Intern Program

ELIGIBILITY: *Undergraduate juniors, seniors, and graduate*
DURATION: *Semester, summer*
ACADEMIC CREDIT POSSIBLE: *Yes*
REMUNERATION OR FEE: *None*
POSITIONS OFFERED: *Varies*
APPLICATION DEADLINE: *October 31*

General Description

The State Department's Bureau on European Affairs Student/Intern Program is designed to provide students planning careers in government and foreign relations with first-hand knowledge of the foreign affairs process. Interns select an area of personal interest, and for approximately three months (a semester or summer's length) work at one of the offices under the close supervision of a Bureau officer. During the course of the internship, participants meet with officers in other Bureaus and Offices of the Department as well as those from other government agencies, including the Agency for International Development, the Arms Control and Disarmament Agency, the United States International Communication Agency, and the Peace Corps.

Applicants should be college juniors, seniors, or graduates and have at least a B+ average. Interns must be sponsored by their college or university, and apply through the institution. Additionally, applicants must submit a faculty-approved statement specifying the area of the Bureau in which he/she would like to work, including objectives and relevant academic and job experience. A transcript is also required, as well as two letters of endorsement from faculty members or administrators at the sponsoring institution. Applications must be received by October 31, as interns accepted into the program must undergo an extensive security clearance which can last up to six months.

Occasionally, opportunities arise in the Bureau's overseas offices for summer interns. These positions, like those based in Washington, are non-remunerative, and the student must also underwrite his/her own living and travel expenses. For overseas positions, interns must receive a physician's approval, and go through the same, lengthy clearance process.

The Inside Word

The intern we contacted was a two-year veteran of the program. Now considering a career in international law and diplomacy, he felt that, "the State Department's work/study program offered a superior internship

experience. The quality of my two summers was in large part determined
by the good fortune of an officer's leave coinciding with my arrival.
Consequently, I was able to pick up as much of a foreign service officer's
day-to-day work as I could handle. In practice, this meant that while in
Washington I answered inquiries from members of Congress and other
government agencies. I also conducted one fairly large-scale research
project and developed a critique of another study being prepared in the
department.''

"I spent the next summer overseas in London, in the Embassy's
political section. My primary responsibility was African affairs, so a
substantial part of each day was spent reading the cable traffic. In addition,
I went frequently to the British Foreign and Commonwealth Office to find
out the British perspective on various topics of common concern in the
area of African affairs, and often sent reports, via a cable, back to
Washington reporting on the meeting.

"One of the least popular jobs in the political section was escorting
visiting American officials around the Foreign Office to see their British
counterparts. As the intern, I was "stuck" with this task which turned out
to be one of the more interesting jobs I had. American officials with widely
varying responsibilities pass through London. As their "control officer"
in London, I was able to sit in on many diverse, and always interesting,
discussions. And if the appointment was in the late afternoon, the British
would always serve tea.''

While his experience with the State Department program is not
representative, most participants believe it is one of the best internship
programs around. It is volunteer because the Department of State cannot
pay anyone who is not a Foreign Service Officer or in one of a handful of
other tightly defined categories. Nonetheless, the program does offer
college credit. Some students obtain grants to offset their costs and keep
the summer from being a financial loss.

Contact:

European Affairs
EUR/EX
Room 9424 NS
Department of State
Washington, DC 20520

CARNEGIE ENDOWMENT FOR INTERNATIONAL PEACE

Washington, D.C.
New York, New York

ELIGIBILITY: *Graduate*
DURATION: *6 months*
ACADEMIC CREDIT POSSIBLE: *Yes*

REMUNERATION OR FEE: *$650/month, transportation costs*
POSITIONS OFFERED: *12*
APPLICATION DEADLINE: *February 1*

General Description

The Carnegie Endowment provides students interested in foreign relations with a working experience. To be eligible for this highly-competitive program, applicants must be endorsed by their college or university.
Interns need not be from a particular academic background, but a knowledge of political science or economics is helpful and an advantage in gaining acceptance.

The Endowment generally receives in the neighborhood of 300 applications. The field is then narrowed to 50, and these candidates are all interviewed before the final selection of 24 (12 to participate in each of the two six-month-long sessions) is made. Once accepted, interns work a full, 9:00-5:00, five-day week.

Two of the 12 interns serve as editorial assistants for *Foreign Policy* magazine, and one serves with the Arms Control Association. Other interns are assigned on an individual basis to assist staff associates. For instance, one intern helped to produce a book on United States policy in South Africa. His responsibilities included monitoring Capitol Hill for hearings, speeches, and bills concerning South Africa, keeping abreast of all related current events, library work, conducting opinion polls, and interviewing U.S. as well as South African government officials.

As a result of such broad experiences, and the high recommendations from program administrators which accompany successful completion of the internship, most interns go on to fill impressive jobs in foreign relations, international business, journalism, and academics. Some are now working for the State Department, and one is currently employed by the National Security Council.

The Inside Word

As the Endowment is extremely competitive, past interns advised playing up any previous experience in international policy. The five-page essay required along with the application is the place to do this. The essay is very important, and involves choosing one of three topics, such as: "Evaluate the role of Congress on foreign policy," "Evaluate the SALT treaty," or "What is the impact of Multinational Corporations in the Third World?"

One intern felt that the major advantage to the program was the good pay and lack of "busy-work." From the moment the intern enters the office, "one is treated as a competent and capable member of the staff," enthused an intern currently in the program. "It's a spectacular internship."

Contact:

The Carnegie Endowment for International Peace
J. Daniel O'Flaherty, Program Officer
11 Dupont Circle
Washington, DC 20036

INTERNSHIPS WITH CONGRESSIONAL   Washington, D.C.
COMMITTEES OR SUBCOMMITTEES

ELIGIBILITY: *Undergraduate and graduate*
DURATION: *About 3 months*
ACADEMIC CREDIT POSSIBLE: *Yes*
REMUNERATION OR FEE: *Little*
POSITIONS OFFERED: *Varies*
APPLICATION DEADLINE: *Generally 3 months in*
    advance

General Description

Among the more prestigious and competitive internships on Capitol Hill
are those with Congressional Committees. Not too many Committees take
interns, and those that do are not very consistent about it. Interns do the
same sort of research that their counterparts in Congressional offices do,
and, similarly, pay is minimal, and academic credit, while possible, is
uncommon. The internship is primarily for upperclassmen and graduates,
but all are free to apply.

The internships exist at legislative whim. Most often they are
available during the summer, but increasingly they are offered during the
school year. Most last about three months, and have spots for four to six
students.

Generally, one should apply with a cover letter and resume sent to the
committee and subcommittee chairmen. They expect the applications at
least three months in advance of when you want to start.

The Inside Word

Getting accepted: The organized way to secure a Committee internship is
to write or call the Committees and Subcommittees you are interested in
four to six months in advance. Hit the Committees whose purpose
corresponds with your academic interests. Find out whether internships
on the Committee or Subcommittee staffs are available, and if so, the
names of the Committee chairmen. Inquire as to whether the Subcommittee internships are awarded by the full Committee or are at the individual

discretion of the Subcommittee Chairmen. In addition, find out what support materials to send and when applications are due.

If you don't get organized this early and run out of time to do anything else but file an application, you can always wing it. Get a hold of a copy of the *Congressional Record* listing the Standing Committees and Subcommittees of Congress and their chairmen and members. The Committees listed at the back of this entry should have internships available, and sometimes have spots open on the Subcommittees as well.

In any case, the Committee will look for a cover letter briefly explaining why you want an internship, how you are qualified, and the details of when and what you are interested in doing. Enclose a resume and perhaps a transcript with the letter. It is helpful but not vital to meet with a Member of the Committee or a staffer.

Getting a sponsoring letter from one of your Senators or Representatives is a hassle, but as one committee staffer explained, "let me be honest with you . . . You've got to have the endorsement of your Senator and Congressman." Write or call their local offices to seek their endorsement.

Follow up your application with a phone call to see what action is being taken and whether they know of anything else available. "It takes initiative and you have to be aggressive about it," explained a staffer.

Each Committee "gets a mass of applications." Generally around the March deadline, they start to sift through them. Sometime in April, when there is a lull in Committee business, the Congressmen authorize their staffs to select a specific number of interns. "We have to make sure that we have adequate activities for them—it's not a paid vacation," explained a Congressional aide. The staff puts together a pool of the hottest applicants, and a special subcommittee of Congressmen make the final decisions.

They are looking for educational interests and coursework related to the Committee's activities. Where an intern stands in school and previous work experience are then examined. One Committee member down played the importance of the transcript, saying, "We're not really interested in whether you got an 'A' in freshman English," although others consider it very carefully. Ask about this early on in your exploratory letter to the Committee.

Daily life: Interns assist the staff in researching potential legislation, digging out documents, and addressing letters. They answer correspondence and the phone. Some manage the Congressional Intern Program. Others programmed projects for the Congressional computers. The very luckiest help draft the Committee reports and "initiate, plan, and organize" Committee hearings. "I'm afraid a lot of it [one Committee's internship] is very disappointing to them. Our work is rather mundane," explained a staffer. Surveying campaign financing, analyzing data, and "catching up on the filing" are all more realistic examples of the Committees's intern assignments.

These internships provide the best view of the legislative process.

From a vantage almost too close, interns watch bills form and reform. While an internship in a Congressional office exposes the *political* side of law making, Committee internships are the best view open to students of the *legislative* process on Capitol Hill.

Where else to look: The following is a list of the Congressional Committees likely to have internships. In addition, several also have Subcommittee internships. Often these are filled by the full Committee staff but occasionally they are handled by the individual Chairmen.

Internship policies change at the flicker of legislative eye, so it's best to go the organized route and call them in advance. Not only will it insure that the internships you are interested in are still available, but it will help you locate others. Internships awarded by the Chairmen usually give preference to residents and students of the Chairman's district. However, if you have ties to the ranking Republican member of a Committee, it would also be helpful to approach him for an endorsement. You should apply three months in advance unless it is specified differently below.

Committee names are listed below. A complete address would read:

Committee on **Government Operations** or **Appropriations Committee;** United States Senate or United States House of Representatives; Washington, D.C. 20515. Included are the telephone extensions of the full Committees. All phone numbers to the U. S. Capitol begin with (1)— 202—22—; individual committee extensions appear following the committee's name.

CONGRESSIONAL INTERNSHIPS WITH A SENATOR OR REPRESENTATIVE
Washington, D.C.

ELIGIBILITY: *High school, undergraduate and graduate*
DURATION: *2 weeks to 1 semester*
ACADEMIC CREDIT POSSIBLE: *Yes*
REMUNERATION OR FEE: *Little*
POSITIONS OFFERED: *Up to 6*
APPLICATION DEADLINE: *Varies*

General Description

Congressional internships are held either in Washington, D.C. or in the Congressman's home-district office. They are available year round, last from two weeks to a semester, and generally pay very little or not at all.

Interns in these offices are paper-pushers. They answer the phone, tally questionnaires, respond to constituent letters, go to hearings, and track legislation.

Find out how to apply by writing to the Congressman from your home or school district. Explain you are interested in an internship, enclose a resume, and ask if there are any other support materials needed. Everyone is eligible, but as these internships are fairly competitive, strong preference is given to residents and students from the Congressman's district. Upperclassmen in college are usually given the first pick. Apply early—three to six months in advance, but don't hesitate to give the office a call late in the game on the off chance that there is an opening.

The Inside Word

Getting accepted: The application procedure for Congressional internships is complicated by guidelines which differ from office to office. Most take on two or three interns during the school year and peak to about six in the summer. Anywhere from 10 to 36 people usually apply for these spots each semester. For some, a call to the Congressman from the right friend will be enough to ensure a spot. Other offices have a formal application; and ask for recommendations, a resume, and a transcript.

During the fall and spring when the competition for internships is less severe, offices often take on interns through special academic programs. These are non-paying and usually last for a school term. Students should arrange for these internships in conjunction with their school.

Applicants are evaluated in a variety of ways. Some offices recognize the political nature of these internships: "To be perfectly frank, if it's somebody who has a personal relationship [with the Congressman], then he gives them first pick." Other offices have a full-blown admissions committee. Good writing and office skills are stressed, and grades are considered. Recommendations also figure in.

One Senate aide said that half of the applicants immediately disqualify themselves because their application packets are incomplete. Of the portion that is left, in "more than half the cases it is obvious that the student doesn't have a command of the English language." Therefore, be thorough in assembling your application packet, get it in the mail on time, and put a lot of effort into the essay questions.

Dr. Donald I. Robinson, director of the Congressional Internship Program, recommends not applying for positions with big-names unless you really enjoy mindless work, and advises students not to look for work on Capitol Hill during the summer. Robinson suggested, "Your best idea is to go to Europe for the summer, and come back to work in the Fall. Summer is a madhouse down here."

To obtain a position, check *American Politics, Congressional Quarterly, Who's Who in Politics* or some similar guide to the Hill to find people for whom you could work. Go to D.C. for an interview appointment with a legislative director or an administrative assistant. Bring a one page resume and brief writing samples. "Washington staffs do not have a lot of time to wade through pages of junk," said Robinson. Look for connections, particularly through school. One former administrative assistant remarked, "when I was going through 50 to 60 candidates for a position, and all other things were equal, it was natural to pick someone with a background I had confidence in."

Plan ahead; to work in the fall, visit offices in the spring. Once an office shows interest, check out what type of work will be expected. Don't be surprised if much of the work seems trivial, but Robinson adds that "you should be able to work out a program that will also give you a good deal of substantive work." Interns warn that people expecting to exert much influence on policy decisions will be frustrated; many factors enter each decision, most of them beyond the control of interns and congressmen.

Daily life: Interns function as the migrant workers of capital offices. Their work ranges from mundane clerical assignments including answering the phone, greeting and giving tours to constituents, and counting question-naires. Work also includes responding to constituent letters in the Congressman's name, taking notes of committee meetings and briefings, researching and writing memos on current issues, and, sometimes, writing issue briefs outlining in short form the Congressman's position on various issues. One office worker quipped, "The interns do the kinds of things the staff doesn't like, and for the frosting on their cake, do the things we take for granted."

Contact:

The Washington office of your Senators or Representative. Who they are and their addresses and phone numbers are available from the Federal Information Centers in major cities around the country. Call directory information toll free ((1)-area code-555-1212) of the nearest metropolitan area with a Federal Building for their phone number.

Dr. Donald I. Robinson
Director, Congressional Internship Program
3717 Harrison Street, NW
Washington, DC 20015
Internship Coordinating Committee
Congressional Internship Program
Room 118
House Office Building Annex 1
Washington, DC 20515

House Committees

Agriculture (52171)

Education and Labor (54527)

House Administration (52061)

Interior and Insular
Affairs (52761)

Interstate and Foreign
Commerce (52927)

Merchant Marine and
Fisheries (54047)

Post Office and Civil
Service (50454)

—Subcommittees have internships.
Address inquiries and applications
to the individual Subcommittee
Chairmen.

Public Works and
Transportation (54472)

Approach both the Committee
Chairmen and the Subcommittee
Chairmen.

Rules (59486)

Science and Technology (56371)

Veterans' Affairs (53527)

—Internships are few and far between.

Ways and Means (53625)

Select Committees

Aging (59375)

—Internships with both the full Com-
mitee and the Subcommittees.

Joint Committees

Economic (45171)

Printing (45241)

—Apply to the Members of Congress
who are on the Committee.

Senate Committees

Agriculture, Nutrition, and
Forestry (42035)

—Apply only through the Chairman
(presently Senator Herman Tal-
madge (D. GA)).

Appropriations (43471)

—Apply only to the Chairman (presently Sen. Warren Magnuson
(D. Wash.)) and submit a Civil Service application, a special application,
and one recommendation, available
from the Chairman's office.

Banking, Housing, and
Urban Affairs (47391)

—Full Committee and Subcommittee internships. Both go through
the full Committee staff.

Budget (40642)

—Only for the summer but with an April application deadline.

Commerce, Science, and Transportation

—Only through the Chairman presently Sen. Howard Cannon (D. Nev.)). Apply early!

Energy and Natural Resources (44971)

—Full Committee internships dispensed only through the Chairman (Sen. Henry Jackson (D. Wash.)). Subcommittee internships open through the Subcommittee Chairmen.

Environment and Public Works 46176

Foreign Relations (44651)

Government Affairs (44751)

—Internships open year round. Apply one month in advance; much earlier for the summer.

Judiciary (45225)

—Apply with a cover letter, resume, and two letters of recommendations, by May 15, Aug. 15, & Dec. 15 for the following semesters. Also, Subcommittee internships are available through the Subcommittee Chairmen.

Veterans' Affairs (49126)

—Apply through the full Committee.

Select-Small Business (45175)

Select-Aging (45364)

—Apply through member Senators.

FEDERAL SUMMER INTERN PROGRAM   *National*

ELIGIBILITY: *College juniors, seniors and graduate students*

DURATION: *Late May/early June to late August/early September*

ACADEMIC CREDIT POSSIBLE: *Yes*

REMUNERATION OR FEE: *GS-4, $193 per week, to GS-9, $326 per week*

POSITIONS OFFERED: *950*

APPLICATION DEADLINE: *Set by intern's university, but near the beginning of March.*

General Description

The Federal Summer Intern Program is the government's largest intern attraction. Over 25 agencies offer positions in everything from cartography to labor negotiation. 3,500 students apply through their schools for 900 to 1,000 internships. The pay scale begins at GS-4, around $193 per week, and works up to GS-9, $326 a week and is established on the basis of an intern's education.

Applicants must meet a variety of qualifications. They must have completed two years or 60 semester hours of college; be in the upper one-third of their undergraduate class, or the upper half of their graduate class; and plan to return to school in the fall after the internship. Sixty-three percent of the internships were in Washington, and 37% were in the field—in regional offices around the country.

The application process is a mini-bureaucracy. You can apply to these internships *only* through your college or university. Different internships are offered to different schools and it seems that only the placement office knows what is available. Therefore, make it a point to see them. They will have more details of what is offered, and be familiar with the idiosyncracies of your school's selection process. By mid-January, participating colleges and universities will know what internships they may nominate students for. By mid-March, nominations must be completed and forwarded to their respective federal agencies. Students are notified of the final selections by the second week in April.

The Inside Word

Getting accepted: The complex thing about these internships is the application process. None of the internships are open to everyone. Instead, the agency offering a spot picks two or three schools that have strong programs in the areas the agency is interested in. Each school publicizes the internship and nominates one or two of its interested students. Nominations are due the middle of March. The agency makes the final choice of an intern and sends acceptance letters out by the third week in April.

Obstructing a Federal Summer Internship are two hurdles—the school's initial screening and the agency's final selection. Your school sets its own criteria for nominating its students; find out about this from your placement counselors early. They will know the most about this phase, and about the positions being offered. In addition, the counselors may be able to tell you how students liked the internship last year.

The "real criteria" agencies used in selecting interns from the nominations centered first on scholastic ability. Next, demonstrated leadership—being a class officer or an official in some student organization—is important. After that, honors, career goals, and special interests are given the appraising eye. "Give [yourself] credit for any achievement at all. When in doubt, put it in!" one counselor recommended.

Daily life: What you actually do in the internship really depends on what agency you are with. The variety of opportunities is vast. Many promise work with "senior staff," and the assignments will always be within the intern's major.

These Federal Summer Internships are a prime opportunity to get an inside view of the division of our nation's bureaucracy involved with your major. If you can negotiate the nomination process, and get accepted as an intern, it is an exceptional way to get a feel for "the day-to-day workings of the federal government through involvement in agency operations."

Contact:

Sylvia D. Cole
Program Manager
Federal Summer Intern Program
United States Civil Service Commission
Washington, DC 20415

OTHER FEDERAL INTERNSHIP PROGRAMS

In addition to the Federal Summer Intern Program, many government agencies offer other kinds of internships. Call the personnel offices of the following agencies or any other you suspect of harboring interesting opportunities and ask for the "Intern Coordinator." The following two listings are good examples of the opportunities available.

DEPARTMENT OF HOUSING AND URBAN DEVELOPMENT
Nonremunerative Intern Program

National

ELIGIBILITY: *Undergraduate and graduate*
DURATION: *6 months*
ACADEMIC CREDIT POSSIBLE: *Yes*
REMUNERATION OR FEE: *None*
POSITIONS OFFERED: *Varies*
APPLICATION DEADLINE: *Minimum of three weeks in advance*

General Description

The Department of Housing and Urban Development (H.U.D.) offers the H.U.D. Nonremunerative Intern Program for undergraduate and graduate students. Held in the regional offices and headquarters of H.U.D., interns are promised work with senior staff in "career-study related employment." The internships can be arranged at any time but cannot last more than six months. Academic credit can be granted, but there is no financial remuneration. Two special forms—a "SF-171" and a "Signed Volunteer Work Agreement"—are required. Additionally, an essay on the applicant's "goals sought through employment" and a statement by the applicant's school relating the internship to its academic requirements are prerequisites for academically credited internships.

Contact:

Christopher Beach
H.U.D. Headquarters Intern Program Coordinator
Room 2243
451 7th Street, S.W.
Washington, DC 20410

NATIONAL BUREAU OF STANDARDS   Washington, D.C.
Academic Summer Employment Program

ELIGIBILITY: *Undergraduate juniors, seniors and graduates*
DURATION: *Summer*
ACADEMIC CREDIT POSSIBLE: *Yes*
REMUNERATION OR FEE: *GS-3, $172 per week to GS-7, $326 per week*
POSITIONS OFFERED: *Varies*
APPLICATION DEADLINE: *Applications are evaluated from mid-January to April 15*

General Description

The National Bureau of Standards has an excellent paying program, using interns as qualified assistants to fill in gaps left by vacationing employees and to pursue short-term projects. Interns must be entering their third year of college or beyond to qualify, and be majoring in a field "appropriate" to the Bureau of Standards. Applicants should be prepared to take the Student Trainee or Summer Employment exams.

Pay ranges from GS-3 for sophomores to GS-7 for some seniors and graduate students. Rolling admissions begin in mid-January and are over by April 15. All of this is outlined in more detail in the Bureau of Standards booklet *Basic Features of the N.B.S. Summer Employment Programs*.

Contact:

Summer Program Coordinator
National Bureau of Standards
Department of Commerce
Washington, DC 20234

THE ROBERT F. KENNEDY MEMORIAL   *Washington, D.C.*
YOUTH POLICY INSTITUTE ANALYST INTERNSHIPS

ELIGIBILITY: *High school and undergraduate*
DURATION: *January through May; June through*
   August; September through December
ACADEMIC CREDIT POSSIBLE: *Yes*
REMUNERATION OR FEE: *$160 per month if you are*
   from the D.C. area; $350 per month if you are not
   from the D.C. area and must live away from
   home.
POSITIONS OFFERED: *10 to 15 each semester*
APPLICATION DEADLINE: *Open*

General Description

The Youth Policy Institute of the R.F.K. Memorial monitors public policy affecting high school age students. A dozen or so interns, each sponsored by a local "youth serving" organization, gather in Washington, D.C. to individually research and present to the Institute an issue that concerns them and their sponsoring organizations. Their findings are then broadcast by the Institute's Student Press Service, "youth forums," and Institute position papers. The internships begin the first Monday of January, June, and September; and end the last week of May, August, or December.

The internships are open to high school or college students (college graduates are discouraged) involved in a youth organization. Two recommendations and a special application completed by the sponsoring youth group are required before a student may apply. Once "on board," the R.F.K. Memorial pays relatively well—$350 a month for those from outside metropolitan Washington, and $160 a month for intown residents. Interns must, however, secure their own housing. Academic credit has been granted by the program in the past but must be arranged by individual students.

The Inside Word

The R.F.K. Memorial is a small rowhouse in Georgetown bustling with ringing telephones, conferences and informal discussions for up to twelve hours a day. It also houses a national youth policy library, perhaps the best resource center of its kind in the country. Youth policy includes juvenile justice, youth unemployment, bilingual education, runaways, youth participation in the issues, and all relevant legislation or innovation affecting youth policy.

Getting accepted: The application process for the Youth Policy Internship is lengthy and bureaucratic. Applicants must first find a sponsoring organization to nominate them. The organization then submits the intern's application, resume, and two letters of recommendation. If you live or go to school near Washington, an interview at the Memorial is required.

Applicants are judged on three criteria: commitment to child welfare, interest in the area they are going to be researching, and communication skills. Those who receive internships are generally the "involved" type—interested in kids, worried about the problems kids are having, and active in helping them to set their problems right.

The R.F.K. Memorial is in the process of forming a network of youth groups and part of the intern's job is to act as a liaison between their sponsoring groups and the Institute. Before being accepted, interns must already have determined a research topic. Normally, the topic is one of particular concern to the intern and his sponsoring organization. The Memorial provides resources, expert advice, and direction. "This forms a double alliance with the organizations and the Youth Policy Institute," said one administrator, "with the intern moderating between them."

Daily life: As part of the program, interns interview government officials and experts in the area of youth policy, and attend hearings to familiarize themselves with the broad issues of public policy. One intern, describing her experiences explained, "Someone is financially supporting you to choose a topic that you are interested in and study it from a federal perspective. This entails talking to all sorts of people, reading, going to hearings, and writing a lot . . . One of the best things about this internship is that it demystified the government, policy-making, and people in general." The intern "required someone willing to be articulate (or learn how to), write, and to explore," she observed. According to another intern, the work was 70 percent interesting and 30 percent dull. "It all depends on your interests and whether you like doing paperwork and research. I discovered that I like direct-service type of work with 'real people' rather than administration."

Interns are also actively involved in establishing and expanding the Youth Policy Institute. There are many opportunities for personal input and self-motivated projects, as the organization is run by and for 'youth' and attempts to be as open and democratic as possible. Drawbacks to the program included a lack of direction and a considerable degree of wasteful and useless paperwork. Said one intern, "many people are 'reinventing the wheel.' Everyone works hard but sometimes it felt like we were chasing our tails."

Overall, the Youth Policy Institute, despite its "growing pains," offers an attractive, purposeful opportunity to be paid to observe the Federal government and its policies regarding youth problems.

Contact:

Michelle Smith
Youth Policy Institute

Robert F. Kennedy Memorial
1035 - 30th Street, N.W.
Washington, DC 20007

MOUNT HOLYOKE COLLEGE   *South Hadley, Massachusetts*
International Internship Program

ELIGIBILITY: *Undergraduate and graduate*
DURATION: *Summer, January term, or semester*
ACADEMIC CREDIT POSSIBLE: *Yes*
REMUNERATION OR FEE: *$10 application fee*
POSITIONS OFFERED: *Varies*
APPLICATION DEADLINE: *October 19 for spring and*
winter; November 26 for summer and fall

General Description

The Mount Holyoke College internship program places students interested in international affairs in United Nations agencies throughout the United States and overseas. Interns work with U. N. officials in specialized agencies, regional organizations, and private international associations.

The Mount Holyoke program, open to students from all colleges and universities, places approximately 60 interns each year. Last year, interns served in situations as diverse as the National Committee on United States-China Relations, Inc., in New York, the Scientific and Technical Committee in Brussels and the Atlantic Institute for International Affairs in Paris.

A background in international politics, and knowledge of a foreign language, where necessary, are extremely helpful when applying; an interview is generally required. Most schools will ask interns to write a paper on the experience in order to receive academic credit.

The Inside Word

One intern we spoke with was placed in the United Nations center in Geneva, Switzerland, working for the High Commission for Refugees: Counseling, Education and Resettlement Division. Her responsibilities included research (reading documents and reports) and analyzing and organizing statistical data. One of the three major projects she participated in involved assembling a file on the refugee situation in Somalia. She stressed the importance of examining all placement possibilities and exploring all options before making any final decision on assignments.

Application must be made through Mount Holyoke College. Approximately 100 applications are received annually, out of which 60 percent of the applicants are selected and placed.

Contact:

Norma O'Meara, Executive Director
International Internship Program
Mount Holyoke College
South Hadley, MA 01075

NATIONAL LEAGUE OF CITIES (NLC)   *Washington, D.C.*
Internship Program

ELIGIBILITY: *Undergraduates and graduates*
DURATION: *Semester; summer*
ACADEMIC CREDIT POSSIBLE: *Yes*
REMUNERATION OR FEE: *Varies; Paid interns receive between $3.50 and $5.00/hour*
POSITIONS OFFERED: *15*
APPLICATION DEADLINE: *March 1 for summer internship candidates*

General Description

NLC is a non-profit, urban affairs organization. It provides services to its 800 member cities by conducting research projects and representing cities legislatively in Washington. For the winter of 1980 internships were available in the following NLC departments: Crime Prevention; Criminal Justice; Fire and Disaster; Solid Waste and Urban Environmental Design. The departments which offer internships may change from year to year depending on whether the department supervisor feels interns are needed. The ability of the various departments to pay interns is determined by the grants they receive from the federal government.

Interns assist Program Directors by researching, compiling, and filing information. Interns also write summaries of urban affairs articles and answer mail. Perhaps the most interesting facet of the internship involves following the progress of legislation influencing the cities. Interns are asked to find where congressmen stand on certain issues and aid a Legislative Counsel in developing effective strategies to lobby for bills increasing funding of various housing and community developments. Interns often do research projects, with the graduate students being assigned the most challenging tasks. One graduate intern studied the effect of rail deregulation on the cities.

Admission to the program is competitive and is decided on the basis of a resume, a personal interview, and the application.

The Inside Word

The interns we spoke with were very satisfied working for NLC. The graduate students were particularly enthusiastic about their work. Undergraduates are generally paid less than graduates and are required to do some clerical work. Yet the undergraduates seemed to accept this state of affairs owing to the greater experience of the graduates and felt they were gaining valuable insight into how lobby groups operate.

As interns are selected by particular departments of the NLC, applicants are advised to design their applications to appeal to more than one of the departments.

Contact:

Mrs. Sharon R. Lucas
Personnel Assistant
The National League of Cities
1620 Eye Street, N.W.
Washington, DC 20006

ORGANIZATION OF AMERICAN STATES   *Washington, D.C.*
Student Intern Program

ELIGIBILITY: *Undergraduate and graduate*
DURATION: *Varies, but usually corresponds to academic semesters, quarters, or the summer*
ACADEMIC CREDIT POSSIBLE: *Yes*
REMUNERATION OR FEE: *None*
POSITIONS OFFERED: *30 to 45 in the summer; 15 to 25 per quarter*
APPLICATION DEADLINE: *2 months before an applicant plans to begin*

General Description

The Organization of American States is a subgroup of the United Nations, providing for the collective defense, social development, and peaceful, diplomatic settlement of conflicts among the U. S. and 20 Latin American countries. "The bulk of the O.A.S. is involved in the technical side of [development] . . . Our work is one of support. Countries come to us for technical development," explains a program administrator. To the O.A.S., "technical" includes everything that can further the economic, social, and cultural advancement of the member countries. They are headquartered in Washington, D.C., where the internship program is based.

Interns participate in research, analysis, writing, and administration, and work side-by-side with the Washington office's professional staff. In addition, for their further edification, mandatory seminars are held weekly on the inner workings of the O.A.S.

Interns must have a thorough working knowledge of two of the official languages: English, Spanish, French, and Portuguese. In addition, a background in international relations, economics, or Latin American studies is helpful. Students with a more technical background in the social sciences and hard sciences are also in demand. Only college upperclassmen and graduate students with a better than 3.0 grade point average and a strong recommendation from their academic advisor are encouraged to apply. Further, interns must find their own way to Washington and locate their own housing. The position is not salaried; although the Organization aids and encourages interns to pursue grants, stipends, or fellowships from other sources to support their stay, and academic credit is usually received for the program.

The internship periods generally correspond to academic terms, and the O.A.S. expects applications to be in two months in advance of when you wish to begin.

The Inside Word

Getting accepted: The application procedure is more or less straightforward. Aside from the dual language requirement, it involves only the usual formal application and two letters of recommendation from a professor, academic advisor, and/or employer.

Acceptance criteria vary depending upon the needs of each O.A.S. division. Applications, after an initial screening by the personnel office, are passed around the departments to determine which applicants have the most useful talents. "We are very dependent on the needs of the various departments" to determine the placement of the interns and their responsibilities." said a program director. It is the departments of the O.A.S. that dictate how many interns are accepted.

The successful applicants are those who are flexible, have a well-rounded education, and were enthusiastic about new responsibilities. "Most supervisors . . . wanted an intern who can take the ball and run with it; students who are independent, creative, resourceful, and also meticulous, since work is not always terribly exciting," confides the director.

There are 20 to 30 applicants for the 15 to 25 spots offered each semester. During the summer, 30 to 35 interns are chosen from a pool of about 70 applicants. Most are political science, military affairs, or Latin American affairs students: "a lot of people with similar backgrounds," as the personnel specialist put it. Consequently the competition for the "political" jobs in the O.A.S. is somewhat intense. The balance of the interns are "technical" students, majoring in everything from engineering to museum or library science.

"Technical" students are those who can help the O.A.S. in the economic, social, and cultural development of the member countries. The O.A.S. "would love to have more people with [training in] business, economics, agriculture, urban and rural administration, nutrition, legal law, education, etc.," said a program spokesman "the opportunities are numerous."

Daily life: According to the O.A.S. flyer, the interns tackle "a great variety of functions." Their work ranges from exciting to tedious—"I would judge the extremes about equal," one intern volunteered. One intern coordinated the O.A.S. Internship Program. Another did "informal abstracting" of information coming into the Educational Affairs Department and wrote for the O.A.S. rural journal. Interns may work on their own or with the professional staff.

All interns rated their supervisors and the working atmosphere very highly. One intern noted the "generous lunch hours, time off; [a] friendly, helpful, nice office" that encouraged the interns to improve things and initiate new ideas. The O.A.S. program was a valuable introduction to the diplomatic bureaucracies that govern international relations today, assessed one intern, "particularly among the U.S. and Latin American countries."

Contact:

Walter Gutierrez
Personnel Specialist
Staffing and Classification Unit
Office of Personnel
Organization of American States
17th St. & Constitution Ave., N.W.
Washington, DC 20006

OR

O.A.S. Student Intern Program
Recruitment and Placement Unit
Office of Personnel
Organization of American States
1735 Eye St., N.W., Rm. 1025
Washington, DC 20006

FOR MORE INFORMATION:
Organization of American States
Attn: Student Intern Program
1889 F St., N.W.
Washington, DC 20006

URBAN FELLOWS PROGRAM   *New York City*

ELIBIGILITY: *College seniors and graduate students*
DURATION: *1 school year*
ACADEMIC CREDIT POSSIBLE: *Yes*
REMUNERATION OR FEE: *$5,500*
POSITIONS OFFERED: *20*
APPLICATION DEADLINE: *February 15*

General Description

The high number of applicants, generous pay, and hefty responsibilities, make the New York City Urban Fellows Program one of the most prestigious internships in city government.

Administered by the New York City Urban Corps, interns receive important assignments in their areas of interest in New York City government. 150 to 200 college seniors and graduate students apply for 20 spots. Applications and support materials are due February 15. The program lasts all year, beginning on September 15 and concluding June 15.

To apply, one must have the academic endorsement of his/her university and be able to take a year off to allow participation. Interns receive a $5,500 stipend, their choice of paid health insurance plans, and travel expenses to New York City. In addition, most interns receive a waiver of tuition and a supplementary grant of at least $500 from their college or university.

The Inside Word

Getting accepted: If you are going to apply to the New York Urban Corps for an internship, a monster application stands in your way. The application form is steeped with essay questions. In addition, they also ask that a transcript and your school's endorsement come directly from the Dean of Students. Three letters of recommendation are also required. All of this is due, postmarked, by February 15.

Applications are pared down to 50 finalists who are flown to New York, expenses paid by the Urban Corps, for interviews. It is from this group that 20 fellows are chosen. The chosen fellows are those that "show the greatest promise of being able to contribute to the city," and would "benefit personally" from the experience.

Daily life: After being accepted, interns are subjected to another series of interviews to place them suitably within the city government apparatus. The offices of Criminal Justice, "Service Delivery," Financial Administration, and Budget Control, each absorb interns. One student conducted studies of patients' rights for the New York City Health and Hospitals Corporation, the largest health system in the United States. Later, he surveyed the corporation's malpractice suits; directing other interns in the search, interviewing city officials, computerizing the data, and finally analyzing and drafting a report on the findings.

When their terms expire, interns often remain in urban affairs. According to one fellow, "A number of my fellow Fellows got jobs in city government after their participation in the program or got related employment as a direct result of this internship."

The New York City Urban Fellows Program offers challenging and extremely responsible positions in the New York City government. "Public service work seems infinitely more rewarding than work for the sake of private gain," said one intern. "I think that I might have ceased believing in this without my experience in the Urban Fellowship Program.''

Contact:

Dominick Cucinotta
Director
The Urban Fellows Program
The New York City Urban Corps
32 Worth St.
New York, NY 10013

OTHER PLACES TO LOOK:

Business
American Assembly of Collegiate Schools of Business

Environment
Environmental Intern Program

Public Service
Atlanta Urban Corps
City Volunteer Corps of Los Angeles
Georgia Governor's Intern Program
National Consumers Affairs Internship Program
National Consumers League
Public Citizen
Resource Development Intern Program
Southern Economic Development

Health

By no means the narrow province of pre-meds and nursing students, the field of health care offers opportunities for students from a wide variety of backgrounds—from physics to graphic arts to business administration. While of course firmly tied to the business of making the sick well and keeping the healthy healthy, this field has room for medical illustrators and public relations specialists as well as physicians.

An important distinction to keep in mind is that of public versus private. Though health care in this country is administered mainly by private institutions, many public agencies have a hand in the business as well. The Department of Health, Education and Welfare (HEW); the National Institute of Health; the Mental Health Administration; plus local and county Health Departments are all responsible for researching and overseeing the way in which health care and health education are dispersed to the masses. Some programs, such as the New York City Urban Corps and Health-PAC (described in the listings), place interns in organizations geared toward research of health care systems in large urban centers. Because of increasing federal pressure for an equitable system of health care nation-wide, work in these agencies is an important and interesting option to consider.

A desire to be more directly involved with delivering health care services will send you in the direction of private hospitals, clinics, and medical centers. Opportunities are diverse, but are here divided into the general categories of administration, patient care, and research. Remember that above all, health care is a crisis-oriented business. This basic fact makes its presence felt in any sector of the field you may sample. You will find a break-neck pace, overworked staff, tight budgets, broken schedules, and demanding work. The complexity, pace and importance of most jobs in the field make professionals leery of giving any of them to novices interested in short-term work. This makes internships difficult to find—but definitely not impossible.

Administration

Organized internship programs for undergraduates in health and hospital administration are few. Most of the opportunities are ones you will have to create on your own. A background in economics, business administration, or public health will put you in a much better position to find an internship than the science student who has suddenly realized that medical school is out of reach. Health administrators are busy people—they are looking for an intern who can produce, not someone who needs constant supervision. Past hospital experience of any kind, familiarity with management systems, or the ability to show *some* knowledge of the health field is very important in landing an internship in administration.

Realize that running a hospital is basically like running any service-oriented business. Administrators spend most of their time planning for the future: building; buying equipment; procuring and managing funds; dealing with employees, patients, and non-patient patrons; and meeting government regulations. In addition to a general knowledge of the hospital working environment, business and management skills are very important, and will help you sell yourself to an employer in this field.

You will want to attack the larger hospitals first—institutions of about 200 beds and up. The larger the medical center the more complex are the administrative tasks, and the more there is for interns. Large institutions have legal and governmental obligations heaped upon them: HEW often requires hospitals to submit reports on compliance with newly legislated regulations or new standards of safety, equal opportunity employment, expenditures for grant-funded projects, etc. Preparing these reports is one area where interns can be of help.

The teaching and research hospitals tend to be the most interesting and most willing to take on interns. Their working relationship with an academic community breeds greater respect for students and the supportive role they can play in an institution. Teaching centers give the student exposure to the functional—and political—relationships between a medical center and an affiliated medical school. The larger teaching hospitals also have better facilities, and are more dynamic in terms of planning and program growth.

The medical schools themselves are another source of internships. Some state schools have grant-funded student-work programs. Though these programs mainly hire science students to work in laboratories, they sometimes offer administrative aid positions as well. In addition, many medical schools have their own out-patient clinics which are connected to a hospital but are managed and controlled by the staff and administration of the school itself. Working in these clinics will give you a relatively narrow view of the field, however. Most of the planning and policy-making regarding patient care and cost containment will be made out of sight back at the dean's office, and you will have no contact with in-patient units.

If you are not near a major hospital, clinic, or medical school—and can't travel—don't lose hope. Investigate the small hospitals and community clinics in your area. They may not have as much going on as the larger facilities, but they often have under-staffed and over-worked administrations that are eager for your help.

Another tack is to investigate local urban planning centers or public health departments. County Health Departments are engaged in cost containment studies and multi-institutional bed reduction studies. Involvement in this type of work will bring you in contact with many different facilities and give you an idea of the immense dollar volume needed to run a public health operation. It will also give you an inside look at the politics which play such a large role in the public health administration racket.

Tips on Landing a Health Administration Internship

Because most of the internship opportunities in health administration are not part of formal programs, landing an internship in this field will take some digging on your own. As we said in the chapter on "Making Your Own," the most important thing in this process is to start by doing your homework. The best way to do this is "interviewing for information." Speak with a hospital administrator if you can, or with any doctors you may know—especially if they have hospital-based practices. If your college or university has a school of hospital administration, see if you can talk to one of the deans. Find out all you can about the field. Ask the dean about an internship or temporary job opportunities for students without master's degrees. Ask doctors and administrators what administrative problems they face; find out what types of projects could be done by interns, saving the staff time and hassle.

Do some reading in your area of interest. Medical school libraries are full of journals containing information on health management problems, current health-related legislation, cost containment studies, systems research studies, openings of new hospitals and medical centers, and community outreach programs. Some particular publications you might look up are: *Hospital and Health Services Administration; Topics in Health Care Financing; Administrative Management; Nursing; Legal Aspects of Medical Practice; Legal Medical Quarterly; Medical Economics; The American Journal of Public Health; Trade Journal of the Medical Group Management Association;* and even the *Wall Street Journal*. These should get you started but there are many more.

Whenever a hospital is in a state of major transition, many new and urgent problems arise which must be taken care of while the old problems continue. Get a copy of the hospital's newsletter or annual report and find out where their troubles lie. Try to tailor your interests to these areas when contacting them and offer to help them out—as cheaply as you possibly can.

Hospital administrators are most receptive to the idea of taking on an intern if the initial inquiry comes from someone at the student's school: an advisor, an internship office, or someone connected with a health-related academic program. If you were able to talk to a dean of a school of hospital administration to find out about the field, you might now return with some specific ideas in hand and ask for his or her help in making inquiries.

If you are unable to find someone from your school to help you out, you will have to go it alone. This means firing off a salvo of cover letters and resumes to hospitals you are interested in working at. If at all possible, address your inquiries to the administrators themselves, rather than the personnel office. Personnel staffers usually have no idea what administrators' current needs are and will never ask them. Moreover, the fact that you do not have a degree in the field will most likely cause a personnel office to immediately bury your request.

In your cover letter, stress whatever previous hospital experience you have had. This is very important; it means that you have some knowledge of the type of system in which you will be working. Hospital administrators will rarely take on someone who is starting at ground zero.

Be precise as to the dates and terms of your availability. If you are able to work for free, say this right away. "I am interested in a volunteer position . . ." will always grab their attention. Then go on to express what areas are of particular interest to you. If you can, say something that relates to that particular institution. If you can get across the idea that you have some familiarity with the detailed needs of the institution, the administrator will recognize that you can make a contribution without having to be constantly supervised. Remember that money is always tight and an administrator's time is precious. If you cannot afford to work for free, your best bet is to keep quiet about pay until they express a firm interest in hiring you; then explain your dire financial situation to them.

Patient Care

Student participation in patient care is limited by legal restrictions and by the complex nature of patient care itself. Unless you have training in nursing or one of the technical or therapeutic fields, your chances of working directly with patients is small.

However, there *are* a number of programs in psychiatry and clinical psychology, where students may act as observers and participants in diagnosis and treatment of patients. Programs offered by the C.B. Wilson Center and the Devereux Foundation are two examples. In programs of this type—involving clinical contact with the patients—it helps to have had some prior clinical experience. This need not be anything extensive (this isn't as much of a "Catch-22" as it sounds), but might consist of some work in hot-line crisis intervention, drug or alcohol rehabilitation programs, the local Veterans' Administration Hospital, or some other volunteer counseling situation.

The Mental Health Administration is a government agency that may be able to place you in one of the Public Health Service hospitals or care centers. Talk to someone in the Psychology Department at your school; they may have connections that could help you get into a program. At the very least they will be able to direct you to programs in your geographic region. These programs are numerous but differ in the amount of actual counseling interns are allowed to do. Once in a program, it is up to you to guage your abilities; if you think you are capable of working with the patients, ask someone to let you do it.

New programs are springing up in arts-related psychotherapy. If you think you have some qualifications in dance therapy or music therapy, consult trade journals to locate these programs and then contact the person in charge. This is a newly developing field, and chances are that energy and fresh ideas will be welcome.

If your clinical interests are medical rather than psychiatric, you may have to settle for an observational position. This still may be worth your while—too many people go on to get a degree without having had actual clinical experience, only to discover too late that they don't really like working with patients. Even an observational position will let you know what you are in for should you go on to acquire the necessary training to handle patients directly.

One way that you can get into direct contact with patients is by working as a nurse's aide. The drawback is that most of these positions require training programs lasting from four to six weeks. Many hospitals are hesitant to train an aide who only intends to stay for the summer, so getting an aide position for the summer might require pulling some strings. The training programs expose students to some of the basic legal, philosophical, and psychological aspects of patient care. They also teach such basic skills as cardio-pulmonary resuscitation (CPR), changing dressings, taking temperatures, emptying bed pans, moving patients, and other basic support skills. The biggest asset about these positions is that they put you in close contact with the patients. Any hospital job which does this is a good one to have—except for delivering food trays and admitting patients. As a Nurse's Aid you would most likely be assigned to a particular patient unit, allowing you to observe your patients over a long period of time. You will have the chance to be around the patients a good deal, talking to them as well as doing the dirty work involved in the job.

If you cannot get into an aide program, there are other possibilities for hospital work. Departments such as Surgery, Renal Medicine, X-ray, and Physical Therapy employ "patient runners" (patient transporters) to take patients from their rooms to various departments for examinations or treatment and return them to their rooms. While this work may be a little on the dull side, it does expose you to a wide variety of departments and to the different patients they serve.

Students have been known to arrange temporary jobs as junior assistants in physical and respiratory therapy—learning and carrying out the less complicated exercises and treatments. These positions are very rare, however, and are obtained only via a close connection with the head of the department; e.g., in the case of Respiratory Therapy you might need an in with the head of the Pulmonary Medicine Department.

You can also find work through a hospital's volunteer services department. This work can be somewhat limited in scope but there *are* a few areas of service that may be of interest, especially in occupational therapy. State laws usually restrict volunteers as to the tasks they may perform and the places they may go. Typically, volunteers may not lift patients, wheel them on stretchers, carry IV's, or transport patients from intensive care or psychiatric wards. They are not allowed to enter isolation rooms, or in some states, the morgue. Occupational therapy is one department that *does* make use of quite a few volunteers. Volunteers are also assigned to run patients and provide general light nursing support. Every hospital runs things a little differently, so go in and speak with the director of volunteer services. Explain what you are after and see what they have to offer. Make sure to let them know that you would like to work as closely with patients as you possibly can.

Research

The opportunities for research internships span a broad spectrum, from clinical studies to neuroendocrinology. Organized programs can be found at private and government labs, medical schools, universities, research hospitals, and centers for the specialized study of medical and bio-ethics. Organized research programs are an excellent opportunity to do advanced work that is far more enlightening than what you see in the classroom. Many of these programs make it possible for you to engage in projects either partially or wholly of your own design. Unless you have outstanding recommendations, high grades are required for acceptance into these programs.

When looking for programs, speak to a professor who knows you and your work well. He may have colleagues in the field who are working in an area in which you are interested and qualified. As always, when looking for an internship, do some extra research and studying in your area of interest. All research programs will take you on only if there is a scientist whose interests match your own. Because most researchers' interests are highly specialized, finding out some details about a particular researcher's work will give you an edge. Asking researchers intelligent questions about their work will both flatter them and let them know that you speak the same language. If you show that you have strong basic science knowledge and laboratory skill, *and* get a particular researcher interested in you, your chances of getting an internship soar.

Read through the scientific journals to find out who is doing research in your area of interest—and where. *Science* and the *Journal of Medical Education* are two such publications. The latter contains extensive bibliographies of research reports and work currently in progress. There are many other medical and biological research journals which can be found at your science library or at a medical school library.

If you are not highly qualified academically and are bent on doing lab work, there are other alternatives. Many labs hire students as laboratory technicians. The work is generally not too complex—you may find yourself mastering a particular technique and then performing the same tasks day after day—but the exposure is worthwhile. Doing technician work now will put you on the road to more substantial research work in the future. A lab tech position will expose you to a professional laboratory situation and give you some contacts in the field. Check with hospitals, clinics, medical research labs, medical schools, and the Department of Public Health to see if an extra technician is needed. There are several government agencies which could employ you: The National Institute of Health has a summer employment program offering lab tech jobs; The Health Resources Administration; the Food and Drug Administration; and the Center for Disease Control.

One final note: The medical profession and its research affiliates are constantly in a state of flux and move at a hectic pace. Professionals in the field are extremely busy and rarely will take the time to make sure that you are learning something worthwhile. If you *do* land an internship in this field, be assertive and ask questions—this is the only way to ensure that your experience will be a fruitful one.

ALLENTOWN AND SACRED HEART HOSPITAL CENTER
Work/Study Program

Allentown, Pennsylvania

ELIGIBILITY: *Undergraduate and graduate*
DURATION: *12 weeks*
ACADEMIC CREDIT POSSIBLE: *Yes*
REMUNERATION OR FEE: *$145/week salary*
POSITIONS OFFERED: *24*
APPLICATION DEADLINE: *March 15*

General Description

The Allentown and Sacred Heart Hospital Center (ASHHC) offers internships in 13 different areas to students who are actively pursuing careers in medicine and research. Internships are offered in the nursing, dietary, engineering, laboratory, library, education, pastoral care, pharmacy, physical therapy, respirator therapy, social service, management, surgery and anesthesia divisions.

ASHHC provides an educational/clinical experience for future medical professionals in a challenging environment. Students work in one of the three Allentown Affiliated Hospitals, which have a combined 970 bed capacity. Each participating department creates a formal program which students follow over the course of the summer. Interns are able to modify their programs to their own interests in consultation with the director.

Each intern participates in a summer-long project which varies in nature depending on the department. In addition to lectures and seminars, students have Friday afternoon meetings to exchange ideas and discuss the workings of the other departments. In fact, students are encouraged to visit and follow interns in other departments when time allows. Where possible, students participate in hospital rounds and conferences.

To be accepted into a given department, a student must be studying in that area. For example, surgery applicants must be medical students, and laboratory applicants might need a completed B.S. in microbiology or some other science field. The positions available and admission requirements change from year to year.

Admission to the program is highly competitive. 250 students apply each year for the 24 positions. Each applicant must complete a work-study application form, submit a transcript of grades, and provide an essay stating goals and expectations for the program. A personal interview with the program director and the participating department head is also necessary.

The Inside Word

Getting accepted: Due to the scope and variety of programs offered, and the fact that each have different acceptance criteria, it is impossible to say exactly what one can do to assure acceptance. However, interns recommend indicating one's enthusiasm and drive in the essay and interview, and expressing realistic goals and expectations. Prepare for both by learning not only about your own department, but about the organization and operation of the entire medical center.

The only complaint about the program came from one student, who, having spent two summers at ASHHC, felt that interns were not as close as a group socially after the program was expanded from 12 to 24 participants. Other students voiced unqualified positive reactions: "A very worthwhile program—I cannot think of any area with which I was dissatisfied, nor any significant way to improve it except to expand it with more participants."

Daily life: Students found that they were quickly absorbed into the hospital routine as staff members. They were not constantly under the hovering wing of supervisors and most of the time were allowed to work independently. "You never felt like a lower employee," said one participant, "on the contrary, people always went out of their way to give you the royal treatment complete with explanations, advice and open doors, whether in your own department or visiting another."

The opportunity to observe all the departments was something interns cited as one of the program's greatest assets. "I always felt free to explore new areas of interest and free to ask questions. It is an excellent learning experience—everyone at Allentown is into teaching."

Students in the program receive the same medical benefits as employees and can purchase delicious hospital food in the cafeteria at a 25% discount. Although housing is the intern's responsibility, none of the past interns had problems finding a place to stay.

Future prospects: Participation in the program has frequently led to permanent jobs with the affiliated hospitals. Other interns were able to accelerate their masters programs as the result of receiving academic credit for their clinical experience at Allentown.

Contact:

Susan Gingrich Knapp
Office of Educational Development
Allentown and Sacred Heart Hospital Center
1200 S. Cedar Crest Blvd.
Allentown, PA 18105

AMERICAN CANCER SOCIETY
Massachusetts Division
Fuller Fellowship

Boston, Massachusetts

ELIGIBILITY: *Undergraduate juniors and seniors;*
  Massachusetts residents
DURATION: *10 weeks, summer*
ACADEMIC CREDIT POSSIBLE: *Yes*
REMUNERATION OR FEE: *$1000 stipend*
POSITIONS OFFERED: *10+*
APPLICATION DEADLINE: *January 15*

General Description

The American Cancer Society, through a grant by the Fuller Foundation, offers undergraduates who are residents of Massachusetts an opportunity to work as research assistants in basic cancer research.

Interns are assigned to one of the numerous cancer research centers in the Boston area, among them Harvard, Sidney Farber, Massachusetts General Hospital, and the Worcester Foundation. They are assigned to a member of the research staff who supervises and aids the student in his work, which usually involves assisting in an ongoing research project.

There is a written report which the student must complete within thirty days of finishing work at the laboratory in order to receive credit for his/her work.

The program accepts students from academic majors such as biology, chemistry, and physics as well as other life science fields. To apply, one must submit a completed application form, college transcript, and two or three letters of recommendation from academic or previous research contacts. The $1000 stipend is dispersed to interns in two $500 allotments: one upon beginning the program and the other upon completion.

The Inside Word

Getting accepted: The Fuller Fellowship seeks students with very high grades—generally about an A average. One thing which is unique about the Fellowship is the large percentage of interns selected from the smaller colleges and junior colleges around the state. "The foundation wishes to give gifted individuals the opportunity to be involved in advanced research which they would not ordinarily have due to lack of facilities or the name of a prestigious school behind them."

In addition to excellent grades, letters of recommendation play a very strong role in helping you get accepted. Remember, they are interested in your research ability, so get your recommendations from someone with whom you have done lab or other independent science work.

Daily life: Students were enthusiastic about the program and their experiences, calling it "an exceptional learning opportunity." They found their work interesting and very challenging as most of them had had very little previous exposure to research.

Students in general spend quite a bit of time working on their own. "I was given a set of experiments to do, and I was expected to make things work and get them done. Everyone in the lab was very helpful and friendly. If I had a question on something and my advisor was not around people would always take time to stop and help me out."

Students are responsible for writing up and analyzing their work on a regular basis. Some said that after discussing their work with their supervisor, and suggesting experiments of their own, their ideas were sometimes incorporated into the project. Students also serve as co-authors of published research papers.

Contact:

Dr. Emil Fry III M.D., Chairman of the Research Committee
American Cancer Society/Mass. Division
247 Commonwealth Avenue
Boston, MA 02116

AMERICAN VEGETARIANS INTERNSHIP   Takoma Park, Maryland

ELIGIBILITY: *Undergraduate and graduate*
DURATION: *Varies*
ACADEMIC CREDIT POSSIBLE: *Yes*
REMUNERATION OR FEE: *None*
POSITIONS OFFERED: *Open*
APPLICATION DEADLINE: *None*

General Description

American Vegetarians promotes vegetarianism as a solution to world hunger, animal suffering, and animal protein related diseases. The organization is supported by contributions as well as by the sale of T-shirts and bumper stickers. An internship with American Vegetarians will teach students ways to influence society by mass media and organizational means.

Interns are employed by the organization in a variety of capacities. Some students have been engaged in lobbying efforts, monitoring Congressional hearings and Federal agency meetings, and analyzing current legislation. Another area of work concerns media-related tasks: writing press releases, reports and summaries of meetings, acting as liaisons with food editors, and working on the organization's newsletter, "Fruitarian Notes." Others aid in organizing compus seminars on vegetarianism, and in research on the merits of vegetables.

The Inside Word

American Vegetarians has never turned away an applicant, and will take on interns for as long a time as they are willing to devote. A sincere interest in vegetarianism or its health related issues is the only requirement; interns need not be vegetarians themselves. A letter or phone call describing an interest is all that is necessary for application.

Contact:

Nellie Shriver, Co-ordinator
American Vegetarians
7202 Trescott Avenue
Box 4333
Takoma Park, MD 20012

APPALACHIAN REGIONAL HOSPITALS   *Kentucky, Virginia,*
Summer Student Employee Program   *West Virginia*

ELIGIBILITY: *Undergraduate and graduate*
DURATION: *3 months/summer or longer by arrangement*
ACADEMIC CREDIT POSSIBLE: *Yes*
REMUNERATION OR FEE: *$2.65 to $3.30/hour*
POSITIONS OFFERED: *50*
APPLICATION DEADLINE: *April 1*

General Description

The Appalachian Regional Hospitals is a non-profit health care organization designed to provide professional health care to those who cannot afford it. The system consists of ten hospitals throughout Kentucky, West Virginia, and Virginia which treat some 50,000 in-patients and 600,000 out-patients annually. The program accepts medical and pre-medical students, and students training in the allied health fields, which include nursing, x-ray technology, and physical, respiratory, and occupational therapy.

The program is designed to provide on-the-job training and experience to students either training in or recently accepted into an accredited course of study. They work a five-day, forty-hour week on the day shift, assisting the hospital staffs and learning departmental procedures.

Students spend their time observing and executing examinations, treatments, and other medical procedures. When performing procedures themselves, the students are under the guidance of a staff member who teaches, observes, and advises the students. .

A resume and a letter stating career goals and your objectives for the program are required initially. Letters of recommendation may be requested later as the selection process narrows. Salaries are determined on a sliding scale depending on the student's level of training. Some staff housing is available to students. Not every student is guaranteed living quarters, however, but the program will assist in finding low cost housing in the area.

The Inside Word

Getting accepted: The avowed purpose of the program is to aid ARH in "training and selecting future permanent employees." For this reason special preference is given to applicants residing in the Appalachian region. A commitment to the provision of rural health care is important. The ratio of applicants to positions is about two to one with a large percentage of those selected being in the nursing field.

Daily life: The program director stressed that the program was primarily a learning experience and that students were not just there to empty bed pans for three months. The program attempts to give students as much opportunity to actively participate as possible. X-ray tech students shoot films under supervision and direction. Pre-meds carry out such duties as working the emergency room, taking patient histories and vital signs, thus becoming acquainted with terminology and procedures.

Contact:

Paul Pickering, Manager
Manpower Development
Appalachian Regional Hospitals
Box 8086
Lexington, KY 40503

DEKALB MENTAL HEALTH AND MENTAL RETARDATION CENTER
Undergraduate Practicum Program

Decator, Georgia

ELIGIBILITY: *Undergraduate seniors only*
DURATION: *3 months*
ACADEMIC CREDIT POSSIBLE: *Yes*
REMUNERATION OR FEE: *None*
POSITIONS OFFERED: *8 per quarter*
APPLICATION DEADLINE: *Open*

General Description

The DeKalb program offers undergraduate seniors a chance to work in a major mental health and retardation center serving the Atlanta area. The program utilizes students in a variety of clinical and administrative capacities. A range of positions allows students to be involved both directly and on an observational basis in patient treatment and care.

The clinical work involves aiding the staff in handling clinical caseloads as counselors and therapists, working to place patients with other social services in the area, and aiding in procuring sources of financial aid. Students observe counseling, therapy and treatment sessions with staff psychiatrists and other staff personnel.

Administrative duties are designed to involve the student in the day-to-day operation of a mental health center. This work entails studies in clinical care programs, studies on consumer satisfaction in which students travel to patients at their homes to determine the effectiveness of care and treatment and the extent to which the patient is satisfied with the results. Students are often responsible for preparing presentations and reports to the advisory council and the state Mental Health Association.

The program accepts students involved in the studies of psychology, social services, special education, and other mental health related fields. The application process is on-going—applications will be screened as they are received—and requires a resume, college transcript, and letters of recommendation from academic advisors or a health-related work contact. An interview is not required.

The Inside Word

Getting accepted: Many of the students accepted have had some previous work experience in mental health care such as work in Veterans Administration Hospitals, hot-line crisis intervention centers, or in other rehabilitative, therapeutic, or mental health counseling-related work. Getting some sort of experience would be beneficial both in terms of acceptance and in what you will actually be able to do when involved in the program. Grades are an important factor, although a weak transcript might be offset by strong recommendations.

Daily life: Interns had mixed feelings concerning the amount of participation they were allowed. Some felt that they were wasting their time, sitting around quite a bit waiting for something to do. Others found their schedules full and demanding, however. Some projects are assigned, but "the thing to do is constantly ask for work and more responsibility in dealing with patients," recommended one intern. "A lot of people come down here and just sit around for three months. . . . I've needed a lot of energy to get permission to do various things, but the experience has been very rewarding and beneficial." Students who made the effort found that they were able to work with a small number of their own clients, setting up daily appointments, planning counseling and therapy sessions, visiting other areas of the center to learn about things such as psychopharmacology, and observing therapy sessions and in-service seminars with the staff.

Contact:

David Truran
Central DeKalb Mental Health and
Retardation Center
500 Winn Way
Decator, GA 30030

U.S. PUBLIC HEALTH SERVICE   *National, International*
Commissioned Officer Student
Training Program

ELIGIBILITY: *Undergraduate and graduate*
DURATION: *Varies*
ACADEMIC CREDIT POSSIBLE: *Yes*
REMUNERATION OR FEE: *Officer's salary and benefits*
POSITIONS OFFERED: *Varies*
APPLICATION DEADLINE: *Open*

General Description

The Commissioned Officer Student Training and Extern Program (COSTEP) offers students a unique opportunity to join a branch of the U.S. Selective Service as an officer—without any obligation to stay longer than four months.

COSTEP is a unit of the U.S. Public Health Service, as well as a branch of the United States Uniformed Services. The Corps is a national health force working to promote the quality and availability of health care.

The Corps is composed of officers, receiving the same pay and privileges as officers in the Army, Navy and Air Force. COSTEP officers serve throughout the U.S. as leaders in health projects, directors of health programs in underdeveloped countries, medical officers for the Coast Guard, heads of research organizations and advisors to states and local communities on health problems.

COSTEP assignments fall into three major categories: Medical and Hospital Services, Research, and Public Health Practice. COSTEP officers assigned to duty in clinical capacities are required to work in several areas, ranging from narcotics addiction and neuro-psychiatric hospitals, to hospitals and clinics maintained for Federal prisoners. Research and Public Health assignments are slightly less formidable, with the Corps offering positions at the National Institutes of Health, the National Insitute of Mental Health, the Center for Disease Control, and other Public Health Service Centers. An officer is not obligated to work for the Public Health Service after completing his professional education.

Active duty under COSTEP is not, however, creditable toward fulfillment of a student's possible obligation to the U.S. military draft.

Applicants must submit their college manuscript along with the standard application. A Medical History Report Form is also mandatory. Applications are due three months in advance of the time period preferred by the applicant (i.e., not later than October 1 for positions during the period January through April). The program also offers positions during May through August, and September through December. COSTEP applicants must all be citizens of the United States, meet the physical standards of the corps, and be under 44 years of age. Applicants must have completed one year of study in a medical, dental or veterinary school, or a minimum of two years of a professionally-accredited program in dietetic, engineering, nursing, pharmacy, therapy, sanitary science or medical record administration studies. Those enrolled in a masters or doctoral program are also eligible. A COSTEP applicant must be returning to college as a full time student, or expect to undergo PHS-approved post graduate training after each COSTEP assignment.

Once accepted, the COSTEP officers are entitled to medical care benefits, Post Exchange privileges, and are eligible to accumulate leave (vacation) at the rate of 2½ days for each consecutive month of service. A tax-free rental allowance is also provided. Pay varies according to an individual's degree or level of training, and is commensurate with corresponding military rank.

Contact:

Public Health Service–COSTEP
Commission Personnel Operations Division
OPM/D.H.E.W. Room 4-35
5600 Fishers Lane
Rockville, MD 20857

THE DEVEREUX FOUNDATION   *Devon, Pennsylvania*
CAREER HOUSE
Pre-Professional Mental Health
Counselor Traineeships

ELIGIBILITY: *Graduating college seniors and*
graduate students
DURATION: *1 year*
ACADEMIC CREDIT POSSIBLE: *Yes*
REMUNERATION OR FEE: *$316 to $409 per month*
POSITIONS OFFERED: *7*
APPLICATION DEADLINE: *Open*

General Description

Graduating college seniors and graduate students who have earned a Bachelor of Arts degree are eligible to intern at the Devereux Career House, working with and assisting post-high school youth with learning and adjustment problems. The program usually begins on June 1 and ends the following June 1.

Seven full-time positions are available at the Career House, located in suburban Philadelphia. The Career House is an innovative, co-ed residential treatment/therapeutic education facility which works with local colleges, career training schools and work placement programs in assisting youths with learning and adjustment problems.

As a Resident Advisor/Counselor, live-in trainees receive supervised training in supportive counseling and milieu therapy, crisis intervention, residential treatment, social rehabilitation techniques, and recreation therapy. Also, trainees benefit from experience in academic tutoring, basic skills improvements, and diagnostic vocational evaluations, as well as from attending clinical conferences and seminars.

Applicants with prior experience in media-related fields may be assigned to the Adjunctive Therapies Program, to work with patients in a therapeutic program of creative expression through art, photography, film-making, campus radio and TV studio operations, and newsletters.

The Inside Word

Getting accepted: As promising as the Career House Program sounds, there are a number of strings attached to acceptance. First, over 200 applications are received by the Foundation, with 7 applicants ultimately accepted. Applicants must be 21 years old, own their own fully-insured car, be able to type reports, and be planning to attend graduate school and/or enter some aspect of mental health work in the near future. Skills in the fields of psychology, sociology and education are preferred, but not mandatory.

The acceptance process is rigid, with preference going to applicants with experience in working with adolescents. Apply early, including college transcripts, a resume, and several solid letters of recommendation from school professors and past employers. Also, an interview with the Career House Director is mandatory—at the Director's invitation and at the applicant's expense. Above all, it is important to apply early, due to the limited positions available, and the large amount of applications being received.

Contact:

Dr. Henry Platt, Director
Institute of Clinical Training
The Devereux Foundation
Devon, PA 19333

THE DEVEREUX FOUNDATION *Devon, Pennsylvania*
INSTITUTE OF CLINICAL TRAINING
Mental Health Pre-Professional Externships

ELIGIBILITY: *Undergraduate and graduate*
DURATION: *10 weeks to 1 year*
ACADEMIC CREDIT POSSIBLE: *Yes*
REMUNERATION OR FEE: *Room and board possible*
POSITIONS OFFERED: *10 to 25*
APPLICATION DEADLINE: *Open*

General Description

The Mental Health Pre-Professional program at the Devereux Foundation offers students the opportunity to work with mentally and emotionally handicapped children for a January term program or a full semester Externship which can be renewed to a full 12-month training period.

Trainees are generally assigned to the Institute of Clinical Training as Pre-Professional Research/Professional Aides, assisting the staff in several "behind the scenes" activities: reviewing audio and video counseling and psychotherapy training tapes, preparing annotated tape catalogues, operating a therapy tape library, and preparing trainee newsletters and clinical training program bulletins.

Service-oriented applied research and writing may include: assisting staff in psychological, vocational and educational testing of patients participating in research projects, follow-up studies on discharged patients, comparative studies on computerized personality tests, as well as preparation of data for research. Trainees may also be invited to audit clinical and educational seminars.

Although the Devereux Foundation may provide limited funding for the trainee's room and board, students are expected to assume their own travel and living expenses during the Externship. On the brighter side, the trainee stands to make up to $350 a month at ICT—tax free.

There is no application deadline, but it is advisable to submit applications well in advance of the time you will be available to start. In addition to the completed application, college transcripts, letters of recommendation, a resume and a few writing samples are required. An interview with one of the program directors is mandatory, with travel expenses paid by the applicant. There are 10 to 25 positions open in the Externship program. Although the application states that the program is open to undergraduates and graduate students over the age of 21, exceptions can be made for "exceptional" applicants. Skills in psychology, communication studies, recreation or teaching are acceptable background. Arrangements for college credit must be made by the Extern applicant. Applicants should be able to type their own reports, and have some clerical experience, as well as experience in working with adolescents. More importantly, the applicant must own his or her own fully-insured car.

Contact:

Dr. Henry Platt, Director
Institute of Clinical Training
The Devereux Foundation
Devon, PA 19333

THE EPILEPSY FOUNDATION OF AMERICA *Washington, D.C.*
Student Intern Program

ELIGIBILITY: *Junior through graduate*
DURATION: *10 weeks to one year*
ACADEMIC CREDIT POSSIBLE: *Yes*
REMUNERATION OR FEE: *None to $100/month salary*
POSITIONS OFFERED: *10*
APPLICATION DEADLINE: *Varies*

General Description

The Epilepsy Foundation of America offers internships to students studying in a variety of fields. Interns act as regular staff members playing a supportive and integral role during their stay at the Foundation. Interns learn through their daily work and by explanation and discussion with staff members. They also attend board conferences and applicable seminars given by the Foundation and in the Washington area by various health related organizations.

Some interns work in the area of media and public education and are involved in gathering information and communicating with the public. This entails writing and editing a newsletter and various pamphlets published by the organization and distributed nationally.

Interns also work in departments such as government relations, client advocacy, and business and accounting. The specific activities depend somewhat on the types of projects the foundation is currently undertaking.

The Foundation is dedicated to teaching its interns and making their involvement a practical learning experience. A year's stay is considered ideal for learning purposes but students are accepted for shorter durations such as a semester or summer. Participants have come from backgrounds in political science, pre-law, communication studies, journalism, sociology, special education, business, social services, law and health administration.

Only about three of the ten positions are salary earning, with the other ten either being non-remunerative or work/study funded. To apply, the student must submit a resume and a letter stating goals and interests. An interview is not mandatory but may be requested.

The Inside Word

Getting accepted: In the past, most of the Foundation's students have come from schools with co-op study programs, although the organization gives no preference to any particular school affiliation; its main concern is the intern's willingness to learn and receive practical experience, as well as sincere interest in the activities of the Foundation.

Daily life: The program director was very supportive of the interns and their work with the Epilepsy Foundation. "We are firmly dedicated to teaching the students something. They, in turn, tend to bring a lot of fresh ideas and energy to us helping us to operate in a more effective manner."

Past interns offered their praise at being able to work independently and having a great deal of personal input in their work. "I really felt as if I were doing something worthwhile there. They gave me a lot of responsibility and set me to work, but were always ready to explain things when I hit a snag or was just curious about something."

One past intern is now in hospital administration. She was involved in gathering information about recently enacted legislation providing mainstreamed education for handicapped children, and personally wrote a 15 page pamphlet which was distributed nation-wide. Other interns, who were involved in government relations, spoke with government officials about legislation to aid and protect the rights of the handicapped, and to increase government involvement in public education.

In order to get the maximum return on an internship at the Foundation, try to make your stay longer than a summer. The director cited that many people are just getting into their work and getting to feel comfortable in their jobs after those few months, and wish they could have stayed longer. Being able to work well on your own is important, as interns are frequently given responsibility for significant projects.

The program is an excellent opportunity to become adept at the ways and workings of D.C.. Foundation interns develop a feel for actual government attitudes and policies toward health care and the methods of effective public education.

Contact:

Janet Levy
Student Intern Director
Epilepsy Foundation of America
1828 L Street, N.W.
Washington, DC 20036

THE HASTINGS CENTER INSTITUTE OF SOCIETY, ETHICS AND LIFE SCIENCES
Internships in the Ethical Issues of Biology and Medicine

Hastings-On-Hudson, New York

ELIGIBILITY: *Undergraduate and graduate*
DURATION: *1 to 3 months*
ACADEMIC CREDIT POSSIBLE: *Yes*
REMUNERATION OR FEE: *Some expenses*
POSITIONS OFFERED: *Varies*
APPLICATION DEADLINE: *January Internship, November 1; Summer Internship, April 15; General Internship, 2 months before proposed period for internship*

General Description

The Institute is a nonprofit research and teaching organization founded for sustained, professional investigation of the social and ethical impacts of biological research. Students pursue independent study in their areas of interest.

Students must submit a proposal for a specific research project to be completed during the internship. Areas of research include medical ethics, health policy, behavior and population control, death and dying, and the use of genetic knowledge in medicine and society. Students must be able to work independently, particularly during the summer months when many staff members are on vacation. The program is not tutorial, although students' work is supervised on a one-to-one basis by resident staff members knowledgeable in the specific field involved. Students are also welcome to attend any workshops, conferences or discussions held during their stay at the center.

The program is open to students actively pursuing a career in law or medicine and interested in doing serious, independent research in biomedical ethics. Applicants must select a project and include the proposal in their applications. This is the most important part of the application process, and should be well organized, demonstrating some familiarity with the topic at hand.

In addition to the proposal, applicant candidates must submit a brief outline of educational direction and career goals, a record of their work experience, a brief essay on their understanding of some of the philosophical or ethical issues surrounding their project area, a writing sample, college transcripts, and recommendations. Very little financial aid is available but is occasionally given to outstanding applicants. The Institute can, however, assist all students in arranging inexpensive housing.

The Inside Word

Getting accepted: The research proposal is the key to acceptance. Administrators state that the project should also be of interest to the staff. Past participants suggest consulting someone with background in the field for help, and in finding articles and information on the subject. Make your proposals very detailed; show that you have put a considerable amount of thought into the topic. Make up reading lists and outlines of the path you plan to follow in research as part of the proposal. Writing ability is important, as is the degree of one's commitment toward the work. Observed one intern, "They all have, and try to instill in you, a very strong missionary sense about the work."

Daily life: Although the admissions requirements are rigorous, the atmosphere is very relaxed at the Institute, "It was more like being invited to someone's home. After arriving there I felt that they were more interested in someone who was a pleasant person to be acquainted with than a super-intellect." Another advantage to working at the Institute is that you meet and rub elbows with some of the leaders in the medical research field.

Students may, to a large degree, determine their own work schedules. Program administrators "foster an unpressured atmosphere" said one intern. His internship was "good training in making good use of my time. It taught me to direct my own activities."

A strong interest and commitment to the work is essential for prospective interns, as everyone at the Institute is highly dedicated to the work. Going into this program with the intent of learning and developing ideas through discussion and practical training is of paramount importance.

Contact:

Tabitha M. Powledge, Intern Director
Institute of Society, Ethics and The
Life Sciences
360 Broadway
Hastings-On-Hudson, New York

HEALTH POLICY ADVISORY CENTER
Health-PAC Internships Program

New York, New York

ELIGIBILITY: *Junior through graduate*
DURATION: *10 to 12 weeks, summer*
ACADEMIC CREDIT POSSIBLE: *Yes*
REMUNERATION OR FEE: *None*
POSITIONS OFFERED: *3 to 12*
APPLICATION DEADLINE: *None*

General Description

The Health Policy Advisory Center (Health-PAC) offers the opportunity to work in an investigative capacity in the area of health systems research. The organization takes a progressive stance on issues in public health, occupational health and safety, health care policy, and, in general, the planning and delivery of health care in the U.S. Health-PAC utilizes its interns, editorial board of journalists, M.D.'s, R.N.'s, health planners and administrators, and occupational health and safety officials to research and publish reports of findings in the Health-PAC Newsletter and the Health PAC Bulletin. These publications are distributed to nurses, physicians, hospital administrators, and public officials throughout the United States and Japan.

Duties of the intern revolve chiefly around gathering and analyzing data and information for on-going research being conducted by the editorial board. Interns meet regularly with the editorial board in seminars to discuss significant issues in the field. The editorial board also coaches and advises the interns on investigative interview techniques and other methods of gathering and analyzing information.

Students obtain their information through reading and interviewing industrial and public health and safety representatives, as well as doctors, nurses, administrators, and patients.

A resume and cover letter stating goals and areas of interest are required when applying, as is an interview upon request. Students work on a volunteer basis, although in the past, work study funding has been arranged through the students' own institutions.

The Inside Word

Getting accepted: The ratio of applicants to positions is about seven to one, so apply early. There is no need to be overly specific in presenting your interests. In fact, the program director indicated that being extremely specific about one area of interest could be limiting and stunt your chances for acceptance. "Health-PAC is looking for change-oriented individuals." Communicating this, as well as the extent of your knowledge and experience with the concerns of Health-PAC, is sufficient. Experience in journalism, economics, public health policy and planning, is also desirable.

Daily life: Students were impressed by the fact that in a job where there is so much independent work involved, that "the staff was so helpful and enjoyable to work with on the whole. They were always willing to discuss your ideas and explain where the studies were leading."

Interns found that a great deal of time was spent out in the field conducting interviews and gathering data. The remaining time went into evaluating the information which had been collected. Interns concluded that while the analytic work became rather tedious after a while, it did add greatly to their understanding and direct input into the project on which they were working. The constant interviewing along with the coaching of the editorial board led to development of a "high level of interpersonal diplomatic skill"; essential when one considers the politics involved in all health care institutions and systems.

Students reported that the staff as a whole was very out-going and easy to work with. The interns themselves "became very good friends and spent a lot of time together when not on the job."

The most advantageous aspect of this program is the thorough exposure it offers to problems and challenges faced by health care officials. Said one intern, "someone who is persistent, observant, and hard-working, can learn an incredible amount."

Contact:

Marilyn Norinski, Director
Health-PAC Internship Program
17 Murray Street
New York, NY 10007

THE JACKSON LABORATORY   Bar Harbor, Maine
Summer Program for College,
Graduate, and Medical Students

ELIGIBILITY: *Undergraduate and graduate*
DURATION: *8 weeks*
ACADEMIC CREDIT POSSIBLE: *Yes*
REMUNERATION OR FEE: *$900 stipend less $550 room and board for undergraduates; $1000 stipend for graduates*
POSITIONS OFFERED: *10 to 15*
APPLICATION DEADLINE: *Early March*

General Description

The Jackson Laboratory, a private institution for research in mammalian genetics, works with genetically-defined mice and rabbits in problem-oriented research. Areas of research range from cytogenetics and immunology to psychobiology and physiology. Summer interns at Jackson work independently on original research of their own design within the scope of their sponsors' on-going programs. The program is open to students currently enrolled in undergraduate, graduate, medical, or veterinary school.

Interns are involved in all aspects of a research project, beginning with design and culminating in a written and oral report of analyzed results. Every intern is assigned to a staff scientist working in his/her particular area of interest. This sponsor provides laboratory space, equipment, animals, and research supervision and guidance. Interns spend the first few weeks working with their sponsors, becoming familiar with the laboratory, and preparing a research proposal which is required no later than the end of the third week of the program.

The amount of independent and supervised work each participant is assigned depends upon an intern's level of experience and expertise. Interns spend most days involved in laboratory and reference work, supplemented with demonstrations, conferences, lectures, and weekly discussion group meetings.

Admission to the Jackson program is quite competitive, with 175 applicants for the 10 to 15 available positions. Applications are not available after the third week in February, and must be received along with evaluations from two science professors, and complete college transcripts no later than the first week in March. All participants in the summer program (unless married) are required to live at Highseas, a 32 room Georgian home located one mile from the laboratory.

The Inside Word

Getting accepted: There is an essay required as part of the application in which you are asked to describe your research interests. Select an area which is compatible with your interests, and indicate your desire to work in that particular field. It may be helpful to study research reports published by the lab staff in "Science" magazine or other publications to gain a more thorough understanding of the "specifics" of their work. This section of the application is especially important to those whose grades are somewhat weak.

Daily life: Jackson Labs boasts a 50-year history in training scientists and students, and its reputation as a prestigious teaching-research institute is well deserved. "For research experience the place cannot be equaled. Most of us found quite a bit more than we had expected." The program is highly praised by both interns and administrators as a rigorous and enjoyable learning experience.

Time commitments vary greatly from student to student, "from almost nil to almost twenty hours a day" depending on personal motivation and the type of research being done. Some students who were less motivated developed a strong penchant for movie-going after tiring of the Acadia National Forest's scenic splendor. Another complaint about life at Jackson was that of residing at Highseas, where there was little privacy and no overnight visitation privileges.

Although some did not find life in the "wilderness" ideal, all agreed that it was a "phenomenal" experience and that the contacts made and the knowledge gained were invaluable.

Contact:

Training Office
The Jackson Laboratory
Bar Harbor, ME 04609

MCLEAN HOSPITAL
Volunteer Program

Belmont, Massachusetts

ELIGIBILITY: *Undergraduate juniors and seniors*
DURATION: *10 weeks*
ACADEMIC CREDIT POSSIBLE: *Yes*
REMUNERATION OR FEE: *None*
POSITIONS OFFERED: *200 (about 120 at a time)*
APPLICATION DEADLINE: *Open*

General Description

The McLean Hospital is a mental health treatment center affiliated with Harvard Medical School, which provides service of both an in-patient and out-patient nature. McLean accepts student volunteers for clinical work and laboratory research.

Students interested in clinical psychology are involved in psychiatric aid work, assisting the nursing staff under the supervision of a staff member in their assigned area. Volunteers are allowed to assume some counseling and therapy work, depending on the amount of their previous experience. The hospital operates a fully accredited high school for students with learning and adjustment disabilities in which interns also participate.

Students interested in research work in on-going projects in clinical and laboratory research. Clinical research involves chart and data survey and observational work. Laboratory research is in the areas of psychobiology and neurobiology, where students are employed as research assistants. There is no formal training program—the experience is one of on-going learning through experience, observation, and explanation.

The program's beginning and ending dates are somewhat flexible, but McLean does ask that the student make a minimum 2½ month commitment for about 20 to 30 hours a week. To be considered for acceptance, interns must submit two to three letters of recommendation and a completed application form obtainable from the hospital's volunteer office. Students are accepted from degree programs such as psychology, social services, special education, biology, chemistry, biochemistry, neurobiology, and applicable life sciences.

The Inside Word

Getting accepted: Admission to this program is not highly competitive although the hospital's name is well known and respected. Only about twenty applicants are turned down yearly. Most students come from good schools and have a solid B average or better.

For clinical work, the program requires special skills in interpersonal communications. Previous counseling experience is the best way to display this. For the research areas, especially in the laboratory, the best bet is to rely on strong recommendations from your college lab instructors.

Daily life: The major problem students found in the clinical areas was in not having much personal involvement in the treatment process. One student spent most of her time simply observing after having a good bit of experience in counseling work prior to coming to McLean. There is a large competent staff at McLean, which led some interns to feel that they were given a very moderate amount of attention. "The place appeared to be overcrowded with professionals—they all seemed very rushed and it was hard to get questions answered. I felt sort of unneeded there about 50% of the time."

Students learned a great deal through observation, but thought that their time at McLean could have been better utilized by the hospital. Said one intern, "The experience was beneficial in terms of learning about how to conduct yourself with mental patients, especially the adolescents who were extremely unpredictable and physically intimidating. I learned about presence and its importance in dealing with patients and how to interact with children in a more relaxed and effective manner."

Contact:

Anne K. Dunn, Director of Volunteers
McLean Hospital
Belmont, MA 02178

THE PENNSYLVANIA STATE UNIVERSITY COLLEGE OF MEDICINE
Pre-Medical Student Internship

Hershey, Pennsylvania

ELIGIBILITY: *Undergraduate juniors and seniors*
DURATION: *3 weeks during January*
ACADEMIC CREDIT POSSIBLE: *Yes*
REMUNERATION OR FEE: *None*
POSITIONS OFFERED: *2 to 4*
APPLICATION DEADLINE: *Open*

General Description

The Pre-Med Student Internship is held at The Milton S. Hershey Medical Center and Pennsylvania State University College of Medicine. It is designed to give students a glimpse of the clinical functions of a medical center as well as its functions in medical education and research.

The internship is a crash course in medicine, where interns are set upon a tight daily schedule for their three-week stay, exposing them to almost every aspect of medicine. The program director contacts students before the beginning of the program to determine their specific interests, and attempts to somewhat tailor schedules to what individuals interns would like to see and do.

Students attend class with the Penn med-students and, in fact, may attend any classes they choose in addition to those they have scheduled. They attend classes including anatomy, pathology, family medicine, animal surgery, and behavioral science, and attend lectures on a variety of subjects, delivered both to the students and to the general hospital staff. The program attempts to expose students to current research in the medical field in various areas (the epidemiology of yellow fever, sleep disorders, etc). Lectures include topics such as "Controversies in Medicine", Images of Aging", and "Red Eye Differential Diagnosis". Interns observe the different departments with physicians and med students on rounds and examinations to learn about clinical procedure.

Admission to the program is extremely competitive and selective. Two letters of recommendation and a complete application form are required.

The Inside Word

Getting accepted: Admission to this program is extremely competitive; unless everything you do is excellent and you have an A average, don't bother applying. The number of candidates is kept small due to the difficult and time-consuming process of devising elaborate schedules for interns within the med-school environment, while giving the individuals' desires and interests close attention. All of the past interns have come from prestigious women's colleges. When contacted in August, the program director stated that several applications had already been received, so early application is a must to allow time to be seriously considered.

Daily life: Interns who took part in the three week session had only the highest praise and enthusiasm for their experience: "It was an excellent learning opportunity. Extremely intensive—but you could see anything you were interested in." Interns suggested regular daily discussion among one another to go over what they had done or seen during the day in class, on rounds, or during lectures. "This was definitely an aid in retaining and developing a more thorough understanding of the areas which I had covered that day, and some of the different areas the others had seen. The exchange of ideas and knowledge was very helpful."

This program offers an extremely rare opportunity for undergrads.

Not only does it give a student a chance to observe diagnostic procedure (without being a patient), but also the opportunity to experience the intensive and highly accelerated realm of the medical school classroom.

Contact:

Mrs. Gaye W. Sheffler
Director, Office of Student Affairs
The Pennsylvania State University
College of Medicine
Hershey, PA 17033

MICHAEL REESE HOSPITAL AND MEDICAL CENTER
Chicago, Illinois

Summer Student Research Training Fellowship

ELIGIBILITY: *Undergraduate and graduate*
DURATION: *10 weeks*
ACADEMIC CREDIT POSSIBLE: *Yes*
REMUNERATION OR FEE: *$1000 tax free stipend*
POSITIONS OFFERED: *20*
APPLICATION DEADLINE: *January 18*

General Description

Twenty of the approximately 85 applicants to the program at the Michael Reese Hospital are selected to work with a research staff supervisor on research projects of both on-going and short term natures. Projects are related to the hemotology, oncology, internal medicine, and endocrinology departments. Summer fellows are integrated into the research work, and assist in analyzing results. Projects are designed to be completed in ten weeks time so that the fellows may participate in the entire research process.

Students in the laboratory areas learn and work with new experimental techniques and equipment. Fellows are urged to attend lectures given by both visiting guests and staff members at Michael Reese. Weekly luncheon meetings allow students to meet and exchange ideas, information, and impressions of their work.

The program accepts students from many areas of scientific study: chemistry, biochemistry, biophysics, biology, nuerobiology, psychology, etc., The only requirement is a strong interest in the areas of academic medicine, biomedical research, or psychiatry, and the desire to continue in either clinical medicine or medical research. Two letters of recommendation from teachers and a completed application form are required.

The Inside Word

Getting accepted: The application process is not particularly involved. There is a one-page application which requests the usual information, including your academic scientific experience, and a brief essay describing interests and personal goals.

Fellows and the director speak highly of the program, citing instances of fellows returning to MR for a second summer of research. Fellows thoroughly enjoyed the opportunity to learn and apply their knowledge in areas "there isn't the most remote possibility of seeing in college. The experience was far superior in terms of education and motivation to anything in school. Sometimes in studying sciences you find certain areas dry and uninteresting. This program can really pull things together and show you how it all applies."

Fellows found their research interesting and rewarding; consisting of either clinical work, involving computer work, and observation on patient rounds, laboratory work, or a combination. Reflected one fellow, "The research staff was helpful and also interested in my ideas. They were always asking if I had either questions or suggestions. If I had suggestions they were discussed seriously. If I had a problem, I could always count on a patient explanation. You felt like they really enjoyed having students around."

The other aspect of the program involves hospital tours to various departments, lectures, and discussion meetings. The program director emphasizes the importance of this element of the program as a means for students to be exposed to Michael Reese's total operation.

Contact:

Clara Gartner
Director for Research/Research Administration
Michael Reese Hospital and
Medical Center
29th St. and Ellis Ave.
Chicago, IL 60616

SYRACUSE UNIVERSITY   *Syracuse, New York*
INSTITUTE FOR SENSORY RESEARCH
Summer Jobs in Neuroscience

ELIGIBILITY: *Undergraduate*
DURATION: *8 to 12 weeks*
ACADEMIC CREDIT POSSIBLE: *Yes*
REMUNERATION OR FEE: *$135/week stipend*
POSITIONS OFFERED: *5*
APPLICATION DEADLINE: *March 15*

General Description

The Institute for Sensory Research (ISR) is a major center for "state of the art" sensory and brain research. A limited number of highly qualified college students studying life sciences or engineering are chosen to participate in on-going research projects in the areas of: sensory anatomy, bio-simulation, psychophysics, and auditory and visual physiology.

The program is offered each year during the summer to offer laboratory research opportunities to students in a relatively new and complex area of research. Interns work with and are supervised by senior faculty. Training and education proceed throughout the summer in lieu of a formal training program with an emphasis on learning the methodology of brain research and the advanced techniques employed in experimentation.

Students are required to submit a college transcript, a letter stating goals and interests, and two recommendations, one of which must come from their major department. While in attendance, students are responsible for their own transportation, meals and housing. Most students find that living in the University dormitories is the best bet due to the short duration of their stay.

The Inside Word

Getting accepted: Past interns tend to be high-powered science students with a strong interest and knowledge in the field. Quite a few students also have previous experience in research and advanced technique of some sort. One of the purposes of the program is to attract students to ISR's Ph.D. program. For this reason, some preference is given to students who have just completed their junior year of college. Recent graduates, who have not been accepted to or enrolled in a graduate program, are also eligible.

Daily life: Students work full time in the lab, located in the college of engineering. Interns said that they enjoyed a close social and working relationship with the rest of the staff, and a relaxed, on-the-job atmosphere. The ratio of senior staff to students is about one to one, "giving one ample opportunity to pick the brains of some of the field's most knowledgeable individuals," reports one intern.

Even though the job keeps a student at the labs for about forty hours a week, some found themselves engaging in survey studies of their own as the facility and its library were available day and night. "There is always a good deal of informal discussion—the staff was more than willing to discuss questions or ideas and direct students in their interests to new sources of information."

New laboratory techniques (such as micro-surgery) and methodology were among the areas examined. One student found that the experience had opened doors for him to do complex independent work at his home institution.

"The work at ISR is challenging and exciting. The only dull work I can remember doing was in the first few weeks when equipment was being set up and tested." The hard work students put into their jobs is not without tangible reward. Of course, there is the money—but there is also the occasional co-authorship and mention on published papers.

Contact:

Dr. Earl Klutsky
Institute for Sensory Research
Syracuse University
Syracuse, NY 13210

WESTERN PSYCHIATRIC INSTITUTE AND CLINIC
UNIVERSITY OF PITTSBURGH SCHOOL OF MEDICINE
Mellon Summer Research Program in Psychiatry

Pittsburgh, Pennsylvania

ELIGIBILITY: *Undergraduate*
DURATION: *8 weeks in summer*
ACADEMIC CREDIT POSSIBLE: *Yes*
REMUNERATION OR FEE: *$900 stipend; travel expenses to and from site of internship*
POSITIONS OFFERED: *6 to 8*
APPLICATION DEADLINE: *March 15*

General Description

Funding by the Mellon Foundation allows undergraduates to engage in eight weeks of research as research associates at the Western Psychiatric Institute and Clinic, one of the specialty hospitals of the University Health Center of Pittsburgh. Interns are involved in psychiatric research of both a clinical and laboratory nature.

Interns work with a preceptor, a member of the research staff, who is either an M.D. or a Ph.D. The individual's preceptor contacts him/her before the beginning of the program to determine what the intern will do. Students have in the past engaged in research in the areas of psychobiology, neuroendocrinology, sleep, population genetics, neurobiology, neurochemistry, psychopharmacology, and neural control of sexual behavior.

The research project is only part of the program, however. There are about 20 seminars given by various members of the staff and visitors; interns are encouraged to take advantage of these offerings to learn about other areas of research being discussed. Interns are also invited to go with M.D.s on rounds and on call in the emergency room, to attend conferences, and to shadow the med-students in their activities.

Applicants must submit college transcripts, two letters of recommendation from academic contacts, and a statement of goals, interests and objectives for the program. Students are accepted from a variety of science fields, although an interest in academic medicine and continuing research in the field is preferable.

The Inside Word

Getting accepted: For the six to eight positions available each year 60 people apply, making admission quite competitive. Most participants come from schools such as the University of Chicago, Yale, St. Louis University, Harvard, Princeton, etc.—all schools with fine science departments and programs.

"The students we accept are extremely bright and advanced in their field." There is no need to be particularly specific as to your areas of interest, or to deliver a detailed research plan along with your goals and objectives. The main concern is an interest in either clinical or laboratory research. Be specific enough so that they are able to place you with someone working in a closely related area. Competency is judged mainly by your grades and recommendations.

Daily life: Both students and program administrators assessed the program as an exceptional learning experience. Said one of the program's administrators: "This really is a tremendous educational facility—we attempt to open up the whole place to the interns and give them run of the house." "After having been involved in the program I highly recommend it," said an intern, "the opportunities for learning are countless."

The amount of personal control the intern has over his/her research project is somewhat dependent on the individual he/she is working with. One student working in sleep disorders was able to work on a project almost entirely of his own design having discussed and worked out the finer points with his preceptor. "It depends on the person you are working with. My preceptor did not have a specific research grant at the time and my ideas greatly interested him, so we worked them out. I think interns who worked with people on grants probably had a little less input into designing the research they were doing."

Interns enjoyed going into the wards and observing rounds and treatment. "There were some students there who were just not interested in the clinical aspects of psychiatry and psychiatric research. No one forced them to get involved in this, but most found it interesting and beneficial to their learning experience while at the hospital. It's good to expose yourself to as much as you can while you're there." An administrator of the program commented, "Some students spend 16 hours a day here; staying on in the evenings for more rounds or emergency room. The hardest thing to do with the interns is to get them to go home and rest."

The staff was out-going, friendly and very interested in teaching and working with the interns, according to participants. One intern thought that everyone seemed eager to be assigned an intern. This observation was shared by one of the administrators, who cited funding limitations, not lack of staff interest, as the reason for the small number of positions.

One intern suggested that applicants check what type of living arrangements have been made on your behalf. "It's a good idea to check on that before arriving. When we got there they had us living in a Frat. It was horrible! After some complaining they arranged to put us in a professor's house, which was great."

Contact:

David J. Kupfer M.D., Director of Research
Western Psychiatric Institute and Clinic
3811 O'Hara Street
Pittsburgh, PA 15261

C. B. WILSON CENTER
Undergraduate Intern Program
Faribault, Minnesota

ELIGIBILITY: *Undergraduate and graduate (minimum 20 years old)*
DURATION: *6 months*
ACADEMIC CREDIT POSSIBLE: *Yes*
REMUNERATION OR FEE: *$50/month salary for first three months, $100/month last three months, room and board*
POSITIONS OFFERED: *16/year*
APPLICATION DEADLINE: *Open*

General Description

The program offers students interested in careers in clinical psychology a chance to be directly involved in the treatment and progress of adolescents with severe learning and social adjustment disorders.

The C. B. Wilson Center works with students between the ages of 14 and 23 years old. Interns live in the dormitories with the students and are responsible for ten of them. Interns help get them to class and aid them in their studies. Interns also plan recreational and social activities to guide students in their development while acting as role models for the disturbed youths.

Interns are supervised by the unit supervisors and the professional clinical staff. Interns meet with the staff on a daily basis for chart review and discussion of the student/patient outside of the clinical environment. The staff and interns exchange information and suggestions on planning future treatment and extraclinical activities, and act as both participants and observers in the scheduled therapy sessions of their students.

Interns receive one day off each week and an occasional weekend, as well as five holidays during their six month stay at the Center. The program accepts students from areas of study such as Psychology, Medicine, Education, Social Services, and Recreational Therapy. The applicant must be at least 20 years of age when beginning the program. Prospective interns must submit a college transcript, 2-3 letters of recommendation, and a completed application form. An interview is mandatory.

The Inside Word

Getting accepted: Only 20% of all applicants are accepted to the program, so it is advisable to apply well in advance. More important than grades are the letters of recommendation. Program administrators are most interested in how you will interact with your counselees. People with well-developed interpersonal communication skills are sought—a quality that is evaluated during the interview.

Daily life: Interns generally applauded the program and the amount of direct input it gave them into the therapeutic process. They found it "an excellent and superior learning opportunity, compared to the classroom". According to a past intern, "There is so much a person can learn there. It gave me a great deal of insight into working with psychiatric patients and to the field of clinical psychology in general. The program is particularly unique because it gives you the rare opportunity to work with and observe the people you are caring for (patients) both in and out of the clinical setting."

Interns can expect to face many stressful situations working in a program of this sort. Living and working with the students involves being available 24 hours a day. "Crisis intervention is almost a daily affair," recalled one participant. Although the interns are almost always working with a grad student or a psychotherapist, the patients need constant help. "You are working with extremely sick individuals there. They are border-line schizophrenics and psychotics, neurotics, and other severely affected individuals—some of the wildest teenagers around," warned an intern. "Expect a good deal of stress and weird hours," she added, "but I wouldn't trade the experience for the world."

There were reports that some interns had not weathered the stress particularly well, and had left the Center rather bitter about their experience. One intern, who spoke favorably of the program, commented it would be advisable to participate in the program only after completing your senior year of college. "I was 21 when I was in the program and that may even be a little young. It would be best to take part in the program after graduation, because after so much of "real life" it seems sort of fruitless to go back to the womb—that nice tidy world of text books."

This program is an excellent opportunity to get some very solid experience in the field and learn an incredible amount. However, you must be prepared for an intense and stressful experience in which you are on call all of the time.

Contact:

Nancy Soth, Coordinator of Undergraduate Internship
C. B. Wilson Center
Box #917
Faribault, MN 55021

WORCESTER FOUNDATION FOR EXPERIMENTAL BIOLOGY
Shrewsbury, Massachusetts
Summer Training Program

ELIGIBILITY: *Undergraduate and graduate*
DURATION: *10 weeks*
ACADEMIC CREDIT POSSIBLE: *Yes*
REMUNERATION OR FEE: *$110/week stipend*
POSITIONS OFFERED: *12*
APPLICATION DEADLINE: *March 15*

General Description

Life Science students are involved primarily in on-going biomedical research in the areas of cell biology, neurology, and endocrinology. Interns have frequently designed their own research projects in these areas, in cooperation with a staff researcher. Interns are employed in the capacity of junior assistants, not simply as lab technicians. There is no "formal" training program to the internship—the experience is designed to instruct by involvement and observation, with training and explanation given as needed. There are occasional seminars and demonstrations within the labs, and frequent discussions on methodology, and technique to enhance understanding of the research and its more complex principles.

Twelve students who have completed their sophomore year of college are selected from approximately 100 applicants to participate in the program which runs from mid-June to mid-August. A resume, college transcript, letters of recommendation, and an application are required.

The Inside Word

Equal consideration is given to all applicants, with interns' goals and areas of interest often the determining factor in admission, so state your objectives specifically. Grades are not unimportant; most students accepted into the program have B+ averages.

The program provides an interesting opportunity to gain research experience of a professional nature while still an undergraduate. This has served as a stepping-stone to graduate school for past interns, particularly those whose interest in medical school is secondary to a career in medical research.

Contact:

Personnel Office
Worcester Foundation for Experimental Biology
222 Maple Avenue
Shrewsbury, MA 01545

OTHER PLACES TO LOOK:

Public Service
Atlanta Urban Corps
Consumer Affairs Department, Giant Food
Mental Health Law Project
National Organization for the Reform of Marijuana Laws (NORML)
Public Citizen

Sciences
Argonne National Laboratory
Brookhaven National Laboratory

Journalism and Mass Media

After Woodward and Bernstein left Washington, D.C. for Hollywood, a host of young writers readied typewriters, rolled up sleeves, and attempted to try a hand at reporting. Consequently, there are few fields in which the competition for internships is as fierce as in newspaper and magazine journalism. As government becomes bureaucratized and as law becomes computerized, the variety and independence of life in the fourth estate becomes all the more attractive.

There are three distinct types of mass media: magazine, newspaper, and broadcast. Each carries with it different implications for the intern. Most competitive, and some say most exciting, is the large New York newsmagazine. Here you will immerse yourself in the Mecca of journalism, experiencing professional reporting, writing, and editing at their glossiest, most refined state. Should you win such a position, the pay is apt to be high; perhaps even high enough to keep pace with the cost of living in New York or Washington. Assignments will be varied and you will work closely with talented, experienced journalists. A large newsmagazine may let you spend considerable time on an assignment, allow a more reflective writing tone, and will often incorporate diverse elements into a story. Certainly a summer with *Newsweek* can prepare an intern for an excellent job in the field following graduation. But *Newsweek* received over 500 applications for six positions last summer, and *Time/Life* invites only a limited number of schools to screen applicants for a program that one former intern termed "exciting" but another branded "very snotty."

While newsmagazine interns may be treated just like regular writers, those newsmagazine writers themselves don't often see more than half of their work in print—and rewritten, supplemented and edited at that. So there is much to be said for seeking a position at the city desk of a daily newspaper. Here the work can be faster; editors tend to be more encouraging of interns' ideas; and interns are able to participate in all phases of newspaper production—from working a regular reporting beat to copy editing to soliciting opinion pieces to laying out pages. Great satisfaction and learning can be obtained from seeing your regular byline on a news page or from seeing your photographs run frequently in the features section.

If a program emphasizes less writing and more copy-editing and fact verification, it will build basic but solid reporting skills. The smaller daily paper will likely require shorter term, more focused articles and will develop your ability to meet hard deadlines as that frantic editor grabs each finished page from your typewriter carriage.

Broadcast Journalism

Internships in broadcasting are less publicized than those with newspapers and magazines, but they are plentiful and not hard to locate. Competition for the available slots is still pretty rough—the most selective have hundreds of applications for just a couple of places—but most are less competitive than internships in written media.

More programs are open to high school students in broadcasting than in the other media, and in most cases, the intern is only required to work a limited number of hours. Programs generally run through the school semester, as well as during the summer. One drawback, though: most broadcasting internships are unpaid, with the stipulation that the student *must* receive academic credit for his or her work. Paying jobs *are* available, but are much harder to find.

The major distinction between broadcast and written journalism is that broadcast journalism demands immediate delivery when breaking a story—reporters must be on top of the news at every moment. Among the various kinds of broadcasting internships, there are also differences: students working in TV stations tend to do much more busy-work and gophering than in radio stations. At the TV station, there is little reporting that the intern can do on his or her own, since access to equipment is limited. But, if a student is reporting for a radio news show, only a tape recorder is required, so the intern can often go on the streets alone.

If you do want to work for a TV station, your best bet is to work for a public affairs talk show, rather than on a news program, since you will generally be assigned more responsible tasks with the talk show. There are usually two kinds of radio internships. One is a "survey course," giving the intern exposure to the various departments within the station. The other requires an intern to specialize in one division, such as music, news, programming, or business. We recommend the former to those students whose knowledge of the field is limited and who don't yet have a specific interest. Only die-hard broadcasting majors who have narrowed down their interests should apply for the latter.

We have included just a sampling of the many broadcast internships available. Interested students should write to radio and TV stations in large cities and to those near their homes or schools—they are bound to come up with programs not listed here.

Know What You Want

Before you apply for internships, decide which of the opportunities and demands of the three journalism types best suits your tastes and aptitude. Concentrate your research and application efforts in this area. Then make some basic decisions concerning the job description you find most attractive. Remember that your duties could include everything from late-night copy-editing or wire service rewriting to early morning police reports to coverage of evening school committee meetings. Know that the high competition among applicants could force you to relocate to a different part of the country. Bear in mind that many organizations will require that you have the use of a vehicle for transportation between assignments. Understand that your commitment could vary from assumption of the long hours of a vacationing *Washington Post* reporter's regular beat to a brief term merely "shadowing" a *Manchester Union Leader* reporter on assignment in upstate New Hampshire.

Before applying visit your library and flip through a national directory of publications for ideas. These guides will not only provide essentials such as addresses and telephone numbers, but will give you some idea of each newspaper, station, or magazine. How big is the circulation or audience? What is their major competition? How is their staff organized? What is the name of the chief editor or manager in the department of your interest? In the newspaper section, you will read of everything from the *Los Angeles Times*, to Boston's alternative weekly, *The Real Paper*, to Florida's *The National Enquirer*. Try to get a sense of the reputation and style, type of coverage, and editorial leanings favored by the operation.

Obtain a few copies of the newspaper or magazine that interests you, or listen to the radio station for which you wish to work. This will help you decide whether your talents and interests will match those of the station or publication. You will then be better able in the application to persuade prospective employers that you have something relevant to offer.

Getting Accepted

But what do editors look for in applicants? The senior editor of the *Tucson Citizen* wants his interns to have "intelligence, a wide range of interests, ambition to advance, thoroughness, accuracy, ability to meet deadlines, excellence in spelling and grammar." Of course, typing skills are a must everywhere. "A person who is well-grounded in liberal arts, insatiably curious, well-mannered in person and on the telephone, a skilled researcher on the street and in the library, and with a basic knowledge about back shop operations" would suit the news editor of the *Indianapolis News*. The requirements and tastes of each editor vary, but the general consensus is best expressed in what one personnel director searches for: "a mental and emotional toughness." If you have these qualities, show them!

Insiders have given us a few hints: newspaper editors prefer a one page resume—two pages only if you're a Rhodes Scholar; the cover letter should be imaginative and personalized, detailing how your experience makes you right for a reporting or editing job; enclose copies of your clippings with your resume. Also, when possible, these materials should be delivered personally. Some editors do not even consider mailed resumes, but rely on recommendations from other editors. Don't hesitate to call to arrange a meeting with an editor, even if only to hand him or her your application.

We cannot overemphasize the necessity of applying to many publications; a Newspaper Fund survey of 1977 journalism graduates shows that those who found full-time daily newspaper jobs sent out an average of 20 applications to land each job. And apply early; deadlines often descend upon you without warning—usually in early December for jobs the following summer. Be prepared to wait as long as three months before hearing from some newspapers or magazines. Others will never even respond to your letters. But stay in touch with several publications at one time, and follow up with calls or letters those jobs which most interest you. Again, smaller-sized newspapers should be the primary targets, because the job turnover there is greater than the larger city newspapers which are swamped with applications.

The words of a former intern ring true: "Do not be a 'job-snob.' There's something to be said for starting at the bottom. Realize that experience is the key to advancement." As an intern, tackle the routine jobs with the same diligence as the more exciting ones; it will teach you something, as well as indicate to the editor something about your capacity for work.

NEWSPAPERS

ARIZONA REPUBLIC NEWS INTERNSHIP   *Phoenix, Arizona*

ELIGIBILITY: *Undergraduate juniors to graduate*
DURATION: *3 to 3½ months*
ACADEMIC CREDIT POSSIBLE: *No*
REMUNERATION OR FEE: *$150/week salary plus work-related travel*
POSITIONS OFFERED: *4*
APPLICATION DEADLINE: *Early February*

General Description

The Arizona Republic is a large metropolitan newspaper, circulation 250,000, which allows interns to try their hand at various kinds of reporting and writing. The summer internship program lasts for three or three and one-half months, depending on the student's schedule. Four students who have completed their junior year are hired each year.

Interns work a 40 hour week—including night and weekend work. Interns are given substantial responsibility, and often cover court and police beats. Every Monday morning, an editor meets with the interns to discuss their progress.

The *Arizona Republic* program is one of the most competitive around: last year over 3000 students applied for the four openings. There is no application form, but resume and writing samples are required. Personal or telephone interviews are conducted with the final round of candidates.

The Inside Word

Both administrators and interns think highly of the program. Students are treated "like regular general assignment reporters—one of the best features of the job. We covered speeches, wrote features, and got about one or two weeks of court beat experience." Interns found the working atmosphere "quite good. The people were generally considerate and didn't talk down to us."

There is room for self-initiated projects in the *Arizona Republic* program, but interns usually follow assignments rather than digging out stories themselves. Despite the emphasis on assigned stories, interns complained that they often received too little direction. "Most of the work was like hanging out in a tomb: opening the mail was the high spot."

The newspaper has hired past interns for permanent positions after they graduate, and students felt that their experience gave them "a foot in the door" for later jobs.

Getting accepted: "Have good clips, good recommendations, be assertive and persistent."

Contact:

Mr. Verne A. Peyser
Assistant City Editor
Arizona Republic
P.O. Box 1950
Phoenix, AZ 85001

BIRMINGHAM NEWS   Birmingham, Alabama

ELIGIBILITY: *Juniors and seniors majoring in journalism or English*
DURATION: *Summer*
ACADEMIC CREDIT POSSIBLE: *Yes*
REMUNERATION OR FEE: *$150/week salary*
POSITIONS OFFERED: *4*
APPLICATION DEADLINE: *March 30*

General Description

The *Birmingham News* has a circulation of 200,000, making it the largest daily newspaper in Alabama. "We expect interns to perform just as another beginning reporter would perform," says the director of the program. The *News* sends interns out on full-time professional beats—and bylines their stories. Editors work closely with each intern, providing supervision and criticism while allowing them to develop according to their own initiative.

Participants tend to be from the South. Thirty-five applied last year. Clippings, an application form, and a cover letter describing background, interest in journalism and experience are required for consideration. A personal or telephone interview is a normal part of the application process.

The Inside Word

The staff looks for high grades and demonstrated ability from applicants. Editors take time to train and to encourage interns' ideas, according to past participants. While beginners receive routine story assignments, hotter news awaits interns after some experience with the paper. One intern described writing about everything from a story on a racial murder, to a review of an Earth, Wind and Fire concert, to a feature about a man who directs traffic for a hobby by the time the summer ended.

Contact:

Birmingham News
2200 4th Avenue North
Birmingham, AL 35204

BOSTON GLOBE

Boston, Massachusetts

ELIGIBILITY: *Undergraduate*
DURATION: *13 weeks*
ACADEMIC CREDIT POSSIBLE: *No*
REMUNERATION OR FEE: *$200/week salary*
POSITIONS OFFERED: *12 to 15*
APPLICATION DEADLINE: *mid-December*

General Description

The internship program at *The Boston Globe,* one of the nation's largest newspapers (circulation: 700,000), is over 20 years old. Students fill in for reporters on vacation, usually working at the metropolitan desk. Last summer, there was one intern in each of the following departments—photo, copy, living, and sports—while others did general assignment reporting. One student was talented enough to be assigned to the statehouse. The stories covered by interns ranged from murder to politics. The work and responsibilities of interns are generally considered to be that of any first-year reporter.

There is an orientation program for interns and several seminars are offered throughout the summer. Each year, between 300 and 400 students apply to *The Boston Globe* internship program. Experience on a college newspaper is a bare essential, and, while not required, most interns seem to come from the Boston area.

The Inside Word

Previous experience seems to be the key factor in getting accepted to this program. One intern suggested that reporters for a school paper should "distinguish themselves with feature articles, not just ordinary news pieces."

The flexibility within the program is emphasized by interns: "In the first two weeks it is important to establish yourself . . . once a city editor trusts you, you're in good shape to work on your own on small stories. There is a very fluid situation for pursuing your own interests. One intern ended up in the business section by getting to know the people who worked there."

As with every other job, this internship has its tedious moments, but assertive and enthusiastic students usually fare best: "Only two people were not fully integrated into the workings of the paper, due to their lack of motivation and initiative." One intern described this internship at the *Globe* as "a very positive experience."

Contact:

Mr. Robert Kierstead
Ass't Managing Editor
The Boston Globe
Boston, MA 02107

BULLETIN SUMMER REPORTING INTERNSHIP PROGRAM   *Philadelphia, Pennsylvania*

ELIGIBILITY: *Undergraduate juniors*
DURATION: *Summer; June 18 to August 24*
ACADEMIC CREDIT POSSIBLE: *No*
REMUNERATION OR FEE: *$150/week salary plus travel expenses*
POSITIONS OFFERED: *5*
APPLICATION DEADLINE: *Fall or early winter*

General Description

The Bulletin is one of Philadelphia's leading daily papers, with a circulation of 500,000. A summer internship with *The Bulletin* allows five students who have at least completed their junior year, to cover and write stories. This training program is for those who have a genuine commitment to journalism as a career and have written for other publications, preferably professional publications. The ten week internship places students at *The Bulletin*'s main office or at any of its bureaus in the Philadelphia area.

The Bulletin depends on its summer interns to fill full-time staff positions in five different departments. The interns write feature articles and self-initiated stories. *The Bulletin* chooses only five interns from an applicant pool of almost 300. There is an effort to have minority representation, as well as a male-female balance. A personal resumé, a transcript of the intern's college record, clippings and copies of writings in publications, and an interview are required. *The Bulletin* also asks that each applicant submit a statement concerning career plans and interests.

The Inside Word

Interns stress that having worked for professional publications is a major factor in getting a job with *The Bulletin*. Most interns feel that this paper has a strong commitment to training journalists: prospective interns will be questioned about their reasons for choosing the publishing field.

The internship begins with what one intern termed "an informal welcome to *The Bulletin*—sort of an orientation." One intern commented that he began by "writing obituaries and other things that you are sort of required to do." *The Bulletin* later designates the same responsibilities to its interns that it gives its full-time staff members.

Usually, *The Bulletin* allows interns to choose where they want to work. The hours are usually "ten a.m. to seven p.m., or ten to whenever you finish." The interns work in a variety of departments, including the features department, and are an integral part of the staff. One intern noted that the paper "is really understaffed and getting the paper out depends a lot on the interns."

The Bulletin "tests you out to see if you can cut it in the publishing world and stay there for the rest of your life." The program is very professional and the interns felt that they "were really treated as one of the staff."

Contact:

Mr. Don Harrison
Director, Summer Internship Program
The Bulletin
30th and Market Streets
Philadelphia, PA 19101

CHICAGO SUN-TIMES   *Chicago, Illinois*

ELIGIBILITY: *Undergraduate and graduate*
DURATION: *3-month periods between Feb. 1 and Nov. 30*

ACADEMIC CREDIT POSSIBLE: *Yes*
REMUNERATION OR FEE: *Varies*
POSITIONS OFFERED: *6*
DEADLINE: *Open*

General Description

The *Chicago Sun-Times* is the second largest daily newspaper in Illinois, with a circulation of 700,000. Applicants with previous intern experience and a strong interest in a career in journalism are preferred. Program administrators emphasize the fact that interns receive on-the-job training with assignments of difficulty according to ability and previous experience. Participants will usually begin with writing news briefs, announcements, and obituaries and then move on to longer and better working assignments. Each works under a city editor or a copy chief. Former interns are often hired full-time upon graduation.

The Inside Word

Past interns complimented the program, noting their editors' receptivity to new story ideas and improvisation. Some remarked positively about the treatment they received from the full-time staff—the encouragement and the general atmosphere that made one intern feel "just as if I was one of them."

Contact:

Chicago Sun-Times
401 N. Wabash Street
Chicago, IL 60611

HOUSTON CHRONICLE   *Houston, Texas*

ELIGIBILITY: *Juniors and seniors; residents of Texas*
DURATION: *Summer*
ACADEMIC CREDIT POSSIBLE: *Yes*
REMUNERATION OR FEE: *$190/week*
POSITIONS OFFERED: *5*
APPLICATION DEADLINE: *March 30*

General Description

The *Houston Chronicle*, a daily newspaper with a circulation of over 350,000, offers internships in many different departments—reporting, advertising, data processing, etc. Interns are delegated a great deal of responsibility in this program; they generally substitute for vacationing staff members, working as "genuine" reporters (with their own bylines) on a variety of beats.

A personal interview is all but required as part of the application procedure for admission into this very competitive program. Applicants must be Texas residents with superior grades and experience on their college newspapers to qualify for the five spots that over 120 applicants vie for each year. Applications should include a resume, clippings, and recommendations from college professors.

The Inside Word

Interns suggest that anyone seeking an internship with *The Houston Chronicle* "pick out a person and try to make personal contact." One intern commented that "the paper is more interested in seeing someone apply what they know—no matter what their background is on paper."

Most interns choose the department they want to work in, and usually their choice is honored—but as one intern noted, "it is all a matter of timing and when you get to the paper." Interns work as reporters, who "work on their own most of the time" rather than in a formal training program. Usually, an intern will work for a staff member for a few days, and then take over the position while that staff member goes on vacation.

Contact:

The Houston Chronicle
801 Texas Avenue
Houston, TX 77002

THE IDAHO STATESMAN · *Boise, Idaho*

ELIGIBILITY: *Undergraduate and graduate*
DURATION: *Summer*
ACADEMIC CREDIT POSSIBLE: *No*
REMUNERATION OR FEE: *Minimum of $140 per week, plus work-related travel and expenses*
POSITIONS OFFERED: *Five or more*
APPLICATION DEADLINE: *Late February or early March*

General Description

The Idaho Statesman, a daily newspaper with a circulation of 56,000 offers summer internships to "help develop the knowledge and skills of journalism students," and to help assume the summer workload. Administrators also like to utilize the internship program as a way of recruiting and screening future employees.

After a training program, interns jump right into reporting and editing positions. They work in many different aspects of daily newspaper production. Every position requires 37½ work hours per week, but the number of weeks each internship lasts is coordinated with individual interns' schedules.

The Inside Word

Approximately 100 people apply for about five positions. Applicants should have some journalistic knowledge and be able to work flexible hours. A resume, writing samples, a portfolio and phone numbers of references are required, and while a telephone interview is optional, previous interns believe it is advantageous to arrange one.

Contact:

James Dean
The Idaho Statesman
P. O. Box 40
Boise, ID 83707

MIAMI HERALD   *Miami, Florida*

ELIGIBILITY: *Undergraduate juniors to graduate*
DURATION: *13 weeks, summer*
ACADEMIC CREDIT POSSIBLE: *No*
REMUNERATION OR FEE: *$200 week salary*
POSITIONS OFFERED: *12*
APPLICATION DEADLINE: *January 30*

General Description

The Miami Herald is a large metropolitan newspaper with a circulation of 450,000. The internships offered include general assignment reporting, sports, features (lifestyle), photo, and copy-editing. In this very successful program, the interns are usually put in regular reportorial positions in the Miami newsroom, in the suburban, or the state bureaus.

An internship with *The Miami Herald* is on-the-job training—the student receives assignments just as if he or she were "a regular staffer." However, interns are given greater feedback and more frequent evaluations than the regular staff members receive.

Applications are accepted from intern candidates beginning each December, and a recruiting trip to between eight and ten colleges is made in late January and early February to interview students. The selection of interns is made toward the end of February. The internships are designed primarily for students who will be returning to school for at least one additional academic period—although graduates are also eligible.

The Inside Word

"We look for students with some reporting experience, either from a prior internship or on a good student newspaper—or both," shared a program administrator. Student comments include: "It was hard as hell, but I learned a lot." It gave me a chance to work on self-initiated projects. I was writing between six and eight articles a week."

"A great many newspapers have patterned their program after ours because of its success," added the administrator. "Between one-third and one-half of our former interns have come back to work for *The Miami Herald* on a full-time basis. Several of them are now in responsible mid and senior level management positions in the newsroom. Others have gone on to successful careers at other newspapers."

Contact:

Mr. Pete Weitzel
The Miami Herald
1 Herald Plaza
Miami, FL 33101

THE MILWAUKEE JOURNAL   *Milwaukee, Wisconsin*

ELIGIBILITY: *Undergraduate*
DURATION: *10 to 12 weeks, summer*
ACADEMIC CREDIT POSSIBLE: *No*
REMUNERATION OR FEE: *$180/week salary plus work-related travel and supplies*
POSITIONS OFFERED: *8*
APPLICATION DEADLINE: *Late January*

General Description

Over 300 people apply for the eight positions available each year at the Milwaukee Journal, a daily paper with a circulation of 400,000, and one of those positions is reserved for a special Newspaper Fund Copy Editing intern. Applicants must be returning to school in the fall and have preferably completed their junior year. The only eligible graduate students are those who will have on-campus work to complete after the internship.

Applicants must intend to pursue a career in journalism and should have experience on their college newspapers or previous part-time newspaper work. Journalism majors are preferred, but liberal arts majors are also considered. Candidates must submit a resume, writing samples and clippings and an application form. They should specify areas in which they hope to work when they submit these materials.

Depending upon their own academic schedules, interns work 10 to 12 weeks, 40 hours every week. There is no formal instruction—interns learn on-the-job by writing and editing news for the daily paper. According to their qualifications, they are assigned to the Metropolitan reporting staff, the Copy Desk, the Sports Department, Spectrum (lifestyle), or the Picture Desk.

The Inside Word

Interns stress the fact that they are treated like any other reporter. This aspect of the internship was attractive because it gave the interns a great deal of input. They felt that their ideas mattered and were pleased with the number of self-initiated articles they were able to write. Another advantage is that interns received a broad range of experience. One woman worked on the state desk, the suburban desk, and sometimes filled in as a police and a court reporter. In addition, interns have weekly meetings with various editors of different sections. The program is made even more attractive by the fact that all the interns' written work is by-lined.

Others, however, felt lost at times. These interns indicated the occasional need for more instruction—but did admit that there were always people around who could answer questions. Editors recognize the problems that can arise when interns are treated like staff reporters and are currently trying to improve the situation. One editor writes: "The major shortcoming has been our failure to provide as much steady feedback on a daily basis as some of the interns would have liked . . . Each year we try to improve the frequency and regularity of critique sessions. I am not sure that we will ever be able to do enough of it to satisfy some of the interns."

Interns feel that the *Journal* internships do enhance their career opportunities. Not only do they gain the real experience, good clippings, and recommendations helpful when applying for jobs elsewhere—but they also have a good chance of becoming a staff member at *The Milwaukee Journal*. According to one editor, more than 25 percent of the interns in the past 16 years have later been hired for full-time positions. He writes, "We use the program primarily as a source of identifying strong prospects for future full-time employment on our staff."

One editor notes, "We almost always end up with 25 or 30 really first-rate applicants in the final selection process and we find it extremely difficult to choose among them." How do applicants fight these odds? Interns and editors feel that an interview helps one's chance for admission because it shows a strong desire for the internship. Interns also advise applicants to show their interest by sending in their applications early and by keeping in touch. Editors suggest demonstrated interest and experience is important: "Experience, which includes the nature and number of clippings of published work, makes an individual stand out."

Contact:

Harry Hill, Assistant Managing Editor
The Milwaukee Journal
P.O. Box 661
Milwaukee, WI 53201

NEWSDAY SUMMER JOURNALISM PROGRAM
Melville, New York

ELIGIBILITY: *Sophomores and juniors*
DURATION: *10 weeks*
ACADEMIC CREDIT POSSIBLE: *No*
REMUNERATION OR FEE: *$150 to $185/week salary*
POSITIONS OFFERED: *31*
APPLICATION DEADLINE: *Mid-December*

General Description

Newsday is the nation's third largest evening newspaper (circulation: 500,000) and is located in a new Long Island plant. Interns replace vacationing staff members for the summer, working as reporters, copy editors, photographers, or artists. Students must be entering their senior year of college, except for artists, who may be entering either their junior or senior year to qualify for this $185/week salaried position. Each summer, five sophomores are also hired as editorial aides and receive $151/week salary.

Editorial aides handle telephone calls and assist editors in newsroom clerical jobs. Some aides are assigned to the library if interested in pursuing a career in that area. Aides are eligible to participate as interns the following summer. No editorial aides are assigned to the photo or art department.

The program also includes a series of seminars in which participants join with regular *Newsday* staff members in informal discussions on such topics as "investigative reporting" and "column writing." Interns are also evaluated regularly by supervising editors.

Newsday has an affirmative action program—40 percent of intern positions are to be filled by women and 20 percent are to be filled by minority candidates. The internship program received 300 applications for the 31 slots in 1979.

One special requirement: interns who work as reporters or photographers must have automobiles.

The Inside Word

Getting accepted: The application package consists of writing a news article from a page of news notes, submitting a biographical statement, and describing one's personal interest in journalism. One intern advised: "Each piece is written to a specified length, so prolixity should be avoided. Spelling and vocabulary proficiency are also necessary. Finally, a strong background in many phases of writing along with care and honesty in your presentation will serve you the best."

Daily life: One student spoke about his duties as an editorial aide: "I performed the low level dogwork that must be done at a big newspaper—sorting and opening mail, typing photo requests, fetching clippings from the library, sending messages to *Newsday* bureaus. The heart of it all, in terms of the most time-consuming, necessary, and interesting/annoying part of the job, is working on the City Desk, where clerks work the telephone lines. Many nights were spent at a visual display terminal, working on articles that were electroncially sent to my station. This did not entail the usual frenzied running-about required of clerks."

The job of a reporter requires different duties and allows for more freedom. "I was left to my own devices. Half my articles were self-initiated—that is, I would present my editor with ideas, and he would indicate the one he would like me to develop. My articles were not written under deadlines, so I could concentrate on thoroughness and style in a relaxed setting. Sometimes, though, I was assigned articles."

Working as a clerk has its drawbacks: "it was frustrating when the phones were ringing, the editors were yelling, and the mail was stacked up by the boxes. At times I thought the summer would have been better spent, in a professional sense, had I gotten a job writing at another paper." But the good points of the job made it worthwhile: "I had the feeling that I really contributed to the operations. The job gave me the opportunity to see a big newspaper up close, and to meet the people involved in its operation. Certainly the chance to return to *Newsday* and write the next summer was the greatest benefit."

The head administrator requests that interns let him know their reactions to the program when the summer ends. Students found this a good way to have input into the operation of *Newsday*. As for future prospects, "the clips and experience of having worked at the tenth largest paper in the country are of incalculable value, certainly more impressive than if I had continued writing for my hometown weekly. The contacts I have made are also of great importance, plugging me right into the New York scene."

Contact:

Mr. Bernie Bookbinder
Senior Editor/Projects
Newsday
Melville, NY 11746

Art Interns:
Mr. Paul Back
Director of Design

Photo Interns:
Mr. Marvin Sussman
Senior Editor / Photography

THE NEW REPUBLIC   *Washington, D.C.*

ELIGIBILITY: *Undergraduate*
DURATION: *Summer*
ACADEMIC CREDIT POSSIBLE: *No*
REMUNERATION OR FEE: *$125 / week salary*
POSITIONS OFFERED: *2 to 3*
APPLICATION DEADLINE: *March 15*

General Description

A weekly paper with 80,000 circulation, specializing in current commentary and reviews, *The New Republic* looks for talented writers and those with experience in journalism. Interns are treated as full staff members and their duties include participation in all editorial discussions and the production of a publishable article every week on an assigned topic or a topic chosen by the intern. *The New Republic* staff numbers around eighteen which provides the intern with the opportunity to work closely with the staff and gain editorial experience first hand.

This program is fairly competitive; about fifty applications are submitted annually. A resume is required, as is an essay of approximately 1000 words in length which demonstrates the applicant's ability to develop an informal topic on some news feature. Articles written for school publications are acceptable as entries.

The Inside Word

The New Republic sends announcements to college newspaper editors in the first months of every new year to publicize their program. Past interns suggest that a background in journalism or free lance writing is essential for acceptance and success in this program.

One intern described the staff at *The New Republic* as "really loose." After the first two weeks the staff provides little "supervision, but is encouraging about ideas." Day to day work includes "reading newspapers and magazines to come up with story ideas, or researching stories in the library, and even some receptionist work." Each intern receives his or her own office or conference room. One intern commented that for an internship "this one was exceptional because it didn't involve any busy work."

The working atmosphere at *The New Republic* is "pleasant" although the staff seemed a "little stiff," one past intern commented, "but the stiffness eased after awhile." Interns felt that this program "improved" their writing skills tremendously.

Contact:

The New Republic
1220 19th St. N.W.
Washington, D.C. 20036

NEWS-JOURNAL PAPERS   *Delaware*
Summer Internship

ELIGIBILITY: *Undergraduate and graduate*
DURATION: *Summer*
ACADEMIC CREDIT POSSIBLE: *No*
REMUNERATION OR FEE: *Varies*
POSITIONS OFFERED: *Varies*
APPLICATION DEADLINE: *Open*

General Description

The *News-Journal* Papers offer summer internships in Wilmington, Newark, and Georgetown, Delaware for students of journalism. Interns write and research stories for the staff along with work on self-initiated projects. The program offered seven positions in 1979, but the number of positions varies with the newspaper's needs, as do the starting and ending dates of the program.

The interns are expected to pull their weight as full-time staff members—working thirty-five hours a week plus some required overtime. They fill regular reporting jobs, do copy editing, and sometimes fill photo spots under the supervision of various editors. The intern's salary varies and includes work related travel expenses.

The *News-Journal* participates in the Summer Program for Minority Students at the University of California at Berkeley. A resume, a transcript, writing samples, and a portfolio are required in the application. An interview is not required—but is suggested, as are letters of recommendation.

The Inside Word

The summer internship with the *News-Journal* Papers is very competitive—thus recent interns recommend that applicants show "why they stand out or are different from others, and stress a willingness to learn." Another intern suggested that applicants should demonstrate "that they are creative—but also have the capacity to follow orders well." Everyone we spoke with emphasized the necessity of displaying "good clips."

The *News-Journal* places interns in any one of their three bureaus— but there are differences between each office. In Georgetown, summer interns work primarily on stories concerning the resort and beach areas which are very busy and crowded during the summer months. In Wilmington, interns work on copy editing. In all offices, the interns feel that the staff provides room for self-initiative and are encouraging about intern's work. One intern who worked in Wilmington warned that interns should be aware that "their schedules will be thrown off because most of the editing is done from six a.m. through noon."

Interns stressed the fact that the staff encourages interns to work on their own and are "always helpful about your ideas and your writing." One intern commented however, that the newspaper holds a "sink or swim attitude" about the intern's progress. The intern should be willing to "start at the bottom and then move up," another suggested, "but they don't stick you in a corner and only commission you to get lunch either."

All interns found the program interesting and feel that they learned many skills. Those who work on copy editing learn to use the Visual Display Terminal machines. Interns recommend that interns should have their own transportation, no matter which bureau they work at because the "public transportation in Delaware stinks."

Contact:

FOR APPLICATION MATERIALS:

Personnel Department
News-Journal Papers
831 Orange St.
Wilmington, DE 19899

FOR MORE INFORMATION:

Mr. Fredrick W. Hartmann
Executive Editor
News-Journal Papers
Wilmington, DE 19899

THE NEWSPAPER FUND
Editing Internship Program

National

ELIGIBILITY: *Juniors*
DURATION: *Summer*
ACADEMIC CREDIT POSSIBLE: *No*
REMUNERATION OR FEE: *$700 scholarship plus variable salary*
POSITIONS OFFERED: *40*
APPLICATION DEADLINE: *Early December*

General Description

The Editing Internship Program is sponsored by the Newspaper Fund, a private organization which serves as an intermediary between interns and the paper where they work. College juniors who will be returning to school in the fall can apply directly to the Fund, which will find a suitable work situation for the intern for the summer. The duration of the internship is dependent upon the student's academic calendar. Interns work on daily newspaper and wire-service copydesks, becoming proficient in all phases of copy editing and headline writing.

Newspapers make advance agreements each year to review applications from Newspaper Fund interns, or to accept the Fund's assignments. Participant's may be asked to contact particular newspapers to arrange employment—but the newspapers make the final decision concerning the hiring of interns and establishing their salaries. Prior to the internship, each intern must attend an intensive three-week training course in copy editing at a university designated by the Fund. An instructor from this editing course will make periodic visits to the intern throughout the summer.

In addition to any salary the intern may receive from the assigned newspaper, a $700 scholarship is paid out upon completion of the interns' final report and his or her immediate supervisor's report. Scholarship and training course costs are paid by the Newspaper Fund and the newspapers hiring interns.

The type of student the Editing Internship Program is looking for "enjoys molding words and phrases into lucid, concise, and informative news stories. He or she wants to check facts in a story, no matter how minute they might be, and has a flair for headline writing, layout, grammar, and spelling." Approximately 350 such students apply each year to this well-established program. Internships offered by the Newspaper Fund are with papers throughout the country and individual experiences differ.

Contact:

Mr. Thomas Engleman
The Newspaper Fund, Inc.
P. O. Box 300
Princeton, NJ 08540

THE NEWSPAPER FUND   *National*
Minority Internship Program

ELIGIBILITY: *Graduate*
DURATION: *Varies*
ACADEMIC CREDIT POSSIBLE: *No*

REMUNERATION OR FEE: *$1000 scholarship plus variable salary*
POSITIONS OFFERED: *10*
APPLICATION DEADLINE: *Early December*

General Description

The Minority Internship Program is sponsored by the Newspaper Fund. It involves minority graduate students, both from journalism and non-journalism areas, who have a demonstrated interest and talent in news reporting and editing. Interns are placed with newspapers or wire services across the country, as with the Editing Internship Program.

Prior to the internship, interns must attend an intensive three-week course in news editing at a university designated by the Fund. An instructor from the course will visit each intern during the summer.

In addition to a salary determined by each newspaper, students receive a $1000 scholarship check, made payable to the intern's school, following a successful completion of the entire summer internship. About 200 people apply to this program each year. Internships offered by The Newspaper Fund are with papers throughout the country and individual experiences differ.

Contact:

Mr. Thomas Engleman
The Newspaper Fund, Inc.
P. O. Box 300
Princeton, NJ 08540

THE PLAIN DEALER
Cleveland, Ohio

ELIGIBILITY: *Junior through graduate*
DURATION: *10 to 12 weeks*
ACADEMIC CREDIT POSSIBLE: *No*
REMUNERATION OR FEE: *Varies, about minimum wage*
POSITIONS OFFERED: *9 summer; 1 fall; 1 winter; 1 spring*
APPLICATION DEADLINE: *Fall, late summer; winter, December 10; spring, March 1; summer, March 10.*

General Description

The Plain Dealer, a daily paper with a 400,000 circulation, has an internship program for undergraduate students in their junior year or above who plan careers in newspaper journalism. In addition to the single spring, fall and winter internships, there are eight reporting internships as well as one photography intern position in the summer program. Interns work for the city editor or for departmental editors on a variety of levels.

Interns work as full-time staff members filling in for vacationing reporters and are sent out on the same assignments and the same beats. Interns work a full forty-hour week, although much of the work and reporting is done at night.

The Plain Dealer recruits some interns from Ohio colleges with journalism programs. A personal interview is required and the applicants receive applications at that time. Clips of writing and a resume are also required as part of the application procedure.

The Inside Word

Most participants in *The Plain Dealer's* internship program have had a fair amount of practical experience in journalism. Most interns have been on the staff or editorial board of their college newspaper, and sometimes have worked for professional papers.

Interns told us that they did a fair share of general reporting along with occasional assignments at places such as the police desk or the seat of county government. Most of the intern's time is spent covering hard news. One intern commented that he "had a few self-directed projects," but mostly the interns are "too busy with assignments."

Interns felt that the staff was encouraging and helpful, "especially the assistant city editor who really helped the interns feel comfortable." Since this program is hard-news-oriented, interns should expect "to hit the ground running" from the moment they arrive at the paper. This is not a training program, but instead it is "experience in reporting and writing as a full time staff member," said one intern. If you are "interested in hard journalism—this is the best place to work."

Contact:

Mr. Vernon Havener
The Plain Dealer
1801 Superior Avenue
Cleveland, OH 44114

THE SEATTLE TIMES   *Seattle, Washington*

ELIGIBILITY: *Undergraduate, Washington residents*
and students only
DURATION: *Summer*

ACADEMIC CREDIT POSSIBLE: *Yes*
REMUNERATION OR FEE: *$300/week salary*
POSITIONS OFFERED: *4*
APPLICATION DEADLINE: *February*

General Description

Seattle's major daily paper (circulation: 300,000), looks for interns who are qualified enough "to step right into a reporter's role." Little orientation is provided to interns who are assigned to a wide variety of stories from the start of their term.

Application includes completing a form, submitting 3 published articles, and interviewing with an editor. 100 applicants competed for the positions last year.

The Inside Word

Previous experience on a daily metropolitan paper or solid deadline experience are the keys to acceptance here. One intern felt that her acceptance was "predetermined because the paper had followed her work on other daily papers." Another suggested that "recommendations are not as important as presenting good clips."

Once accepted, interns report that they were sent to work at regional bureaus. One intern stated, "I dreaded the thought of working at a regional bureau, but I really enjoyed it." At the main office, interns are assigned general stories by editors, and each intern must take a turn at morning releases. The releases were termed "drudge work" by one intern because they included obituaries, births, and weather, but another intern said that she only did the morning releases a few times all summer.

The staff at *The Seattle Times* was described as receptive to the interns, but some interns felt that the atmosphere was "impersonal until you proved yourself." The general assignments were usually good stories, and the interns felt that they were treated as staff reporters rather than interns. "Some stories can be trivial or on trite subjects," one intern commented, "but the editors are all honest and open and they try to cut stories like that."

Interns have felt "intimidated" at first, but they suggest that "interns work and talk with editors, and become journalists rather than temporary reporters." There is a one-day orientation at the beginning, and the paper asks for an optional intern critique at the end.

Contact:

Seattle Times
P.O. Box 70
Seattle, WA 98111

THE SENTINEL STAR
Orlando, Florida

ELIGIBILITY: *Undergraduate*
DURATION: *10 weeks, summer*
ACADEMIC CREDIT POSSIBLE: *Yes*
REMUNERATION OR FEE: *$135/week salary*
POSITIONS OFFERED: *8*
APPLICATION DEADLINE: *Late December*

General Description

The *Sentinel Star* is a daily newspaper with a circulation of 200,000. Approximately sixty to one hundred people apply for the eight positions offered each summer. Interns work forty hours per week from the first or second week of June through the first or second week of August. Starting at the Metropolitan desk doing mostly clerical work for one or two weeks, interns then move on to the departments that best suit their interests and abilities. Every three or four weeks they change departments so as to learn about all phases of editorial work. Interns have their own by-lines on any written work.

Reading, writing, and typing skills are necessary for these internships. Applicants must submit a resume and writing samples. Interviews are preferred, although they are not necessary.

The Inside Word

Interns say that this program is very beneficial for those who are motivated. In the beginning there is some boring work—answering phones, taking dictation, working on obituaries. However, one intern told us, most do not do this busy work for long: "The people stuck at the Metro desk lacked initiative." Most of the interns are allowed to devote the majority of their time to the areas they are interested in. Everyone has to do some desk and reporting work—but a great deal of the work is suited to individual talents and tastes. As one intern said, "All the work can be interesting if you have the initiative to go where you want."

Interns enjoy the range of experience possible in this program. Not only do they work for different departments—but each week the department heads discuss with the interns the particular advantages of their specialties.

Concerning the career opportunitites that result from this program, one intern said, "the internship puts you half-way there." She told us that interns get contacts and good recommendations as a result of their involvement. The administrators and interns agree that their record in job placement is very good—many of *The Sentinel Star* staff members were once interns themselves, and a great number of interns have moved on to good jobs elsewhere.

Contact:

Nancy Taylor
The Sentinel Star
633 North Orange Ave.
Orlando, FL 32802

WALL STREET JOURNAL   New York, New York

ELIGIBILITY: *Undergraduate*
DURATION: *Summer*
ACADEMIC CREDIT POSSIBLE: *Yes*
REMUNERATION OR FEE: *$200/week*
POSITIONS OFFERED: *10*
APPLICATION DEADLINE: *March 30*

General Description

Interns work in New York and in bureaus nationwide as full-time reporters. Competition for the program is surprisingly low for such a distinguished journal—only 100 applied last year. A resume, clippings, and a cover letter constitute the application. Interns are often hired as full-time reporting staff following graduation. "We hope to attract a broad spectrum of applicants," said one administrator.

The Inside Word

Past interns gave this one a gold star rating. "It was an excellent internship," said one who had found a Time/Life program less than satisfying the year before. "I can't say enough good things about it." Another former participant said "they don't lead you around by the hand. Usually they will start you right off on front page, bylined feature stories after only two weeks of preliminary training in spot news."

Interns characterized the program as a "doing internship" in which room existed for participants to suggest and carry through their own story ideas. Bureaus are small and personable. Writing quality is reportedly the ticket to the job, and program directors are willing to admit applicants with no "connections." A past intern summed it up with the comment, "the real goal is to find people for future employment."

Contact:

Larry O'Donnell
Managing Editor
Wall Street Journal
22 Courtland
New York, NY 10007

WASHINGTON POST   *Washington, D.C.*

ELIGIBILITY: *Undergraduate and graduate*
DURATION: *10 weeks, summer*
ACADEMIC CREDIT POSSIBLE: *Yes*
REMUNERATION OR FEE: *$180 to 200/week*
POSITIONS OFFERED: *10 to 15*
APPLICATION DEADLINE: *December 31*

General Description

Washington Post interns replace vacationing staffers, working for national, state, local, sports, style, and business desks. Positions are also available in photography and copy editing. Requirements include an interest in journalism, writing ability, previous experience on a college and/or commercial newspaper, and typing skills. No personal interviews are given. The last date for requesting applications is November 1, and all decisions are made in April. Applications are first screened by the personnel office, then reviewed by reporters and editors in the different areas. Intern hours vary: they "could be anywhere from night to early morning," cautioned an administrator. The internship program includes an orientation in the Post offices, a tour of Washington, D.C., and help in finding housing.

The Inside Word

The Washington Post program has been called "the Cadillac of newspaper internships," and it is one of the most competitive around. Between 2000 and 3000 students apply yearly for the 15 positions. One intern commented that "since we are filling in for full-time reporters, the work is real and demanding." Most interns at the Washington Post have worked on professional publications previously, so novices face a definite disadvantage in the hiring process.

Contact:

Personnel Department

The Washington Post
1150 15th St., NW
Washington, DC 20071

THE WICHITA EAGLE AND BEACON   *Wichita, Kansas*

ELIGIBILITY: *Undergraduate and graduate*
DURATION: *May to August*
ACADEMIC CREDIT POSSIBLE: *No*
REMUNERATION OR FEE: *$185/weekly salary plus work-related travel expenses*
POSITIONS OFFERED: *8*
APPLICATION DEADLINE: *Varies*

General Description

The Wichita Eagle and Beacon (circulation: 175,000) offers summer internships for students who have completed their junior year or who are in graduate school. The program is geared towards students with a good deal of campus journalism experience behind them, or those who have participated in a previous journalism internship.

The Wichita Eagle and Beacon offers eight positions: six in reporting, one in copy editing, and one in photography. This internship is a full-time, forty hour a week job that runs from mid-May to mid-August. The interns in this program are active in reporting, editing, and writing, and function as integral members of the staff under the supervision of various department supervisors. Occasional intern sessions address different aspects of newspaper journalism and help the intern gain a better understanding of the field. Approximately forty to fifty students apply to this program each year. A resume, writing samples, and an application are required, and an interview is preferred, but not required.

The Inside Word

One past intern told us that applicants should stress "any previous job that shows them your interest in journalism" on their application. Another intern told us that she had been accepted because she "had experience in radio interviewing" and they thought that this experience would help her in newspaper journalism. An intern with minimal experience in journalism, but a strong writing background was accepted to this program—experience in journalism is not essential as long as your experience illustrates some "self-initiative."

Interns, two-thirds of whom are usually undergraduates, concentrate on writing and reporting in this program rather than editing. One intern said that she "spent half the time collecting facts and the other half writing." Everyone we spoke with said they were encouraged to come up with ideas, although stories were generally assigned. All commented that they had a "good rapport" with the staff who were "generally helpful."

One intern advised all future interns to "make the extra effort, no matter how dull the story assigned, and it will be more rewarding." Another told us that "familiarity with the geographic area enriches the experience and enables you to initiate more projects."

Contact

Mr. Keith Ashley
Assistant to the Executive Editor
The Wichita Eagle and Beacon
825 East Douglas
Wichita, KS 67202

MAGAZINES

CHICAGO MAGAZINE INTERNSHIP PROGRAM
Chicago, Illinois

ELIGIBILITY: *Undergraduates*
DURATION: *Summer - 3 months; school year - 1 quarter*
ACADEMIC CREDIT POSSIBLE: *Yes*
REMUNERATION OR FEE: *$150 per week*
POSITIONS OFFERED: *1 editorial, 1 art*
APPLICATION DEADLINE: *March 1 for summer*

General Description

Chicago Magazine, an associate of WFMT (FM), offers 2 internships during the summer and an occasional internship for one-quarter of the school year.

The editorial intern acts as a staff editor and is assigned regular articles, assists the senior editors, and does research and back-checking. The art intern assists the art director, designs advertisements and layout, and does some illustrating.

Applicants should send a resume, cover letter, and samples of writing or art work in the early spring. An interview is required for finalists.

The Inside Word

Most of the interns have completed their junior or senior year, and a number remain with the magazine. Selection for the news intern is based on both writing skills and editing experience. Before an interview, candidates should become familiar with *Chicago Magazine* and prepare some article ideas. A desire to stay with the magazine and a knowledge of Chicago are also factors in selection.

Contact

Steve Glittelson
Chicago Magazine
5000 North Michigan Avenue
Chicago, IL 60611

MAGAZINE INTERNSHIP PROGRAM   *New York, New York*

ELIGIBILITY: *Undergraduate juniors*
DURATION: *Summer*
ACADEMIC CREDIT: *No*
REMUNERATION OR FEE: *$150/week salary*
POSITIONS OFFERED: *40 to 45*
APPLICATION DEADLINE: *December 15*

General Description

The Magazine Internship Program places college students who have completed their junior year in summer positions with many of the nation's leading magazines. The student must be in New York by early June, and be able to stay in the city through mid-August.

Students who have strong backgrounds in journalism and writing are selected to work as junior staff members in magazine editing. Intern responsibilities include handling reader mail, evaluating unsolicited manuscripts, research and learning the basics of magazine editing. The interns are supervised by the senior staff of the magazine. A three-day orientation seminar on The Magazine Internship Program, magazine journalism, and living and working in New York City takes place in early June before interns are sent to their respective magazines. Most internships are with consumer and business publications in New York, although a few may be located in other parts of the country. Students report back once a week to the Magazine Internship Program for lectures, and all students are required to submit a written evaluation at the end of the program.

This program is very competitive. Candidates are usually from journalism schools or liberal arts colleges and have a strong background in campus journalism. Approximately 175 students apply for the 40 to 45 positions available. Interviews are not required, but the American Society of Magazine Editor's application, some writing samples, and letters of recommendation are necessary.

The Magazine Internship Program hopes that interns will return to their schools and generate interest in magazine journalism or actively participate in magazine journalism after they have completed this program.

The Inside Word

All the interns interviewed were excited about the program. One student said that this was "*the* program for magazine journalism." Most of the students chosen to participate in the program were journalism and communications majors, while students from liberal arts colleges felt that activity in campus journalism was helpful in getting accepted.

The emphasis in this program is on learning magazine editing skills— not writing. Both the program director and the past interns say that "You really won't enjoy this program if you go to work with writing in mind. You must realize that you will be editing, not writing articles."

Two interns told us that the applications should not just list all activities and experiences in journalism, but rather—should include good writing samples. One intern told us "they are more interested in quality than in lists."

Once accepted, each intern gives three magazine preferences and is usually sent to one of the three listed. Usually, students seem more interested in the big name magazines—*Time, Newsweek, People*, etc.— but as one intern said: "Working on a large magazine is no good unless you want to be told what to do constantly . . . a good, small magazine is more fun and worthwhile."

Once at the magazine, experiences differ. One intern felt that her work was "slow" for three weeks before becoming interesting, while another intern "felt she was a member of the staff from the moment she walked in the door." Most interns we spoke with said that they were supervised closely and usually given projects rather than initiating them. Their duties varied from telephone reporting, to picking mail for publication, to editing manuscripts. Acceptance of the intern by the magazine staff seems to rely on whether the magazine usually employs interns and on the size of the magazine.

The two and a half day orientation at the American Society of Magazine Editors in early June "deals with magazine production and was not very worthwhile," said one intern. On the other hand, the weekly reunions for all the interns at the society were called "fascinating because all the big names in publishing and editing came to speak and were really interesting."

Contact:

Mr. Robert E. Kenyon, Jr.
Magazine Center
American Society of Magazine Editors
575 Lexington Avenue
New York, NY 10022

THE NATION   *New York, New York*

ELIGIBILITY: *Undergraduate and graduate*
DURATION: *6 weeks to 3 months*
ACADEMIC CREDIT POSSIBLE: *Yes*
REMUNERATION OR FEE: *Work-related travel expenses*
POSITIONS OFFERED: *5*
APPLICATION DEADLINE: *Varies*

General Description

The Nation is a weekly magazine (bi-weekly during the summer months) that has a circulation of 32,000 and specializes in current commentary.

The internship program is a summer and January term program which gives interns an opportunity to edit, write, and publish *The Nation* under the supervision of the assistant editor. The program is open to undergraduate and graduate students with an interest and a background in politics and current events. The minimum internship length for the January program is six weeks and the maximum length is three months during the summer.

Interns will be writing and researching articles, working with the senior staff of the magazine, and doing some general clerical work. The program can be connected to an academic program and thus earn academic credit for the intern. The internship is full time, forty hours a week, and the only remuneration is for work-related travel expenses. There are five internships during January and five during the summer. Approximately sixty people apply each year and special consideration is given women, the handicapped, and minorities. An interview, a resume, a transcript and writing samples are required.

The Inside Word

The Nation looks for students who have had journalism experience. One intern recommended that applicants should "spell out an idea for an article" in their application to show their interest. Interns find most enjoyable the opportunity to research and write their own articles, some of which are published in the magazine.

The interns usually spend the first three months "reading incoming manuscripts and writing responses to queries about these manuscripts." If the intern has a story idea in mind, the second three months are usually spent working on it. The staff is generally "encouraging and if you have a lot of initiative and discipline yourself, you could gain invaluable experience in this unstructured environment."

The staff at *The Nation* is "good hearted" and interns can continue contributing to the magazine after they have finished the program. The staff has helped some interns find their present jobs in publishing. The final word on this program is "be rich because they don't pay you a cent" and "try to get the program attached to academic credit."

Contact:

Kai Bird
The Nation
72 Fifth Avenue
New York, NY 10011

NEWSWEEK   *New York, New York*

ELIGIBILITY: *Undergraduate through graduate*
DURATION: *13 weeks, summer*
ACADEMIC CREDIT POSSIBLE: *No*
REMUNERATION OR FEE: *$280/week salary*
POSITIONS OFFERED: *6*
APPLICATION DEADLINE: *March 1*

General Description

This program attempts to give aspiring student-journalists a view of the operation of a national newsmagazine, while allowing editors to look at potential future employees. The sponsors hope to attract "increased numbers of qualified minorities and women into the ranks of major publications," according to a published statement.

Competition is heavy—over 500 applications were received last year. The best time to apply is January or February; personal interviews are conducted in early March and selection is usually completed before the end of the month. Applicants should include a cover letter to the program director which expresses an interest in the internship, clippings indicating the breadth of the applicant's reporting experience and writing style, a complete resume, a 500-word autobiography, and a "My Turn" article similar to what appears as a regular column in the magazine.

Interns are placed in bureaus ranging from Washington, D.C. to Los Angeles where they work very closely with bureau chiefs on a variety of research and writing assignments. Successful interns are frequently employed full-time following graduation.

The Inside Word

"Very good writing ability is the main thing I look for," said one editor of the application review process. "We want our interns to be able to jump right in."

Interns do jump right in, according to former participants. But their writing does not often end up in print. "What gets into print is what would normally get into print from a beginning correspondent," said one past intern. In a national newsmagazine, the normal quantity of published writing appearing in publication is dictated, according to another, "by luck, the content of your story, and by the quality of your writing."

Interns, as regular correspondents, work on "files" which are forwarded to the New York office for rewrite and combination with files of other reporters. In those cases in which an intern's work forms the exclusive basis for a story, a byline is used. Bureau chiefs work closely with interns, making what might easily become an overwhelming and impersonal organization into "basically a supportive kind of system," according to a past intern. Quantity of work depends on the particular bureau location. Washington, for example, is known for a high story volume with a resulting "here's the assignment; go out and get it" approach from busy editors. Interns stress the real responsibility of the job. "If you blow a story, you have blown it for both yourself and the magazine," said one. "There's no back-up."

Contact:

John L. Dotson
News Editor
Newsweek
444 Madison Avenue
New York, NY 10022

ROLLING STONE   New York, New York

ELIGIBILITY: *Juniors and seniors*
DURATION: *Summer; fall and spring semester*
ACADEMIC CREDIT POSSIBLE: *Yes*
REMUNERATION OR FEE: *None*
POSITIONS OFFERED: *3 summer, 3 fall, 3 spring*
APPLICATION DEADLINE: *Open*

General Description

Rolling Stone is a bi-weekly newspaper, circulation 600,000, that reports on contemporary culture, politics, art, and music. *Rolling Stone* sponsors an annual competition among college students for the best published article in the following categories: 1) General 2) Investigative 3) Entertainment. The winners of the contest become summer interns. The semester programs are filled by application including a resume, cover letter, transcript, references, and a personal interview, as are programs with the new *Rolling Stone College Papers* publication.

Interns work as assistants to editorial assistants in the Features, Editorial, and Music departments, according to program directors. Issue indexes are compiled, record collections kept current, readers' letters are answered, writers' stories are researched. Duties in the Art and Production department involve work with dummy sheets and clerical functions. "Interns shouldn't count on writing by any means," said a staff member. Fifteen of the 300 applicants were granted personal interviews. Occasionally interns are retained as full time staff.

The Inside Word

"O.K., there's a lot of busy work," said one former intern, "but then again it really is very interesting. By keeping your eyes and ears open you learn a lot. I learned more here than I did in four years of college." A current intern agreed that "a lot depends on individual initiative." "You learn a lot from hanging around. The bottom is a good starting point, I guess." She noted, however, that "with the 40 to 45 hours of work per week they give you, it is hard to do the amount extra that would be required for you to break into writing; they have you between a rock and a hard place." Both participants agree that the basic reporting skills they acquired are solid enough to earn them passage into the world of national magazines.

Contact:

Rolling Stone
745 Fifth Ave.
New York, NY 10022

SATURDAY REVIEW   *New York, New York*

ELIGIBILITY: *Undergraduates and some graduate
  students*
DURATION: *Three months*
ACADEMIC CREDIT POSSIBLE: *Yes*
REMUNERATION OR FEE: *None*
POSITIONS OFFERED: *6*
APPLICATION DEADLINE: *Open*

General Description

Saturday Review accepts interns into both its Art and Editorial departments. Art interns help with layout, do photographic research, deliver packages and help out wherever necessary. Editorial interns type, proofread, check facts and do odd jobs. The work delegated to an intern depends upon his/her abilities and the department he/she is working in. In addition, the magazine plans to begin hiring interns as reporters for the summer.

Interns generally work 40 hours per week for a semester or approximately three months. The program is offered year-round. Because there is no application deadline, applications are handled on a first-come-first-serve basis. The magazine receives about 50 applications each month. Applicants must submit a resume and a cover letter explaining why they want to work at *Saturday Review*. Interviews are required.

The Inside Word

An intern told us that she spends most of her time doing research for articles to be written. She investigates background material and checks facts, but she does not actually write articles. In addition, interns are required to submit article proposals. If their proposals are accepted they get to do the research on their topics but they do not actually write the finished product.

However, different editors delegate varying amounts of responsibility and creativity to interns. Some editors do let their interns write small segments for publication. An administrator told us that most interns are not given much responsibility because they don't stay at *Saturday Review* long enough to become truly effective. One intern told us that she sometimes feels "exploited" because she works long hours and tries to do her job well—but receives no salary. She thinks that *Saturday Review* is "not in great shape financially" and takes on interns to fill editorial assistant positions without having to pay them. This intern added that because the magazine is small the atmosphere is very friendly. She feels that the interns have been treated like equals. "They make us feel like they couldn't manage without us," she said.

An administrator told us that interns are evaluated on the basis of their resumes and their cover letters. She told us, "We don't ask for work samples because we hope to avoid the Catch-22 that says you can't work if you don't have experience. We look for an intelligent cover letter instead."

Contact:

Susan Von Hoffman
Saturday Review
1290 Avenue of the Americas
New York, NY 10019

SCIENCE
NEWS   *Washington, D.C.*

ELIGIBILITY: *Graduate*
DURATION: *Varies*
ACADEMIC CREDIT POSSIBLE: *Yes*

REMUNERATION OR FEE: *$500 to $1600/semester*
POSITIONS OFFERED: *1 per semester*
APPLICATION DEADLINE: *Open*

General Description

Science News, a weekly magazine with a circulation of 175,000, offers internships in science reporting and writing. One student is hired full-time each semester and summer, and the dates for the program are flexible. Interns are required to have a BS/BA and must show science writing ability by including clips in their application.

An editor informally supervises the intern's work, and some students work closely with a particular writer. Almost all work is self-initiated, except for occasional assignments to articles that may be part of a special issue or an addition to another writer's piece. Interns take part in every aspect of the magazine's operation: layout, proofreading, choosing pictures, paste-up, editing copy, and general "gophering" in addition to reporting and writing.

There is stiff competition for admission to the program. Approximately 20 people apply each year for a total of three positions. The internship receives academic credit at the University of Missouri School of Journalism, and is usually connected with academic programs at other journalism grad schools.

The Inside Word

Two interns we contacted went on to get full-time professional jobs with *Science News.* All the interns "enjoyed everything" about their internships: "very little writing for this magazine is tedious or uninteresting because there are virtually no assigned articles—you cook up your own news." The internship allows students "to become full, functioning professionals, and helps them make contacts for getting a permanent job."

Before applying for a science writing internship, be sure you want to write for the science buff and science professional, rather than for the lay audience. You must know your science forwards and backwards: "there are no fact checkers or researchers on the staff; the mistakes you make are your own, and the audience will catch every one and write in, to your great embarrassment." It certainly helps to have a good science background in college; a degree in the fields of physical or environmental science is invaluable to writing technical articles.

Probably the best way to go about getting accepted into *Science News'* internship program is to be connected with University of Missouri's Journalism School or other academic programs with ties to the magazine. But students from outside these schools are certainly welcome to apply independently. Other positive factors include the ability to work without much guidance, "a little craziness, and a particularly friendly-aggressive personality."

"*SN* is a very casual, low-key, somewhat schizophrenic operation. People here are all young, all a little weird in their own loveable ways, some renegades from the 60's, but all very interesting and mostly talented. The staff, while not bowling you over with friendliness, will always respond to one's advances."

In the words of one intern: "you can do as much or as little as you want and no one will say anything—but the more you do, the better off you'll be."

Contact:

Mr. Robert J. Trotter
Science News
1719 N. St., N.W.
Washington, D.C. 20036

RADIO

CORPORATION FOR PUBLIC BROADCASTING (CPB)
Summer Internship Program

Washington, D.C.

ELIGIBILITY: *Undergraduate and graduate*
DURATION: *September-December; January-April; June-August*
ACADEMIC CREDIT POSSIBLE: *Yes*
REMUNERATION OR FEE: *None*
POSITIONS OFFERED: *5*
APPLICATION DEADLINE: *March 1 for summer program; open for others*

General Description

CPB is a private, non-profit organization established to promote the growth of non-commercial television and radio stations. The corporation maintains liaison with Congress and members of the executive branch concerned with broadcasting policy, while also managing the funds of non-commercial networks.

Internships were recently offered in the following CPB departments: Radio Activities, Legislative Affairs, Communications Research, and Public Affairs. Interns in Public Affairs are usually journalism students who edit, research, and are occasionally asked to write articles for CPB publications. Communications Research interns contact various agencies to determine what cross-section of the population is viewing certain programs and collect data on target audiences for prospective shows.

Legislative Affairs interns assist a legislative counsel in lobbying efforts, often attending hearings to find where congressmen stand on issues affecting non-commercial broadcasting. Interns involved in Radio Activities read about, write on, and research issues pertaining to non-commercial radio stations.

According to Director of Personnel, Lily A. Okura, every effort is made to ensure the intern is assigned a specific project before coming to Washington. By making such preliminary arrangements, Ms. Okura hopes to avoid unsatisfactory situations.

Applicants specify which CPB department most interests them. If the particular department is in need of an intern, the department draws up the guidelines for an internship project. The applicant accepts or declines the internship depending on what he/she thinks of the project.

CPB will not accept any applicant who is not affiliated with a college or approved by a placement officer. Ms. Okura prefers to have interns working for academic credit and feels a responsibility to assign challenging work because they are doing so.

Interns are required to write a paper after their tenure with CPB in which they comment on what they have gained from their internship experience.

The Inside Word

Overall, the interns gave a favorable impression of their work for CPB. One intern was exceptional in his view that he felt interns were given rather tedious and uninteresting tasks. He had complained to Ms. Okura who responded by asking the other interns if they too were dissatisfied. She claims the others found their work quite stimulating. The same positive sentiments were echoed by the interns in our personal interviews with them. The interns overwhelmingly agreed that they were gaining valuable practical experience in their field.

Several former interns have continued to work for CPB. One man is presently doing work for the Corporation in the Midwest, while a woman who was an intern for two semesters has just been offered a paying job with the organization.

Contact:

Lily A. Okura, Director of Personnel
Corporation for Public Broadcasting
1111 16th Street, N.W.
Washington, D.C. 20036

GROUP W WESTINGHOUSE BROADCASTING COMPANY STATIONS   New York, New York

ELIGIBILITY: Graduate
DURATION: 9 months

ACADEMIC CREDIT POSSIBLE: *No*
REMUNERATION OR FEE: *Varies*
POSITIONS OFFERED: *12*
APPLICATION DEADLINE: *Open*

General Description

Although Group W stations are located across the country, the headquarters are in New York, and it is here that a student applies. Since interns must work full-time, they cannot also be attending school. Salary is determined by the location of the station to which the intern is assigned and by his or her position, and ranges from $210 to $250 weekly. Interns spend the first three months training in general broadcasting. The remaining six months are spent specializing in an area of the intern's choosing. This internship program is currently being re-evaluated and not presently accepting interns, but is expected to begin again soon. Some Westinghouse stations offer summer positions, and interested students should write either directly to the station or to the headquarters, which will foward all inquiries.

The Inside Word

The Westinghouse Program has been described as "a good source of training. Interns are treated like any other employee and are assigned responsible work." Many interns go on to apply for permanent positions.

Contact:

Eleanor Brown
Group W Westinghouse Broadcasting Co. Stations
90 Park Ave.
New York, NY 10016

KNBR BROADCAST INTERN PROGRAM
San Francisco, California

ELIGIBILITY: *High School through graduate*
DURATION: *8 to 13 weeks*
ACADEMIC CREDIT POSSIBLE: *Yes*
REMUNERATION OR FEE: *Minimum wage*
POSITIONS OFFERED: *10 to 14*
APPLICATION DEADLINE: *Open*

General Description

The Broadcast Intern Program is a competitive and comprehensive introduction to radio broadcasting for people of all ages. It requires excellent communication skills, typing ability and a willingness to do one's best at the boring as well as the more exciting features of the job.

The station usually hires college students, graduates, older men and women looking for a career change, and even a few high school students. The internship program is offered both during the summer and the school year.

KNBR requires a firm time commitment and prefers those who can work full-time. When this is not possible, interns must be able to guarantee certain hours when they will be available—even though the station can not promise that hours will be steady.

Instead of being assigned to a specific project or to assist a staff member, interns form a central pool to assist in all aspects of broadcasting. Assignments vary in length from hours to weeks. The amount of responsibility that goes with each project depends on the department, the intern's experience, and the specific task.

A large part of the internship, especially in the beginning, is definitely busywork. Trainees stuff envelopes, answer telephones and mail, and run whatever errands need to be done. While all interns have their share of these less demanding but necessary tasks, they also get a chance to run promotional events, help in the newsroom, set up interviews for public affairs shows and eventually produce news programs. As the program's director said, "Someone who works hard at the tedious jobs is likely to be trusted with the demanding and exciting ones. By making the most of every assignment, the intern will learn most and go furthest."

It is helpful, but not essential to have majored in journalism or broadcasting. Many interns with no journalism background have been very successful in the program and were hired permanently by the station. Clear expression of ideas, the ability to type 50 words per minute, and enthusiasm are of utmost importance. Many interns have later been hired by KNBR and other radio as well as television stations.

The Inside Word

The interns who got the most out of the internship were those who looked for a general smattering of knowledge and were willing to work long hard hours. One intern said, "Don't expect a glamorous job as a sportscaster or anchorman—it's just not that kind of experience." Enjoyment and satisfaction can be found in less demanding tasks. An intern who helped screen telephone callers during a talk show said "It's not terribly demanding—but it's fun. You wouldn't believe some of the kooks who call in."

Former interns praise the program on two counts. For most, it was a stepping stone leading to other positions in the broadcast field. In addition, these interns said that they felt appreciated—and were never taken advantage of. The friendliness of the staff made even the most boring tasks tolerable.

Contact:

Ms. Jane Morrison
Station KNBR
1700 Montgomery St., Suite 400
San Francisco, CA 94111

NATIONAL CITIZENS COMMITTEE FOR BROADCASTING

Washington, D.C.

ELIGIBILITY: *Undergraduates, graduates, law students*
DURATION: *About 10 weeks; September-December, January-March, June-August.*
ACADEMIC CREDIT POSSIBLE: *Yes*
REMUNERATION OR FEE: *None*
POSITIONS OFFERED: *Generally 7 in fall and spring; 15 in summer*
APPLICATION DEADLINE: *April 1 for summer*

General Description

NCCB is a national media reform group chaired by Ralph Nader. Interns are involved in the following NCCB activities: research and writing for *Access Magazine* (bi-weekly magazine of media reform); preparing booklets on consumerism; analyzing complaints registered with the FCC and determining what action, if any, has been or should be taken; developing alternative communications policy positions; meeting with decision-makers; and routine office work.

According to program director Samuel Simon, each intern ideally publishes at least one article in *Access* during his tenure. Additional papers may be required by the intern's school if academic credit is being received. Work Study Programs are occasionally arranged in which the intern receives a salary paid jointly by his academic institution (30%) and NCCB (20%).

Approximately 20 percent of the intern's time is taken up by office work. An intern will often work four days straight on a project and spend the next day filing, typing, etc. Recent intern projects include studies of the Trade Association and compiling statistics of the telephone industry.

Admission to the program is competitive and is based on interviews, resumes, and writing samples.

The Inside Word

The NCCB is a small, dedicated organization with only seven permanent employees, three of whom are attorneys. They regularly work six days a week from nine in the morning till eight at night. Because of the great amount of work to be done and the small staff, interns receive little supervision; it's essential that the intern be able to pursue a project independently.

One intern felt the program would be ideal for a student concentrating on broadcasting or communications; he came to Washington with a specific project in mind. Other interns with little background in the media have also benefited from the program.

The interns we spoke with were enthusiastic about the program. One intern commented, "We obviously wouldn't be here [working without pay], if we didn't think it was worthwhile." Another intern felt she had more interesting work than interns with whom she had talked who were involved in other programs in Washington. "If you're comfortable with a public interest perspective, work independently, and have some outside means of support, NCCB internship is ideal," said a program veteran.

Contact:

Samuel Simon or Sally Steenland, Project Directors
National Citizens Committee for Broadcasting
1028 Connecticut Ave., N.W.
Washington, D.C. 20036

UPI OF CHICAGO   Chicago, Illinois
Broadcast Journalism Summer Intern Program

ELIGIBILITY: *Undergraduates and graduates*
DURATION: *10 to 16 weeks—summer*
ACADEMIC CREDIT POSSIBLE: *Yes*
REMUNERATION OR FEE: *$238/week*
POSITIONS OFFERED: *Varies*
APPLICATION DEADLINE: *May 1*

General Description

The intern's work at UPI of Chicago consists of rewriting news copy into broadcast material. This work must be willingly done at all hours of the day and night. Rarely will interns work on outside stories and projects.

Applicants are selected on the basis of a personal interview, scholastic standing, and a news writing test in which they are given an hour to write four or five stories. Some background in broadcast journalism is required.

The Inside Word

Program director Bill Ferguson feels that interns gain an understanding of what a career in broadcast journalism involves: "If the kids enjoy the program it's successful, and if they don't, it's still successful because they have realized broadcast journalism is not for them while there's plenty of time to change career decisions."

Contact:

Bill Ferguson
UPI of Chicago
360 North Michigan
Chicago, IL 60601

WBCN NEWS INTERNSHIPS   *Boston, Massachusetts*

ELIGIBILITY: *Undergraduate*
DURATION: *Fall semester, spring semester, and summer*
ACADEMIC CREDIT POSSIBLE: *Yes*
REMUNERATION OR FEE: *None*
POSITIONS OFFERED: *Maximum of 4*
APPLICATION DEADLINE: *July 31 for fall; November 31 for spring; April 31 for summer.*

General Description

WBCN is a progressively oriented FM radio station emphasizing "alternative news." It broadcasts to a target audience of 18 to 25 year-olds.

Interns learn to use taping equipment and write for radio news shows. They do some in-the-field reporting, rewrite stories, and keep wire services up-to-date.

Generally 20 to 30 people apply for the four positions the station offers. WBCN seeks interns who have had some previous experience in writing and journalism or who have demonstrated familiarity in a topic such as political science or foreign affairs. Interns come from colleges and the local community.

Applicants should send a résumé and cover letter explaining why they want to work for WBCN. Samples of previous work are helpful and an interview is required.

The Inside Word

The intern interviewed was very enthusiastic about the WBCN program. She said that she was receiving solid training in the basics of both production and reporting and has the opportunity to do everything but actually be on the air. She does very little clerical or busy work.

Contact:

Ms. Lorraine Ballard
WBCN
5005 Prudential Tower
Boston, MA 02199

WFYR INTERNSHIPS   *Chicago, Illinois*

ELIGIBILITY: *Undergraduate*
DURATION: *News up to one year; public affairs up to
    two years*
ACADEMIC CREDIT POSSIBLE: *Yes*
REMUNERATION OR FEE: *$3.10/hour salary*
POSITIONS OFFERED: *2 news, 2 public affairs*
APPLICATION DEADLINE: *Open*

General Description

WFYR is an FM radio station with a staff of 42 which offers internships in either news or public affairs.

News interns learn to use taping equipment, report in the field, and write for radio. Public affairs interns write public service announcements, sit in on conferences, participate in production work, research special features and documentaries, and share in the general office work.

WFYR seeks interns who have previously demonstrated an interest in a broadcasting career. Selection is based on the applicant's sincere desire to gain valuable experience and on potential skill as demonstrated through an interview and writing samples.

The Inside Word

The news intern interviewed spent the majority of his time in the field covering everything from fires to basketball games. The habits and tips he received from working closely with experienced reporters have "prepared him well," and he will soon move on to another station as a full-time sports reporter. He mentioned other interns who have made similar moves or remained with WFYR as full staff members.

Contact:

News—Ron Davis

Public Affairs—Leslie Isenberg
WFYR
130 East Randolph
Chicago, IL 60601

WHN BROADCASTING INTERNSHIP   New York, New York

ELIGIBILITY: *High school through undergraduate*
DURATION: *Semester*
ACADEMIC CREDIT POSSIBLE: *Yes*
REMUNERATION OR FEE: *None*
POSITIONS OFFERED: *4 to 8*
APPLICATION DEADLINE: *Open*

General Description

The WHN Broadcasting Internship is designed for those without any
extensive experience in broadcasting. Its two main requirements are an
interest in broadcasting as a possible career and a statement from the
intern's academic institution guaranteeing that he or she will receive
academic credit for the semester's work.

WHN patterns the internship like a college course. The trainee is
expected to contribute between five and eight hours throughout the week,
preferably not all in one day. At the end of the term, the intern receives an
evaluation from the station's employee with whom he/she was in close
contact throughout the semester.

There is no formal application or deadline. The usual practice is to call
the station and set-up an interview, which is intended to be both evaluative
and informative.

The Inside Word

Interns become acquainted with the doings of all those around them, but
usually choose to concentrate on one field. There are a variety of areas
from which to choose: researching sports and music, writing and producing news, operating the technical equipment, etc. In all fields the intern
becomes familiar with the station's broadcasting rules and scheduling
format.

Contact:

Carol McGuire
Station WHN
400 Park Ave.
New York, NY 10019

WPIX New York, New York

ELIGIBILITY: *High school, undergraduate*
DURATION: *Semester*
ACADEMIC CREDIT POSSIBLE: *Yes*
REMUNERATION OR FEE: *None*
POSITIONS OFFERED: *Varies*
APPLICATION DEADLINE: *Open*

General Description

WPIX is a contemporary music station. Internships are offered on a semester and summer basis, and students must receive academic credit for all internship work. Interns are assigned to one of a number of areas: news, production, sales, and, primarily, music. Approximately eight positions are available at any one time and several hundred students vie for these spots. It is advisable to apply about three months before you wish to begin work.

The Inside Word

The interview is the deciding factor in gaining admittance. Administrators look for "a desire to learn and to fit in." A good deal of "busy work" is to be expected no matter which department an intern works in—but responsible tasks are assigned as well. Interns working in the news division for instance, have been involved in editing tapes and gathering story information. Many interns return as full-time employees in the future.

Contact:

Ms. Betsy Buckin
WPIX
220 E. 42nd St.
New York, NY 10017

WRVR New York, New York

ELIGIBILITY: *Undergraduate*
DURATION: *Semester*
ACADEMIC CREDIT POSSIBLE: *Yes*
REMUNERATION OR FEE: *None*
POSITIONS OFFERED: *Varies*
APPLICATION DEADLINE: *Open*

General Description

Interns at WRVR, primarily a jazz radio station, must receive academic credit for their work at the station. Positions are available during both the summer and the school year. Typically, there are three to six interns during any one period. It is possible to work either full-time or part-time depending upon the student's schedule or willingness to take off time from college. Help is needed in several areas: music, news, and production, among others. Interns spend an equal amount of time in each division, unless they have specifically requested one division.

The Inside Word

Interns responded positively to the WRVR program and their exposure to the various aspects of programming. The people at the station were described as "friendly and responsive—they appreciate the intern's help." The work is "a combination of responsible tasks and busy-work." Interns claim the interview is the most important factor in the application process. Prospective interns should try to show basic broadcasting knowledge in these interviews. The success of WRVR's internship program is evidenced by the fact that most interns come back to apply for permanent jobs.

Contact:

Ms. Sandy Jackson
WRVR
41-30 58th St.
Woodside, NY 11377

WYSP   *Bala Cynwyd, Pennsylvania*

ELIGIBILITY: *High school through undergraduate*
DURATION: *Semester*
ACADEMIC CREDIT POSSIBLE: *Yes*
REMUNERATION OR FEE: *None*
POSITIONS OFFERED: *Varies*
APPLICATION DEADLINE: *Open*

General Description

WYSP is a rock and roll station located just outside Philadelphia. At least five interns work during a semester or summer, and must receive academic credit for their work. A minimum of 10 hours per week must be logged by the intern. The student rotates departments every two weeks, gaining exposure to the music, sales, accounting, programming, and engineering divisions. Each department grades the intern on his or her work. It is advisable to apply early since approximately 50 people vie for the positions each semester.

The Inside Word

In the interview, applicants should stress their interest and their available hours, since those students who are most accessible to the station and are most enthusiastic about their work fare best in the job. Interns commented that "a lot of it's busy work and unless you're a hard worker, they don't like to give you responsible tasks. The program could be improved if the staff took out more time to show interns what to do, but everyone's really busy. Still, they try to make the interns as comfortable as possible." More recent participants in the program claim that "it is much more organized, and the interns are happier." Students have occasionally been offered permanent jobs during the course of their internship.

Contact:

Ms. Sandy Shields
WYSP
1 Bala Cynwyd Plaza–Suite 424
Bala Cynwyd, PA 19004

ADDITIONAL RADIO INTERNSHIPS

You might also try the following stations for information on their less structured internship programs:

KIRO
3rd and Broad
Seattle, Washington 98121
(206)624-7077

WCAU—Radio
Mr. Goodman
Cityline and Monument Rds.
Philadelphia, Pennsylvania 19131
(215)839-7000

KSFX
1177 Polk St.
San Francisco, CA 94109

WCBS
51 W. 52nd St.
New York, New York 10019
(212)975-4321

KYW
5th and Market Sts.
Philadelphia, Pennsylvania 19106
(215)238-4700

WDVM
4001 Brandywine St. NW
Washington, DC 20016
(202)686-6000

WNBC
Mr. Pete Porello
30 Rockefeller Plaza
New York, New York 10020
(212)664-4444

WPVI
4100 Cityline Ave.
Bala Cynwyd, Pennsylvania 19004
(215)878-9700

WNMR
19th and Walnut
Philadelphia, Pennsylvania 19103
(215)561-0933

WCYC (Spanish language station)
José Gaspar
2801 South Ridgeway Ave.
Chicago, IL 60623

TELEVISION

WNET-TV
College Internship Program

New York, New York

ELIGIBILITY: *Undergraduate juniors and seniors*
DURATION: *Fall, spring, and summer*
ACADEMIC CREDIT POSSIBLE: *Yes*
REMUNERATION OR FEE: *None*
POSITIONS OFFERED: *120/year, 40/semester*
APPLICATION DEADLINE: *November for Spring;*
  February for Summer; May for fall.

General Description

The internship program at WNET is open to any college junior or senior
with an interest in television production. No special skills are required
because WNET assigns interns to departments suited to the intern's
interests. Those applicants who have worked out academic credit for this
program are given first preference.

The internship is divided into three programs: the fall program runs
from September to January; the spring program from January to May; the
summer program from June to August. The specific starting and ending
dates depend on the intern's academic schedule. The internship takes
place at the WNET office building or at their studio, both of which are in
Manhattan.

The internship at WNET requires interns to work a minimum of
twenty-one hours per week and a maximum of forty hours. Two weekdays
of work must be consecutive. Interns will be required to write and do
research, regardless of the department in which they are placed.

Approximately 450 to 500 people apply to this program each year and
special consideration is given to women and minorities. WNET does not

offer any remuneration for the fall and spring programs, but summer interns are paid the cost of their initial transportation to WNET. A resume, letters of recommendation, and a portfolio (if the applicant is an art student) are required.

The Inside Word

During the interview at WNET, interns are given an evaluation written by a past intern and are asked how they might be able to get more out of the program. Through this process, WNET hopes to provide a unique opportunity for each intern to work in a program that is pertinent to his/her skills and interests.

Interns attend meetings once a week, in which they have control over topics of discussion and guest speakers. Each intern is also required to sit in on an editing session, a taping of The Dick Cavett Show, and a taping of the McNeil-Lehrer Report.

Last year, interns worked in thirty-three departments at WNET. Interns must submit a mid-progress report describing how they have contributed to the program along with a five-page evaluation at the end of the program. The program director recommends that each intern have typing skills.

Contact:

Internship Administrator
WNET
356 West 58th Street
New York, NY 10019

WNEW-TV   New York, New York
Internship Program

ELIGIBILITY: *Undergraduate and graduate*
DURATION: *10 to 12 weeks*
ACADEMIC CREDIT POSSIBLE: *Yes*
REMUNERATION OR FEE: *None*
POSITIONS OFFERED: *90/year, 28/semester*
APPLICATION DEADLINE: *Late summer for fall; late*
    November for spring; March for summer.

General Description

The WNEW-TV internship program is organized for students interested in communications who are juniors or seniors in college. Students work in many of the various departments of the station, and the position they are given depends on their previous experience and skills. Positions are either full-time or part-time, but interns are required to work at least three full days a week.

Interns work under the supervision of the department head or a supervisor designated by the department head. Interns attend a four-hour orientation seminar at the beginning of the internship. After the seminar, interns in production are required to work 35 hours per week, and all others must work at least 24 hours during the course of the week.

The program is usually ten to twelve weeks long. Applicants must have a written statement from their college either granting academic credit or agreeing to record the internship on students' transcripts. A resume is also required before the mandatory interview can take place.

The Inside Word

Interns at Channel 5 come from a variety of academic backgrounds and most have had previous experience in television production. It was noted by one intern, however, that this experience was not essential to be successful in the program: "Channel 5 doesn't really want you to use any of your past experience—they want you to observe and learn new things."

An intern in the programming department described her activities as "anything that needs to be done—reading viewer mail, screening commercials, screening cable television, etc." Another intern in the community affairs department described his day-to-day activities as "answering phones, screening commercials, watching production, screening calls, and helping work on the production of a children's show." All interns advised "leaving your own department and going as many places as you can." And one intern noted that "if you get accepted early enough they will let you choose the department you want to work in."

The staff at Channel 5 is "helpful and receptive—and if you realize that you are last on the totem pole but have the ambition and initiative, you can really learn a lot."

Contact:

Mr. Michael Stephens
WNEW-TV
205 E. 67th Street
New York, NY 10021

OTHER PLACES TO LOOK:

Business
American Association of Advertising Agencies
C. Paul Luongo Company
Wakefield Washington Associates

Public Service
Public Citizen

Law

If you think getting into law school is tough, try getting an internship with a law firm. Despite the strenuous efforts of legislators to expand the number of laws and of litigious Americans to pack the courts, the competition for positions of any kind in private law firms is tough.

Moreover, many of the jobs that students *can* fill are boring. Finding a good internship, as one lawyer says, "is mainly getting in a position of close observation, and that is a very haphazard kind of thing." For a close-up of life in the law, another lawyer advises observation of his colleagues in court defending clients. "Seeing what goes on in the courts is good exposure to the real business of the law," he explains, "because so much else that lawyers do seems on the surface dull and tawdry."

Internships in private firms are usually called "summer" or "part-time" jobs, and are extremely hard to get. Most firms simply don't hire students until they have completed one, or usually two, years of law school. "Until then, students just don't know how to think like lawyers," complains one corporate law partner.

But there *are* exceptions, especially for those with connections. "It all depends on how heavily leaned on you are," says a big-firm lawyer. "If an important enough client calls and says, 'My son is looking for a law job. He's desperate for something to do this summer. Can you find him something?' then we hire him and we *make* something for him to do." Start thinking about who you know.

There are other opportunities open to people not yet in law school—or who aren't even sure they want to go—but they take some looking.

A word about motivation: If you're looking for a legal internship to get you into law school, think again. Most admissions officers don't pay much attention to "pre-legal" experience. To them, grades and test scores are far more important admission yardsticks. But don't be put off. A legal internship might give you the experience you need to make up your mind about law schools. And you won't be alone—a large percentage of first-year law students do not enter directly from college.

Chances for an internship vary around the country. New York seems to have many; Chicago very few. In all cases, persistence is the key. If you can wrangle an interview with one of the big fish of the organization, veterans say, your chances of getting a position skyrocket.

Paralegals

Paralegal positions are one route into a firm. Lawyers who don't understand the word "intern" are often glad to talk about letting you do

276

paralegal work, particularly in smaller firms. However, be prepared to make a minimum commitment of one year: "We don't want to train someone as a paralegal who is going to disappear inside a year."

Most paralegals (sometimes called "legal assistants") are still professionals, having gone to school anywhere from eight weeks to 18 months for the job, and are often specialists, such as in insurance adjustments. But small firms often cannot afford this kind of expertise and will turn gladly to articulate students who can learn fast, while even prestigious firms have taken on recent college grads who seem earnest in their interest in the law.

One graduate of a selective New England college, now helping an associate in a major New York firm, researches cases, writes memoranda, and even drafts briefs. "I got the job after two tries at other places," he says. "I gave them a resume, I told them I was pretty sure I wanted to go to Harvard Law School, but that I wanted a chance to see what lawyers really did before committing myself. They not only gave me this job— they're paying me, too!" As a paralegal you can expect to serve as a kind of assistant lawyer, doing routine tasks like organizing and analyzing documents, drawing up wills, and drafting simple court pleas.

Does paralegal work give you a good sense of the life of a lawyer? "Probably not," says Richard Badger, Dean of Students at the University of Chicago's Graduate School of Law, "but it is better exposure to what lawyers do than anything else."

Another area to investigate: work in a firm's library or docket department ("These people really get to know the court system"). These positions have two advantages: they require no training, and have no minimum time commitment.

Work in the library means locating references, and re-shelving. Docket department jobs require that you keep track of the firm's pending cases, obtain files (and then refile them), and, on rare occasions, file minor motions in court. ("There is some concern that this is practicing law without a license," says one attorney, "but that has never really been tested yet").

Second only to paralegal work, these positions provide a good, albeit worm's eye, view of a law firm.

It is difficult to generalize about *what* you will be observing in a private firm. Corporate law employs legions of the country's lawyers, where tax law, advice on government guidelines and restrictions, and litigation head the list of common activities. But most big firms also have *pro bono publico* (public interest) divisions which offer free counsel to all kinds of non-corporate interests. Smaller private firms outside big cities, on the other hand, are often pre-occupied with individual clients who need wills drawn up, property conveyed, divorces accomplished and landlords sued.

To get a feeling for the law, though, you needn't work for a law firm. Major corporations have their own "in-house" legal staff. A bit off the beaten path of big-city law, they often prove more welcoming. Also, court-connected agencies, like Parole and Probation Offices or the juvenile court, are good places to try.

One court-connected agency that often takes interns on a regular basis is the District Attorney's Office. If you are interested in criminal prosecution, try the D.A.'s office in your area. At the end of this chapter, you'll find a detailed description of the Staten Island District Attorney's program, which is one of the best. This should give you an idea of what you are likely to discover at other D.A.'s offices around the country.

Public Service Law

The best way to become acquainted with our convoluted system of jurisprudence is to work for any one of a number of public service law agencies. Ranging from the American Civil Liberties Union to the local legal aid clinic around the corner, these places offer an intimate look at our country's laws, courts, and counsel from the perspective of clients who often walk in off the street not knowing how to fight for their rights. Interns in these agencies usually do intake work—interviewing potential clients, organizing the facts for the staff attorneys, and following up with phone calls and letters to see that the claims have been rectified. Many of these agencies have an ideological bent (the Chicago chapter of the A.C.L.U. promises to convert its interns into civil libertarians), and few of the organizations can afford to pay much. But at the same time they offer the best opportunities—short of actually being a lawyer—to see the nuts and bolts of U.S. law and courts in action.

In the following pages, you'll find detailed information on working in legal aid clinics, and a description of the internship program of the Chicago chapter of the American Civil Liberties Union — representative of programs in other A.C.L.U. chapters around the country.

AMERICAN CIVIL LIBERTIES UNION   Chicago, Illinois
Chicago Chapter Internship

ELIGIBILITY: *Undergraduate*
DURATION: *Usually summer*
ACADEMIC CREDIT POSSIBLE: *Yes*
REMUNERATION OR FEE: *None*
POSITIONS OFFERED: *6*
APPLICATION DEADLINE: *February for the summer, or
2 months in advance of desired starting date*

General Description

A.C.L.U. interns are at the service end of a special interest law agency. They don't work as much with the law as with the people who have been wronged by the law. Interns do intake work, answer the phone, follow up on A.C.L.U. action, and put out fliers.

Internships are available all year and can run any length of time. The hours are flexible—both full-time and part-time spots are open. To apply, give the A.C.L.U. a call and then to write them. Your best chances for snaring a spot are in February or March, but don't hesitate to contact them after that—often things open up later on.

The organization gets around 15 applicants for the six summer spots. Juniors and seniors in college are preferred.

The Inside Word

Qualifications: The A.C.L.U.'s ideal intern likes people. Interns must have a good phone voice and be reliable. Communication skills are important, as interns spend a lot of their time writing letters and answering questions. Most importantly, an intern must be cooperative and willing to listen and learn. No previous legal experience is necessary.

Getting accepted: The A.C.L.U. is looking for a good interviewer and a good business letter writer. During the interview, they are watching how you deal with people, and checking on your "demeanor." Intelligence and maturity are expected. Also, since they are "primarily concerned with constitutional liberties," a lot rides on your open-minded examination of civil libertarian issues. It would pay to read up on current A.C.L.U. activities, and be familiar with the issues.

It's recommended that you apply early in order to have the best shot at a position.

Responsibilities: An intern's primary duty is to research and present complaints to the staff lawyers. This means greeting clients who telephone or walk in off the street, and taking their stories. Half of an intern's time is spent interviewing clients, usually in person. The other half is generally spent as a receptionist—holding down the phone, responding to letters, and introducing everybody who wanders into the office.

Interns do the "pushing" for the A.C.L.U. After they have presented a case to the staff attorneys and it is resolved, the interns follow up on it. They write letters and make phone calls to see whether a landlord or employer is now complying with the law, or whether a victim is getting proper recompense. From these tasks comes a healthy sense of the importance of civil liberties. Interns often go on to law school.

Limitations: The A.C.L.U. internships are not without their problems. Interns have little input into what's going on, and their work is sometimes tedious. Furthermore, with most interns working part-time, they seem to flit from task to task without having to take much responsibility.

Interns explain that the best jobs are in "intake" and advise people to apply for that section only. Otherwise, you are likely to get stuck, as one intern did, doing fund-raising and new membership mailings. The excitement of outlining and researching a flier on the military draft failed to outweigh the tediousness of the mailing work.

Contact:

Babette Joseph
American Civil Liberties Union
5 South Wabash
Chicago, IL 60602

CORPORATE LAW INTERNSHIPS

In corporate law firms, interns are at the bottom end of a very tall totem pole. They run the errands and do the chores that the legal secretaries don't have time for. Once restricted to occasional summer jobs for establishment children, internships with corporate law firms are beginning to open up to a wider variety of applicants. Though you will find hirings to be still dominated by nepotism, there *is* a small chance that you can land a job without connections. The work these jobs entail might not be exciting in itself—sorting mail and filing documents is nobody's idea of a good time—but they remain the only way for students to get a glimpse of corporate lawyers in action.

Most of the internships are in the summer—that's when the students are free. Occasionally, someone will work in the fall, winter, and/or spring, working part-time or taking time off from school.

Law firms call the internship for pre-law college students "summer employment." Discover good law firms to apply to by delving into the *Martindale-Hubbell Law Directory* (available at the public library). Find out who you should contact from the firm's receptionist, write or hand deliver your resume and cover letter requesting a job. Wait two weeks, then call to set up an interview.

Pay ranges from nothing to $230 a week and averages around the minimum wage. Count yourself lucky if you get a job, and don't press your employer for too much pay.

The Inside Word

Interns in law firms never touch the law. More likely, they will be dispensing the mail, pulling, sorting, and filing documents, or working in the library. Seldom do the projects involve personal initiative and input, but often interns do work on their own.

Most interns index documents. Others distribute mail and occasionally file documents in court. Some put together digests and chronologies of potential evidence. Often they work in the firm's law library. These are important activities but seldom very stimulating. "Law firm internships are usually boring. Besides filing and other menial tasks, (or, if you know enough, working as a librarian), there is nothing you can do without two years of law school," an intern explained.

Despite the drudgery, these internships have clear benefits. They are an excellent exposure to the world of the most professional lawyers. One intern learned "a great deal about how a corporate firm operates—important in deciding to be a lawyer." For some it is a helpful transition to law school: "It helped me to get away from an academic framework, while giving me an insight into a large New York law firm."

LEGAL AID CLINIC INTERNSHIPS

One of the most likely places to get experience with the law before you head off to law school is in a Legal Aid Clinic. Often operating on a shoestring budget and always with a heavy caseload, the clinics usually welcome interns when there is space and supervision for them.

Legal aid clinic interns do the preliminary research work for busy staff attorneys. This includes interviewing witnesses, investigating cases, basic legal research, and compiling office publications. Because the clinics are usually understaffed, the interns are expected to do clerical work as well. One intern took care of all the intake and pre-trial work-up of the family law cases and, additionally, helped with the general clerical work.

Usually, there's little pay and rarely is there any of the prestige that comes from working for a big law firm. Instead an intern gets an excellent up-close, "hands-on" look at how the law operates.

Finding a legal aid clinic internship isn't always easy. The first problem is locating clinics that are likely to take you on. Search through the local yellow pages under "Lawyers; Legal Aid" or "Lawyers, Legal Assistance." Call the local bar associations (also in the yellow pages) to see if they can help, and, when you are desperate, contact the Legal Services Corporation, the umbrella funding organization of legal aid, in Washington, D.C.

Most places you call won't have formal programs, so you might have to make your own internship (see the section on *Making Your Own*). Most will, however, have had interns come in before and will be open to the idea of more. Visit and apply to a variety of clinics, so as to keep your bases covered.

The Inside Word

The number of internships and the competition for them vary from clinic to clinic. Some will have only three openings with an equal number of applicants, others will have a dozen slots and four dozen applicants. The programs are usually informal and do not have pre-set beginning and ending dates. In most places a letter with a transcript or resume, and perhaps a visit, will be enough of an application.

Getting accepted: When being considered for an internship, some negative factors, such as inavailability of office space and supervision, will be out of your control. Therefore, when you apply, underscore your independence, your ability to fit in without trouble, and your research and writing competence—the skills needed to prepare the case backgrounds. Someone who can carry through on assignments well, quickly, and with little supervision will appear most attractive. An intern's duties are varied. To be hired you must be able to handle—effectively and without complaint—everything from the office work (including emptying waste baskets) to case work. Patience and resourcefulness will serve you well.

Law for the poor: Legal aid clinics dispense law to poor people—that's their job by charter—and an intern should be able to deal with the poor public in a friendly, helpful way. One clinic summed up the qualities they were looking for as a "concern for the poor; good writing and analytical skills; and human relations abilities."

Work at a legal aid clinic is challenging. Under adverse circumstances, the staff and interns must prepare sound legal advice without many resources to support them, and must dispense it for people who are poor and relatively unsophisticated about the ways government and the laws work. "It's a very useful glimpse for anyone who will be a lawyer," one intern commented. It's also quite a challenge.

STATEN ISLAND DISTRICT ATTORNEY
Staten Island, New York
Summer Internship

ELIGIBILITY: *Undergraduate and law school students*
DURATION: *June 1 to August 15*
ACADEMIC CREDIT POSSIBLE: *Yes*
REMUNERATION OR FEE: *None*
POSITIONS OFFERED: *5 to 7*
APPLICATION DEADLINE: *Beginning of January*

General Description

The Staten Island District Attorney's interns work side by side with Assistant District Attorneys: investigating cases, working on memos, responding to court motions, monitoring hearings, and helping with jury selections. All cases involve prosecuting criminals arrested in Richmond County, New York.

To apply, send in a letter and a resume and then arrange for an interview.

The Inside Word

Getting accepted: The five to seven interns are chosen from a pool of 30 to 40 applicants. Though training in criminal justice is a big plus, untrained undergraduates might be able to get by with a good show of enthusiasm. Said a program administrator: "A prime concern in choosing the interns was their interest in the field and eagerness to work. Whether they had taken pertinent courses such as criminal law and procedure was an important, but not overriding, consideration."

Interns recommend showing a sincere interest in criminal prosecution, and being enthusiastic during the interview.

Daily life: Interns fill in on projects that would otherwise be assigned to assistant D.A.'s. Some of it is dull; one intern explained that "legal research is generally uninteresting." But often it is very rewarding. "Knowing that your effort was put to practical use was extremely satisfying," observed another.

The supervision is excellent. Said one intern: "The Chief Assistant D.A. was very charming, instructive, and a fine example of a prosecutor and a boss. He was always available for questions."

Interns have to be open minded and willing to work, but it is a "congenial, dynamic atmosphere." Interns' contributions are carefully recognized: "Frequently, interns were asked their views of a particular issue, and serious consideration was given to their suggestions."

Future prospects: After wrapping up the Staten Island Internship, most students went on to law school and then returned enthusiastically to become Assistant District Attorneys in their own right. Looking back on the internship, they couldn't improve it. One past intern extolled: "I can't think of a thing to change; it was excellent."

Contact:

William L. Murphy
Chief Assistant District Attorney
Office of the District Attorney
Richmond County
36 Richmond Terrace, Rm. 206C
Staten Island, NY 10301

OTHER PLACES TO LOOK:

Business
Massachusetts State Banking Department Consumer Assistance Division

Public Service
Business and Professional People for the Public Interest
Common Cause
Indian Law Seminar and Intern Project for Indian Law Students
Mental Health Law Project
National Committee Against Discrimination in Housing
National Organization for the Reform of Marijuana Laws (NORML)
Public Citizen
Public Defender Service

Public Service

Public service organizations, while encompassing an indefinably broad range of concerns, can be typified by their shared commitment to social change, and by their non-profit status. Interns in such agencies, more so than in any other field, play an integral role in the existence of these groups. Were it not for their internship programs—and virtually every public service organization operates one—many organizations could not function. Given the extensive amount of work to be done, capable volunteer help, as provided by interns, makes it possible for public service organizations to survive.

It follows that, despite the varied and challenging opportunities to be had in other fields, work with a public service organization provides *the* quintessential internship experience. Public service organizations are thoroughly dependent upon their internship help, and the contributions of interns is felt in all phases of their operation. The work, warn most administrators, if often less than glamorous, but all workers—regular staff and interns alike, share fully in both the interesting and the mundane tasks. "It makes for a real sense of community in the office—I became very close to the other workers and interns because things tended to be pretty non-hierarchical" reflected one former intern.

Internships in public service are not suited for everyone. The commitment asked of participants is often a near-total one. Interns work hard at what can be tedious assignments, and generally receive little or no compensation. These are considerations one should take into account before applying, suggests a college internship coordinator, "I wouldn't encourage everyone who comes into my office to try public service—it definitely takes a student who is motivated and knowledgeable—both about the work that goes on at an organization and about how he/she will be expected to fit in."

Although it may be said, with considerable accuracy, that public service organizations are more similar to each other than they are different, the fact remains that all agencies are not alike. Some programs have a definite environmental bent—interns conduct research and lobby on issues related to environmental protection. Others are best suited for those with special skills; the Institute for Local Self-Reliance, for example, looks for students with backgrounds in architecture to investigate new uses for solar energy in the construction of homes. Many agencies work closely with Congress—monitoring legislation and promoting various causes. In some cases, such as the City Volunteer Corps of Los Angeles, interns actually work out of a government office to support public service organizations and activities.

The point is, public service programs can be very different, and the role of an intern in these organizations can vary accordingly. Another factor, in addition to the nature of the work, that should be considered before pursuing a given internship, is whether or not you can afford to work without pay. Most programs accept interns strictly on a volunteer basis. Those needing to make money for school tuition, or having to support themselves for the duration of the internship, should check first to see if the internship could be scheduled around a part-time job. Occasionally, students are able to arrange for work/study funding through their schools, or are eligible for scholarships or grants administered by schools and private organizations. Check with your school's career development office for information on how to subsidize your internship, and how and where to apply for financial assistance.

While never a particularly lucrative proposition, there are, however, several groups that modestly compensate their interns. Some offer a stipend, and many others pay for an intern's job-related travel expenses. Organizations which are essentially clearinghouses place interns with other agencies which will then pay them a regular salary. For the most part, however, interns should not expect their labors to be rewarded in cash. "The personal satisfaction made my experience more than worthwhile" commented one volunteer intern "it would have been nice to be paid, but I think I learned as much or more than I would have had I been in school last semester, so in that sense, it was really worth it."

The Breakdown: What Is Available

The programs listed in the following chapter represent only the very tip of the iceberg in terms of the numbers and kinds of programs and experiences available. This chapter describes programs ranging from an organization that monitors national security institutions to one which gives would-be parks and recreation professionals an on-the-job look at the field. Because of the dependency of these and other public service organizations on interns, most programs in this field tend to be well-defined and have standardized admissions procedures. However, there are numerous opportunities to strike out on your own (see section on "Making Your Own"). Most social service and consumer agencies welcome students who are willing to plan and direct their own internships. For listings of other programs not included here, see the Chapter, "Additional Sources of Information" at the back of the book. Several of the organizations listed here (Public Citizen, National Public Interest Research Group) have affiliated groups in a number of states. Washington *is* the internship capital, but opportunities abound in every locale for enterprising students. Arranging an internship close to your home or school will often provide as illuminating and rewarding experience as a Washington position, and will help solve the financial dilemma as well.

Research, Writing, and Public Service Interns

After reading this section, you will no doubt swear that each listing mentioned the "research and writing" an intern would be responsible for. Past interns assure us that these ubiquitous tasks are far from boring or monotonous. Usually, an intern will be researching and composing a project of his/her own creation. In other cases, interns are given responsibility for gathering crucial data on issues as significant as defense spending and nuclear energy. Even if the "desk work" does become tiresome, "the skills I acquired in doing research for my project and then writing it helped my schoolwork" claimed an intern. In fact, none of the interns we contacted felt that the amount of time spent in the library or at the typewriter was excessive. Field work, lobbying, counseling, attending seminars, etc., were all equally prominent features of most programs.

As a result of the abundance of opportunities, and most organization's inability to pay their interns, admission into all but the salaried programs tends to be non-competitive. Directors don't accept just anyone, however. Sincere interest in and commitment to the goals of an organization is the primary requirement of all programs—more important than scholastic or extracurricular achievements. The best advice for gaining admission, therefore, is to apply only to those agencies for whom you sincerely desire to work, and go to them with a set of objectives mapped out, or with a specific project in mind.

"Achieving social change is a slow process—it requires a good deal of patience" warns the director of a statewide public service organization in Connecticut. "It's a great business: we help a lot of people, but it can be the most frustrating work in the world."

ATLANTA URBAN CORPS INTERNSHIP PROGRAM — Atlanta, Georgia

ELIGIBILITY: *Undergraduate and graduate*
DURATION: *Varies*
ACADEMIC CREDIT POSSIBLE: *Yes*
REMUNERATION OR FEE: *Varies*
POSITIONS OFFERED: *Approximately 1000*
APPLICATION DEADLINE: *Two to three months in advance for summer internships, one month in advance any other time*

General Description

The Atlanta Urban Corps is the city of Atlanta's internship clearinghouse. From an annual applicant pool of 1200, 800 to 1000 interns are placed in agencies in and around Atlanta. Aiming to extend students' educational experience beyond the classroom and into the surrounding community, the Corps works with 150 agencies, placing interns on a year-round basis. Participating agencies fall into four categories: medical and mental health, government and community service, arts, and education. The positions available are catalogued in an "Internship Index" enclosed in the application packet.

There is no formal application deadline, but for the more competitive positions, placement is decided on a first-come, first-serve basis. As a general rule, program director Dennis Doherty recommends that applications be submitted two to three months ahead of time for summer positions, and at least one month beforehand for internships during the fall, winter, and spring.

Applications go directly to the Urban Corps office for an initial screening. Some agencies leave the entire placement procedure up to the Corps, while others screen applicants in their own personnel office. Writing ability and a clear sense of purpose are especially desirable, says Doherty.

The Inside Word

Getting accepted: The Urban Corps program is geared toward students on work/study programs, and gives preference to those students who are able to make such arrangements through their college or university. If possible, arrange to participate in the Corps's program during the school year; the ratio of accepted candidates to applicants is significantly higher. One need not be a resident of Atlanta to participate in the program; however, in such cases interns are responsible for locating their own housing.

The Corps requires an interview of all candidates, and occasionally hires interns for its own office to supplement the full-time staff of four to five coordinators. One such intern, a part-time receptionist who is also studying fashion design, feels his experience has been "invaluable. I am learning to talk to and deal with people in a variety of circumstances— something that will be important to me later on. It has taught me to be versatile."

Contact:

Dennis Doherty
Atlanta Urban Corps
Box 671
University Plaza
Atlanta, GA 30303

BUSINESS AND PROFESSIONAL PEOPLE FOR THE PUBLIC INTEREST INTERNSHIP

Chicago, Illinois

ELIGIBILITY: *Undergraduate and graduate*
DURATION: *Varies*
ACADEMIC CREDIT POSSIBLE: *Yes*
REMUNERATION OR FEE: *Little*
POSITIONS OFFERED: *About four*
APPLICATION DEADLINE: *Two to three months in advance*

General Description

Business and Professional People for the Public Interest (B.P.I.) is a Chicago alliance of executives, public-spirited law firms, and community groups promoting projects that will have a "significant, beneficial impact" on the quality of metropolitan life. B.P.I. acts as a catalyst, providing local organizations and concerned citizens with the legal advice, staffing, and office space needed to fight effectively to improve their city.

Interns do research work to assist the staff or work on public relations and development. Pay is minimal and often the competition for admission to the program is rigorous.

Apply by writing B.P.I. to say that you are interested. Follow up with a phone call, and expect to be interviewed. The internships are open to college and graduate students, begin at any time, and last for three to four months. One should apply two to three months in advance.

The Inside Word

Daily life: B.P.I. is looking for interns with communication and research skills. An ability to deal effectively with people is also important, said one administrator.

Interns at B.P.I. are treated as "equal staff members," in the opinion of one intern—able to offer advice and to criticize as they see fit. One intern felt that even the long and tedious scanning of regulations was an important and interesting task. His experience at B.P.I. was, he felt "more practical and more useful than any college course I could have taken during that time."

Contact:

Alexander Polikoff, Executive Director
Business and Professional People for the Public Interest
109 North Dearborn, Suite 101
Chicago, IL 60602

CENTER FOR COMMUNITY ORGANIZATIONS
Intern Program

Washington, D.C.

ELIGIBILITY: *Undergraduate junior*
DURATION: *Varies*
ACADEMIC CREDIT POSSIBLE: *Yes*
REMUNERATION OR FEE: *None*
POSITIONS OFFERED: *5*
APPLICATION DEADLINE: *Open*

General Description

The Center for Community Organizations trains and organizes community and neighborhood groups to effectively combat urban problems. The CCO, which is financed by public and private grants, also generates its own income by publishing pamphlets and books on community group organizations, and by developing urban programs. As a training, technical assistance and research organization, it holds conferences, workshops, and provides on-site technical assistance. The organization has a network of community action consultants and a management training staff.

Interns are given the responsibilities of a full-time staff member. They work with residents and organizations directly, teaching and helping to organize political action groups. Interns also plan workshops and write and edit manuals on "how to" organize specific community political organizations.

The internship opens many doors to similar work. Interns are exposed to the field of community political action, and, according to one CCO staff member, the training received makes "someone who's been there very valuable." Interns learn writing skills and how to develop specific programs. They also acquire fund raising, research, and communication skills, and a knowledge of federal programs for community organizations. The internship requires a self-motivated person who is able to work independently of others. He or she also must be "aggressive" and "willing to go out there and do what needs to be done."

The Inside Word

Daily life: Interns generally enjoy the program because of the considerable responsibility they are given. They actually do the writing and research for major programs and go as far as organizing their implementation. Most interns intend to go into volunteerism as a career, and this internship seems to be a big foot in the door for full-time staff jobs in the field.

An ability to write well is essential to the job, according to most interns. Knowing how to research topics is also important as well as just a general affinity for "volunteerism, activism and social action." Interns do the work of full-time staff people and practically no clerical work. They spend their days either researching certain community political action organizations, or traveling around the country learning or teaching specific programs, e.g., a community organization to combat crime.

There is no application deadline, but the CCO does require a resume and cover letter of applicants. Approximately 50 students apply for the five available positions. Students majoring in political science, sociology, urban studies, or public administration are given preference in the admission process.

Contact:

Center for Community Organizations Intern Program
1214 16th Street, N.W.
Washington, DC 20036

CENTER FOR DEFENSE INFORMATION   *Washington, D.C.*

ELIGIBILITY: *Undergraduate and graduate*
DURATION: *3 months*
ACADEMIC CREDIT POSSIBLE: *Yes*
REMUNERATION OR FEE: *$400/month*
POSITIONS OFFERED: *8*
APPLICATION DEADLINE: *Mid June for fall; Mid November for winter; End of March for summer*

General Description

Seeking to provide objective analysis of current military issues and related public policy questions, the Center for Defense Information works with journalists, congressional staffs, and the general public. Interns at the Center assist with research and in producing the Center's newsletter, *Defense Monitor.*

The internship is open to all; no college background or specific training of any nature is necessary, although administrators look for sincere interest in the field when screening applicants. Eight positions are available each year—two in the fall, two in the winter, and four during the summer. Each lasts three months, during which time interns receive a monthly stipend of $400.

The Inside Word

Getting accepted: Administrators stress that genuine interest in military and public policy issues is the primary requisite for the Center's program.

Whether demonstrated by one's academic background, work experience, or general knowledge of the field as evidenced during the suggested interview, directors look for a sense of understanding and commitment to the organization's goals among applicants.

While applications are requested two to three months in advance of the time the intern wishes to begin, administrators say that these guidelines are flexible. Applicants must submit a transcript, resume and writing sample.

Daily life: The CDI office is relatively small, with only 12 full-time staff members. Among the special projects interns have been assigned are: evaluating the role of the Department of Energy in national defense policy; the development, deployment, and importance of tactical nuclear weapons, and investigating and reporting on the MX missile. Interns have also participated in public education programs about nuclear weapons, and recently, students assisted in producing a film on the projected consequences of nuclear war.

Contact:

Dr. Tom Karas
Center for Defense Information
122 Maryland Ave. NE
Washington, D.C. 20002

CENTER FOR NATIONAL SECURITY STUDIES

Washington, D.C.

ELIGIBILITY: *Undergraduate and graduate*
DURATION: *10 to 12 weeks; fall, spring, summer*
ACADEMIC CREDIT POSSIBLE: *Yes*
REMUNERATION OR FEE: *None*
POSITIONS OFFERED: *12*
APPLICATION DEADLINE: *Varies*

General Description

Located at the heart of the Washington political scene on Capitol Hill, the Center for National Security Studies is devoted to the investigation of national security institutions and policies. The Center is primarily concerned with the maintenance of individual civil liberties through public reassessment of the policies of the F.B.I, C.I.A., and the military establishment.

Interns assist the permanent staff of 15 in conducting research for CNSS projects. They are responsible for writing or contributing to at least one paper during their term at the Center.

To apply, candidates must submit a resume and writing sample. Directors ask that application be made two months before you will be available to begin. There are three different sessions: fall, spring, and summer. Three interns are accepted for each semester, and six are hired during the summer. Undergraduate upperclassmen and graduate students are preferred.

The Inside Word

Getting accepted: Administrators look for research and writing skills in applicants. Academic and work experience in fields related to the Center's work is helpful, as well as some specified interests which will indicate the type of role an intern might fit into. Many receive academic credit for the program, but participants must make such arrangements on their own.

Daily life: Because of the small size of the regular staff, interns play a vital role in the CNSS operation—collecting and disseminating information, monitoring legislation, and working on the Center's monthly newsletter, *First Principles*.

Specific projects undertaken by interns have included: C.I.A. and Covert Action, Project on National Security and Civil Liberties, Southern Africa and Security, and Executive Prerogative. Interns have published articles in *First Principles* on the Freedom of Information Act, and on their coverage of Congressional hearings.

Participants are assigned as staff assistants in the legislation, publications, library, litigation, or research divisions. Interns attend weekly seminars on the evolution of the national security state, and frequent staff meetings where the Center's activities are updated and projects are coordinated.

According to past interns, the program "was valuable. I learned a great deal about how to organize an office and how to budget my time. Also, I became familiar with various aspects of the legislative process and the Washington scene in addition to the information and skills I acquired in the course of doing my research". Said another, "I particularly benefited from working with experienced professionals in the field".

Contact:

Florence Oliver, Intern Coordinator
Center for National Security Studies
122 Maryland Avenue, N.E.
Washington, D.C. 20002

CITY VOLUNTEER CORPS OF   *Los Angeles, California*
LOS ANGELES
Internship Program

ELIGIBILITY: *Undergraduate and graduate*
DURATION: *Varies*
ACADEMIC CREDIT POSSIBLE: *Yes*
REMUNERATION OR FEE: *Some meals, work-related travel*
POSITIONS OFFERED: *Approximately 40*
APPLICATION DEADLINE: *Open*

General Description

The City of Los Angeles sponsors this volunteer program to promote citizen participation in city government and the local community. The C.V.C. is largely a clearinghouse organization, and matches participants with government and social service agencies in the Los Angeles area.

The program is geared toward college students, although it can involve any community member with volunteer time to contribute. Application to the program is made by filling-out a "skills bank" form. A member of the C.V.C. staff then contacts applicants and suggests volunteer projects based on the individual's interests and abilities. A volunteer position can be simply a one-shot deal, or a long-term internship.

In the past, interns have been involved in projects as diverse as locating and arranging funding for a day care center, and investigating low cost housing and solid waste recycling.

A more specialized program, open strictly to college students, involves interning in city government positions. These positions differ from the C.V.C. program, in that candidates apply directly to the Mayor's office. Positions are flexible and placement is based on the immediate needs of city offices. Applicants must submit an application form, resume, and a cover letter detailing their interests and the periods when they will be available.

The Inside Word

Getting accepted: Most participants in both programs come from the Los Angeles area—mainly for practical reasons in that the C.V.C. does not provide housing for interns or volunteers. Program director Barry Smedberg looks for students with planning and writing skills, and observes that most participants are from academic backgrounds in political science, advertising, communications, media, business, or finance. The number of interns admitted at any given time into the open-ended program depends on the projects underway in the Mayor's office and the amount of work that needs to be done. Generally, however, "there are more needs than applicants" says Smedberg.

Daily life: Interns work closely with staff people in the Office of the Mayor and in other city government positions. Many have done research for the Mayor and City Council on city planning, have monitored constituent concerns, and have participated in studies on the City's economic climate.

Interns are expected to contribute at least ten hours each week to the program, which is designed around each individual's academic and career interests. Many students have arranged to receive academic credit for their work, and some have been granted work/study funding through their colleges or universities.

Contact:

Barry Smedberg
City Volunteer Corps of Los Angeles
City Hall, Room 2403
Los Angeles, CA 90012

COMMON CAUSE   *Washington, D.C.*

ELIGIBILITY: *Undergraduate and graduate*
DURATION: *Semester or summer*
ACADEMIC CREDIT POSSIBLE: *Yes*
REMUNERATION OR FEE: *Daily transportation costs*
POSITIONS OFFERED: *120*
APPLICATION DEADLINE: *Fall, August 15; Spring,*
    December 15; Summer, April 1.

General Description

The national office of Common Cause in Washington, D.C., employs interns to serve as staff assistants and liasons between the central office and the 50 Common Cause state agencies. Among the foremost citizen lobbying organizations in the nation, Common Cause defends the rights and interests of the citizen-taxpayers on both a local and national level. The Washington office disseminates information to the state chapters and actively lobbies on Capitol Hill on issues of nationwide concern.

Interns can be assigned to issue development, litigation, legislative correspondence, or legislation. The responsibilities in each area vary, however, a good deal of research work and report drafting is involved in all divisions. Interns in issue development generally work on a specific research paper or on collecting data for an investigative study. Litigation department interns compile tactical data for law suits and help to prepare court cases. Interns working as legislative correspondents prepare responses regarding legislative issues to be distributed to Common Cause affiliates and the general public. In the course of the extensive research and writing involved, students acquire a thorough knowledge of Common Cause issues, the status of legislation, and organizational issues. Interns in the legislation department monitor Congressional Committee hearings and bill drafting sessions.

Thirty positions are available each semester and during the summer. Approximately 100 students apply for the spring and fall programs, and over 300 apply each summer. Many participants receive academic credit, if willing to make the arrangements on their own. While Common Cause offers no stipend outside of paying for daily transportation costs, past interns have held part-time jobs on the side.

Administrators request a cover letter, resume, two letters of recommendation, and writing samples (a research or term paper), in addition to the application form itself. An interview is not required.

The Inside Word

Getting accepted: Administrators look for students with academic backgrounds in political science, government, history, communications, journalism, or education. Indicating your superior organizational skills and solid writing and communications abilities will set your application apart. In the application, students are asked to estimate the amount of time—in terms of part-time or full-time availability—and the date on which they can start. Those who can make a weekly commitment of four to five days for a full summer or semester are given priority over those with more limited periods of availability.

Daily life: Assignments to divisions are based on students' preferences as well as applicants' academic interests and work experience. Interns are an integral part of Common Cause's operation. They work closely with the national staff in lobbying activities and keep close contact with the statewide Common Cause offices.

In their function as liasons, interns "tend to spend a lot of time on the Watts line" said one participant. "It's crucial that we maintain constant contact with our regional affiliates in order to keep them abreast of our progress with national issues."

Issue development interns are assigned a research paper which involves exploring an issue's pros and cons, and, ultimately, offering recommendations for Common Cause action. Recently, one intern examined the issue of term limitations for members of Congress, while another focused on developing proposals for state Civil Service reform. Other interns are involved solely in investigative studies "designed to dramatize the need for certain reforms with careful, detailed research." Interns have documented the Senate's somewhat cursory attention to the confirmation of Presidential appointees, as well as the effects of special interest lobbying on the President's energy package, among other projects.

Litigation interns are assigned to whatever projects the department is concerned with at the time of a student's participation. Past interns have analyzed testimony of witnesses, conducted research on governmental waste, investigated the compilation of amounts of franked mail sent by individual Congressmen to determine whether mailing patterns have political motivations, and researched the political use of Congressional staffs.

Interns in legislative correspondence are usually responsible for collecting information on current projects and communicating this information to state organizations. Often, legislative correspondence interns participate in lobbying as well, and always work closely with the entire legislative staff.

Legislative department interns are responsible for submitting written reports summarizing the essentials of testimony, questioning, and opinions of members of Congress, and all action and votes taken during bill drafting sessions. Many have conducted short-term research projects related to Common Cause issues.

Contact:

Allan Zendle, Director of Volunteer Services
Common Cause
2030 M Street, NW.
Washington, D.C. 20036

CONSUMER AFFAIRS DEPARTMENT INTERNSHIP
Landover, Maryland
Giant Foods, Inc.

ELIGIBILITY: *Undergraduate and graduate*
DURATION: *3 months*
ACADEMIC CREDIT POSSIBLE: *Yes*
REMUNERATION OR FEE: *$500 stipend*
POSITIONS OFFERED: *4*
APPLICATION DEADLINE: *One month in advance of each session*

General Description

Giant Foods, Inc., a retail supermarket chain with 120 stores in the Washington D.C., Virginia, and Maryland area, hires four interns each year to assist in the firm's Consumer Affairs department. One position is offered each season, and lasts for a three month period. During that time, interns work with the full-time staff as liaisons between the Giant management and the public in addressing consumer concerns.

The consumer program was established in 1970 to facilitate customers' access to product information and to provide an avenue for consumer redress. The department provides consumer information materials, including nutrition education programs, and holds regular advisory meetings with a group of consumers.

Approximately 20 people apply each year for the four positions. Applicants must submit a resume and arrange an interview in order to be considered. Applications should be sent at least one month before the start of the desired session.

The Inside Word

Getting accepted: Students majoring in consumer affairs, nutrition, business, or food science are given preference in admission says Odonna Matthews, program director. "Unless you are in one of those areas I don't think the program is really suited for you." Applicants should be capable writers and public speakers, and enjoy working with people.

Daily life: Interns participate in the department's ongoing efforts to establish positive rapport between the Giant management and its customers. In the past, students have helped to develop nutrition programs for people on special diets and have worked with the F.D.A and manufacturers in testing goods and implementing regulatory measures.

Interns generally complete several small projects or one major endeavor during the internship. In addition, the interns work closely with the consumer advisory committee, meet regularly with the Giant management, prepare radio advertisements, and give speeches to local school and consumer groups.

"I was treated like a full-time staff member," stated one former intern. "I was given a wide range of responsibilties that really allowed me to apply the consumer economic theories I learned in school."

Interns' projects are determined on the basis of the student's interests and the needs of the department. The program requries a minimum of 15 hours a week during the three-month period, and Giant provides a $500 stipend to help students cover housing and transportation expenses. Participants have usually arranged to receive academic credit from their home institutions for the program.

"Interns can pretty much determine how worthwhile their experience is going to be," said a participant. "It depends on the project you select and the amount of time you are willing to devote." In terms of future careers, Odonna Matthews finds that most participants go on to careers in consumerism—some even with Giant Food. "Take me, for instance—I was the first intern the department hired and now I'm in charge!"

Contact:

Odonna Matthews
Consumer Affairs Department
Giant Food, Inc.
P.O. Box 1804
Washington, D.C. 20013

CONSUMER FEDERATION OF AMERICA   *Washington, D.C.*

ELIGIBILITY: *Undergraduate and graduate*
DURATION: *Varies*
ACADEMIC CREDIT POSSIBLE: *Yes*

REMUNERATION OR FEE: *None*
POSITIONS OFFERED: *10 per year*
APPLICATION DEADLINE: *Open*

General Description

The largest consumer advocacy agency in the country, the Consumer Federation of America (CFA) is an organization of over 200 national state and local groups dedicated to promoting consumer rights. CFA lobbies before Congress, the President, regulatory agencies, the courts, and industry on behalf of consumers, and has been cited as one of the ten most effective lobbying groups in Washington.

CFA employs a full-time staff of only six members; therefore, interns assume a major share of the office activities. Interns, say program directors, are vitally involved in gathering facts, analyzing issues, and disseminating information to the public, regulators, and legislators. "The CFA is the consumer's voice in Washington" states the organization's pamphlet, a cause in which the ten interns hired yearly by CFA figure prominently.

There is no application deadline, nor is there a fixed length to the program. However, applicants should send a resume and cover letter at least six weeks before the date they will be available to start.

The Inside Word

Getting accepted: Admission to the CFA intern program is based on "competence and enthusiasm," says Steve Brobeck, Associate Director of CFA. It is not a terribly competitive process; a commitment to consumer rights is as impressive a recommendation as a solid transcript.

Daily life: Interns are given real and worthwhile responsibilities to fulfill. They work with the staff, researching government contracts, lobbying in Congressional offices, and updating member organizations on current and important legislation. Past interns cite improved writing and speaking skills, increased self-confidence, and the satisfaction of having contributed to the public interest as the program's greatest rewards. "The contacts I made in the field got me my present job," added one pragmatist. Veterans of the program suggest a knowledge of consumer affairs, an understanding of the legislative process, and public relations experience as good background preparation for the CFA program.

Contact:

Steve Brobeck, Associate Director
Consumer Affairs Federation
1012 14th Street, N.W.
Washington, DC 20005

FRIENDS COMMITTEE ON NATIONAL LEGISLATION

Washington, D.C.

ELIGIBILITY: *Graduate*
DURATION: *11 months; Labor Day - end of July*
ACADEMIC CREDIT POSSIBLE: *Generally no*
REMUNERATION OR FEE: *$6,000 stipend*
POSITIONS OFFERED: *3*
APPLICATION DEADLINE: *April 15*

General Description

Friends Committee on National Legislation is a lobbying agency supported by the Society of Friends (Quaker Church), which seeks to make Congress responsive to their religiously-based concern for peace and human justice.

Interns can expect an intense and somewhat austere experience. Prospective candidates are warned in the application materials that the day-to-day work can be less than glamorous, "sometimes to the point of frustration", however, the positions are important and responsible ones. FCNL attempts to distribute the mundane office tasks fairly among all staff members, not just interns, but admits that during particularly busy periods, interns' individual projects might have to take a back seat to office priorities.

Interns typically serve as legislative assistants, working closely with one of FCNL's full-time lobbyists. Legislative priorities are decided at an annual meeting, and interns take part in fulfilling these organizational aims by preparing short-term reports, developing long-term research projects, keeping up on current legislative activity in an assigned area, writing newsletter articles, and attending meetings of various interest groups. Administrators suggest that interns initially focus on a special interest as a means of approaching the program and familiarizing themselves with the organization.

The FCNL accepts three interns yearly out of an applicant pool of about 20. Applications must be submitted by April 15, and while an interview is not required, it is recommended.

Interns receive a $6,000 stipend for the 11 month program, as well as a leave period of 11 days, and membership in a group health insurance plan. FCNL does not provide housing, but will assist interns in locating accomodations.

The Inside Word

Getting accepted: Members of the Society of Friends are given priority in admissions, however, anyone is eligible to apply. According to Administrative Secretary Nick Block, FCNL looks for individuals with "a tough hide". Tact is an essential quality, as well as communications skills and a heartfelt commitment to the issues FCNL deals with.

Daily life: The FCNL is a dedicated group of 14 permanent staff workers. Legislative representatives, with whom the interns work, have recently been active in organizing protests against the reorganization of the draft, and in examining the Middle East situation, Indian concerns, and the Federal budget.

Interns attend weekly staff meetings to "get a sense of what others are doing." Also at these meetings, strategy, problems related to information-gathering, publications, and general administrative matters are discussed.

Administrators warn that interpersonal relationships within the office may become strained at times, a result of the intensity with which most employees approach their work. Said one intern, "We all share the committed feeling about what we're doing, so everyone tends to be understanding." The work load and range of responsibilities is challenging, and the length of the time commitment exhausted at least one intern. "Worthwhile though the program was, it's a major commitment. I'd recommend it under any circumstances, however."

Contact:

Nick Block, Administrative Secretary
F.C.N.L.
245 Second Street, N.E.
Washington, D.C. 20002

GEORGIA GOVERNOR'S INTERN PROGRAM

Atlanta, Georgia

ELIGIBILITY: *Undergraduate and graduate*
DURATION: *10 weeks*
ACADEMIC CREDIT POSSIBLE: *Yes*
REMUNERATION OR FEE: *$500 stipend for undergraduates; $1,000 stipend for graduates*
POSITIONS OFFERED: *Approximately 600*
APPLICATION DEADLINE: *Open*

General Description

The Governor's office of the State of Georgia's administers this extensive program, designed to match public service-oriented college and graduate students with public agencies in need of assistance. The Governor's office acts both as a clearinghouse for the placement of students, and as an intern employer as well. Jobs are with state and local government in addition to private and public social service agencies.

Candidates must include a resume along with their applications, and recommendations from college faculty members. An interview is usually required. 80 percent of the interns receive academic credit for their work, and all receive a generous stipend for participation in the ten-week program.

The Inside Word

Getting accepted: Although any student "in good standing" at his/her college or university is eligible for the program, preference is given to residents of Georgia. Program directors do encourage any qualified student, Georgian or otherwise, to apply. Selection is based on the interview and application, with particular attention being paid to "extra-curricular activities" and "employment background."

The program is broken-up into a series of ten-week sessions continuing year-round, so one can apply at any time. Administrators recommend having your application in the mail at least six weeks before the period during which you will be available to ensure consideration.

Daily life: The program was created to make the resources of colleges and universities more accessible to the community, and consequently, the interns work closely with their sponsoring institutions throughout their participation. A final report on their experiences in the program must be submitted by all interns within 30 days of completing the internship.

Interns are required to attend several seminars in which participating students discuss their experiences in the program and exchange ideas on the success and merits of their involvement.

Students are placed in such a wide variety of positions that it is impossible to generalize about the type of experience one might expect; however, one intern, who has been working as a press aide in the governor's office, considered her internship "credible and worthwhile. I was given a substantial number of important tasks—writing speeches for the Governor, attending press conferences, researching for committees, reporting information to radio stations, and was encouraged to pursue individual interests as well." Another intern agreed that the program was worth recommending, "I haven't had time to waste time, and I have yet to hear any of the other interns complain about boredom either. I have always been interested in government, and this experience has really convinced me to pursue my interest further."

Contact:

William D. Cloud, Director
Georgia Governor's Intern Program
111 State Capitol
Atlanta, GA 30334

INDIAN LAW SEMINAR AND INTERN PROJECT FOR INDIAN LAW STUDENTS

Western U.S.

ELIGIBILITY: *Native American Indian graduate students in law*
DURATION: *10 weeks, summer*
ACADEMIC CREDIT POSSIBLE: *Yes*
REMUNERATION OR FEE: *$4.75 an hour; travel expenses*
POSITIONS OFFERED: *Varies*
APPLICATION DEADLINE: *Varies*

General Description

The American Indian Lawyer Training Program provides support for Indian lawyers and aids in the development of Indian law. Specifically, it trains Indian lawyers in Indian law and provides resources for solving Indian legal problems. Since its inception in 1973, the program has promoted the ideals of tribal sovereignty and self-determination.

The Inside Word

Daily life: Interns are placed in tribal governments, court systems, legal service offices on reservations and with Indian lawyers to learn Indian law and its institutions first-hand. Most interns spend their days in a tribal court working with a tribal judge.

Interns also submit research reports on the needs and problems of the tribal court systems. These reports, which are often quite extensive, attempt to analyze the effectiveness of the legal system at meeting the needs of the Indian people. One such project was published as a book entitled *Indian Self-Determination and the Role of Tribal Courts.* The book was completely researched and written by law student interns.

The most attractive benefit of the program is the familiarity one gains with Indian law. The intern is in contact with Indian legal systems on a daily basis, which, according to one AILTP employee, "puts life back into their studies." It takes actual involvement in the Indian legal system to understand it well, but it also takes an intern who is committed to Indian law.

The program is open only to native American Indians in their first or second years of law school. The number of positions available varies from year to year depending on funding, but generally no more than eight interns are accepted. Most participants receive academic credit for the intensive, ten-week program. Interns can expect to work a full, 40-hour week. To apply, submit a resume, transcript, and references along with the application form. Interviews are requested.

Contact:

Diana Martinez
Indian Law Seminar and Intern Project for Indian Law Students
319 McCarthur
Oakland, CA 94610

INSTITUTE FOR LOCAL SELF-RELIANCE *Washington, D.C.*
Internship Program

ELIGIBILITY: *High school, undergraduate, and graduate*
DURATION: *Varies*
ACADEMIC CREDIT POSSIBLE: *Yes*
REMUNERATION OR FEE: *None*
POSITIONS OFFERED: *Varies*
APPLICATION DEADLINE: *Open*

General Description

Designed to provide technical assistance to residents of urban areas working on community development, the Institute for Local Self-Reliance attempts to demonstrate that an informed and involved community can become self-reliant. The ILSR suggests means for urban communities to recycle wealth within neighborhoods, and ways of using new technological advances to stimulate locally-based production.

"Because of the complexity of the task, our work program is a varied one, stressing research, outreach, demonstration projects, technical assistance, and policy review" states the agency's brochure. The Institute's efforts are divided among four "project" areas: energy, urban agriculture, waste utilization, and publications. Intern assignments within these areas can last anywhere from two months to a year. Participants are matched with specific projects within one of these areas, on the basis of their interests, skills, and goals.

Energy project interns assist the Institute staff in teaching community groups about weatherizing and insulating homes, and in installing solar heat and hot water systems. Also, interns research other energy alternatives, and investigate the potential for organizing community-based energy-related industries, such as cellulose insulation manufacture.

Interns in urban agriculture set up community gardening programs in low-income urban neighborhoods. Together with staff supervisors, ILSR interns have been involved in planning and developing community parks.

Students also help tend the experimental greenhouse on the Institute's roof, and explore new methods of urban gardening.

A community-based recycling business was started in the Washington area by participants in the waste utilization project. Interns have provided advice and technical assistance to other urban groups and city and state officials for setting-up such a program, and also work on several educational projects on recycling and solid waste.

Publishing constitutes a major aspect of the ILSR's work. They produce a bi-monthly magazine, *Self Reliance*, and have published over 30 original works on local self reliance, helpful technology, and neighborhood economic development. Institute staff and interns have also prepared numerous slide shows.

There is no limit to the number of interns accepted—the number admitted is based on the nature of the projects in progress at a given time. The cover letter and application should explain one's interest in the Institute's work, and any special skills or abilities that relate to the ILSR program. Letters of recommendation are required, as well as an interview.

The Inside Word

Getting accepted: Students majoring in economics, political science, architecture, or engineering might be best qualified for the program, although one's academic background is not necessarily a key factor in admissions. Interest and special skills of some kind are the acceptance tickets for this internship. Interns suggest applying for a spring internship as there is generally more to do, the competition is less intense, and new projects are just beginning.

The ILSR is very flexible in terms of numbers of positions offered and the duration of an intern's stay. The hours an intern works each week also varies, although most work about 40 hours a week.

Daily life: One staff member we spoke with had started out at the Institute as an intern. He had just graduated from college with a degree in architecture, and was assigned to a project teaching home-owners how to implement solar heating systems. He has since worked on designing solar greenhouses, recreational play facilities, planning a city park, and renovating an abandoned warehouse.

Contact:

Harriet Barlow
Institute for Local Self-Reliance
1717 18th Street, N.W.
Washington, D.C. 20009

JOINT CENTER FOR POLITICAL STUDIES

Washington, D.C.

ELIGIBILITY: *Undergraduate and graduate*
DURATION: *1 month*
ACADEMIC CREDIT POSSIBLE: *Yes*
REMUNERATION OR FEE: *None*
POSITIONS OFFERED: *8 to 10*
APPLICATION DEADLINE: *Open*

General Description

This organization is engaged in formulating analysis of major policy issues of importance to minorities and the poor; developing a core group of minority experts in the public policy field, and in making visible to the general public the special needs of minorities within the public policy arena.

Interns assist in researching public policy issues, small town planning, urban development, drug abuse, housing needs of the elderly black, and black political participation. Other assignments include helping staff specialists in print and broadcast journalism; accumulating data on resources available to aid cities in economic and community development; and analyzing campaign financing, election monitoring, competency-based education, and urban programs.

The Center accepts eight to ten interns yearly for one month periods; interns are expected to devote 20 hours per week to the program. While the Center offers no monetary remuneration, students are often eligible for work/study funding from their college or university, and in most cases receive academic credit for the program.

The Inside Word

Getting accepted: Students of political science, black studies, urban affairs/planning, economics, public affairs/administration, sociology, history, statistics, education, law, journalism, advertising, public relations, marketing, and business are encouraged to apply. The program's primary requisite, however, is an interest in and commitment to helping minority groups. Program administrators expect applicants to speak and write with better-than-average proficiency.

Daily life: Projects completed by former interns include: an analysis of Congressional voting records; a census of black elected officials; the compilation of the *Directory of Black State Legislators*; studies on campaign financing, the E.R.A. and minorities, and financial management problems of elected officials.

Interns function as regular staff members at the Center, and are given a full behind-the-scenes view of the workings of a public service organization as well as the frustrations of dealing with governmental bureaucracy on a daily basis.

Contact:

Dr. Louise Taylor
Joint Center for Political Studies
1426 H Street, N.W. Suite 539
Washington, D.C. 20005

MENTAL HEALTH LAW PROJECT   *Washington, D.C.*

ELIGIBILITY: *Second or third year law students*
DURATION: *Semester, summer*
ACADEMIC CREDIT POSSIBLE: *Yes*
REMUNERATION OR FEE: *None*
POSITIONS OFFERED: *6*
APPLICATION DEADLINE: *Open*

General Description

The Mental Health Law Project is a non-profit organization advocating the rights of the mentally disabled. The Project works to protect the mentally ill, and to promote better treatment, rehabilitation, and mainstreaming programs.

Interns assist the regular staff of eight attorneys in selecting test cases to demonstrate the problems of the mentally ill. They serve as volunteer legal assistants to individual project attorneys involved with specific mental health cases.

Most participants are in their second or third year of law school and spend either a summer or school semester working at the project. There is no formal application deadline but administrators advise applying early—at least two months before you will be available to start.

The Inside Word

Getting accepted: Most participants are students with a strong interest in civil liberties or a background in the mental health field. Program directors look for applicants with strong research, writing, and analytical skills.

Daily life: Interns draft briefs, do background research work on cases, and develop a close professional relationship with their sponsoring staff attorney. Participants point to the rigorous but rewarding nature of the work as the program's great advantage, "Not once during my entire time there was I stuck with busy work—I always had substantial responsibilities to fulfill, and was treated as a full-fledged member of the operation." Past interns felt that their experience gave them significant exposure to the requirements of mental health legislation and allowed them to establish valuable connections in the field.

Contact:

Patricia Bell, Office Manager
Mental Health Law Project
1220 19th Street, N.W.
Washington, DC 20036

NATIONAL COMMITTEE AGAINST DISCRIMINATION IN HOUSING

Washington, D.C.

ELIGIBILITY: *Undergraduate and graduate*
DURATION: *Varies*
ACADEMIC CREDIT POSSIBLE: *Yes*
REMUNERATION OR FEE: *None*
POSITIONS OFFERED: *2*
APPLICATION DEADLINE: *Open*

General Description

The National Committee Against Discrimination in Housing is a 29-year-old civil rights organization devoted to research, public information, technical counsel, legal services, and monitoring the enforcement of fair-housing laws. Interns are assigned to a research project concerning housing and discrimination. Often their work involves investigating red-lining cases and fair-marketing writs. The agency publishes a bimonthly report which interns help to prepare.

The program is open-ended and interns are hired year-round for varying periods. There are positions open for legal interns also. Generally law students, these interns are involved in the litigation aspect of the agency's work.

The Inside Word

Getting accepted: The most successful applicants come from backgrounds in the social sciences; however, experience in demography, banking, finance, or economic analysis is helpful in conducting housing investigations. Writing and presentation skills are important criteria for admission, and administrators and interns agree that one's abilities in these areas will have improved greatly by program's end.

Daily life: Interns work closely with the paid staff of about 20 members, assisting in research, counseling, and reporting. Interns must also complete their individual research projects during the course of the program in order to be recommended for academic credit. Often, interns will be asked to monitor housing bills, and occasionally participate in investigative field work to assess the degree to which fair housing legislation is enforced.

Contact:

Ernest Erber, Director of Research and Planning
National Committee Against Discrimination in Housing
1425 H Street, N.W.
Washington, DC 20005

NATIONAL COMMITTEE AGAINST REPRESSIVE LEGISLATION

Washington, D.C.

ELIGIBILITY: *Undergraduate and graduate*
DURATION: *3 months*
ACADEMIC CREDIT POSSIBLE: *Yes*
REMUNERATION OR FEE: *Work-related travel*
POSITIONS OFFERED: *1 per semester or summer*
APPLICATION DEADLINE: *Open*

General Description

The National Committee Against Repressive Legislation was established in 1960 as the National Committee to Abolish the House Un-American Activities Committee, and has since evolved into an influential watch-dog agency committed to the defeat of legislation threatening to our basic Constitutional freedoms. In recent years, NCARL has worked to repeal anti-riot, preventive detention, wiretapping, and immunity statutes. Other activities include development of a program for the control of abuses of Constitutional rights by intelligence agencies.

The organization is based in Los Angeles, with regional offices located in California, Boston, and Chicago. The national legislative office in Washington, D.C. is the site of the NCARL internship program. NCARL serves as an information clearinghouse to other public service organizations, providing literature, speakers, and other forms of non-financial assistance to others concerned with the defense of First Amendment freedoms.

Interns at NCARL attend Congressional hearings, research pending legislation, and work closely with the permanent staff in a variety of other functions. Applications must be submitted at least one month in advance of the time you are available to start, and must be accompanied by a resume and writing samples.

The Inside Word

Getting accepted: Administrators look for students interested in politics and those who share a commitment to the defense of Constitutional liberties. "Independence, self-motivation, writing ability, office skills, an inquiring mind, and the ability to relate positively to many different kinds of people" are distinguishing qualities in successful applicants, according to program administrators. Applicants who can guarantee a three-month time committment are given first consideration.

Daily life: Interns assist the Washington Coordinator in all aspects of NCARL's work: organizing, office work, legislative analysis, research, and writing. Students represent NCARL to supporters and other public service organizations, attend meetings with affiliated agencies, answer correspondence, and write newsletter articles.

All comments from past interns were positive, with students pointing to the extent of responsibility they were given and the interesting nature of the work as the program's most attractive features.

Contact:

Esther Herst, Washington Coordinator
National Committee Against Repressive Legislation
510 C Street, N.E.
Washington, D.C. 20002

NATIONAL CONSUMER AFFAIRS   *National*
Internship Program

ELIGIBILITY: *Graduate*
DURATION: *January—May; May—August;*
    August—December
ACADEMIC CREDIT POSSIBLE: *Yes*
REMUNERATION OR FEE: *$1625 stipend,*
    transportation costs
POSITIONS OFFERED: *30*
APPLICATION DEADLINE: *November 30 for spring;*
    April 15 for summer; July 31 for fall

General Description

Now in its fifth year of existence, the National Consumer Affairs Internship Program (NCAIP) pairs graduate students interested in consumer affairs with business and government agencies to learn about consumer issues and concerns.

The program, based in Tucson, Arizona, is divided into three sessions of 15 weeks each. Applicants must be nominated by a faculty member—

who is willing to supervise an internship project—at his or her home academic institution. The faculty sponsor must also be willing to make arrangements for the student to receive academic credit for the program. Approximately 40 students apply each session for the 30 positions available. Selection is based on faculty recommendations, two brief essays, and a college transcript. Applications are screened by a panel of faculty advisors, but the final selection is made by the host organizations.

All participants attend a pre-internship conference where interns meet consumer leaders and consumer affairs professionals in business and government, and learn about the policies and procedures of the program they are about to start.

Individual projects vary and are worked out in cooperation with the intern, the host organization, the faculty sponsor, and the NCAIP director. The project must receive academic credit, and be suited to the needs of the organization and the interests and qualifications of the intern.

Interns receive $125 each week for the 13 weeks (following the conference) when they are actually on-the-job in a host organization. Interns are also given a $200 relocation allowance, and are compensated for travel expenses to and from the conference and their work site.

The Inside Word

Getting accepted: Getting the enthusiastic support of a faculty member is the key to the success of a candidate's application. If your faculty sponsor can demonstrate his/her excitement and confidence in your abilities to NCAIP directors, and you have the skills and credentials to support the hard-sell routine, your chances for acceptance are excellent. Past interns urged that applicants take pains to see that the application essay on how the internship will figure with your career plans is interesting and concise. "I was told that the people screening the applications paid particular attention to your response to that question" said one veteran participant.

Daily life: Past interns have worked in a wide variety of organizations performing an extensive range of tasks. One student, working for Westinghouse Corporation, developed a consumer information booklet with answers to the questions most frequently asked of the company; another prepared a pamphlet on waste disposal, and evaluated available information on nuclear energy. Another intern worked at the National Highway Traffic Safety Administration, serving as special assistant to the chief of consumer participation. He prepared briefing papers on state safety programs, developed a resource guide for the State of Florida, and responded to consumer inquiries on safety and auto repair.

Contact:

Dr. Currin V. Shields, Director
National Consumer Affairs Internship Program
Box 40445
Tucson, AZ 85717

NATIONAL CONSUMERS LEAGUE   *Washington, D.C.*
Legislative Intern Program

ELIGIBILITY: *Undergraduate juniors and seniors*
DURATION: *3 months*
ACADEMIC CREDIT POSSIBLE: *Yes*
REMUNERATION OR FEE: *$3.10 per hour*
POSITIONS OFFERED: *4 to 5*
APPLICATION DEADLINE: *May for summer; August or December for semester programs*

General Description

The National Consumer League (NCL) is the oldest organization of its kind in the country, and also the smallest. Seven staff members work full-time at monitoring consumer issues and bills, and overseeing the application of federal agencies' rules and regulations.

The Legislative Intern Program provides interns with an opportunity to observe the legislative process, and to become familiar with current consumer issues. Interns attend Congressional hearings, track legislation through Congress, and research consumer issues. They also assist in lobbying Congressmen and sometimes represent the NCL at White House meetings.

The NCL deals centrally with the broad categories of consumer participation and representation, labor standards and product safety, and consumer education. Interns write press releases in connection with their investigations of specific consumer issues within these broad categories.

The Inside Word

Interns are free to initiate projects; for example, one intern spent a semester researching and attending federal hearings for a project entitled "The Impact of Inflation on Small Business." Another intern worked on methods to increase consumer participation in the governmental process.

Internships are generally arranged on a summer- or semester-long basis, and rarely exceed three months in length. Most participants receive some form of academic credit from their college or university. Said one intern of the program, "It was fascinating . . . the immediacy of my involvement made the internship a tremendous experience. I was given pretty important responsibilities, and was able to do a lot of significant things. Just being in Washington, in contact with government agencies and legislators, made for a real education in the workings of the political process."

Applicants should submit a resume and cover letter along with their application at least one month prior to the time they will be available to participate.

Contact:

National Consumers League
Legislative Intern Program
1522 K Street, N.W., Suite 406
Washington, DC 20036

NATIONAL ORGANIZATION FOR THE REFORM OF MARIJUANA LAWS (NORML)

Washington, D.C.

ELIGIBILITY: *Undergraduate and graduate*
DURATION: *1 to 4 months*
ACADEMIC CREDIT POSSIBLE: *Yes*
REMUNERATION OR FEE: *None*
POSITIONS OFFERED: *Varies*
APPLICATION DEADLINE: *Open*

General Description

NORML promotes the liberalization of existing marijuana laws through lobbying, research, and legal and public education. Interns work with the six paid staff members, conducting medical and legal research, following up on related court action, and lobbying efforts. Frequently, interns write for NORML publications and assist in aiding victims of marijuana laws.

The program's beginning and ending dates are open, although most interns stay for an average of three months.

The Inside Word

Getting accepted: Interest in and commitment to the purposes of the organization are the real admission requirements for interns at NORML. Enthusiasm, initiative, and speaking skills are important attributes, say administrators, who hire approximately eight interns yearly. Those students interested in law, business, administration, politics, or public interest "might be best suited for the program," suggests a former intern, who found that his experience at NORML "provided a unique opportunity to acquaint himself with the Washington machinery."

Daily life: Interns are given a substantial amount of responsibility, and are an integral part of the NORML operation. "Tasks tend to be divided up pretty evenly among interns and staff," said one participant. "It's definitely a group effort." In addition to a "good deal of time spent lobbying on Capitol Hill," she wrote frequently for the agency newsletter and participated in several education projects. "Interns get a chance to see the legislative system in operation at NORML, and get a shot at changing the system.''

Contact:

Mark Heutlinger
Intern Director
NORML
2317 M Street, N.W.
Washington, DC 20037

NATIONAL PUBLIC INTEREST RESEARCH GROUP

Washington, D.C.

ELIGIBILITY: *Undergraduate*
DURATION: *Varies*
ACADEMIC CREDIT POSSIBLE: *Yes*
REMUNERATION OR FEE: *None*
POSITIONS OFFERED: *4 to 5 per semester, summer*
APPLICATION DEADLINE: *Mid-May for summer;*
    Mid-August for fall; Mid-December for spring

General Description

A non-profit agency dedicated to promoting constructive social change, National P.I.R.G., with a network of statewide affiliates, conducts research, produces two newsletters, and provides resource materials and organizational assistance to their state offices and the general public. National P.I.R.G. is also involved in neighborhood development and consumer advocacy as a means of social change.

The duration of the internship is usually negotiated by each individual; students often receive academic credit for their volunteer work.

Interns take part in research, development of resource materials, legislative analysis; they report for the newsletters, and assist in organizing fund drives. Recent projects have included testing and surveying the public on issues of concern to National P.I.R.G., and monitoring the development of and public reaction to nuclear power facilities.

National P.I.R.G. is essentially a clearinghouse of information for the local P.I.R.G. offices. Many regional offices also have intern programs; for more information on opportunities available locally, check in the phone book. Applications to the national office's program must include a resume and writing sample, and be submitted at least one month prior to the period in which you wish to work.

The Inside Word

Getting accepted: "We're looking for people with a good deal of self-motivation, who are willing to put in long hours—in other words, hard workers" says a program spokesman. P.I.R.G. is a student-funded and supported organization, with a half million students in 27 states on 200 campuses either participating actively or financially supporting P.I.R.G.'s efforts. National P.I.R.G., therefore, gives preference to applicants from member schools.

Directors of the program look for applicants with strong interest in consumer affairs and consumer advocacy, combined with strong writing skills.

Daily life: Interns assume the role of a full-time staff member while at National P.I.R.G.. They share in the responsibility of assisting the state organizations and keeping them informed of issues and policy developments. Specific projects students have completed include examining the accuracy of ETS testing, assembling a series of resource guides for P.I.R.G., conducting teach-ins on nuclear power, and lobbying on Capitol Hill on a variety of issues.

Contact:

Nan Shapiro
National Public Interest Research Group
1329 E Street, N.W. Suite 1127
Washington, D.C. 20004

NEW CASTLE COUNTY DEPARTMENT   Wilmington, Delaware
OF PARKS AND RECREATION
Student Field Work Program

ELIGIBILITY: *Undergraduate sophomores*
DURATION: *May 1-August 31*
ACADEMIC CREDIT POSSIBLE: *Yes*
REMUNERATION OR FEE: *None*
POSITIONS OFFERED: *Varies*
APPLICATION DEADLINE: *March 1*

General Description

The Department of Parks and Recreation of New Castle County, Delaware sponsors a ten-week summer Field Work program for college sophomores planning careers in parks, recreation, and/or conservation.

Students participate in the supervision and maintenance of the County's 131 parks and over 200 recreation programs.

The program is divided into two parts: general orientation and major emphasis. General orientation covers the first five-week phase of the internship and is designed to give each student a comprehensive overview of the seven department divisions: Parks, Operations, Maintenance, Construction, Forestry, Design and Development, and Recreation.

For the second phase of the program, each intern selects a major emphasis option which involves concentrated study in one of the divisions. During this phase of the program, each intern is required to research a field program or project area in order to make a final presentation to the department's professional staff.

The program is open to students seriously interested in careers in parks, recreation, and conservation. "Only those applicants who exhibit potential as a future parks and recreation professional will be considered for selection," warns the program manual. Write a "letter of interest" to the department regarding the program to receive application materials. Applicants must complete an interest questionnaire along with the employment application, and submit a college transcript and resume.

Students from the University of Delaware have usually been given credit for the program. Administrators recommend that students from other universities make their own arrangements to receive credit.

The Inside Word

Getting accepted: Delaware residents are given priority for the "variable" number of positions open each summer, but good credentials and an active interest on the part of out-of-state candidates can even the admission odds. Administrators are looking for "people-oriented interns," who can work well with others and lead recreational activities. Good writing skills are also sought, as students will frequently be asked to draft reports in addition to preparing their major project.

Daily life: Upon selection, students are assigned a host or hostess from the department with whom they will meet regularly throughout the General Orientation, and who will assist them in selecting the topic for their major project. Attendance at several meetings; one county council meeting, one division head meeting, one Delaware Parks and Recreation Society meeting, two civic association meetings, and all department supervisor staff meetings is required of participants in addition to daily assignments within their divisions.

Interns felt that while the program was demanding, they learned "an incredible amount about the field." The program is non-remunerative, and outside employment is discouraged during the ten-week program. The department does not provide housing, but does help students to locate living quarters. As travel throughout the County is necessary, access to a car is a must.

Contact:

Patricia C. Johnson, Executive Assistant II
New Castle County Dept. of Parks and Recreation
102 Middleboro Road
Wilmington, DE 19804

PUBLIC CITIZEN   *Washington, D.C.*

ELIGIBILITY: *High school, undergraduate, graduate*
DURATION: *Varies*
ACADEMIC CREDIT POSSIBLE: *Yes*
REMUNERATION OR FEE: *Usually none, possible $50*
    or $80 stipend
POSITIONS OFFERED: *Approximately 60*
APPLICATION DEADLINE: *Open*

General Description

Perhaps the premier public service organization in the country, Public Citizen, Ralph Nader's consumer advocacy organization, is based in Washington. It employs some 100 people in ten different divisions, and offers positions to approximately 60 interns yearly. Public Citizen is an umbrella organization for ten public interest/consumer advocacy offices: Congress Watch, a group which monitors Congressional activity and the voting records of individual Congressmen with regard to consumer issues; the Tax Reform Group; the Critical Mass Energy Project and Journal, dealing with the nuclear power issue; the Center for Auto Safety; the Health Research Group; the Center for Study of Responsive Law, the Washington Visitors' Center, an information bank of what is going on, on Capitol Hill and in Washington; the National Citizen's Commission for Broadcasting; the Clean Water Action Project; and the Litigation Group.

With the exception of the Litigation Group, which specifically involves law students in preparing suits against alleged transgressors of consumer rights, and the Health Research Project, which is geared for medical and law students, interns can participate in any of the divisions in research, writing, and organizing capacities. Florence Dembling, intern coordinator for all the Public Citizen agencies, matches applicants with agencies on the basis of students' preferences, the immediate needs of the various groups, interns' academic and work backgrounds, and applicants' special skills or abilities. "We try to make the experience meaningful" says Dembling.

Applications are screened on a rolling basis. Generally, several hundred students apply for the 60 or so positions available. Dembling requires that students be able to make a full-time commitment for at least a ten-week period in order to be considered. To apply, submit a writing sample, resume, and cover letter stating your interest. The internships are volunteer positions, although students have occasionally received work/study funding from their colleges, or been awarded a $50 or $80 stipend by Public Citizen for their work.

The Inside Word

Getting accepted: The most important factor for consideration is an interest in and awareness of the consumer advocacy movement, says Dembling. "I look for some degree of sophistication in applicants, in the sense that he or she knows what's going on. Also, something unique in an applicant's background will make that application stand out. Flexibility is also important, but basically, we want interns who are active and reactive individuals."

Dembling suggests indicating your placement preference on the application, but advises applicants to be flexible. "Often, because of the needs of the various groups, I'm forced to decide where an intern could be used most effectively and have the most rewarding experience."

Daily life: Interns work alongside the permanent staff as full-fledged researchers, lobbyists, and consumer advocates. Assignments differ from group to group, but all interns can expect to respond to consumer complaints, conduct research, and draft reports on the group's activities. Public Citizen works closely with other Washington-based public service groups, National Public Interest Research Group (P.I.R.G.) in particular; occasionally, interns are assigned to assist those organizations or to work on joint projects.

Contact:

Florence Dembling
Public Citizen
2000 P Street, N.W. Suite 711
Washington, D.C. 20036

PUBLIC DEFENDER SERVICE
Investigative Internships
Washington, D.C.

ELIGIBILITY: *Undergraduate and law students*
DURATION: *12 weeks*
ACADEMIC CREDIT POSSIBLE: *Yes*
REMUNERATION OR FEE: *None*
POSITIONS OFFERED: *40 per term; 120 per year*
APPLICATION DEADLINE: *Open*

General Description

Interns at Public Defender Service act as staff research assistants for the 37 attorneys in the Washington-based public law clinic. The program is open to students with an interest in law and criminal justice, and involves 40 participants during each of the three annual terms.

Interns attend intensive training seminars in investigative techniques and procedures prior to being given assignments as staff assistants. Having completed the orientation program, interns become eligible to assist in the "representation of indigent persons charged with criminal offenses."

Students also participate in seminars with representatives of the FBI, U.S. Attorney's Office, and Lorton Correctional Institute and Medical Examiner's Office.

There are no set beginning or ending dates for the program; terms correspond roughly with academic semesters and the summer session. There is no application deadline and applicants must submit a resume along with the application form.

The Inside Word

Getting accepted: Demonstrated intelligence, responsibility, autonomy, a capacity for decision-making, writing ability, and good speaking and interviewing skills are qualities program administrators cite as most desirable in applicants. As interns often have complete responsibility for pre-trial investigations—gathering evidence, interviewing witnesses, and doing legal research and writing—the program is geared toward highly-motivated self-starters.

Interns must remain for a minimum of 12 weeks, usually receiving academic credit for their time. The Service does not compensate its interns; however, some students have been able to arrange work/study funding through their college or university.

Daily life: Interns accompany attorneys in every official capacity. From conducting interviews with and obtaining signed statements from potential government and defense witnesses, to testifying at motions hearings or trials, interns share fully in the Service's operation. In fact, say program directors, the staff attorneys utilize interns for conducting the major part of their investigative research. One former intern spoke of her "amazement" at the level and importance of the responsibilities she was assigned. "I received such a thorough education in the workings of a public defender's office that I was able to decide confidently to pursue a career in law. It was an incredibly exciting experience."

Contact:

Ray Denison, Coordinator of Investigation
Public Defender Law Service
451 Indiana Avenue, N.W.
Washington, DC 20001

RESOURCE DEVELOPMENT INTERNSHIP PROJECT

Midwestern U.S.

ELIGIBILITY: *Juniors, seniors and graduates*
DURATION: *Varies*
ACADEMIC CREDIT POSSIBLE: *Yes*
REMUNERATION OR FEE: *Educational grant*
POSITIONS OFFERED: *50 to 60*
APPLICATION DEADLINE: *Open*

General Description

The Resource Development Internship Project is a function of the Public Careers Internship Placement Center of Indiana University. Each year, the agency places 50 to 60 students in public service-oriented organizations in the Midwest in order to give interns "practical experience and professional maturity by employing technical skills learned in college to solve the hard problems of reality."

Internships vary in length from 12 to 26 weeks, and are full-time positions. Each participant is assigned a project advisory committee, consisting of representatives of the host organization, a faculty member from Indiana University, and a technical advisor with related experience. The committee assists interns in defining project objectives and planning methods of approach. Interns are matched with host organizations which have expressed a need for intern help, and design a project based on some aspect of the work they will be involved in.

The Inside Word

Getting accepted: Between 200 and 300 students apply to the RDIP each year, most from Midwestern schools. The program is open, however, to all undergraduates having completed two years of school and graduate students. Interns must be nominated by their college or university, a host agency, or a faculty member, although some participants have applied independently. Final selection of candidates is made by host organizations after reviewing applicants' resumes and application folders.

Daily life: As the RDIP is essentially a clearinghouse for public service agencies, the experiences interns have had are wide-ranging. In the past, interns have been placed with the Bureau of the Budget of the State of Illinois, the Department of National Resources of Michigan, the Division of Planning of the City of East Chicago, and the Ohio Mid-Eastern Governments Association.

Interns, having chosen a project to pursue, must submit progress reports to the RDIP and their home campuses. Final reports can take whatever form an intern chooses to present his/her findings and in so doing synthesize the varied experiences the internship has involved.

According to a program director, the RDIP was organized both to enhance the educational experiences of college students, by providing forums for practical application of abstract classroom theory to real problems, and to promote a closer relationship between educational and societal institutions. Academic credit is usually awarded participants in the program, and although circumstances vary, most interns receive educational grants—generally tax-free—with which to support themselves during their tenure as interns.

Contact:

The Public Careers Internship and Placement Center
School of Public and Environmental Affairs
The Poplars, Room 223
Indiana University, 400 East Seventh Street
Bloomington, IN 47401

SOUTHERN ECONOMIC DEVELOPMENT   *Southeast*
Internship Program

ELIGIBILITY: *Undergraduate and graduate*
DURATION: *Semester or summer*
ACADEMIC CREDIT POSSIBLE: *Yes*
REMUNERATION OR FEE: *Varies*
POSITIONS OFFERED: *50 to 100*
APPLICATION DEADLINE: *Open*

General Description

Funded by the Economic Development Administration of the U.S. Department of Commerce, the Southern Economic Development (SED) program assists organizations in solving problems related to economic development. Foremost among SED's objectives is to utilize the resources of educational institutions to meet the specific needs of economic development organizations in the South.

Subsidiary organizations in Alabama, Arkansas, Florida, Georgia, Kentucky, Louisiana, Maryland, Mississippi, North Carolina, South Carolina, Tennessee, Texas, Virginia, West Virginia, and Washington, D.C. submit proposals to the central SED office in Washington, suggesting projects they would like to undertake that will require the help of an intern. SED then selects the best proposals, and chooses applicants, in cooperation with faculty representatives of several colleges and universities, to fit the needs of the various member agencies.

The program operates year-round for varying periods, but generally coincides with academic semesters and the summer. SED pays part of each intern's stipend, with the remainder paid by the host organization.

The positions can be part-, or full-time, depending on the availability of the intern. Application should be made well in advance of the time one is available to begin work, and should include a resume.

The Inside Word

Getting accepted: SED is looking for students with strong writing and research skills, preferably upperclassmen or graduate students with backgrounds in economics, urban studies, planning, business, or political science. Final selection, however, is made on the basis of the needs of the individual agencies. Applicants who are residents of one of the 15 states involved in the program are given priority. Past interns suggest stressing any job experiences or course work that has prepared you for work in economic planning and development. One advised sending a writing sample with the application, and, if at all feasible, arranging an interview with program director Jane Kendall.

Daily life: Projects vary from agency to agency, but generally involve research and field work related to stimulating the economic climate in small Southern communities. Most participants receive academic credit for their work, and must compile a report or submit a project at the end of their internship, which is suitable for publication and distribution.

Students who have completed the program pointed to the "valuable experience of having practically applied the skills learned in school to meeting real problems" as among the program's great strengths.

Interns felt that because they were matched to a project at the outset, their time was well-spent. "I didn't have to sit around waiting for direction—I was told first-off exactly what would be expected of me." While much of their work was done independently, "a supervisor or director was always around to answer questions and make suggestions."

Contact:

Jane C. Kendall, Director
S.E.D.I.P.
1735 Eye Street, N.W. Suite 601
Washington, D.C. 20006

U.S. STUDENT ASSOCIATION   *Washington, D.C.*

ELIGIBILITY: *Undergraduate and graduate*
DURATION: *September-December; January-May;*
    June-August
ACADEMIC CREDIT POSSIBLE: *Yes*

REMUNERATION OR FEE: *None*
POSITIONS OFFERED: *30*
APPLICATION DEADLINE: *Open*

General Description

Representing 3.5 million American college students from 350 member schools, the U.S. Student Association "carries the student's voice to the Federal government." The Association trains student government and campus leaders in students' rights and lobbying, in addition to presenting student concerns and representing student sentiment on legislative issues.

Interns choose to work in one of a variety of areas: legislative, women's desk, third world desk, TRIO desk, or communications and administration. Each participant is required to select a specific aspect of his/her work, research the area, and write a report on the subject to be published as one of U.S.S.A.'s *Target Reports*, which are sent to member schools. Interns also help to plan and oversee the U.S.S.A.'s annual eight-day National Student Congress, to which hundreds of student leaders come to discuss issues of student concern.

Most participants are able to receive academic credit for the internship if willing to make the necessary arrangements themselves. Positions at U.S.S.A. are volunteer, although many participants have arranged to receive work/study funding or grants from a sponsoring agency or academic department.

There is one paid position open each semester at the TRIO desk—a Federally-funded program providing career counseling, tutoring, and increased academic opportunities to students from disadvantaged backgrounds. TRIO interns conduct research, prepare testimony in support of TRIO, meet with members of Congress and lobby for increased appropriations for TRIO programs. Applicants for the TRIO position should direct their application to that program specifically, at the U.S.S.A.'s address.

To apply to the general program, include a resume, writing samples, recommendations and a statement on your interests in addition to the application form. Although there is no application deadline, candidates are advised to apply well in advance.

The Inside Word

Getting accepted: Students from backgrounds in political science, economics, history, or English have traditionally made the best use of the program opportunities and, consequently, are the most appealing candidates. The program is "not that competitive" assures administrators, who stress their desire to involve as many qualified students as possible in this student-run organization. U.S.S.A. gives preference to students from member schools, women, and minority applicants. In reviewing applications, directors pay most attention to students' extracurricular activities and any courses they have taken which are relevant to the program. "Particularly attractive are candidates with academic concentrations in black studies or women's studies. Basically, though, what we seek are students committed to social change."

Daily life: Interns are primarily involved in organizing lobbying efforts on Capitol Hill, and in communicating with member schools to assist in organizing campus activities. Of late, interns have worked on setting-up a series of teach-ins on member campuses dealing with the draft, and have helped to coordinate such events as Earth Day, the National March for the E.R.A., and Big Business Day. "We're pretty much non-hierarchical. It's a student organization so we rely on student energy to get our projects done" explains one staff member.

Contact:

Frank X. Vissiano, Executive Director
U.S. Student Association Internship Program
1220 G Street, S.E.
Washington, D.C. 20003

VOLUNTEER BUREAU OF SAN FRANCISCO

San Francisco, California

ELIGIBILITY: *Undergraduate and graduate*
DURATION: *Varies*
ACADEMIC CREDIT POSSIBLE: *Yes*
REMUNERATION OR FEE: *None*
POSITIONS OFFERED: *2*
APPLICATION DEADLINE: *Open*

General Description

The Volunteer Bureau of San Francisco / Voluntary Action Center acts as an internship clearinghouse for the area's 500 social service agencies. The Bureau itself hires two interns per semester to assist in intern placement: one as an aide in the Youth Development division, and another in Transition-Individual Recovery.

In addition to the specific responsibilities in each division, interns help the six full-time staff members to develop new methods of placement and to publicize the Bureau's services to regional organizations. Interns generally work at the Bureau at least 20 hours per week during the course of the program, usually arranged to coincide with academic semesters or the summer.

The Inside Word

The Bureau requires a resume and interview of applicants. Interns outline a program, under the guidance of a staff person at the start of the internship, and must participate in an evaluation session upon completion.

Interns at the Bureau take part in educational workshops to develop volunteer management skills. Interns in the Transition-Individual Recovery division assist in placing emotionally-troubled patients in volunteer positions in the community upon their recoveries. Interns are responsible not only for making the placement assignments but for following-up on the individual's progress.

In the Youth Development program, interns speak to high school and youth groups to recruit students for volunteer positions. They are then responsible for placing the students in social service agencies.

According to interns, the program offered a rare opportunity to work closely with social and rehabilitative agencies in a vital, responsible way. "The staff was extremely helpful and supportive," commented one intern, "they allowed me to be very flexible and determine my own program around my interests—which changed as I became further involved in the program."

Contact:

Mary Culp
Volunteer Bureau of San Francisco
Voluntary Action Center
33 Gough Street
San Francisco, CA 94103 .

WASHINGTON PEACE CENTER   *Washington, D.C.*

ELIGIBILITY: *Undergraduate and graduate*
DURATION: *2 to 9 months*
ACADEMIC CREDIT POSSIBLE: *Yes*
REMUNERATION OR FEE: *Work-related travel*
POSITIONS OFFERED: *4*
APPLICATION DEADLINE: *Open*

General Description

The Washington Peace Center is an organization of Washington area residents concerned with militarism in our society. The Center "works for a more just society, one based on respect for life, the inviolability of the individual, and the equitable sharing of the world's resources."

The Center's program involves educating the public on militarism, and lobbying for a more humane American foreign policy. The Peace Center works closely with other social change organizations in the

Washington area. The Center's operation is divided into four areas of concern and activity. Interns may work in the disarmament, speakers bureau, youth and military, or newsletter phases of the Center's program. Interns work with four permanent full-time staff member and four high school student volunteers.

The disarmament program lobbies to "end the arms race, commence a reduction in arms, and zero nuclear weapons growth as needed first steps toward disarmament." Activity is divided among five areas: organizing community support to urge Congress to transfer funds from the military to meeting human needs; promoting international arms reduction and disarmament talks; halting arms sales abroad; protesting the development of new weapons systems, and educating the public on the pervasiveness of military-based industry. Interns participate in all aspects of the program.

The speakers bureau is a service the Center offers to local groups; experts on a wide variety of subjects lecture on the activities of the Peace Center. Interns help to coordinate these speaking engagements, and assist in the presentations.

The youth and military program works to inform area youth of the harmful aspects of life in the military. Interns and staff members work with counselors, teachers, and parents to increase their awareness of the "extent of the military's influence and presence in the public schools."

The organization publishes a monthly newsletter on which interns work extensively. The publication reports the Center's and other local peace activities, and deals with national and international issues related to the Center's work.

Program applicants must submit a resume and essay on why they are interested in the Peace Center along with the application form. Beginning and ending dates are flexible, as is the weekly time commitment. Applications are accepted and screened on a rolling basis.

The Inside Word

Getting accepted: There are no admission requirements outside of sincere commitment to the Center's work, say program administrators. The Peace Center hires four interns each semester, and assigns each to an individual project based on past academic and job experiences. In addition, each intern is given specific daily responsibilities within his/her division.

Daily life: Interns step right into the thick of the Center's workings, immediately assuming significant responsibilities ranging from studying the effect of military budget spending on the metropolitan Washington area, to organizing the annual Hiroshima memorial, to lobbying against reinstitution of the draft. Of late, interns have been involved in collecting campaign information and issuing statements on each presidential candidate's position on military and defense spending.

Interns found the program to be "challenging—intellectually, physically, morally. I became so involved with the work I was doing that it was difficult to leave once my project was completed."

Contact:

Jane Midgley
Washington Peace Center
2111 Florida Avenue, N.W.
Washington, D.C. 20008

YOUTH OPPORTUNITIES UPHELD, *Worcester, Massachusetts* INC.—INTENSIVE ADOLESCENT SERVICES

ELIGIBILITY: *Undergraduate only*
DURATION: *September to June; summer*
ACADEMIC CREDIT POSSIBLE: *Yes*
REMUNERATION OR FEE: *None*
POSITIONS OFFERED: *10*
APPLICATION DEADLINE: *Open*

General Description

The Intensive Adolescent Services internship, which is part of Youth Opportunities Upheld, Inc., is especially suitable for someone interested in educational and social counseling. The agency, supported by the Worcester Juvenile Court, provides a wide range of activities for youthful offenders and their families. The project's goal is to provide a safe and friendly setting where troubled kids can learn skills and practical knowledge to build self-esteem and channel their energies more constructively.

Staff members and interns help students with arts and crafts projects and with recreational sports; they work together to explore educational and job opportunities. Interns spend free time getting to know the kids, getting them involved and praising their efforts. In a sense, they teach by being a role model during this unstructured time. The intern is expected to devote between eight and ten hours a week to the program's various activities.

In addition to interacting with the kids, interns work closely with the staff. They participate in a general initial orientation to the program's goals and a more specific orientation to their role as interns. Throughout the year they meet weekly to discuss the roles of teacher and counselor. They also meet individually with their assigned supervisor to talk over problems and suggestions. At the end of each semester they receive a written evaluation.

Y.O.U., Inc.—I.A.S. accepts only those 18 years of age or older who will be attending school during the internship. Those eligible should call the agency and set up an appointment.

The Inside Word

Interns agree that because of the type of kids they work with, the experience is very challenging and worthwhile. One intern cautioned, "You should be prepared to be assertive, firm, and not easily upset by crude language and insults." The work can be very rewarding: "You can see their self-confidence and willingness to learn to grow with the support you give them."

Interns credit the teachers and clinical staff for their patience, willingness to answer questions, and for allowing interns flexibility in pursuing their own interests. However, one intern felt that there could have been more communication between staff and interns. "I wish the counselors had told us more about the individual kids before we worked with them. If we asked, they would tell us about specific cases, but this information would have been more helpful if we had it sooner."

Another complaint was that the intern's role was too limited. Some would have liked to learn more about the actual counseling therapy in which interns do not participate. The program directors feel that more experience is needed for this work.

One final word of advice which interns offered, "It is much easier at times to do things for the kids than watch their frustrated efforts. However, it is most important to have the patience to let them try because it demonstrates your confidence in them."

Contact:

Ms. Sara Whiteman
Y.O.U. INC.—I.A.S.
75A Grove St.
Worcester, MA 01605

OTHER PLACES TO LOOK:

Architecture
Eastern Tennessee Community Design Center

Environment
Center for Renewable Resources
The Conservation Foundation
Environmental Intern Program
Friends of the Earth
The Georgia Conservancy
National Wildlife Federation
New England Sierra Club
Technical Information Project, Inc.

Government
Americans for Democratic Action
Robert F. Kennedy Memorial Youth Policy Institute
National League of Cities
Urban Fellows Program of New York

Health
American Vegetarians
Epilepsy Foundation
Health Policy Advisory Center

Journalism
Corporation for Public Broadcasting

Law
American Civil Liberties Union, Chicago Chapter
Legal Aid Clinic Internships

The Sciences

The main problem in finding science internships is that there are lots of other budding science students out there trying to do the same thing. It seems that science students fall roughly into two categories (if you believe in crude generalizations): the Hot-Shots and the Not-So-Hot-Or-Luke-Warm-Shots. The Hot-Shots are the ones who forget to take their calculators off before going to bed and do their math homework in their head during breakfast. If you're a Hot-Shot science student, you probably don't need this book to find an internship or a summer job. But if you don't have all A's in your Math and Science courses and haven't demonstrated a precocious talent in the laboratory, the situation becomes somewhat more difficult. A little ingenuity and perseverance are needed.

First of all, there are what have traditionally been called the pure sciences. If you are interested in scientific laboratory research, there are two major places to find it. The first is in college or university laboratories; the second is in government laboratories. The two are very often intertwined: university labs often function with federal funding, and government labs are often administered and run by academic institutions. If you are a student, the first and easiest place to look is in your own college or university. See what kinds of research are being done at your school, and whether there is a need for research assistants. Read department bulletin boards; they often contain notices of undergraduate research opportunities. Check with your faculty: they might have colleagues in research labs, in industry, or at other universities who need help with their research projects and might be able to hire an assistant. By all means take advantage of these connections, for personal contacts are the surest way to employment in the science-biz, or any biz, for that matter.

The National Science Foundation and The Department of Energy

Once you have exhausted the academic channels, it's time to look to Uncle Sam for some help. The two major sources of funding for under-graduate research programs are the National Science Foundation (NSF) and the Department of Energy (DOE). Each year, NSF awards grants to college and university faculty, departments, and students, for under-graduate summer research programs. These provide research oppor-tunities for over 1,700 students each year. A more complete description of NSF Student Oriented Programs and where to write for more information can be found later in this Chapter.

The Department of Energy operates some twenty-one laboratories and research centers throughout the country. These labs carry out fundamental and applied energy-related research in most all of the "hard sciences." Well-established internship programs at some of these laboratories are an excellent opportunity to become involved in energy-related research. In addition, DOE labs are beginning to carry programs in some of the "softer," more policy-oriented areas, and to accept interns from backgrounds other than the hard-core math-science type.

A word of warning: competition is intense for places in the well-established programs funded by NSF and DOE (last year, the Solar Energy Research Institute summer program received 400 applications for 15 places). Perhaps the application forms should be stamped at the top: "For Hot-Shots Only." If you are not immediately recognizable as a "Promising Young Scientist with Demonstrated Research Potential," your chances of being accepted into one of these programs is rather slim. Much emphasis in the selection process is placed on *demonstrated* interest and competence in your field, compatibility of your interests with ongoing work at the laboratory, and strong letters of recommendation from your faculty.

If you feel you might qualify for hot-shot status, then by all means apply for these programs. Your chances will be improved through aggressiveness and ingenuity. If you have expertise in a specific area, say Josephson tunnel-junctions in semi-conductors, you would do well to call or write to the lab and find out exactly who is doing work in a project related to your area of experience. Contact this person; get him or her interested in you. If you can attack the selection process from both sides, by getting someone inside the lab to pull for you while carrying strong recommendations from your own faculty, you'll stand a much better chance of being hired.

Remember, a research scientist would much rather hire an intern who shows some interest and enthusiasm in hunting down a position than one who simply remains a mute name on a list of equally well-qualified candidates. Perhaps the cardinal rule of internship-hunting bears repeating: never simply leave your fate in the hands of a personnel department. Repeated personal inquiries are the surest way to securing a position.

For the Not-So-Hot-Or-Luke-Warm-Shots

If that's you, all of the above attempts will fail, and you'll find yourself thinking that a summer washing dishes wouldn't really be all that bad. Don't give up yet. Not until you've tried that golden book of opportunity: The Yellow Pages. Don't snicker. If you don't seem to be cut out for the research-biz, it's time to go the applied science route. For example, if you are interested in solar energy, you just might find someone interested in hiring you. Realize that it's always a numbers game: send out dozens of resumes and you might get a few maybes, but keep on plugging. Remember that whereas research labs might be interested in learning and knowledge for its own sake, a business' main concern is to make a profit.

Businesses that deal in highly technical products are still businesses, and the old profit incentive is never far from anyone's mind. You must convince the company that you can make a real contribution. See the "Business" Chapter for more information and for listings of programs in industrial science.

Most scientific outfits are looking for engineering-type students with an applied-science background. A liberal-arts student walking into an engineering firm is likely to meet with scepticism. Don't give them the impression that your approach to the job is one of typical non-commital liberal-arts intellectualism. Show them that you want to work. If you want to do a little carrot-dangling of your own, you must have particular skills (can you use an oscilloscope?) that you can sell to the firm.

Energy Buffs

If the film, "The Graduate," were being remade today, the man who had only one word to say to Dustin Hoffman would have urged him to think about "Energy," rather than "Plastics." Energy is today's buzz-word, and lots of things are happening in the energy field.

If you're interested in the energy business (designing, manufacturing, and selling wind machines or solar panels, for example), try the Yellow Pages. Also check out your local or regional utility company; they sometimes hire engineering students to do temporary work, and many of them now carry research and development programs in alternative energy sources, and in energy conservation and public education. Oil distributors also are becoming involved in conservation education, better home heating programs, and home energy audits.

If you're after more fundamental energy research, the national laboratories run by DOE and described below all carry out extensive energy research programs.

On the federal level, write to your senators or congressmen and find out who on their staffs is researching energy issues. See if they need any help.

Call or write to your State Energy Office (most states have one by now). These offices are involved in the public policy and legislative aspects of the energy problem on the state level. There is often a need for specialized, short-term work on the part of interns (researching a specific issue such as tax-credits for the purchase of solar water-heaters, for example). A technical background, facility with numbers and graphs, and familiarity with a particular energy technology or public policy issue can be very useful. It always helps to have a specific project in mind when you apply for a position. There is always a need for people who want to get something done, whereas those who merely have a vague interest and want to "help out somehow," will find themselves less useful. For more contacts, get hold of the *Directory of State Government Energy Related Agencies,* available from the National Energy Information Center, Washington, D.C. 20461.

Also on the state level are the State Public Utility Commissions, which are responsible for regulating the utility industry within the state. These commissions play an important role in the implementation of statewide energy strategies, and might have need of student help on short-term projects.

On the local level, find out if your city or town has an energy manager. See what kind of conservation and public education programs are underway. Perhaps you could help out, or design one of your own and sell the town on the idea. Be ingenious.

THE NATIONAL SCIENCE FOUNDATION   *National*

There is probably not one area of scientific inquiry that has been ignored by the National Science Foundation (NSF). In addition to supporting professional scientific research in all fields, NSF provides funding for Student Oriented Programs, which are part of the Foundation's Division of Scientific Personnel Improvement.

NSF administers federal funds, but does not actually run any programs itself. Interested parties—college departments, faculty members, or students themselves—submit grant proposals to NSF. If funding is approved, the grantee is then responsible for running the program, buying necessary equipment, selecting the participants, etc. Funding is available for three types of Student Oriented Programs: Student Science Training (SST) for secondary school students, Undergraduate Research Participation Projects, and Student-Originated Studies.

Student Science Training

These summer programs for high school students are designed to identify and encourage young scientific talent. Designed both for students with excellent as well as those with limited educational backgrounds, the projects allow students to do ten to twelve weeks of laboratory research under the supervision of a college faculty person. Greater emphasis is now being placed on programs for students from ethnic groups that have been historically deprived, and for students with physical handicaps. The programs are held mostly at colleges and universities, and allow about 2500 students to participate each year. Application deadlines for students are usually April 15.

For a listing of programs, request the brochure on the Student Science Training Program, available from the National Science Foundation, Washington, D.C., 20550.

Undergraduate Research Participation

These are summer programs for college undergraduates between their junior and senior year. Participants must be full-time students when they apply. Stipends of up to $1000 may be available, paid out at a rate of $100 per week.

The programs allow faculty members or industrial scientists to bring talented students into their research activities. Students gain first-hand research experience by collaborating with professional research scientists.

The individual projects are very specialized and usually receive many applicants. Selection of participants is made by the scientists themselves, *not* by NSF. You should personally contact whoever is running the program to discuss the possibility of your being accepted. Before applying, find out whether you are really qualified to work on the particular project. A few preliminary phone calls might save a lot of time filling out applications for research programs that are way out of your league. For instance, a scientist looking for a student to help out with research on Metal-Oxide-Semiconductor Tunnel Junctions will have little interest in taking on a student with no experience in semi-conductor physics.

There is a good chance, however, of finding at least one program within your area of expertise. Each year NSF funds well over one hundred projects in all different fields, providing summer research opportunities for over 1,200 students. Write to NSF for their brochure on Undergraduate Research Participation Projects, The National Science Foundation, Washington, D.C. 20550. This contains a listing and brief description of current projects, along with the names and phone numbers of the persons running them. The brochure is usually available in January or February.

Student-Originated Studies

This is perhaps the most exciting and innovative of NSF's student-oriented programs. It provides funding for student-initiated, -planned, and -directed study of environmental and social problems. Last year, projects included: "Factors Influencing the Application of Solar Technology in Connecticut," "Prospects for Development of Day Care for the Aged: Champaign County, Illinois," and "Organic Chemical Pollution in Western New York Drinking Water."

Each study is conducted by a team of up to 10 students, headed by a student project director and advised by a faculty member. The team must be interdisciplinary and must be composed primarily of undergraduates. While the faculty advisor is paid for his or her contribution to the project, the real initiative and responsibility rests on the students. Students receive a stipend of $100 per week for 10 or 12 weeks of summer work.

After completing all research and/or field work in the summer, the group must write up a project report. The preliminary report is due in October. In December, two members of the group are given an expense-paid trip to Washington, where they give a 15-minute presentation of their project before a national SOS symposium. A Final Technical Report is due in February.

Writing an SOS proposal: Student project directors tell us that the most important thing in writing an SOS proposal is to "make a strong case for its social relevance." The importance of this should be clear if you read the application booklet carefully. "You must convince them (NSF) that your project will really be worth something to somebody, and won't just end up sitting on a shelf." The best way of proving that a project is worthwhile is to solicit letters of support from the people to whom the study will be useful. "If you have letters from people saying that your study will be important to them, you'll have a much better chance of getting it approved," said one project director.

Student directors also advise applicants to "keep the proposal from being too broad. Keep in mind that you have only three months to work with. NSF wants a feasible project, one that gets results." Though the selection committee might make suggestions on how to focus the project once it has been approved, "every effort should be made to narrow the proposal down before submitting it."

Another piece of advice: "Be aggressive. Let the people in Washington know who you are. Make a few phone calls to the people in charge of reviewing proposals, tell them about your proposal, ask questions. They'll remember you; you'll be surprised."

Even if you do not initiate a program yourself, it is possible to get involved in projects started by others. Write to NSF for a listing of SOS projects. You can then contact the student directors of projects that interest you to see if they need any more people for their group.

A word of warning comes from one project director: "everyone loves to do field work, but when it comes to writing up the report, people tend to lose interest." Realize that these projects are a fairly long commitment, extending well beyond the summer months in which you get paid. If you are planning on heading up a project, make sure you have a firm commitment from each member of the group to stick with the project to the end. One strategy: "you might even want to withhold the last two weeks pay until they've written up their section of the report."

For more information, request the brochure and proposal forms for Student-Originated Studies, The National Science Foundation, Washington, D.C. 20550.

U.S. DEPARTMENT OF ENERGY   *National*
EDUCATIONAL PROGRAMS DIVISION
Student Research Participation

If working in a big lab is for you, a DOE program is bound to be an excellent introduction into the world of professional energy research. The Department of Energy (DOE) operates dozens of laboratories and research centers throughout the country. At least twenty of these offer summer research programs for college juniors and seniors, as part of DOE's Student Research Participation program. Some labs offer programs during the academic year, as well, and there are also opportunities for graduate students.

The idea is to train young scientists in fields related to national energy problems by letting them pitch in for a summer with professional energy researchers. If you are a better-than-average student in any of the physical and life sciences, there is probably a program for you. There are three main clearing-houses for information on student research programs, depending on the region you're interested in.

South and South-East: Oak Ridge Associated Universities, University Programs, P.O. Box 117, Oak Ridge, Tennessee, 37830. Northwest: The Northwest College and University Association for Science (NOR-CUS), Joint Center for Graduate Study, 100 Sprout Road, Richland, Washington, 99352. Western and Rocky Mountain: Associated Western Universities, Inc., 136 East South Temple, Suite 2200; Salt Lake City, Utah, 84111.

DOE labs range from broad multidisciplinary labs such as Oak Ridge and Argonne to specific mission-oriented or single purpose labs such as the Pittsburgh Energy Technology Center, which focuses on coal research. The labs typically employ over 1000 professional scientists in huge, often unattractive complexes. One intern at the Lawrence Berkeley Laboratory said that "you have to be able to deal with shuttle-buses and cafeterias—you really feel like one of the scientific masses. You get a sense of just how huge is the federal scientific effort."

The following pages include detailed descriptions of some of the larger of DOE's student programs which will give you an idea of what goes on at other large DOE facilities. Several other programs are then described in less detail. Finally, we've listed some seven more Doe labs that offer Student Research Participation programs.

ADDITIONAL DOE LABS

The following laboratories all carry Student Research Participation Programs for college undergraduates:

Energy & Environmental Division
Lawrence Berkeley Laboratory
University of California
Berkeley, California 94720
(415) 843-5433

Associate Director for Education
Department of Radiation Biology
 and Biophysics
University of Rochester
Rochester, New York 14642
(716) 275-3891

Monsanto Research Corporation
Mound Laboratory
P.O. Box 32
Miamisburg, Ohio 45342
(513) 866-7444 ext. 7147

Director of Education Program
Savannah River Ecology
 Laboratory
P.O. Box E
Aiken, South Carolina 29801
(803) 824-6331 ext. 2959

Professional and University
   Relations
Savannah River Laboratory
E.I. duPont de Numours &
   Company
Aiken, South Carolina 29801
(803) 824-6331 ext. 2821

Center for Energy and
   Environmental Research of the
   University of Puerto Rico
Caparra Heights Station
San Juan, Puerto Rico 00935
(809) 767-0350

Morgantown Energy Technology
   Center
P.O. Box 880
Morgantown, West Virginia 26505
(804) 599-7511

AMES LABORATORY
Summer Student Trainee Program

Ames, Iowa

ELIGIBILITY: *Juniors and seniors*
DURATION: *10 weeks, summer*
ACADEMIC CREDIT POSSIBLE: *No*
REMUNERATION OR FEE: *$125 to $150/week*
POSITIONS OFFERED: *30*
APPLICATION DEADLINE: *Mid-February*

General Description

The Ames Lab offers summer research positions each year in the fields of Chemistry, Physics, Metallurgy, Ceramic Engineering, and Chemical Engineering. Operating with DOE funds, the program is oriented toward energy-related projects. Laboratory staff line up projects for students to work on for the summer. Once started on a project, most students work independently.

The Inside Word

Ames Lab is a smaller, "less intense" lab than some of the larger DOE facilities such as Argonne and Oak Ridge (described above). It functions in a close relationship with Iowa State University—many laboratory staff members also teach at the university. The lab is very well funded, causing one student to remark "I could have pretty much any equipment or supplies that I needed."

   Though most students step into projects that are waiting for them when they get there, there is the possibility of designing a different project if your assignment is not to your liking. According to one student, "after a week they ask you if you want to continue with the project. When I was there, only one student out of the group decided she wanted to do something different.''

Because much of the work is in on-going research, the majority of students do not see their project come to any culmination, and no final report is required. However, several students each summer do complete a sufficient amount of work to write a paper, often publishable.

Most participants live in the dormitory housing available to out-of-town students, within walking distance of the lab. Ames has a population of 50,000—of which 20,000 are students at the university—so that numerous films and lectures provide interns with some activity outside of the lab. Still, commented one student, ''Ames isn't the most fun place in the world to be; a lot of the students like to travel.''

Contact:

Curtiss Roberg, Director
Summer Student Trainee Program
Ames Laboratory
Iowa State University
Ames, IA 50011

ARGONNE NATIONAL LABORATORY   *Argonne, Illinois*
Summer Research Participation
Academic Year Research Participation
Summer Employment

ELIGIBILITY: *Undergraduate*
DURATION: *Summer or semester*
ACADEMIC CREDIT POSSIBLE: *Yes*
REMUNERATION OR FEE: *Summer $135/week plus travel; Academic year $100 honorarium plus housing.*
POSITIONS OFFERED: *Varies*
APPLICATION DEADLINE: *Summer, February 1; Fall semester, April 1; Spring semester, October 2.*

General Description

Argonne National Laboratory (ANL) is one of DOE's major research centers. It employs over 5000 people and is located on two sites: one 27 miles southwest of Chicago, and one 40 miles west of Idaho Falls, Idaho. Argonne began as a center for nuclear reactor research and development, and still devotes much of its funding to nuclear reactor safety, waste disposal, breeder reactor development, and fusion energy research. In recent years, ANL has diversified its areas of research, and now carries programs in solar energy research, advanced batteries for electric automobiles, magnetohydrodynamics, biomedical and environmental research, and the atmospheric and human health effects of energy-related pollutants. ANL has also been involved in educational programs designed to help American Indians make informed choices on energy resource development within reservation lands.

Summer program: The Student Research Participation program is aimed at honors-caliber students of science, engineering, and mathematics who intend to enter graduate or professional school. Applicants must have a B average or better. Argonne does not itself grant academic credit. If credit is desired, arrangements must be made by the student with his or her own school.

During the first week of the program, the student and supervisor agree on a project. For the next few weeks, the student's supervisor provides considerable assistance, and after that, the student completes the project on his or her own initiative. Students are required to submit a final research report on the project, and the Argonne program coordinator sends a performance evaluation letter to the student's adviser on campus after the program ends.

Housing for single students is available in a college dormitory.

The program has been running for 12 years now, and its director claims that "over 90% of our participants have had successful research experiences."

Academic year program: This has the same structure as the summer program, but is extended over a 16-week period. Students are housed free of charge in six-person units consisting of three bedrooms, two baths, and a kitchenette-living room. Students are responsible for buying and cooking their own food, and for all other incidental expenses. A car is a must, as the nearest grocery store is three miles away.

Summer employment program: Students may also be selected for summer employment as Student Aides at Argonne, where they will provide technical assistance to a scientist or engineer. Student Aides are paid a taxable salary which is larger than a summer research participant's salary and which is determined by the number of terms of undergraduate study.

Contact:

FOR APPLICATION MATERIALS:

*Undergraduate Research
   Participation Programs*

Argonne Center for Educational
Affairs
9700 South Cass Avenue
Argonne, IL 60439
(312) 972-3366

BARTLESVILLE ENERGY TECHNOLOGY CENTER
Bartlesville, Oklahoma

Student Research Participation

ELIGIBILITY: *Sophomore through graduate*
DURATION: *8 to 16 weeks, summer*
ACADEMIC CREDIT POSSIBLE: *No*
REMUNERATION OR FEE: *$135 to $150/week, plus transportation up to $200*
POSITIONS OFFERED: *Varies*
APPLICATION DEADLINE: *April 15*

General Description

Bartlesville is involved in petroleum production research, and in research on the efficient use of oil and natural gas. Advanced research includes the thermodynamics of coal liquids and hydrocarbons from fossil fuels, characterization of syncrudes from coal, and performance testing of synthetic fuels.

Contact:

FOR APPLICATION MATERIALS:

Associated Western Universities, Inc.
136 East South Temple
Salt Lake City, UT 84111
(801) 364-5659

FOR MORE INFORMATION:

Barbara Barnett
Spec. Asst. to the Director
P.O. Box 1398
Bartlesville, OK 74003
(918) 336-2400

BARTOL RESEARCH FOUNDATION
Cosmic Ray Research Program

Antarctica

ELIGIBILITY: *Seniors*
DURATION: *14 months*
ACADEMIC CREDIT POSSIBLE: *Yes*
REMUNERATION OR FEE: *$11,000/year salary*
POSITIONS OFFERED: *2*
APPLICATION DEADLINE: *Mid-February*

General Description

This program sends you to Antarctica. That's right. Each year two graduating seniors in physics, engineering, or astronomy are selected to spend 14 months "On the Ice," performing basic cosmic ray research. The interns are placed either at the McMurdo Sound research station or at a smaller, high-altitude station sitting atop the South Pole itself. Credit can be arranged for graduate study in physics and astronomy.

The Bartol Research Foundation is part of The Franklin Institute of the University of Delaware. It operates the most advanced research facility of its kind—taking advantage of the unique potential of the Antarctic region for observing cosmic rays and performing basic cosmic ray physics.

Applicants are carefully screened. The pool is usually narrowed to less than 12, and these are brought to the University of Delaware (expenses-paid) for a mandatory three-hour interview. Here the applicants—often fewer than 12 because some students decide to withdraw their applications—are shown some of the sophisticated electronic equipment that they will be dealing with at the research station. Those students who are finally selected—and decide that they want to stick with it—are then sent to Washington, D.C. (also expenses-paid). In Washington they are turned over to the Navy for psychological testing—the same as that performed on prospective submarine crew members. The rigors of confinement in the research station during the long winter months require a certain degree of psychological stability. Once past these tests, interns are given a course of cold weather training and then shipped off to The Ice. The program lasts 14 months, from August to November.

The Inside Word

Isolation: When winter closes in on The Ice there is no escape. Past November, transportation to and from the pole becomes impossible. This is why the program director says that participants "should have a fair amount of imagination" to keep themselves occupied. The summer-time population of 1000 souls at the McMurdo Sound station shrinks to 50 during the winter, and at the South Pole Station the crew is reduced from

50 to 20. But don't worry—the program director tells us that no one has cracked up yet. The careful screening process that preceeds your trip to The Ice ensures your ability to handle the isolation.

One person we know of brought a complete harpsichord kit to work on while he was down there—taking advantage of the excellent wood-shop and machine-shop facilities the stations must have in order to be self-sufficient during the winter months.

Daily life: Most interns enjoy their stay, and in fact "never get bored." The physics is interesting—but not painfully academic, and there is always plenty of exploring to do in the outdoors. "It is an unforgiving environment," remarked one intern, "but with the training they give you it is fairly safe." The medical facilities are quite good—a lucky thing for one student who had to be thawed out after falling into the frigid ocean while chasing penguins.

Aside from the work, there is plenty of time for "loafing." The program provides participants with certain amenities, such as candy bars, toothpaste, and—get this—free beer. Sound appealing? This program could be a once in a lifetime opportunity to travel to the far reaches of the planet.

Contact:

The Director
Bartol Research Foundation
University of Delaware
Newark, DE 19711

BROOKHAVEN NATIONAL LABORATORY   *Upton, New York*
Summer Student Program

ELIGIBILITY: *Juniors and seniors*
DURATION: *11 weeks, summer*
ACADEMIC CREDIT POSSIBLE: *No*
REMUNERATION OR FEE: *$125/week plus travel expenses up to $150*
POSITIONS OFFERED: *Varies*
APPLICATION DEADLINE: *January 31*

General Description

This is a prestigious summer research program for hard-core math and science students. Students majoring in applied mathematics, physical and life sciences, engineering, and scientific journalism are eligible. Applicants must have a B average or better, demonstrate a "genuine interest in research or teaching as a career," and must be in a field which coincides with research in progress at the lab.

Ongoing projects are in various areas of chemistry, physics, engineering, biology, nuclear medicine, applied mathematics, high and low energy particle accelerators, and science writing.

Contact:

Dr. Glenn A. Price
Office of Scientific Personnel
Brookhaven National Laboratory
Upton, NY 11973

GRAND FORKS ENERGY TECHNOLOGY CENTER
Student Research Participation

Grand Forks, North Dakota

ELIGIBILITY: *Sophomore through graduate*
DURATION: *8 to 16 weeks, summer*
ACADEMIC CREDIT POSSIBLE: *No*
REMUNERATION OR FEE: *$135 to $150/week, plus transportation up to $200*
POSITIONS OFFERED: *Varies*
APPLICATION DEADLINE: *April 15*

General Description

Grand Forks is a coal research center. Research focuses on coal liquefaction by the co-steam process, coal gasification by the slagging fixed bed process, and coal combustion and combustion products. Additional work includes the environmental-biomedical assessment of the impact of coal conversion and combustion technology, and study of work-place safety and health hazards in synfuel processes.

Applicants should have backgrounds in Chemistry or in Engineering (Chemical, Mineral, Petroleum, Mechanical).

Contact:

FOR APPLICATION MATERIALS:

Associated Western
Universities, Inc.
136 East South Temple
Salt Lake City, UT 84111
(801) 364-5659

FOR MORE INFORMATION:
Philip G. Freeman
Staff Scientist, Grand Forks
Energy Technology Center
P. O. Box 8213, Univ. Sta.
Grand Forks, ND 58202
(701) 795-8000

KITT PEAK NATIONAL OBSERVATORY   *Tucson, Arizona*
Summer Research Assistantships

ELIGIBILITY: *Junior through graduate*
DURATION: *10 to 12 weeks, summer*
ACADEMIC CREDIT POSSIBLE: *Yes*
REMUNERATION OR FEE: *$561 to $829/month salary,
    plus transportation*
POSITIONS OFFERED: *8*
APPLICATION DEADLINE: *February 15*

General Description

For students committed to a career in astronomy or astrophysics, this is an opportunity to work with some of the best optical equipment in the continental United States. Students work with a staff scientist on an on-going project compatible with their interests and abilities.

Kitt Peak houses a large number of optical telescopes including a four-meter scope and an 84-inch scope. Students work in areas such as high resolution astronomical spectroscopy, photometry, design, and construction of astronomical equipment, observation, data reduction, and computer programming. There are also limited opportunities for work in astrophysics and solar physics, as the observatory has a solar scope and is a complete solar facility.

Students' salaries are dependent on their academic level. Students live either on-site at the observatory or in Tucson itself. Applicants must submit college transcripts, three letters of recommendation, and an application, including an essay describing relevant academic and research background, goals, and preferred areas of research.

The Inside Word

Getting accepted: Admission to the program is very competitive, with 250 applicants for the meager eight positions offered. Early application is advised as well as *some* previous research experience. In your essay, be thorough but concise in describing your interests and why you want to work in the program. Not only will this boost your chances of acceptance, but it will ensure that, once in, you'll be given work that you will enjoy. Applications are circulated among the research staff members, who pick out those students whose interests match their own.

General comments: Students find the opportunity to engage in professional research work a very worthwhile experience, and recommend the program to anyone interested in optical astronomical research. "The staff is fantastic, very easy to work with, and extremely knowledgeable in the field. There are some fine brains to pick at the observatory, and they don't mind giving out answers." The top-notch staff is also an excellent source of valuable recommendations for the future.

Living conditions: If you're going to be living at the observatory site, rest assured that you will be very comfortable. "The on-site living facilities at Kitt Peak are beautiful, some of the best I've ever seen," said one well-travelled astronomer. The Tucson area itself is beautiful, and lends itself to exploration, backpacking, and rock climbing adventures.

Contact:

The Office of the Director
Summer Research Assistantship Program
Kitt Peak National Observatory
P. O. Box 26732
Tucson, AZ 85726

LARAMIE ENERGY TECHNOLOGY CENTER
Laramie, Wyoming
Student Research Participation

ELIGIBILITY: *Sophomore through graduate*
DURATION: *8 to 16 weeks, summer*
ACADEMIC CREDIT POSSIBLE: *No*
REMUNERATION OR FEE: *$135 to $150/week, plus transportation up to $200*
POSITIONS OFFERED: *Varies*
APPLICATION DEADLINE: *April 15*

General Description

Laramie conducts research in the *in situ* processing of shale oil, in the characterization of shale oil products, in the *in situ* gasification of coal, and on the environmental effects of shale oil processing. Students should have backgrounds in Chemistry, Physics, Geology, Engineering (Chemical,

Mineral, Petroleum, Mechanical), Environmental Sciences, or Mathematics/Computer Science.

Contact:

FOR APPLICATION MATERIALS:

Associated Western
Universities, Inc.
136 East South Temple
Salt Lake City, UT 84111
(801) 364-5659

FOR MORE INFORMATION:

Jack D. Raymond
Spec. Asst. to the Director
Laramie Energy Technology
  Center
P.O. Box 3395, Univ. Sta.
Laramie, WY 82071
(307) 721-2256

LOS ALAMOS SCIENTIFIC LABORATORY
Los Alamos, New Mexico
Graduate Research Assistant Program

ELIGIBILITY: *Graduate*
DURATION: *Summer*
ACADEMIC CREDIT POSSIBLE: *No*
REMUNERATION OR FEE: *$1300 to $1500/month salary*
  plus travel
POSITIONS OFFERED: *About 130*
APPLICATION DEADLINE: *November 30*

General Description

Los Alamos Scientific Laboratory (LASL) is run by the University of California for the Department of Energy. Research and Development programs seeking Graduate Research Assistants are: Laser Research and Technology; Controlled Thermonuclear Research; Nuclear Safeguards, Reactor Safety, and Energy Technology; Detonation Physics; Field Testing; Health Research; Geoscience/Geothermal Energy; Materials Research and Technology; Chemistry/Nuclear Chemistry; Computer Research; Energy and Environmental Systems, Analysis, and Assessment; Design Engineering; Accelerator Technology; Experimental Nuclear Physics; and Theoretical Research and Design.

Contact:

Patricia Beck
GRA Program DIV. UM
Los Alamos Scientific Laboratory
P.O. Box 1663
Los Alamos, NM 87545

LOS ALAMOS SCIENTIFIC   *Los Alamos, New Mexico*
·LABORATORY
Skills Training Employment Program

ELIGIBILITY: *Undergraduate and graduate*
DURATION: *1 year*
ACADEMIC CREDIT POSSIBLE: *No*
REMUNERATION OR FEE: *$1200 to $1400/month salary*
POSITIONS OFFERED: *About 30*
APPLICATION DEADLINE: *October 1*

General Description

This program is aimed at those who don't have the experience needed to compete successfully for jobs in their chosen field. It is open to both degreed (B.S. in a scientific/engineering field) and non-degreed applicants. Participants work for one year under the guidance of senior staff in a position that offers career development potential. Applicants should have a definite career goal in mind and be able to show that they have taken positive steps to fulfill that goal.

For degreed participants, positions are available in the physical sciences, biological sciences, engineering, and mathematics/computer science.

Non-degreed candidates can apply for training in the following areas: Electronic Data Processing, Motion Picture/Video Production, Drafting, Data Analysis, Programming, Illustration, Technical Writing, Administration, Technology—mechanical, chemical, electronics.

Contact:

Elmer H. Salazar
Personnel Department
Los Alamos Scientific Laboratory
P.O. Box 1663 MS-280
Los Alamos, NM 87545

Arecibo, Puerto Rico

NATIONAL ASTRONOMY AND IONOSPHERE CENTER ARECIBO OBSERVATORY
Summer Student Program

ELIGIBILITY: *Junior through graduate*
DURATION: *June 1 to August 18*
ACADEMIC CREDIT POSSIBLE: *Yes*
REMUNERATION OR FEE: *$550 to $740/month salary plus transportation*
POSITIONS OFFERED: *Varies*
APPLICATION DEADLINE: *Mid-February*

General Description

The Arecibo Observatory is the home of the world's most powerful radio telescope—with a dish 1000 feet in diameter. Students are assigned to research staff scientists to assist in observation, data reduction and analysis, plus equipment development and testing in ongoing research projects. In the past, students have been involved in projects such as ionospheric research, mapping the surface of planets, studying quasars and pulsars, and searching for primordial galaxies.

In addition to research involvement, students have the opportunity to attend a series of seminars and lectures given by the resident staff and by distinguished visiting scientists. This allows students to extend their knowledge beyond the area in which they are working.

Three recommendations from faculty or from previous research contacts are required, as is a completed application form and college transcript.

The Inside Word

The eighth wonder: The enthusiasm expressed by one intern about the Arecibo program fell just short of that of a drop-to-your-knees Baptist prayer session: "Arecibo is like the eighth wonder of the world. It's an incredible learning experience." Because it is the best radio observatory in the world, Arecibo draws the world's finest observational personnel. Consequently, students are exposed to some of the greatest minds in the field. Working with this high-caliber staff proves to be pleasant as well as stimulating. "Most people were pleased with the research they were doing and the person they were working with. If you are not satisfied with what you are doing the place is big enough so that it is easy to arrange work with someone else," said one intern.

Students intimated that "the research project might not be the best part of the learning experience at Arecibo." You may find yourself doing a fair amount of computer work and other things which may be relatively dull. However, interns stress the value of being exposed to the excellent staff and hearing lectures delivered by the brilliant researchers who are continually flown in from all over the world.

Life on the island: Not only is the program a great scientific experience, "it is an amazing cultural experience as well," commented one intern. Students are housed by the program, close to the site of the observatory. "The area is the Appalachia of Puerto Rico. The neighbors' chickens and cows wander around outside your house—and every once in a while a lizard will skitter across the floor," said one student. The island is covered with dense, lush jungle, cliffs and beaches. There are endless possibilitites for scuba diving, sailing, and exploring.

Contact:

Office of the Director
National Astronomy and Ionosphere Center
Space Sciences Building
Cornell University
Ithaca, NY 14853
(607) 256-3734

THE NATIONAL RADIO	*Charlottesville, Virginia*
ASTRONOMY OBSERVATORY	*Green Bank, West Virginia*
Summer Research	*Tucson, Arizona*
Assistantship	*The New Mexico Desert*

ELIGIBILITY: *Juniors and seniors*
DURATION: *10 weeks, summer*
ACADEMIC CREDIT POSSIBLE: *Yes*
REMUNERATION OR FEE: *$550 to $700/month salary*
    plus transportation
POSITIONS OFFERED: *15 to 20*
APPLICATION DEADLINE: *February 15*

General Description

The National Radio Astronomy Observatory (NRAO) has been giving students the opportunity to be directly involved in astronomical research since 1959. Students work closely with staff scientists in observation, data reduction and analysis, equipment development, and theoretical study.

The program accepts students with backgrounds in astronomy, physics, engineering, computer science, and mathematics.

NRAO places students at any of its four sites, depending on whom they have for an advisor, but most students are placed at either Charlottesville or Green Bank. The Green Bank facility is outfitted with a three-hundred-foot transit radio telescope; three 85-foot radio telescopes and a 45-foot portable telescope normally used together as an interferometer; and a precision 140-foot radio telescope. Students at the Green Bank Facility are expected to spend a week assisting with public tours of the observatory.

Kitt Peak is the home of NRAO's Arizona facility, which utilizes a 36-foot scope operating at milimeter wavelengths. Charlottesville is the administrative and computing headquarters, carrying out a great deal of data reduction and analysis. The most unusual of the four sites is the New Mexico project, known as VLA (for Very Large Array). VLA is an array of 27 radio telescopes located in the New Mexico deserts. It is both the most expensive and the most sensitive astronomical project in the world, having incredibly high resolution (accurate to within ¼ arc-second).

The application process requires: a completed application form; a letter stating background, goals, and scientific experience; college transcripts; and three or four letters of recommendation.

The Inside Word

Entrance to the program is extremely competitive, with about 350 applicants for the 15 to 20 positions offered each summer. Applications are subject to committee review.

The program is highly recommended by participants. In addition to a great program run by excellent staff, the series of 20 to 25 lectures delivered by visiting scientists are quite valuable.

Participants' individual experience will depend to a large part on where they are placed. The Arizona and New Mexico sites offer beautiful scenery, and the Very Large Array is said to be an extremely impressive facility. Interns at the Green Bank facility say they "don't mind giving tours to the public." And though one student called Green Bank a "hick town," it is reported that there are some good bars in the area. The Charlottesville site boasts daily volley ball and the infamous Mouse Trap bar—"it's the only place to go."

Contact:

National Radio Astronomy Observatory
c/o Dr. W. B. Burton
Summer Student Program
Edgemont Road
Charlottesville, VA 22901

NORTHWEST COLLEGE AND UNIVERSITY ASSOCIATION FOR SCIENCE (NORCUS)
Laboratory Cooperative Program

Richland, Washington

ELIGIBILITY: *Sophomore through graduate*
DURATION: *January, summer, year*
ACADEMIC CREDIT POSSIBLE: *Yes*
REMUNERATION OR FEE: *Student Trainee (summer) $150/week plus travel; January $100/week plus travel*
POSITIONS OFFERED: *Varies*
APPLICATION DEADLINE: *January 10, for summer; November 1, for January*

General Description

NORCUS places high-caliber math, engineering, and science students, who have completed their sophomore year, in temporary positions within major DOE contracting laboratories and industrial firms. Because these labs are private contractors, students gain insight into research methods in industry. Participants work on energy-related assignments, under the guidance of senior research scientists.

The labs are all in the Richland area. They are: Pacific Northwest Laboratory, Boeing Computer Services—Richland, Inc., Hanford Environmental Health Foundation, Rockwell Hanford Operations, United Nuclear Industries, Inc., and Westinghouse Hanford Company.

Two programs are offered: the student trainee program lasts for 10 weeks, usually during the summer, although other times can be arranged; the academic year program runs during the month of January.

Contact:

The Northwest College and University
Association for Science
Joint Center for Graduate Study
100 Sprout Road
Richland, WA 99352

OAK RIDGE NATIONAL LABORATORY
Student Research Participation

Oak Ridge, Tennessee

ELIGIBILITY: *Juniors*
DURATION: *10 weeks, summer*

ACADEMIC CREDIT POSSIBLE: *No*
REMUNERATION OR FEE: *$125/week stipend plus travel allowance*
POSITIONS OFFERED: *About 80*
APPLICATION DEADLINE: *Early January*

General Description

A summer program at Oak Ridge is an opportunity to pursue independent research under the guidance of Department of Energy staff scientists at one of DOE's major research centers. Students majoring in mathematics, engineering, and the physical, life, and social sciences are eligible.

Students participate in ongoing research at the lab. They are placed in positions which best match their skills, experience, and education to a particular research project. The first two to three weeks are spent with a staff scientist, becoming familiar with the particular project and learning whatever techniques will be necessary to performing the research. Students begin working independently as soon as possible, and the major part of the program consists of carrying out independent work and writing up a report at the end. Many times, students appear as co-authors on papers published by laboratory personnel and present talks about their research at regional and national scientific meetings.

This program is one of the most prestigious in the country; competition is stiff. Each year between 70 and 80 students from colleges and universities across the country are selected from a pool of about 250 applicants. The main criteria for selection are sincere interest in energy-related research, a combination of course and laboratory work that qualifies a student for doing research, and recommendations from faculty members. A college transcript, letters of recommendation, and a completed application form are required.

The Inside Word

Getting accepted: Choosing the right area to work in is a major factor in getting accepted into the program. It is also essential to the program's being worthwhile once you're there. Both students and program administrators alike tell us that regardless of your qualifications and experience, you are unlikely to be accepted if there is no one in the lab who is working in your area of expertise.

One student tells us: "It's important at Oak Ridge to apply to an area where students are *wanted*. Thoroughly investigate the area in which you apply to work. I recommend trying to contact someone in your chosen area previous to formally applying. You may pick an area that sounds like your thing, but unless someone in that field wants a summer student, you're out of luck."

Also, "references are very important. Be choosey about who you ask to recommend you for the program, preferably someone who has seen your lab work."

Motivation and sincere interest in laboratory work are perhaps most important: "I think my extra-curricular experiences—working in a biology lab at school, doing independent research, etc.,—helped more than course work and grades in getting accepted."

Program success: Everyone involved speaks highly of the program. The program director cites the many instances of student co-authorship of research papers as a measure of the success of the program: "The percentage of students who feel they have made a real contribution is quite high." One intern said that programs such as the one she participated in at Oak Ridge are "superior to any education you receive inside the classroom."

The program stresses independent work, and encourages personal input: "I think I would have been given the opportunity to embark on any related project I wanted to, and encouraged to do so."

Daily life: Students can live at Oak Ridge, but most find housing through the University of Tennessee in nearby Knoxville. On the night life: "Oak Ridge is pretty tame—not a lot to do for people my age. Knoxville may be a little better." Students are made to feel welcome: "I felt very comfortable with the people in the lab. At no point was I put down for being a student or part-timer. As best they could, my co-workers made me feel like an equal—a much warmer reception than I expected." "The people in charge of the program are fantastic—very helpful and friendly."

Contact:

Student Research Participation
University Programs
Oak Ridge Associated Universities
Box 117
Oak Ridge, TN 37830

PITTSBURGH ENERGY TECHNOLOGY CENTER
Professional Internship Program

Pittsburgh, Pennsylvania

ELIGIBILITY: *Undergraduate*
DURATION: *Varies*
ACADEMIC CREDIT POSSIBLE: *Yes*
REMUNERATION OR FEE: *Sophomores, $800/month; juniors, $900/month; seniors, $1000/month; plus travel expenses*
POSITIONS OFFERED: *Varies*
APPLICATION DEADLINE: *3 months before desired starting date*

General Description

The Pittsburgh Energy Technology Center (PETC) focuses on research and development for both the industrial use of coal and its derived synthetic fuels in an environmentally sound manner. Ongoing projects include coal-oil mixture combustion, chemical cleaning of coal, coal liquefaction, direct combustion, gasification and magnetohydrodynamics.

The internship program provides on-the-job work experience for undergraduates majoring in chemical engineering, mechanical engineering, chemistry, computer sciences, biology, journalism, and business administration. The directors are most eager for chemical engineering students; they will be given preference. Some project assignments require that students be juniors.

This is a "co-op" program: pairs of students will be assigned to the Center, with one student in residence at any one time while the other remains on campus. At the appropriate time and in accord with the school calendar, the students will change. Applications from pairs of students on alternating schedules are encouraged.

The program is administered by Oak Ridge Associated Universities.

Contact:

Oak Ridge Associated Universities
Professional Internship Program
University Programs
P.O. Box 117
Oak Ridge, TN 37830

WOODS HOLE OCEANOGRAPHIC INSTITUTION
Summer Student Fellowship Program

Woods Hole, Massachusetts

ELIGIBILITY: *Junior through graduate*
DURATION: *12 weeks, summer*
ACADEMIC CREDIT POSSIBLE: *Yes*
REMUNERATION OR FEE: *$1,650 stipend*
POSITIONS OFFERED: *15*
APPLICATION DEADLINE: *March 1*

General Description

For 30 years Woods Hole Oceanographic Institution—one of the world's foremost oceanographic research centers—has offered summer fellowships to students interested in the study of the oceans. Though an interest in oceanography is required, fellows may have backgrounds in biology, chemistry, engineering, geology, geophysics, mathematics, meteorology, physics, *and* oceanography.

The positions are called "fellowships" rather than "internships" because program participants work only on their own independent projects. They are not required to provide any services to the Institution during their stay, but are there to take advantage of the excellent facilities and personnel that the Institution has to offer. (Students have access to over 200 practicing scientists and engineers.) Fellows are carefully matched to a research "sponsor," however, who helps the student select a project that is both meaningful to the student and feasible in a summer's time.

At the end of the summer, fellows are required to present an oral report of their research project and to submit the results in a paper for staff criticism and approval.

In addition to working on their projects, students are urged to take advantage of the series of seminars and colloquia given by staff and visiting scientists on many aspects of marine science.

The application must include three letters of recommendation, college transcripts, and a concise statement of the applicant's research interests, future plans, and reasons for applying to the program.

The Inside Word

There is little question that the Woods Hole program is tops in its field. One fellow said that it was "one of the best things I've ever done." In addition to an excellent opportunity to do interesting research—his project in processing seismic refraction data took him on a data-collecting cruise—the series of some 25 lectures and seminars exposed him to "lots of great ideas."

One fellow claimed that grades were *not* the key admission criterion. "Interest, imagination, independence, and strong recommendations from your faculty are the most important things."

Woods Hole, on Cape Cod, is in a beautiful location. Though the area is invaded by tourists and sun-seekers each year, interns still find it "a great place to spend the summer." Housing is available through the Institution in both dormitories and private housing, at reasonable rates.

Participants stress that the main purpose of the program is to expose promising science students to the Institution and to oceanography in general. Said one fellow, "don't worry about producing Nobel-Prize-quality work—you're there to see if you like it."

Contact:

The Fellowship Committee
Education Office, Clark Laboratory
Woods Hole Oceanographic Institution
Woods Hole, MA 02543
(617) 548-1400

OTHER PLACES TO LOOK:

Architecture
The Nacul Center

Arts
Alexandria Archaeological Research Center
Note: Chemists with an interest in art history and art restoration can find
  internships with the conservation and restoration departments of art
  museums

Business
Control Data
Dupont Summer Professional Program
International Association for the Exchange of Students for Technical
  Experience (IAESTE)
Phillips Petroleum
Texas Instruments
3M Company Cooperative Work/Study Program
3M Company Summer Technical Program
Wakefield Washington Associates

Health
American Cancer Society, Massachusetts Division
Jackson Laboratory
The Hastings Center Institute of Society, Ethics and Life Sciences
Michael Reese Hospital and Medical Center
Syracuse University Institute for Sensory Research
Western Psychiatric Institute and Clinic
Worcester Foundation for Experimental Biology

Journalism
Science News

Fellowships

Four years of college may have left you feeling you've discovered the perfect life style. If so, the answer to "what to do *next?*" may just be—more of the same.

Fellowships and scholarships are often the prelude to a professional career in academe. But that's not the whole story. The fellowship and scholarship route also leads in another direction: toward what can be an important and satisfying break between college and career. Offering a rare opportunity to step out of the treadmill of grades, careers and ambition for a year or two, the so-called National Fellowships—as well as similar awards given locally—are the door to a precious moratorium you won't have a chance to repeat.

What are the national fellowships? "National" refers to the competition: all of them are open to students anywhere in the nation, or at least, from a field of colleges spread across the country. Beyond that, definition is difficult; a big part of their attraction is their diversity, with the choice ranging from a decidedly *non*-academic year touring the world on a Watson Travelling Fellowship, to the relatively intense academic work expected of Fulbright Scholars. But a few common characteristics do stand out: they all give the lucky winners unforgettable experiences abroad, generous stipends, and a great deal of prestige.

Paid for by private philanthropies, governments, and corporations, the general objective of each of the national fellowships is to find students with the specific combination of outstanding talent, leadership ability, intellect and imagination prescribed by the sponsoring organization. The award itself gives the winner a valued credential, often further training in his/her specialty, and, of course, a hell of a good time for a few years—usually at a foreign university.

Fellowships are not like internships. They are generally not on-the-job experiences, not a way to sample a potential career, and do not put a foot in the door for you in any particular occupation. They are similar to internships, however, in giving you a time-out.

Getting one of these awards is not easy in the face of intense competition. No matter which you apply for, you'll be up against people with the best qualifications in the country. But despite the competition, it's important to remember that each of the national fellowships is looking for different characteristics, and that all are hoping to find individuals who break stereotypes. You may not think much of your passion for South American funghi, but that may be just the thing to captivate a Rhodes Committee bored with reading about candidates who want to "become a corporate lawyer while remaining deeply concerned about the little guy."

This section describes only National Fellowships—an all-purpose term covering various nationally offered scholarships and grants as well. There are three reasons for this limitation. First, scholarships and fellowships in specific fields offered by individual universities or career organizations—i.e. AMA scholarships to med school—are too numerous to name, and in any case are sure to come under your eye as you scout around for graduate schools.

Second, it is the national fellowships which are peculiar in the special ferocity of competition, and in putting a lot of weight on non-academic qualifications.

Third, the whole area of national fellowships is quite often ignored by undergraduate administrators and counselors who otherwise rush to advise students about the future.

This section describes the major fellowships and the experiences they can provide. It also gives essential advice about what to expect in the application process, and how you can do your best.

Students who attend the small handful of eastern colleges which make a business of distributing this information in order to win a big chunk of the fellowships each year may have heard a lot of this advice already. But to the rest—read on. No one else is going to tell you. A word to you underachievers: maybe you already know you can find your Shangri La without winning a Fulbright. Good for you. But we have culled the experiences of students who have actually applied for and won national awards to bring you word from the horses' mouths which is just as useful in applying for *any* scholarship or fellowship. Many colleges offer their own "in-house" awards similar in design to the national awards described here. And applications to graduate schools of all kinds require the same kinds of personal essays, "honors and activities" summaries, and interviews which are covered here. No matter what sort of graduate program you are applying for, the people who sit on the other side of the table and select are close to unanimous on one thing: students have little expertise in any of these areas, and it shows. So you can profit from the experience of the over-achievers condensed in this section, even if you decide to avoid their ulcers.

For more information about other fellowship opportunities, see the sources listed at the end of this section.

What to Apply for, When, and Why

The best test of whether to bother with national fellowships in the first place is to get the advice of people you trust who have first-hand experience with the process—former Marshall scholars, Watson fellows, and the like. College advisors can be helpful, but *only* if you can be sure they know the score—many really do not. Don't trust your own judgment too much, particularly if you are inclined to self-deprecation. Selective indeed are the various committees, but they are not looking for the *übermensch*. If you have any doubts, *apply*. The only cost is your time, a stamp, and possibly a small dent in your ego if you lose; a dent easily repaired when you realize you are in good company. Suppose your grades are staggering, your activities reminiscent of Ben Franklin, your potential recommendations enough for a judgeship. You are sure you should apply for *one* of these awards. But which one, and when?

The answer, in part, is not to settle on just one. If you think you would be in the running for any of them, chances are you'll be competitive in one of two other competitions with similar criteria. Rhodes and Marshall scholarships, for example, are different in emphasis but alike enough that you can probably get away with the same essay for both. So apply for as many as you seem to have a shot at: your odds will improve, and once you've written one application the others will be easy.

When to apply is a harder question. Most people choose their senior year in college—but that could be a big mistake. Your credentials at that point may not be nearly as impressive as they will be a year or two hence, and in most cases the age limits set by national fellowships will allow you to apply for several years after graduation.

The reason to wait, then, is because you might become more interesting. If you've just had an offer to run a high school in Africa after graduation (as did one recent Rhodes Scholar) it makes sense to do that first, *then* apply.

On the other hand, if your undergraduate years have been breakneck, and your graduate plans mainly focused on slowing down, it's probably smart to apply while you look hot in your senior year. A few more terms in law school are not likely to bowl over any fellowship committees.

Remember, too, that the wide age limits for most fellowships mean that if you don't win in one year, you can try again later. Sometimes the reason you lost is that your credentials were not competitive enough—but sometimes it's simply because lots of people were qualified and the committee had to flip a coin.

APPLICATIONS IN GENERAL

All the major fellowships have a similar screening process. Preliminary screening is undertaken by individual college fellowship committees, which are supposed to encourage promising candidates and discourage obviously inadequate ones. In a few instances—the Watson, for example—the college is required to trim the applicant pool to a few names which are then sent on to the national committee.

Next, applicants send in their forms, transcripts, essays, activities and honors lists, and the names of people they've asked to write recommendations. After a look at this material, the committees invite candidates that interest them to interviews—sometimes to just one grilling, sometimes to a series of interviews.

After pondering whatever intangibles it is they ponder, the committees issue their verdicts: some, like the Rhodes, literally minutes after the interviews; others, like the Marshall, after weeks of mysterious committee huddles.

Where to Begin:

By early fall, decide which fellowship you have a shot at and obtain the application forms. No matter which you choose, three items are essential, in addition to a transcript:
— letters of recommendation
— a list of honors and activities
— a personal essay
Before beginning to work on any of these items, sit down for a good think. *Now* is the time to come up with a strategy, and to take a hard look at yourself as others will be looking at you.

This is the most important step in the application process, and it pays to do it well.

There are two objectives:

1) Decide exactly which of your qualities, interests and activities to emphasize—and establish the weak strokes in your portrait that you will either subdue, or try to turn to your advantage.

2) Sketch a complete approach weaving your strengths, the specific criteria of the fellowship, and the letters of reference you can expect, into a solid pattern that sparks curiosity.

Looking at yourself from outside in is one of the trickiest feats of analysis to perform. That's why most fellowships require it in their applications. No cookie-cutter method can be applied, but a few examples suggest the best approach. Consider these questions as suggestive, then, of the sort to ask yourself:

— Why have I taken specific courses in college? Is there any pattern or progression? Which ones were pivotal in my academic career?

— Is there any connection between course work and outside interests? Has academic work led to involvement in extracurricular activities, or *vice versa*?

— Am I involved in activities entirely outside college life—hometown community affairs, state politics, e.g.—and if not, why not?

— What relation is there between college work and plans for the future? Do I even know what I want to do in the future? Can family or other background be understood as a major influence on my expectations?

Whatever questions you raise for yourself, there is one area that must not be ignored. Be sure to ask:

> What am I clearly uninterested or deficient in? And why have I not done things which the rest of my record indicates would be logical or sensible?

Such inconsistencies, omissions, and the like should not necessarily be skirted when it comes to writing your essay. On the contrary, they may be the most interesting elements of your life story.

It is dull to hear about a guy who has always known he wants to be a doctor, has parents who are doctors, spends his vacations in hospitals and builds pace-makers for a hobby. On the other hand, a varsity tennis player whose greatest love is mountainclimbing, who is a first-rate magician, and who wants to do a two-year politics degree at Oxford and *then* go to medical school is interesting indeed. (He also won a Marshall.)

Furthermore, unexpected twists and turns in your background have a ring of authenticity. Few people follow a master plan through life. You'll strike the committee as wise beyond your years if you recognize that, by taking the time to identify contradictions as well as coherency in your background.

Grand strategies: Once you've taken a hard look at yourself, formulate a strategy for presenting yourself to others.

The aim is a complete application, forming a tight web of distinct strands. The essay will present personal reflections and a sense of how significant bits of your experience are tied together. The list of activities and honors and a transcript will be concrete evidence of your accomplishments. Letters of recommendation will confirm these accomplishments, and turn the one-dimensional perspective you offer of yourself into a three-dimensional image constructed through the judgments of others.

To get this result, advance planning is necessary. For instance, maybe ten people in the world can write the detailed, enthusiastic endorsements you want. But even that select crew must be whittled down, and to do it right, you need to know exactly what parts of your background need the most support, and who can best give it. Several professors may be ready to predict a brilliant career for you—but which one will say so despite the two poor grades you received from his department?

Likewise, look carefully at the criteria of the award. Lots of sterling qualities probably cling to your record, but not all will fit the fellowship in question, and a few might even look like drawbacks.

Before you sit down to write, have a firm idea of the themes you will sound, the connections you'll make among different elements of your experience, and the relation of the whole to the fellowship criteria.

With this planning done first, the resulting application will be easier to write and tightly constructed. You will know, for instance, that you needn't say much about last summer's work in your essay, because your employer is writing a letter—but that there is lots to be said about your solo journey down the Nile, since no one can tell *that* story but you.

THE ESSAY

With one voice, national fellowship applicants say this is the hardest act in a tough performance. It is also the most important. Charming and witty though you may be in person, those assets can't help you if you don't get asked to an interview. And it is the essay which is likely to be the deciding factor in who *does* get asked. Two questions are favorites on fellowship applications:

— explain your activities, interests, and plans for the future.

— explain why you want to pursue a particular project or course of study in a specific place.

Some fellowship applications tell you to answer both in a single essay.

Writing about yourself is always hard; doing so with extremely tight constraints on length is more challenging still. You have about 1,000 words to play with—four double-spaced pages. You cannot afford extraneous remarks.

The no-b.s., be-concrete approach: Start by throwing out most of your undergraduate essay methodology. There is no room for the long introduction of a college paper, for purple prose, or for complicated arguments. (See our sample "bad" essay for an example of this.)

The sentences themselves should be direct and fairly simple, avoiding any ornamentation that will make a reader suspect he is getting verbal fireworks in place of substance. The finished item should be a fast, firm read—something close to a well-argued column on the New York Times editorial page.

Getting to the point is always hard. One way of doing it quickly is to write an introductory paragraph, then a following one. Now throw out the first paragraph. Usually that "second" paragraph will get you off to a crisp start. Try to find a novel way of beginning the essay: don't repeat or paraphrase the question a la Miss America.

Be specific: You want to express ambitions, values, concerns, and the language which first comes to mind is general and vague. Resist! Don't *explain* yourself—*demonstrate*, with concise and pointed examples.

> *"It has been a long-standing concern for the urban poor which has kept me involved in working to remedy the economic inequities of the inner city . . ."*

This is long-winded, empty and boring—but typical of attempts to compress lots of ideas and attitudes into a small space. There is an alternative:

> *"My work in the Los Angeles mayor's office this summer put me in daily contact with problems of the inner-city poor, an experience which led me to help organize the city's first community-run employment center . . ."*

Through a specific example, concern about inner-city problems is expressed without sounding patronizing, while concrete initiatives taken are spelled out.

You are off to a good start. But with the essay underway, two massive roadblocks to eloquence are likely to arise. We can call them "The Chronological Order Syndrome" and "The Problem of the Overloaded Ark."

The chronological order syndrome: This is the affliction of most novice autobiographers. Symptoms are an "essay" which is really a verbose time-line, with events and activities strung along like beads on a chain. When the gilt is stripped away, you are left with "First I was born, and then I went to high school, where I directed the school play, and then I went to college . . ." This approach can work if the question really is "write a brief autobiography," but most fellowship applications want more.

The paths out of this mess are many, but not easy. Almost anything you can do instead will be an improvement, but a number of successful applicants agree: first establish some imaginative, genuine links between different elements of your background and interests. Then write the essay around those links, filling in with additional material to cover the important bases. Consider the chart below:

CHRONOLOGICAL	THEMATIC
born & raised in rural Georgia school in Ga. until 16 age 16, AFS program to France age 18, return to Ga. to finish High School & go to work 1 year in auto factory age 19—freshman at Georgetown U. Freshman: soccer, begin work in Senate office, work on rural issues important course: "Western European Intellectual History"	—*conservative southern small-town upbringing strongly affected by year in Paris with French family* —*realize strong interest in issues of rural south, but also develop strong interest in foreign affairs, especially European politics—college coursework crystalizes this interest* —*work in senate office & discover understanding of rural problems*

Sophomore: summer work as U.N. intern; organize Georgetown students for summer school program for rural children in Ga. (etc.)

can be put to work in national legislation, as result contemplating future involvement in politics
—but also recognizing some divergent goals: on one hand, finding skills in organizing on grass-roots level; on the other, U.N. experience confirms desire & ability to work on national, even international policy issues. (etc.)

By establishing the thematic points, this hypothetical resume can· be turned into an interesting essay which will touch on the important events and activities without sounding like a laundry list, and in the process will demonstrate an ability to be self-critical. It *can* move chronologically, but importantly, it doesn't have to.

Your list of activities and honors will be read with your essay. That means you do not have to tell all in the essay, and can rely on the list for details. Instead of wasting precious space to say

"In 1979 I spent 5 months working for Senator X from California in his Sacramento office . . ."

you can simply write

"While working for Senator X in Sacramento . . ."

The problem of the overloaded ark: Confronted with lots of material and little space, you are likely to push a panic button without even realizing it, but with dangerous consequences. Paragraphs will fill with superficial detail, and you will leap from one interest, accomplishment, or idea to the next like a mountain goat, under the impression you can avalanche the reader into recognition of your many talents. Not so.

Instead, pick a few ideas and hit them hard. Three guidelines will help make your essay attractive to the people who will read it:

1) **Keep ideas clear and simple.**
   Committees want to discuss your ideas, not spend lots of time figuring out what you mean in the first place.

2) **Limit discussion of issues to a few, clear motivating factors behind your ideas/interests.** You can easily generate a confusing mess of an essay by trying to talk about all the conflicting impulses which affect your thinking on world hunger. Isolate a few of those impulses to indicate the kinds of concerns you have.

3) **Structure the whole essay with clarity as the principal objective.**
   Committees may read 100 essays or more. Write so they will

remember you for a few, clear, distinctive points. If they remember you also for some wit and eloquence, so much the better. *Do not* let them remember you as sounding confused, pedantic, or excessively mannered in style.

Essential last words: So much for the basics. Now for some final pieces of advice from veterans on fine-tuning your essay:

1) Concentrate on giving personal significance to the themes of the essay. As one Marshall Scholar puts it, "You probably have outstanding achievements in your background, and it is better to let them speak for themselves—or to let your references tell the tale in their letters. So use the essay to say the unexpected, and to say how particular things affected you personally: the importance of a teacher who was also a friend, or why you like the hazards of stock car racing."

2) Be absolutely certain you can talk about every aspect of the essay. This is vital in the event you get an interview. Don't mention books you remember only vaguely, don't mention political theorists whose ideas you don't quite understand, and so on. You'll get screwed if you do.

3) Ask two or three people whose advice you trust and whose own writing is polished to read and criticize your essay. Tell them to be tough: this is not another college essay, but a finished piece. Some of your teachers may fit the bill.

4) Plan on writing at least three drafts. (One sample essay we've included was revised 12 times!) No matter how well you do in your first draft, you can do better, and criticisms of the second draft will generate important revisions for a third version.

5) Get someone else to proof-read the final copy—someone who knows English grammar and can spell. A few stupid spelling errors or a non-sentence can destroy your essay.

6) Stick to the length asked for. One thousand words means absolutely no more than 1,100. Committees may even refuse to read essays much exceeding the limit.

ACTIVITIES AND HONORS

All applications require a list of your extracurricular achievements and a description of honors, academic and otherwise. This is straightforward business, for the most part. *However,* keep in mind the influence you can exert by the way you order your list and the kind of description you give. For example: if most of your significant activities outside of college involved dramatic arts, you can create a special section, "Drama," and list your credits there.

And do not make the mistake of being too brief in describing your activities. This list should be terse, but complete. The committee should not have to ask you what it was exactly you were doing in that Washington law firm—it should be able to see:

> Summer, 1979—Law Firm of XYZ, Washington, D.C.;
> assistant to senior partner.
> Drafted briefs to clients including
> Common Cause and the Dept. of the
> Interior; accompanied senior partner
> as aide in testimony to Senate
> Foreign Relations Committee.

Remember to use the list to your advantage, by pointing out how your activities fit the bill of the particular fellowship.

Discretion is obviously required here—it will not do to include a category of "Leadership Ability" in your Rhodes application. On the other hand, if you are a jock as well as a gentleman and a scholar, make the most of it and satisfy Cecil Rhodes's fondness for "physical vigor" with an impressive category of "Sports."

RECOMMENDATIONS

Says one Eastern committee member for a prestigious scholarship, "The only things I trust are essays and letters of recommendation. And if the letters don't cut it, no essay is going to win me over."

He may be a bit of a fanatic, but there is truth to what he says—and who knows, he might be on *your* committee.

Put yourself in the committee's position for a moment: naturally you will give greatest weight to the candidate's essay, but you will look to letters of recommendation to flesh out details, and to give you some idea how this candidate compares with other highly qualified people. If the letters are lukewarm, or have a standardized smell to them, or seem to have suspicious gaps in areas where the candidate claims great experience or interest, you will have serious reservations.

It is time to recall the importance of strategy: the objective is a comprehensive picture of your strengths and interests—a completed jigsaw puzzle of essay, transcript, recommendations and activities. Your recommendations are key.

There are a few general truths about these sorts of recommendations:

> —Choose people who can comment on things you cannot talk about adequately in your essay, or whose words will make abundantly clear how overwhelmingly responsible, talented or whatever you were in a given area. This is particularly important when it comes to activities common to many college students. If you worked in

Washington but were *not* the average slave tied to a xerox machine, be sure you get a letter from the administrative assistant saying you personally constructed Senator X's lauded agriculture bill. Otherwise you risk having the whole experience dismissed as the usual Washington Intern summer fun.

—If you must decide between people who know you well, and people who are well known but know *you* only slightly, *always* choose the former. Example: one scholarship winner worked in the lab of a Nobel prize winner, on an experiment the celebrity was supervising. He knew the hot shot fairly well, but worked directly under a younger scientist. He asked the younger guy to write the recommendation—because he knew that although the hot shot would say nice things, the younger guy could be *more specific* and *more personal.*

Generally, committees are on the lookout for name droppers, and do not like them. If you get a letter of recommendation from a celebrity that is even mildly impersonal or vague, you will create a distinctly negative impression. On the other hand, if you do have a genuinely close relationship with a star, by all means ask for a letter. It is the best recommendation you can have.

—Not everyone who knows you well can write a good letter. Good recommendations are an art that few people master. Effusive, cloying nonsense can flow from the pens from folks otherwise levelheaded and reserved, and will hurt your chances considerably. Committees look not only for remarks *about* you in these letters; they are also trying to figure out what sort of company you keep, and all they have to go by is the personality conveyed on the written page.

Unfortunately, there is no fail-safe way of avoiding a mistake. But good judgment on your side can help—and maybe a look at other writing of the potential referee.

Once you have sorted out who should write recommendations for you, there are several things you can do to make their letters most effective.

—Give them a list of activities and honors, transcript, and—if you've finished it—a copy of your essay.

—If possible, talk with them briefly to make sure they understand the criteria of the specific scholarship in question. Offer suggestions; *coach* them.

—Be absolutely sure they have sent a letter by the required date. A polite note or two which presumes they did send it but suggests that

just possibly the press of business might have led them to forget . . .
can do the trick. A late letter is often no use at all.

It is sad but true that students from small, expensive, private colleges
in the northeast have a leg up in the recommendations arena. This results
from four years of close contact with a faculty that can afford to know their
students well, and is versed in the twists and turns of national scholarship
competition. They know exactly what the committees are looking for, and
can shovel it out with just the right balance of tactful reservation and
fulsome praise.

Candidates in different circumstances cannot do much about this, but
they should be aware of what they are up against.

In particular, if you do not have the prof over regularly for dinner, be
especially careful to impress on referees the necessity of considered,
personal, concrete letters. You may want to take special care to round up a
compelling set of recommendations from outside your college, if the
harvest from academe looks a bit thin.

THE INTERVIEW

It's not worth worrying about this hurdle till you reach it. Congratulations,
if you have.

Let's assume you have been invited to interview. Depending on
where you come from and which fellowship it is, this means your
credentials alone have distinguished you from some proportion of your
fellow competitors. But whether you are one out of 5 or one out of 50, you
can proceed to the interview with one psychological advantage: for
whatever reasons, the committee preferred you over a lot of other people.

Before you meet the lion at the gate: When people tell you to "be
yourself" in an interview, tell them to take a walk. It is *impossible* to "be
yourself" when your hands are shaking, when you feel like you may lose
your breakfast at any moment, and when the scenario resembles Bill
Buckley's "Firing Line." *Interviews are performances*—they have to be.

And because they are performances, you can prepare for them. You
do want to "be yourself" in one sense only: you want to present in
concentrated form the best qualities that set you apart from other people.

How to do this?

First, by anticipating the balls that will be pitched in the upcoming
game. Committees usually stick to the material you give them, with an eye
to the criteria of the fellowship. Read your essay again, this time, with an
eye to the question marks it raises. If you make value judgments—and you
should—you can be sure someone will ask you about them. If there are
apparent contradictions in your goals, your training, etc., have some
answers ready.

A favorite approach of interviewers is to fasten on a general interest
expressed in your essay and to pose a question about a current problem

that is related. Example: you write that you worked in a biochemistry lab over the summer, and did research in genetics.

Interviewer asks: "Your colleagues have stirred controversy over genetic research and the responsibility of scientists to their communities for the consequences and methods of their research. What approach would you take in an article for the New York Times 'Science' section on this issue?"

By going through your essay critically, you can anticipate the areas that will be hit hard and come up with general positions to take. And despite the fact that you, of course, cannot anticipate every question, you will have contemplated broad lines of attack—a tremendous psychological advantage.

Second, you can steal a march by prepping on current events. Typical questions usually ask you to relate your interests and opinions to specific contemporary problems, *or* to specific texts or schools of thought in academic subjects. It therefore pays to have a good general knowledge of world events and issues of the year, and to have specific knowledge of developments in fields you claim as special interests. The way to do it efficiently is to:

1) Read the past few months of the news magazines and Sunday issues of the New York Times. If you are applying in your home state and haven't been back for a while, be sure to look at local papers as well.
2) Scan *Facts on File* or similar world news summaries in your local library. These treasurehouses compress significant news and editorial comment for the year into easily digestible chunks which you can devour in a few hours of hard reading.
3) Survey a sample of principal journals in your academic fields of interest—*Daedalus* is an excellent general resource, and for sciences, *Scientific American. New Republic, Harper's* and *Atlantic Monthly* do the trick in public affairs and all-around intellectualizing.

The advantage this preparation gives is twofold: you are ready to field questions in a broad range of subjects with facts and arguments fresh in your mind; more importantly, you *know* you cannot be utterly surprised, and will consequently be more confident in every response.

Third, make sure your referees do not torpedo you with their praise. Ask them to tell you if they mentioned specific books, arguments, etc., or told any anecdotes. If they wrote good letters they probably did all of the above, and you should know about it. Not only do referees frequently make mistakes about what you actually read, thought, etc., but more often bring up actual incidents or ideas which you have forgotten. Of course, if someone did make a mistake, and expounded on your completely fictitious expertise in theories of knowledge, you have no choice but to do some quick reading. But that is better than getting caught cold.

You're on! After all the preparation you have now done, this routine should be as easy as tying your shoes. It won't be, of course—but there are ways of making the interview itself go as well as possible.

Winners, losers and interviewers all agree: *you are most likely to blow it by talking too much*.

Confronted with two to six people listening attentively and a question which could be the basis of a book, nothing is easier than to begin babbling while your mind is in neutral, shift gradually into gear and grind ahead until you run out of gas.

Your approach should be the opposite. Resist the inclination to leap into the breach! What you might think sounds like a snappy answer is more likely to sound hasty to your audience. Pregnant pauses are always shorter than you think, and they are immensely effective in conveying a tone of deliberation and level-headedness.

Use that pause to marshall your thoughts. Chances are, the question is one you have already asked yourself, or is in a form similar to the sort mentioned above.

Pare down your response. Most likely, there are lots of angles you can take in answering. Do not feel you have to hit them all. Instead, offer one concise opinion.

It is usually best to take a stand on an issue. Simply giving two opposing points of view on a question about the morality of corporate investments in South Africa will not satisfy your interviewers.

One successful Watson applicant described his one-on-one experience: "I was sure my interviewer would be a distinguished gray-hair with a deceptive, crushing handshake and an imperious gaze. Since he turned out to be a smiling, affable 30-year-old with a lot of interests similar to mine, I instantly felt at ease. Imagining the worst can be helpful, I suppose, but it's probably better to find out what you can about the interviewer. If you can subtly and tactfully bring the conversation around to areas in which the interviewer has interest (without exposing yourself to be a cretin on the subject), you're in good shape."

The next question is almost certainly going to be, "but what do *you* think?" and you will win points for being sensible enough to move on to what they really want to hear from the start: *your* ideas.

Remember: these people like asking questions. They probably have more than enough for a few hours of talking. Yet you are in there for 20 minutes to an hour. If they want you to elaborate a point, they will say so. But don't waste time with long involved answers that could a) turn out to be misinterpreting the question or b) bore your interviewers or c) lead you unwittingly onto shoals you would rather avoid.

More generally: There is no need to regard the experience as a confrontation—even if some of the interview panel do. Instead, as one advisor told a successful Rhodes applicant, "Remember that the six people you will be talking with are possibly the most interesting group you are going to meet in one room in your life. Treat the occasion as a potentially fascinating discussion, and they are likely to do the same."

This is another way of saying that your behavior can substantially determine the tone and direction of your interview. True, the panel asks the questions, but as a look at "Face the Nation" or "Meet the Press" will underscore, control of the answers is a powerful tool. Some inquisitors may indeed try to intimidate you—but if you can stay unruffled, or point out that the question is really too broad, or can conjure a witty rejoinder, they will respect you, and maybe even smile. And more likely, your interviewers will turn out to be wise, warm and accommodating. Have a good time!

SAMPLE ESSAYS

The first two essays printed below give you a "before and after" look at the process of writing a successful fellowship essay. The first, though it contains some of the same ideas that end up in the final version, is bogged down by the sort of flatulent prose you should avoid at all costs. The final version was a winner (it came twelve drafts later!), and is printed as the second sample.

The third sample is another essay that worked. It does not give you any short cuts to follow in writing your own, but it will give you an idea of how various ideas can be bolted together into a successful pattern.

Their best lesson is that you do not have to fit any rigid essay mold. If essays as different as these helped with Rhodes and Marhsall scholarships, whatever style is comfortable for you can do the trick too. (Names and places have been deleted to preserve some degree of anonymity.)

First Sample (Bad Essay)

It is paradoxical indeed that history, which is so deeply rooted in chronology, in fact destroys temporal boundaries. But it is precisely in this process of transcending time that the aesthetic appeal, fascination and significance of history rests. Although it is impossible to reconstruct the past exactly as it was, it is still incumbent upon us to discuss its value, to relate historical knowledge to meaning.

For me as a scholar, the whole idea of comprehending the past has unfolded as an exercise in self-knowledge. First, as memory is the knowing image of the "individual self" history reflects the knowledge of the "collective self." But second, and of more importance, historical writing necessitates an ordering of otherwise diverse pieces of evidence. As an individual, this process of imposing a structure upon materials has forced me to search within myself. And the particular framework thus produced is but a reflected image of that self. It is this understanding, revealed by a fundamental comprehension of the past and of the present, that I have found worthy of pursuit. However, a search for self-knowledge is in no way restricted to the life of the mind. Revelation is possible through athletic competition, through public discussion and representation, and through the remaining spectrum of individual and collective actions.

Although this process of knowing is self-generated and internally directed, it is inextricably entwined with those areas of action that have given my life some measure of public meaning. Athletics, for example, have always been and will continue to be an integral part of my life, from intercollegiate competition to non-competitive participation. It is of great importance for me to be physically active, to share the camaraderie of team competition as well as the solitude of the more isolated 'individual sports.' Athletics have been not only a means to discover my limits, but have also been a means to discover how those limits can be extended, a means to overcome pain and discouragement—a means to assert accomplishment over limitation. Even further, athletics contain an element that is found in all aspects of my life, an element too often neglected in formal discussions of this kind—the sheer enjoyment of competition, exertion, participation and accomplishment.

This enjoyment of group and individual interaction is reflected in the political as well as in the athletic world. Political action has been the translation of the general into the particular, the distillation of theories and ideas debated in the academic world into questions of practical applications and social programs. It has crystallized concepts of individual dignity into statements of rights and obligations. As a group effort, it has been the striving toward a definite goal based upon a common set of beliefs, standards or desires. Through political action I have become increasingly aware that the old distinctions between individuals and groups are quickly dissolving. In politics, for example, this evolution has manifested itself in the increasing confusion of principles separating the Republican and Democratic parties. On a larger scale, even nations once separated by long traditions of animosity are being drawn closer together by forces not wholly in human control. Almost all aspects of my education, both in the United States and abroad, have led to the realization that this movement toward internationalism is inevitable. It is a movement that has already generated problems whose solutions require international cooperation, a movement that demands leaders of universal vision and outlook. Leaders must once again become men of international perspicacity, for too long the leaders of our country have been dominated by domestic consensus politics.

My interests in internationalism and politics are partially tied to a revival of interest in American history and the moral base of American politics, a revival engendered by recent political crises. These crises underscore the fact that the great figures of our national past were often men of universal human outlook and creative ability, an enlightened tradition that has not been sufficiently maintained. It is toward this tradition that my seemingly disparate interests converge and through it that a coherent neo-Renaissance pattern emerges. For just as I find it insufficient to study only those disciplines that bear directly upon my chosen vocation, so too I regard a strictly American legal training as a similarly unsatisfactory education. The study of literature, philosophy and foreign languages is as necessary to me as the reading on cost overruns, budgets and government theory, for all contribute to the formation of that necessary universal outlook.

I have tried to prepare myself to face those problems that require for their solution the sort of knowledge and skills that transcend specialization and technical proficiency. The solutions to such problems demand a perspective and an international experience that enable one to escape national limitations and, in part, the prison of individual history. It is now my goal to concentrate on the study of jurisprudence and through it philosophy. The two are, as Jefferson remarked, ". . . as necessary as law to form an accomplished lawyer . . ." And to be an accomplished lawyer is only one step in the continuing process of becoming a complete person. To these ends it is my intention to read jurisprudence at _____ University.

This program will constantly be guided, as it has been here, by an intention to return to the United States to complete an American law degree and from that background to seek and to hold public office at the highest levels. My reading of jurisprudence will thus be not simply a procedure to order the past and the present, but above all will be a means to prepare myself for the future.

Second Sample (Twelfth Draft)

As my record indicates, my activities and interests have been concentrated in the areas of politics and European Studies. Although this political experience has been primarily domestic and these studies primarily foreign, the two came together to form one major interest in internationalism. More specifically, a combination of these two areas has made me aware of a lack of international vision in American leadership, a lack that could be avoided through a greater diversity of backgrounds and experiences.

In France, as a student at the _____, as a worker, as a part-time television host and as an inhabitant of Paris, I was exposed to a variety of circumstances and situations that I would have missed had I remained in the United States. Through this experience, and through my studies of Europe, I have become aware of and interested in a number of problems, ideas and solutions to problems not yet widely discussed in the United States. For example, three major political questions now facing the United States as new problems have already been institutionalized in Europe with varying degrees of success—central economic planning, national health care and government support of the arts. It was partially to study these sorts of questions that I have chosen to study Europe and its separate countries. More generally, I have tried to study the view that the French have of themselves, of their society and of their world. My study of Europe has been based upon an interest in the complete culture of a country, an interest that has led me to study the poetry and literature of a country as well as its "politique-economique."

One of the things that struck me most strongly in Paris was the awareness of the students of their country's role in a world that is constantly evolving and their knowledge of the world as an international community. Through my domestic political experience I have become aware that not only are Americans unsure of their role in that evolving world, but that American leaders also lack the vision that can come from international experience. As a delegate to a state Constitutional Convention and as the floor leader on two major questions—the death penalty and the (constitutional) right to bear arms—I was reminded that the variety of experiences and ideas found in other countries was lacking in American political discussion. On these two issues there was almost no discussion (none at all except my own speech) of the results that other countries had discovered when they discontinued one or the other. And there was no discussion at all of countries that had long traditions without either one. The second of my major interests is to apply what I have learned in my international studies to my personal and professional lives.

The American character and institutions are certainly unique, but I have found that too often we deprive ourselves of the exprience of the rest of the world. For example, one of my interests as a Parisian was the manner in which the government handled the cities. The administration of the parks and suburbs, the decentralization of power, and the overlapping of local and central authorities are policies that merit our evaluation and close inspection. I am not suggesting that the United States imitate Europe in all respects, but I am suggesting that the United States not discount the European experience by ignoring it.

My interest in politics, from the lowest local levels to the planning of a presidential campaign strategy, has been aimed at the idea that a broader background will lead to a better set of answers to the problems that can be solved by our political system. The more I become involved in politics, the more I realize the value of an international perspective. Yet the questions that interest me and the reasons for which I intend to study abroad are neither purely structural nor purely political. In all of my interests there is a potential for self knowledge that cannot be satisfied except through the discovery of a greater variety of situations and personalities.

I seek now to read jurisprudence, in particular comparative law, at _____ University, for I view such study as essential to the formation of a more universal outlook. I would like to live and to study at _____ not just to acquaint myself with comparative law, but to understand as much as I can of the life and people of England. From that understanding I would not only be able to see myself with greater clarity, but would be able to bring an international perspective to the solution of problems as an international lawyer, as a politician and as an individual.

Third Sample

Since my transcript and letters of recommendation provide adequate information on my academic background, this statement focuses on some of the extracurricular activities that have been meaningful to me. It is my hope that you will find my record to be one of self-reliance, leadership, and dedication to the well-being of others.

My experience as a Big Brother has been very important to me. My sharing the good times and troubles of two young boys, I have learned much about the struggle of reaching out to help where help is needed. It *is* a struggle to make the kind of human contact necessary to be of real service to people, but it is a struggle made worthwhile by the joy of that contact once achieved.

In my employment, I have been willing to take initiatives and accept responsibility for my own welfare. From organizing and managing a tennis club while in high school to entering into a weathered lumber business last summer I have invented various projects and carried them through successfully. Even my school year job of buying and selling pizzas requires some determination and risk—I had to eat the losses.

The project I was involved in this summer had potentially much greater losses and required a much deeper commitment than any other on which I have worked. I have lived all my life in a lower middle class neighborhood. In recent years the neighborhood has started to become integrated and most of the better-off residents have moved or are moving to the suburbs. Growing fears in the community over the declining property values and the future unknowns of continuing integration prompted the formation of a number of bi-racial citizens' groups over the last year in an effort to save the community spirit; however, very little had been done to stop the decay of the physical environment.

Coming home from college during vacations I was perhaps struck more profoundly by the empty stores and unkempt lots in the local shopping center than were others who had seen only a series of small day-to-day changes that added up to the big change I saw over the interval of months. This summer, I developed some ideas for rejuvenating the shopping center and presented those ideas at a meeting of one of the citizens' groups and later to the city bureaucracy; I met with people in Parks and Recreation, the Community Economic Development Department, the City Planning Department and the Mayor's office. It became clear through the discussions that while community support was an important factor in influencing the funding for shopping center development projects, the businessmen in the area would have to be organized to apply for the funds themselves. With the support of the community groups I then organized a business association by talking individually with all 120 business people in the proposed project area, explaining my ideas and asking them to meet and discuss what steps should be taken to improve the business district. At the meeting, the merchants formed an association, elected officers and established a committee to send a proposal to the Block Grant Program. A request for $2.5 million on behalf of the business association and the neighborhood groups was submitted in the last week of September.

My experience with this neighborhood project is closely related to one of my academic interests—the role of the modern, urban man in society and his ability or inability to affect his environment. What is the place of the individual in the industrialized Western world and what are the factors that shape or limit individual expression and identity in that world?

My courses—including the independent study I am doing this semester on the growth and decay of American cities—have enabled me to look at this question from several angles, but I would like an opportunity to go into the subject further, aided by the range of perspectives available in the study of Philosophy, Politics and Economics at _____. The exposure to British culture afforded by such an opportunity can only enrich my study in this area.

Another matter of special interest to me has been the interaction of ideas of justice with ideas about utility. The demands of moral principles are often in conflict with the calculus of economic efficiency. How can the differences be reconciled? Can an economic system be modified to include a value for justice? What do justice and morality mean in a world of different cultures and beliefs? A course I recently took on the theory of political obligation tried to meet the cultural relativist argument by contending that morality and justice are indeed absolute and cut across all cultures and times. Economics, on the other hand, by the very definition of utility, assumes not only a cultural relativism but an individual relativism.

My desire to pursue a career in law with concentration on problems related to economics grows out of my interest in this interaction of the moral and the utilitarian. For the same reason, I also hope to remain active in community and public service.

It is my understanding that the academic system at _____, while focusing one's studies in a specific field, also leaves room for independent study in areas of tangential interest. One of the things I would like to study, tangentially, is architectural history. I know nothing about architecture other than what I learned this summer about barns and farm houses. The opportunity for travel associated with the Scholarship would certainly allow me to expand my knowledge of architectural history.

I have a tendency to reach out in many different directions, yet I possess a drive to synthesize and compare. Two years at _____ would give me a chance to reach for some ideas and experiences I cannot find in another environment, and a chance to ponder my assortment of thoughts longer and more deeply. I think I have both the energy and the intellectual potential needed to make good use of a _____ Scholarship. I hope you will find I have the leadership and human potential to merit the honor.

FULBRIGHT-HAYS

ELIGIBILITY: *B.A. degree by time study begins*
DURATION: *1 year*
ACADEMIC CREDIT: *Yes*

REMUNERATION: *Varies by country (generous)*
NUMBER & TYPE OF AWARDS: *Approx. 500 for
full-time graduate work*
DEADLINE: *For obtaining application, Oct. 15; For
submitting application, Nov. 1 or sooner; ask
campus advisor for details*

General Description

Uniting a vast range of scholarships and fellowships abroad under one
program, the Fulbright-Hays is by far the biggest set of awards available.
It is also the most comprehensive: sponsored by the U.S., foreign
governments and private donors, full grants including travel, tuition and
living expenses for study at universities in over 50 countries are offered,
plus a limited number of supplementary travel grants for students on other
scholarships. The catch: most awards are reserved for advanced graduate
students, so the senior fresh out of college is up against stiff competition.

Unlike some other national awards, the Fulbright is emphatically an
academic program—your plans for study and current academic record
will be decisive factors in the competition. But the range of projects you
can attempt is wide: everything from advanced chemical research to folk
studies and creative arts is fair game.

The Fulbright carries with it a good deal of prestige. In particular, it is
a hefty credential in the academic world if you aspire to teaching or
research, and a door opener in visual and performing arts, too.

What You Need to Know

There are three stages to the application process: first you submit your
completed application to the campus Fulbright advisor—those out of
college send it directly to the Institute of International Education (I.I.E.)
then it is reviewed by a U.S. panel, and if you are lucky, forwarded to a
committee in the country you chose, which makes final decisions. There is
no interview.

Gargantuan and government sponsored, the Fulbright program suf-
fers from a relatively minor case of bureaucracy. To avoid headaches the
indispensable aid through the labyrinth is *Grants for Graduate Study
Abroad* issued by I.I.E. or available from your campus fellowship advisor.

Read the booklet carefully: although the application for all awards is
standardized, provisions for different countries are not the same.
Mauritania, for example, expects you to pursue Public Administration
''with practical application for Mauritania,'' but Japan hopes you will look
into Contemporary Japan.

Language training will narrow your choices immediately. Although
some countries provide intensive language courses, the selection committee generally expects basic knowledge of the language of the country
you choose, and prefers fluency.

The Inside Word

On top of good grades and recommendations, your chances of winning as a soon-to-graduate senior depend strongly on careful research on your proposal for study. Fulbright screening committees do care about your personality and interests—in part, they expect you to be an example of America's finest—but the meat of the matter is the required essay you must write on what you plan to do for the year.

If you don't already have a research project in mind, you probably shouldn't apply. But assume you do: flesh it out. Talk with professors knowledgeable on the subject, to learn which country will offer the most in your field. Be sure to contact universities in that country, to find out which handles your specialty, who you could work with—and if no existing program covers your interests, whether you can make special arrangements.

Good essays in this competition are ones which reflect an imaginative approach—plans to "study English Literature" will not impress the committees—so demonstrate the connections between the project idea, your undergraduate courses or interests, and the specific country you want to visit. The I.I.E. booklet describes what each country can offer, so play up the connections between those strengths and your project. Even though you may have little interest in Luxembourg *per se,* your interest in the role of neutral nations in international affairs could make it the ideal place to study, while appealing to the committee's preference for students "whose work will contribute to a better understanding of Luxembourg in the United States."

Fulbright scholars also recommend liberal name-dropping in your essay. "Tell them who's the best in the field; tell them why it's the only country in the world with the problem you're studying; tell them why that particular university is the only one with the program you need—it's what the committee wants to hear," says one scholar, and advisors familiar with the problem agree. But make sure your info is accurate: promising applications end up under the eye of professors from the country of your choice, where B.S. is sure to be detected.

And remember: *where* you want to study can be crucial. Only 1 out of 6 applicants overall won a grant in 1979—but for Turkey it was a near-failsafe 5 out of 7, while for France, a depressing 75 out of 492. The I.I.E. booklet breaks down the odds for each country's competition, so study that page carefully. You might think England is the logical place to examine the welfare state, but a look at the numbers could encourage you to try Denmark instead.

Contact:

Information and Counseling Division
Institute of International Education
809 United Nations Plaza
New York, NY 10017
(212) 883-8279

LUCE SCHOLAR'S PROGRAM

ELIGIBILITY: *Upper age limit 29. Must attend or have
attended one of approximately 70 participating colleges.*
DURATION: *11 months; late August to July*
ACADEMIC CREDIT: *No*
REMUNERATION: *Travel and living expenses, plus
salary; varies from year to year*
NUMBER AND TYPE OF SCHOLARSHIPS: *15 awarded
annually for work in the recipient's profession in
an Asian country.*
APPLICATION DEADLINE: *Early December*

General Description

Under the auspices of the Henry Luce Foundation, the Luce Scholar's
Program provides the novel, exciting opportunity for 15 Americans to
work for a year in their chosen professions in Asian countries. The
Foundation picks the place of work after consultation with successful
candidates. The stipend varies from year to year, but is about the salary of
a junior faculty member at a major university.

No prior knowledge of Asian Culture or language is required for the
Luce. To the contrary, applications are not accepted from specialists in
Asian Studies, International Relations, or other individuals whose careers
or interests are likely to lead them to Asia. However, sincere interest in
other cultures, and a proficiency for learning languages can help in the
competition. Academic and extracurricular distinctions are expected of
applicants from all fields; strongest weight is given to the promise of
professional and community leadership. Successful candidates, in addition to having strong academic records, usually command professional
and community respect.

Scholarships are not offered in Burma, the People's Republic of
China, or Vietnam. Luce Scholar-designates are urged to study the
language of their host country in the summer prior to their departure. The
Foundation expects that Scholars will gain more in cultural awareness
than in professional achievement during their year abroad, and that the
Asian experience will broaden their personal outlooks and professional
perspectives after their return.

What You Need to Know

At a time in which knowledge of Asia is becoming more desirable, so is the
Luce Scholarship. Competition is keen. Candidates must first be nomi-

nated by participating colleges, universities, and graduate schools. Luce nominees do not have to be students; applications from alumni and junior faculty are also accepted. The process begins with a written application and an hour-long interview with a Luce representative in a city near you. Following these interviews, 45 finalists are selected and assigned in groups of 15 to regional panels in New York, Washington D.C., and Los Angeles—where they are flown at the Foundation's expense for the final interviews.

Though the Luce Foundation accepts applications from college seniors, few are selected as scholars. The scholarships are awarded to applicants from a diverse range of geographic and professional backgrounds. For example, a lawyer from Georgia was placed in Tokyo; a journalism student from Princeton was dispatched to Seoul. Applicants may name their preference of location, but will not necessarily be placed there.

The Inside Word

The written application: The Luce judges unabashedly admit that they are looking for future leaders in professions, communities, and the nation. A solid record in leadership positions, mighty ambitions, personal charisma, and association with individuals and institutions with clout count for a lot in the Luce competition. Stress all these in your application. If you can get meaningful recommendations from well known people, do. Above all, stick your most dynamic foot forward and if you have two dynamic feet, all the better.

Fully aware that Americans can find Asian cultures foreign and adjustment difficult, Luce panels seek good diplomats who can adjust well to strange environments. Try to show evidence of your attempt to struggle with the complexities of other cultures. For example, one successful applicant for a Luce Fellowship in journalism discussed in his essay the difficulties that non-minorities face in covering minority issues. Previous travel, either in the U.S.A. or abroad helps, but is not essential. Proficiency in a foreign language would underline your willingness to master an Asian language, obviously an expectation for Luce Scholars.

The final interview: The regional panels are composed of such notables as Vernon Jordan, head of the National Urban League, and William Bradley, Jr., U.S. Senator. The panelists are in the business of detecting leadership qualities in young people, so there's no fooling them. For the interviews, collect data about the most outstanding individuals in your field. Expect questions like "where do you see yourself at the peak of your career," to which the answer should be something like President of Yale University, or Dean or Harvard Law School or Managing Editor of *The New York Times,* depending on your profession.

Finally, brush up on your knowledge of national and global events, even if they do not relate to your main interests. Leaders are supposed to know these things.

Contact:

The Henry Luce Foundation, Inc.
111 West 50th St.
New York, NY 10020
(212) 489-7700

NOMINATING INSTITUTIONS:

Amherst College
Bowdoin College
Brown University
California Institute of Technology
Carleton College
Carnegie-Mellon University
The Claremont Colleges
College of Wooster
Colorado College
Columbia University and Barnard
   College
Cornell University
Dartmouth College
Duke University
Emory University
George Washington University
Grinnell College
Hampshire College
Harvard University and Radcliffe
   College
Haverford College
Howard University
John Hopkins University
Massachusetts Institute of
   Technology
Morehouse College and Spelman
   College
Mount Holyoke College
New York University
Northwestern University
Occidental College
Princeton University
Rice University

St. John's College
Smith College
Stanford University
State University of New York
Swarthmore College
Trinity University
Tuskegee Institute
University of California at
   Berkeley
University of California at Los
   Angeles
University of Chicago
University of Denver
University of Illinois
University of Massachusetts
University of Miami
University of Michigan
University of North Carolina
University of Notre Dame
University of Pennsylvania
University of Southern California
University of Texas
University of Washington
University of Wisconsin
Vanderbilt University
Vassar College
Wake Forest University
Washington and Lee University
Washington University
Wellesley College
Wesleyan University
Williams College
Yale University

MARSHALL SCHOLARSHIP

ELIGIBILITY: *No lower age limit, upper limit 25; U.S.*
   citizenship and B.A. by time of taking award
   required
DURATION: *2 years (option of 3rd) October to June*
ACADEMIC CREDIT: *Yes*

REMUNERATION: *£4,000 in '79; to rise substantially 1980*
SPECIAL REQUIREMENTS: *Preference given to unmarried applicants*
NUMBER & TYPE OF AWARDS: *30, at choice of British university*
DEADLINE: *Applications to regional British consulate by mid-October*

General Description

Marshall Scholarships share distinction with the Rhodes as the most competitive and respected national awards in the country. Like the Rhodes, Marshall scholarships are awarded on the basis of a combination of personal qualities and academic achievement, but the Marshall seems to pay greater attention to academic distinction.

The scholarship sends winners to the British university of their choice for two and sometimes three years of undergraduate or graduate work. The stipend, which will be radically increased to cover new overseas student fees in Britain, covers living and educational expenses plus travel.

Marshall applicants undergo a rigorous application process including an interview before regional committees for finalists and a further screening of credentials by the Marshall Commission in Britain.

Successful applicants combine outstanding undergraduate academic records with serious "self-starter" activities in and out of college. Marshall scholars typically display strong scholarly interests fused with public policy concerns, artistic ability, or other non-academic pursuits. The scholarship is a distinction which opens doors in almost every profession.

What You Need to Know

Begin thinking about applying early in the academic year: the mid-October deadline is preceded in most colleges by campus screening and advising. College endorsement is required if you are an undergrad. If you're not, an "at large" category is open to applicants out of college: apply directly to your region for applications.

Applicants are handled by region, and each region screens candidates independently. Overall, about 125 applicants are interviewed, and of total applicants, 30 win the scholarship.

Although people with academic backgrounds ranging from English Lit. to astro-physics win Marshalls, a disproportionate number go each year to the big and little Ivies and to other prestigious northeastern schools. Scholars are free to choose any university in Britain, and do, with Marshall Scholars spread from Dublin to Sussex and all points between.

Marshall Scholars also seem free to choose any career they like when they are done. A high proportion end up in "public policy" positions, but the Marshall's emphasis on academic distinction shows through it the many scholars who end up as educators.

The Inside Word

Academic excellence is taken for granted in this competition. Beyond that, your essay is the single most important element of your application, assuming your five required recommendations are outstanding.

If you're applying for the Marshall you should be applying for the Rhodes Scholarship as well. As one applicant for both put it: "The two things are so similar you can practically xerox a Marshall application and mail it off to the Rhodes people."

The essay: But although the two competitions are similar, they are not identical. Many candidates argue that you should take a more scholarly tack in the Marshall essay, stressing the influence of *academic* interests on your activities. Likewise, links between academic interests and career plans (though by no means necessarily in academia) can be explained, and you should include concrete reasons for your choice of university and subject to be studied under the Marshall.

It is particularly important to avoid a laundry-list essay: for example, one successful candidate's essay centered around his desire to be an accomplished mountaineer, and left achievements as Big Brother Program administrator, tennis letterman, and academic star to other parts of his application.

The regions: If you live in one region but attend school in another, you may apply to either region: evaluate very carefully your chances in both places. Generalizations are impossible, but the regional committees are not all the same. Different regions have different numbers and calibre of applicants; they also have distinctive selection committees. Broadly:

1) If you choose your home region, you should have spent some time there recently, or be knowledgeable about local affairs. While Pacific and Northeastern committees are said to be tolerant of globe-trotters and prodigal sons, some others have been known to be more provincial, favoring home-town boys and girls.

2) To find out what you will encounter, shop around to learn if any acquaintances have been on the committee, or if college advisors know the score. Another source: through your college or on your own, contact former Marshall scholars in your area and ask their opinion.

The Interview

What's the interview like? Pretty pleasant, report surprised survivors. "Gentle and friendly" is how one scholar put it, and another summed up the committee he encountered in one word: "genteel." Unlike some other fellowships, Marshall committees seem intent on putting you at ease. But that doesn't mean they ask easy questions. Be prepared for some of the, "suppose you were President. What would you do about . . .?" genre; also for quite specific queries on academic subjects. One Marshall candidate expressed an interest in T. S. Eliot; he was asked to describe the course he would teach on the poet.

Choosing a British University

The application asks you to name the college(s) of your choice for study in Britain. Unless you have compelling reasons, you are better off not applying for Oxford or Cambridge. Committees look for explicit reasons for your choice in the essay, and may pursue the matter in the interview. They will expect you to apply for the place best suited to your academic interests, not the one with the big name or fancy architecture. Cambridge, for example, is not the best place for International Relations, but London arguably is.

Consequently, one special bit of preparation you should do is to beef up on the places you list in your application. Ask professors for names of people you can say you'd like to study under, and go into your interview with a good grasp of the peculiarities of the British educational system: knowing that undergraduate degrees are considerably more specialized there than in the U.S., for example, and that Oxford and Cambridge are actually composed of numerous small, autonomous colleges. Cocktail party trivia, but it will come in handy.

Contact:

Your campus Fellowship advisor, or the British Consulate at the address listed for your region:

Mid-Eastern Region: (Connecticut, Delaware, D.C., Kentucky, Maryland, New Jersey, New York north of 42nd parallel, Pennsylvania, West Virginia) 12 South 12th Street, Philadelphia, PA 19107, Tel: (215) 925-2430.

North-Eastern Region (Maine, Massachusetts, New Hampshire, New York south of 42nd parallel, Rhode Island, Vermont): 4740 Prudential Tower, Prudential Center, Boston, MA 02199, Tel: (617) 261-3060.

Mid-Western Region: (Illinois, Indiana, Iowa, Kansas, Michigan, Minnesota, Missouri, Mebraska, North Dakota, Ohio, South Dakota, Wisconsin) 33 North Dearborn Street, Chicago, IL 60602, Tel: (312) 346-1810.

Pacific Region: (Alaska, Arizona, California, Colorado, Hawaii, Idaho, Montana, Nevada, New Mexico, Oregon, Utah, Washington, Wyoming) Equitable Building, 120 Montgomery Street, San Francisco, CA 94104, Tel: (415) 981-3030.

Southern Region: (Alabama, Arkansas, Florida, Georgia, Louisiana, Mississippi, North Carolina, Oklahoma, South Carolina, Tennessee, Texas, Virginia, Canal Zone, Puerty Rico, Virgin Islands) Suite 912, 225 Peachtree Street, N.E., Atlanta, GA 30303, Tel: (404) 524-5856.

RHODES SCHOLARSHIP

ELIGIBILITY: *Men and women who have passed their 18th birthday but not passed their 24th birthday by October 1st; must be unmarried, a U.S. citizen; must have B.A. or be sufficiently advanced to obtain it before beginning scholarship (i.e., in senior year in most colleges)*

DURATION: *2 years (option of 3rd); October to June academic year*

ACADEMIC CREDIT: *Yes*

REMUNERATION: *£4,500 stipend per year, approximately; includes travel expenses, tuition, fees, room & board, living allowance (will be substantially raised pending decision on increased overseas student fees in Britain)*

NUMBER & TYPE OF AWARDS: *32, as full-time undergraduates or graduate student at a college of the University of Oxford*

DEADLINE: *October 31*

General Description

The grand prize in the fellowships sweepstakes, the Rhodes each year skims the top of the fellowship crop. Academically accomplished, Rhodes Scholars are better known for being all-around good citizens.

Like the Marshall competition, the Rhodes looks for a winning blend of character, activities, and grades, but the balance is decisively tipped in the direction of non-academic attributes, successful scholars say. "Marshall scholars can write but can't run, Rhodes scholars can run but can't write" is a popular dictum among snooty Oxford dons, but although it is true that a varsity letter on your chest will go over well with Rhodes committees, playing field heroes are actually a minority among the average crop of Rhodes Scholars. Confesses one Rhodent: "I think I spent 90 percent of my college career in the bio lab. When I saw that interview committee, my first reaction was, 'My God, this is more people in one place than I've seen in four years.'" So much for the notion that all Rhodes scholars are social butterflies, too.

For the record, we may as well say what everyone believes, and *does* happen to be true: after a Rhodes Scholarship, you can pretty much name your career. For an inordinate number of scholars, the careers they name boil down to law and politics—which is not surprising, given that the man behind the award, colonialist and philanthropist Cecil Rhodes, made clear his hope that his scholars "would come to esteem the performance of public duties as the highest aim."

What You Need to Know

This is another award that requires early planning—with a late October deadline and earlier campus advising sessions, you should start working on your application in September.

Note that a college endorsement is *not* required; however, the selection committees do ask that colleges screen candidates if possible, and the endorsement of a fellowship committee can't hurt.

One of Cecil Rhodes's philanthropic extravagances with the proceeds from highly profitable colonial enterprises (*Rhodesia*, e.g.), the scholarship sends scholars to Oxford each year from all over the world; mainly, from old British colonies.

Competition for the 32 scholarships assigned annually to the U.S. begins within each state. After interviewing about 12 candidates the state committees generally recommend 4 to go on to one of eight district committees, which interview again and the same day announce the new scholars for the year.

Despite the fact that each year one or two schools are added to the roster of scholar-producing colleges, the bulk of scholars come from a handful of top east coast institutions. Although they are undoubtedly well qualified, some critics suggest that this may be related to the preponderance of east coast-educated members on selection committees.

For long a reminder that once upon a time women were not considered worth educating, the scholarship is now open to females—an overdue adjustment which required an Act of Parliament to accomplish. At present, women make up about one-third of the annual contingent.

It is also worth remembering that the relatively high upper limit on age makes this an award you can think about for several years after college. In particular: if you are now a senior but anticipate a mind-boggling couple of post-graduate years running a senate campaign or being an olympic champion of whatever, think seriously about waiting until you've done it before applying.

A few dismaying statistics: of about 1,200 highly qualified applicants, only 600 are usually interviewed, and roughly 2.5% of the total end up as winners. But keep in mind that the intensity of competition varies markedly between different districts (see below).

The Inside Word

The interviews: On windy nights when the fire burns low, old Rhodes scholars gather round to retell the tale of the applicant who went to the interview, got so nervous he lost his lunch on the table—and went on to win the scholarship.

It has happened more than once, and in all fairness that sort of extreme reaction has more to do with the candidate than the committee. Nevertheless, Rhodes committees tend to be aggressive, fast with their questions, and are inclined to test your resilience with unexpected or unanswerable queries. "Do you have a death wish?" inquired one committee member of a nonplussed applicant with a history of dangerous sporting enterprises, and most interviewees can expect at least one question of this sort.

The snappy style and occasional booby-traps of Rhodes interviews make the Golden Rule of Brevity and a moment's pause before answering especially important. Interviewers generally expect to ask a lot of questions in a brief space of time, and short pointed replies will keep them happy and keep you from saying more than you know. Likewise, a pause to collect your thoughts before answering will give you time to decide whether "I don't know" might be more effective than bullshitting a response to "how can we reduce unemployment and inflation at the same time?"

The regions: But before worrying about interviews, think about where to apply in the first place. Northeastern and mid-Atlantic states generally have the largest number of applicants each year; Massachusetts, New York, and New Jersey lead the pack. If you have a choice between a 'tough' state and a less competitive one (say you go to college in New York but have a legal residence in Kansas), however, don't automatically choose the one that seems easier. Western, mid-western and southeastern regions are said to be suspicious of candidates who disappear into eastern prep schools and colleges, only to return at fellowship time for an easy ride.

Another tip from experienced interviewers: while the Northeast tends to stress academic credentials, the South, Southwest and Mid-west will often put more stock in sports and other extracurricular achievements, and a few committee members complain privately of an anti-intellectual streak in those regions.

How to decide where you will apply? Your best bet is to do some preliminary scouting among old Rhodes Scholars in the two areas, and anyone else who can test the water for you, then take a gamble on which district will be more hospitable to your strengths. And for those who live in

New York City and go to Columbia—good luck! At least you don't have any choices to make.

The essay: As for the essay, the Rhodes application stresses its importance, and most interviews are devoted entirely to points it raises. Unlike Marshall committees, the Rhodes seems relatively unconcerned about the details of what you want to study at Oxford, and far more interested in the personal goals and interests you emphasize.

And save your fancy verbal footwork for a college paper; Rhodes committees are looking for clarity of thought above all, and are suspicious of anything smacking of cuteness.

Finally, remember that there are really only two reasons to prefer a Rhodes over a Marshall: the cocktail party the Rhodes people throw the night before your interview, and the stylish Atlantic crossing on the QE II tossed in *gratis*. Beware of the party, however—committee members often take that opportunity to size up your social graces under the influence.

Contact:

Your Fellowship Committee or Career Office on campus, or

The Rhodes Scholarship Office
Wesleyan University
Middletown, CT 06457
(203) 347-9411 or (203) 346-7640

ROTARY EDUCATIONAL AWARDS

ELIGIBILITY: *Varies with award*
DURATION: *1 academic year*
ACADEMIC CREDIT: *Yes*
REMUNERATION: *Varies by school; includes room, board, tuition, travel, books and supplies, and intensive language training if necessary. $300 for educational travel.*
SPECIAL REQUIREMENTS: *Married students may apply in all categories except undergraduate scholarships.*
NUMBER AND TYPE OF AWARDS: *At least one awarded in every U.S. Rotary district for Graduate Fellows, Undergraduate Scholarships, and Technical Training Awards. 150 awards worldwide in Journalists and Teachers of the Handicapped categories.*

DEADLINE: *March 1 of the year prior to effective date of award*

General Description

Considering that they provide a veritable free ride for a year at a foreign institution of the recipient's choice, the Rotary awards are surprisingly unsought after in many areas of the country. In fact, some of the district Rotary chapters find themselves without a competitive number of applicants to choose from.

Original application should be made to local Rotary Clubs. After team interviews, the local clubs forward endorsements to district Rotary clubs, which conduct a further round of team interviews and nominate one individual for awards in each of five categories—Technical Training, Graduate Fellowships, Undergraduate Scholarships, Teachers of the Handicapped, and Journalism Awards—to the Rotary Foundation based in Chicago.

Usually, nominees in the first three categories receive rubber stamp approvals, while 150 out of all the nominees worldwide are chosen in the latter two categories. All applicants are notified in early September, one year prior to the date the award becomes effective. Winners receive full tuition, room, and board at an institution of their choice so long as it is in a country which hosts Rotary clubs. The award also includes funds for books, supplies, and living expenses.

Eligibility varies in each category as follows:

Technical Training Awards: High school graduates, 21 to 35 years of age, with at least two years employment in a technical field.

Graduate Fellowships: College graduates from 18 to 28 years of age.

Undergraduate Scholarship: Age 18 to 24, with at least two years of college level study.

Teachers of the Handicapped Awards: High school graduate, age 25 to 50, with at least two years full-time employment as a teacher of the mentally, physically, or educationally handicapped.

Journalism Awards: High school graduates, age 21 to 28, with two years employment; *or* at least two years of high school and evidence of planning to enter a career in journalism.

What You Need to Know

Keep the dates straight. Most important, remember that awards are made a full year before they become effective. You must apply to local Rotary clubs by March 1; sponsoring clubs must forward endorsements to District clubs by April 1; the District clubs must approve of nominations by May

15; and awards are made in early September for the following academic year.

Some districts are more competitive than others. You may apply in either district or that of your home school, so any homework you do to determine which of the two areas is the less competitive is worthwhile. Usually local Rotarians can give you a sense of the competition for the awards in their district.

You are responsible for gaining admission to your chosen school, wholly outside of the application process for the award. Having the award may boost your chances of admission to some schools, in that funding is guaranteed, but the Rotary Foundation does not offer assistance in the admission process except for informal advice. Rather, they assume that if you are savvy enough to win a Rotary Award, you are smart enough to get into the school you want to attend.

There are a few countries (South Africa, Cambodia, etc.) where Rotary does not allow clubs, and applicants are not allowed to use Rotary awards in those countries. Find out what they are so as not to embarrass yourself.

Rotary award winners are unofficial diplomats and may be asked to speak at Rotary clubs and to have dinner with families in the host country. In most instances they have the option of living with Rotarians while abroad or finding private housing. When they return to their country of origin they are expected to speak before the sponsoring club, and perhaps before a gathering of district club members. Beyond that, they have no obligation to the club.

The Inside Word

Know something about the Rotary Club. Rotarians are, by and large, small businessmen and middle-level bureaucrats. It helps to acquaint yourself with the principles of the organization and the kinds of activities its members pursue. Rotary's overt exclusion of women from membership, for instance, is an issue that candidates for awards may be asked to address in one form or another.

Notorious good-old-boy back-slappers, Rotarians look for good humor and well-roundedness as much as at grades, recommendations, and extracurricular activities. After describing his vigorous daily schedule in a district interview, one candidate was asked "don't you leave any time for a beer with the guys?" Personal charm is likely to count more heavily here than in other competitions. Stay clear of volatile political subjects in your essay; be cheerful in the interview. Use any connections you might have among members of the local chapter. Although relatives of Rotarians are not allowed to apply for awards, having a friend on the inside is likely to help your chances.

Although the Club does not place restrictions on the number of people given awards for study in any given country, remember that the awards are meant, in part, to encourage understanding and cooperation between peoples in the many different countries that host Rotary clubs. Applying to a place like Tanzania, for instance may boost your chances, simply because so few applicants do. The Rotary awards provide an excellent opportunity for study in African and Asian universities which do not offer the equivalent of Rhodes Scholarships.

Contact:

The Rotary Foundation of Rotary International
1600 Ridge Avenue
Evanston, IL 60201

THE THOMAS J. WATSON FELLOWSHIP PROGRAM

ELIGIBILITY: *Must be in senior year at one of approximately 50 participating colleges.*
DURATION: *1 year*
ACADEMIC CREDIT: *No*
REMUNERATION: *$8,000; $11,000 for married students. Includes travel and living.*
SPECIAL REQUIREMENTS: *All applicants must be college seniors, at one of the institutions listed below, and receive the school's nomination.*
NUMBER OF AWARDS: *70 each year*
APPLICATION DEADLINE: *Early November*

General Description

Often just the right pause for the creative, initiative college senior to take after graduation, the Watson allows its Fellows to pursue their most passionate *wanderjahr* desires abroad. Candidates design their own year-long program, involving travel through one or more foreign countries. The Foundation provides the funds and sometimes a few connections.

Some of the tamer projects have included pounding out poetry on Spain's beaches, learning about facilities for the handicapped in Scandinavia, and following the routes of Old World Believers in North and South America and the U.S.S.R. Some of the wilder ones: Sex Linked Mimicry in Butterflies (Kenya); Herd Dog Lore and Training (Wales); Open Air Museums (England, Scandinavia, Holland); Martial Idealism (Israel and Japan); Studying Chinese Opera (Taiwan); Marionettes and Puppeteers (the World.)

The only requirement made of Watson Fellows is that they submit a short report of their activities when the year is up, along with an accounting of their expenses. They also attend a final all-expense paid four-day conference in Maine featuring panel discussions, slide-shows, performances, and talks.

What You Need to Know

Projects should stem from long term interests and you should do your homework before writing your proposal. Be aware of language and/or travel difficulties, cultural differences, and whether the project, or one like it, has been accepted before. Because the most imaginative projects can be the most difficult to do, practicality as well as innovation must play a role in your proposal.

Be flexible. Don't make a proposal that can be conducted in only one country. One candidate applied to study agriculture in Iran, only to have his interview during the very week in which the Shah fell. Be prepared to make last minute plan changes if necessary.

To get a better feel for the types of things Watson Fellows do, write for a list of past projects, or see if your campus Fellowship Office has one.

To be eligible for a Fellowship, you must be nominated by one of the participating colleges. These include small colleges (see list below) and exclude the Ivies and big universities because travel grants already offered by many of the larger schools.

Check with your Fellowship Office about deadlines for the campus competition. Participating colleges may nominate only a limited number of candidates and on-campus competition can be keen. All college nominees (totalling about 170) are then interviewed on campus in late fall or winter by a representative of the Watson Foundation, usually a former Watson fellow.

Unlike other Fellowships, the Watson does not require strong overall academic records in applicants. They look instead for achievements in a chosen field, both in and out of the classroom. More than that they seek imagination, will, and spunk. The best candidates are usually good students who have made their real mark in some extra-curricular way. Your reasons for proposing a particular project must be seen in both your personality and your work achievements.

The Inside Word

Past participants laud the Watson for its flexibility, a quality that they say encourages unrivalled experiences. The "project" can be highly academic, involving extensive reading and research—such as studying European investment trends in the U.S. or Sri Lankan foreign policy—or it can be highly nonacademic—such as an apprenticeship to an Indian sitar craftsman. It can be the capstone to a long, involved study of a field, a prelude to an interest of great personal concern in the future, or an aberration and interlude between college and Life After. It may involve travel to twenty nations on four continents; it may lead to the writing of magazine articles or a book; it may bring greater maturity, self-awareness, and understanding of other peoples and the world.

Successful applicants advise tailoring initial applications to the whims of the college committee, based on past nominations or particular school emphasis. If grades are important (they are not so important at the national level), stress your good ones and minimize the lower ones. Try to show why your proposal is original, how you are uniquely qualified, and why you are so deserving. Following nomination, national applications should be more lengthy; the result of detailed research of your proposed project. Study the literature provided by the organization for cues on the kinds of ideas shared. Show the committee that your idea is innovative, flexible, timely; that you are responsible enough to live for a year on your own and carry out the project, and that your projected plans are specific and realistic. From all reports, the Watson committee looks for students with applied expertise in areas related to their proposal.

Watson Fellows tell us that the funding provided is adequate in most cases to cover all travel, food, lodging, medical, and clerical expenses, as well as some extra for souvenir and entertainment purposes. (One recent wanderer noted that the money provided now can't touch the $6,000 supplied in 1969 when low inflation and favorable exchange rates enabled Fellows to live in luxury and buy cars they could take home.)

Every Fellow spends some time in a country in addition to the one(s) proposed; unplanned experiences outside the original scope of the proposal are encouraged as much as those planned. One person tested the committee's patience by mailing them letters from his travels in Afghanistan and Nepal, when his project called for photographing Jews in Eastern Europe. The actual requirements are minimal; enjoyment and flexibility are at a premium.

Contact:

The Thomas J. Watson Foundation
217 Angell Street
Providence, RI 02906
(401) 274-1952

PARTICIPATING INSTITUTIONS:

Amherst College
Antioch College
Bowdoin College
Brandeis University
Bryn Mawr College
California Institute of Technology
Centre College of Kentucky
Carleton College
Claremont Men's College
Colby College

Colgate University
Colorado College
Connecticut College
Davidson College
Emory University
Fisk University
Franklin and Marshall College
Gallaudet College
Goucher College
Grinnell College

Hamilton College
Haverford College
Harvey Mudd College
Hobart and William Smith
   Colleges
Kalamazoo College
Kenyon College
Lawrence University
Middlebury College
Mills College
Morehouse College
Newcomb College of Tulane
   University
Oberlin College
Occidental College
Pitzer College

Pomona College
Reed College
Rice University
Scripps College
Spelman College
St. John's College (Md. and
   N.M.)
St. Lawrence University
Swarthmore College
Trinity College (Conn.)
Trinity College (D.C.)
Union College
Wesleyan University
Whitman College
Williams College

ENGLISH-SPEAKING UNION STUDY GRANT

ELIGIBILITY: *B.A. usually required*
DURATION: *Varies*
ACADEMIC CREDIT: *Yes*
REMUNERATION: *Varies*
TYPE OF SCHOLARSHIPS: *To British university*
DEADLINE: *Consult nearest English-Speaking
   Union chapter*

General Description

There is no central body in charge of these awards—instead, local chapters handle them individually. Grants are similarly varied: one winner got $2,500; another, $5,000.

In all cases, however, you are expected to study at a British university, and it is up to the candidate to get accepted at the school of his choice.

Application: Format varies because of the decentralized system of chapters, but two essays—one on "why study in England" and one on academic/personal background and plans—plus a transcript, list of activities, and recommendations are usual.

Interviews are generally part of the process: "a relaxed, informal talk with two people from the local chapter—we chatted about my favorite authors," recollects one winner now at Oxford.

Although rarely substantial enough to find a full degree course in Britain, ESU grants can give a needed boost to other funds, and when adequate for one year's study, can be combined with another award (from your own college, e.g.) to create a two- or three-year package.

Contact:

The local chapter of the English-Speaking Union or:
Mary Ann Davis
Education Department
English-Speaking Union
16 East 69th Street
N.Y., NY 10021

INTERCOLLEGIATE STUDIES INSTITUTE
Weaver Fellowship

ELIGIBILITY: *B.A. by start of fellowship*
DURATION: *1 year*
ACADEMIC CREDIT: *Yes*
REMUNERATION: *Varies*
NUMBER OF AWARDS: *10*
DEADLINE: *January 15*

General Description

"A Right-wing, reactionary academic institution, fundamentally monarchist, arch-catholic and anti-communist" is how one applicant describes the sponsors of this award. At least they know where they stand.

Aside from the politics of the Institute, the Weaver Fellowship is interesting because it sends you anywhere you want to go for a year of graduate study—well, anywhere in the Free World.

Application: A transcript, three recommendations, and an essay on "What is Liberal Education" are all that is required; there is no interview. Suggested approach: read Richard Weaver's essays on Philosophy—you'll pick up some helpful ideas on the nature of a proper liberal education (it should impart eternal verities, for one thing) and you'll also be able to pass on to your referees a few hints on the kind of person who fits the bill for this fellowship.

Despite the doctrinaire tone of the organization, it seems to be truly rather liberal in making its awards, so long as your essay does not stray too far from Dick Weaver's line.

Contact:

Intercollegiate Studies Institute
14 South Bryn Mawr Avenue
Bryn Mawr, PA 19010
(215) 525-7501

FURTHER SOURCES OF INFORMATION

GENERAL
The Grant's Register.
St. Martin's Press, New York. 1978. Expensive—obtain from library.
Fellowships, Scholarships, and Related Opportunities in International Education. From Division of International Education, 205 Alumni Hall, University of Tennessee, Knoxville, TN 37916
Foundation Directory. Foundation Center, New York. 1975. Expensive—obtain from library or college development office.
Scholarships and Fellowships for Foreign Study: A Selected Bibliography. Free from Institute of International Education, 809 United Nations Plaza, New York, NY 10017. Describes sources of financial aid.

BY COUNTRY OR REGION

AFRICA
Director of Financial Aid in Higher Education for Africans and Americans Studying about Africa. From the African Studies Assoc., Epstein Service Center, Brandeis University, Waltham, MA 02154

ISRAEL
A Guide to Israel Programs. From the Jewish Agency, World Zionist Organization, Publication Dept., 515 Park Avenue, New York, NY 10022

JAPAN
Life and Study in Japan for Japanese Government Scholarship Students. Free from Japanese Ministry of Education, Student Exchange Division, 3-2-2 Kasumigaseki, Chiyoda-Ku, Tokyo, Japan.
Study in Japan. Free from Office of the Director, Division of International Education, Office of Education, U.S. Dept. of Health, Education, and Welfare, Washington, DC 20202

MIDDLE EAST & NORTH AFRICA
Study and Research in the Middle East and North Africa. From AMIDEAST, Inc., 1717 Massachusetts Avenue, N.W., Washington, DC 20036

SWEDEN
Travel, Study and Research in Sweden. From the Heritage Resource Center, P.O. Box 26305, Minneapolis, MN 54426

U.S.S.R. AND EASTERN EUROPE
Research and Study in Eastern Europe and the U.S.S.R. From Office of the Director, Division of International Education, Office of Education, U.S. Dept. of Health, Education, and Welfare, Washington, DC 20202

WESTERN EUROPE
Fellowship Guide for Western Europe. From Council for European Studies, 1429 International Affairs Bldg., Columbia University, New York, NY 10027

Fellowships in Western Europe. Free from Social Science Research Council, Western European Fellowship Program, 605 Third Avenue, New York, NY 10016

BY AREA OF INTEREST

Art Education: An International Survey. From UNIPUB, P.O. Box 433, Murray Hill Station, New York, NY 10016

World Directory of Environmental Research Centers. From R. R. Bowker Co., P.O. Box 1807, Ann Arbor, MI 48106

The Musician's Guide: The Directory of the World of Music. Expensive—obtain from library or from Music Information Service, Inc., 310 Madison Avenue, New York, NY 10017

International Theater Directory: A World Directory of the Theater and Performing Arts, Leo B. Pride, Ed. Expensive—obtain from library, or from Simon and Schuster, 1230 Avenue of the Americas, New York, NY 10020

Additional Sources of Information

This chapter lists some of the additional publications we found useful in our search for interesting and worthwhile programs. Most include names and addresses of programs and some contain descriptive information as well. The basic difference between these publications and our *Guide* is that we have expanded the brochure-type information and include comments and advice from actual program directors and participants.

Many of the publications are updated annually to provide the latest information on what is available. Some deal with specific interest areas, and correspond to the related chapters in this book.

These reference guides are available by writing to the addresses provided with each listing. They range in price from being free to $75; contact the publishers for details. Most career libraries at accredited colleges and universities have these books plus other useful sources of information in their collections; you'll save time and money if you check there first.

Several of the publications listed in this bibliography are put out by the National Society for Internships and Experiential Education (NSIEE), a major clearinghouse for information on internships. NSIEE is a valuable source of information on internships of all kinds, and will provide material on additional programs and further advice on those listed in their many directories.

General

Bolles, Richard N., *What Color Is Your Parachute? Job Hunters' Manual,* Ten Speed Press, Box 7123, Berkeley, CA 94707. The most widely-used guide to job hunting, this book contains valuable practical information for those seeking work in any field. While not specifically geared toward internships, much of the advice on job hunting is applicable to prospective interns.

Directory of Internships, Work Experience Programs, and On-the-Job Training Opportunities, Ready Reference Press, Specialized Indexes, Inc., 100 East Thousand Oaks Blvd., Suite 224, Thousand Oaks, CA 91360. This catalogue and its first supplement edition list over 1000 programs offered nationwide. It provides general program descriptions, and information on remuneration, deadlines, eligibility, etc. Also included are lists of job information centers throughout the country.

Directory of Undergraduate Internships, National Society for Internships and Experiential Education, 1735 Eye Street, N.W., Suite 601, Washington, D.C. 20006. This directory, a listing of a variety of internship opportunities throughout the country, provides information about program design, admission requirements, application procedures, remuneration and academic credit.

Directory of Washington Internships, National Society for Internships and Experiential Education, 1735 Eye Street, N.W., Suite 601, Washington, D.C. 20006. A listing of Washington-area programs, this publication contains helpful information on living and working in the Nation's capital, as well as brief descriptions of a collection of internship opportunities.

Eis, Jennifer and Ward, Don, *Taking Off: An Organizational Handbook and Comprehensive Resource Guide for Non-Traditional Higher Education,* Center for Alternatives In/To Higher Education, 1118 South Harrison Road, East Lansing, MI 48823. The *Handbook* contains resume information plus an extensive listing of internships and alternative learning opportunities, with important general information on each program.

Hecht, Joy, *Where to Look: A Source Book on Undergraduate Internships,* American Association for Higher Education, One Dupont Circle, Suite 780, Washington, D.C. 20036. A brief guide to internships, Hecht's book focusses on shaping personal and career interests to available internship opportunities. Listings of where to find campus resources, and an annotated bibliography of further internship information are also provided.

Internship Opportunities, Wellesley College Career Services Office, Wellesley, MA 02181. A brief listing of internship programs. Also included in the publication is a bibliography of internship directories and information on resume writing.

Invest Yourself, Commission on Voluntary Service Action, c/o Circulation Office, 418 Peltoma Road, Haddonfield, NJ 19104. A catalogue listing volunteer internship opportunities with national and international organizations in a variety of fields. Contains basic information and program descriptions.

1980 National Directory of Summer Internships for Undergraduate College Students, The Career Planning Offices of Bryn Mawr and Haverford Colleges, Career Planning Office, Haverford College, Haverford, PA 19041. This listing of internship programs contains general descriptions and information on deadlines, eligibility and remuneration, plus a bibliography of other reference sources.

Sexton, Robert F., editor, *Dimensions of Experiential Education,* National Society for Internships and Experiential Education, 1735 Eye

Street, N.W., Suite 601, Washington, D.C. 20006. An examination of the role of internship and experiential education programs, this book explores the usefulness and potential of internships and on-the-job experience programs as part of the higher education process.

Arts

Exploring Visual Arts and Crafts: A Student Guide Book, Technical Education Research Centers, Inc., 44 Brattle Street, Cambridge, MA 02138. This volume is an introduction to career internship opportunities in visual communication, commercial graphics, video, architecture, etc., A variety of programs and interest areas are explored and compared.

Government

Brier, Donald E., *A Guide to Federal Internships for Students,* National Institute of Public Management, 1612 K Street, N.W., Suite 810, Washington, D.C. 20006. A list of various government-run internship programs, containing general information and brief program descriptions.

Franzich, Stephen E., *Storming Washington: An Intern's Guide to National Government,* American Political Sciences Association, 1527 New Hampshire Avenue, N.W., Washington, D.C. 20036. A guide to living in Washington and making the most of government internships, this book contains information on where to find information, people to see to arrange an internship, and programs to take advantage of in the area. The *Guide* primarily lists university-sponsored internship programs.

Murphy, Thomas P., *Government Management Internships and Executive Development,* Lexington Books, 125 Spring Street, Lexington, MA 02173. This guide reveals the peaks and pitfalls of internship experiences in government management positions from a student's point of view. It addresses academic questions related to internships and surveys the historical development of legislative, city manager, and urban internships.

Ruemelin, Charles, *Guide to Government and Public Service Internships,* Office of Career Services and Off-Campus Learning, Harvard University, 54 Dunster Street, Cambridge, MA 02183. A guide offering advice on how to find exciting government and public service internships, it also includes a listing of programs in these areas along with basic program information.

Health

The American Hospital Association: Guide to the Health Care Field, American Hospital Association, 840 North Lake Shore Drive, Chicago, IL 60611. This central reference source contains all AHA registered care centers, listed by state and including contact addresses and descriptive data. Also included is a complete listing of related organizations, agencies, and accredited educational programs.

A Guide to the Health Professions, The Office of Career Services and Off-Campus Learning, Harvard University, 54 Duster Street, Cambridge, MA 02183. A career guide which looks at various areas of health care and lists available work/study opportunities. It also contains specific information on opportunities for employment in many areas of the field, and advice on how and where to pursue graduate studies.

Health Services Administration Education 1980, Association of University Programs in Health Administration (AUPHA), Suite 420, One Dupont Circle, Washington, D.C. 20036. This index of graduate programs in health services and administration in the United States and Canada also provides complete, up-to-date information on internship opportunities in the field.

Journalism

Clayton, Ronald H. and Powell, B.A., *The Student Guide to Mass Media Internships,* Intern Research Group, School of Journalism, University of Colorado, Boulder, CO 80302. A book cataloging a variety of internship programs in radio, television, magazine production, and specialty, weekly, and daily newspapers, program listings include a general description and basic application information.

Public Service

A Directory of Public Service Internships: Opportunities for the Graduate, Post Graduate and Mid-Career Professional, National Center for Public Service Internship Programs, Suite 601, 1735 Eye Street, N.W., Washington, D.C. 20006. A listing of 123 programs with descriptions and application information. Also includes a bibliography of related publications and a listing of clearinghouses of internship information.

Jobs in Social Change, Social and Educational Research Foundation, 3416 Sansom Street, Philadelphia, PA 19104. This publication contains lists of public interest groups throughout the country and what they do. Plus information on the Foundation's interests, plans, and projects.

Rosenbaum, Allan, *Public Service Internships and Education in Public Affairs: Administrative Issues and Problems,* National Society for Internships and Experiential Education, 1735 Eye Street, N.W., Suite 601, Washington, D.C. 20006. This publication provides information on public service internship opportunities, along with insights into administrative concerns and discussion of the role of internships in the educational process.

Ruemelin, Charles, *Guide to Government and Public Service Internships*. See description listed under "Government".

Fellowships

A Selected List of Major Fellowship Programs and Aid to Advanced Education for United States Citizens, Publications Division, National Science Foundation, Room 235, 1800 G Street, N.W., Washington, D.C. 20050. This book lists undergraduate, graduate, and post-doctoral fellowship programs, as well as other sources of funding for post-graduate study in a variety of areas.

Send us a letter!

If you've heard about, or participated in an internship or fellowship program, please fill out this form and send it to:

Amherst Student Special Publications
Box 234 Station #2
Amherst, Massachusetts 01002

YOUR NAME: _____

ADDRESS: _____

TELEPHONE: _____

PROGRAM NAME: _____

INSTITUTION/ORGANIZATION: _____

PERSON TO CONTACT: _____

ADDRESS: _____

_____

Additional comments on the nature of the program, etc.: